SECOND EDITION

Child Welfare

A Multicultural Focus

Neil A. Cohen, Editor
California State University, Los Angeles

and Contributors

Allyn and Bacon

Boston ▪ London ▪ Toronto ▪ Sydney ▪ Tokyo ▪ Singapore

Senior Editor, Social Work and Family Therapy: Judy Fifer
Editor in Chief, Social Sciences: Karen Hanson
Editorial Assistant: Julianna M. Cancio
Marketing Manager: Jackie Aaron
Editorial Production Service: Chestnut Hill Interprises
Manufacturing Buyer: Julie McNeill
Cover Administrator: Jennifer Hart

Copyright © 2000, 1992, by Allyn & Bacon
A Pearson Education Company
160 Gould Street
Needham Heights, MA 02494

Internet: www.abacon.com

Between the time Website information is gathered and published, some sites may have closed. Also, the transcription or URLs can result in typographical errors. The publisher would appreciate notification where these occur so that they may be corrected in subsequent editions.

Library of Congress Cataloging-in-Publication Data

Child welfare : a multicultural focus / Neil A. Cohen, editor. — 2nd ed.
    p.   cm.
  Includes bibliographical references and index.
  ISBN 0-205-29890-7
  1. Child welfare—United States. 2. Children of minorities—
Services for—United States. I. Cohen, Neil A.
HV741.C498 1999
362.7'0973—dc21   99-26271
                                            CIP

Printed in the United States of America

10 9 8 7 6 5 4 3 2 1   04 03 02 01 00 99

Photo Credits: Page 1: Texas A&M Early Childhood; page 15: Library of Congress; page 41: AP/Wide World Photos; pages 87, 165; page 117: Lawrence Migdale/Stock Boston; page 145: Jean-Claude LeJeune/Stock Boston; page 193: Felicia Martinez/PhotoEdit; pages 227, 257: copyright 1999 PhotoDisc, Inc.

CONTENTS

PREFACE

Children, youth, and their families have been subjected to rapid social change over the past 25 years. As a result, child welfare professionals and their respective agencies and programs are increasingly called upon to provide social services and benefits that are more efficient, ethno-sensitive, more creative, more comprehensive, and more supportive. There is increasing emphasis on incorporating a strengths model, i.e., working with client system assets rather than deficits, and continuing attempts to be proactive, rather than reactive. This demand is made during a period of social program retrenchment and a laissez-faire attitude on the part of the government and disturbingly large segment of society.

In spite of the myriad of child welfare texts and readers written during the past twenty years, there is a marked absence of a child welfare book specifically directed to the undergraduate learner/practitioner interested in developing a working knowledge/skill base in the field.

This book, therefore, is intended primarily for the undergraduate student (particularly in social work and human services) and child development majors, and entry-level children's services practitioners. The first chapters discuss the history of child welfare in the United States and the present social changes, issues, and problems facing children, youth, and families. Attention is then focused on those child welfare policies, programs, and practices that attempt to address these problems, including family support and family preservation services for the family while the child(ren) are in the home, foster care, and adoption settings.

It presents specialized chapters by child welfare experts who endeavor to provide an integrated approach to ethno-sensitive child welfare services and generalist practice theory including: child welfare and African-American families; Asian-Pacific families; Hispanic families; and a newly prepared chapter on Native American families for the second edition. Included also is a comprehensive chapter on child maltreatment, including physical abuse, emotional abuse, sexual abuse, and neglect. This book also contains a unique chapter on child welfare programs and practice in rural America.

Found throughout the chapters is an explicit multicultural focus emphasizing the role inequality has played in generating the need for, and form of, child welfare services in this country. The book blends contemporary child welfare concepts—including rights of children, the best interests of the child, family support and family preservation, prevention and intervention, empowerment, quality of care, managed care, permanency planning, deinstitutionalization, continuity of care, and normalization—with "hands-on" practice skills and case examples.

Throughout, readers will be challenged to develop an analytic perspective, one that requires sensitivity to simultaneously trying to meet the needs and wants of the child, parents, agency, social work profession, and society. This perspective is reinforced by the presentation of case examples and discussion to illustrate the application of child welfare practice, knowledge, and theory.

We would like to thank the following professionals who reviewed this book at various stages: Kenneth J. Herrmann, Jr., State University of New York, Brockport; Karen S. Knox, Southwest Texas State University, Carol Rippey Massat, University of Illinois at Chicago; and M. Jenise Comer, Central Missouri State University.

This book is dedicated to the child welfare workers—past, present, and future—who endeavor to make life more worthwhile for children, youth, and their families. A special "thank you" to my wife Bonnie and to all the families of the authors who have provided support, encouragement, and understanding over the many, many months of preparation. And to Judy Fifer, series editor, Karen Hanson, editor-in-chief, social sciences, a special thanks for their advocacy, support, and professionalism in all matters related to the publication of this book. Responsibility for the content, of course, rests solely with the authors.

ABOUT THE CONTRIBUTORS

Neil A. Cohen is Professor in the Department of Social Work at California State University, Los Angeles. He received his M.S.W. from the University of California, Berkeley, and his Ph.D. from the Mandel School of Applied Social Sciences, Case Western Reserve University, Cleveland, Ohio. Dr. Cohen has taught in both the undergraduate and graduate social work programs in the areas of child welfare, collaboration for children, social policy, services for children, youth and families, and homelessness in society. He has been a consultant for human service organizations concerning issues of organizational evaluation, management training, and quality of care. For the past 15 years he has coordinated and taught in a social services certificate program for Head Start social services staff. Dr. Cohen has been a keynote speaker on the subject of child welfare at numerous conferences. His practice includes being a child welfare worker and supervisor for a number of years for the Los Angeles County Department of Public Social Services.

Charles L. Baker is the President and CEO of the Presbyterian Child Welfare Agency-Buckhorn Children's Foundation that provides a wide range of services to children and their families in Kentucky and Ohio. The Agency has a growing national reputation for the successful management of violent behavior in children and youth. A native of Appalachia, Mr. Baker received his M.S.W. from the University of Louisville. He also currently serves as the Mayor of the Village of Buckhorn, KY. His experience includes teaching, training, consultation and the management of programs in foster care, developmental disabilities and a school for delinquents.

Dr. Cynthia Crosson-Tower is Professor of Behavioral Sciences and Director of the Child Protection Institute at Fitchburg State College in Massachusetts. She received her Masters in Social Work from the University of Connecticut and her doctorate from the University of Massachusetts. Dr. Crosson-Tower is the author of numerous publications including: *Understanding Child Abuse and Neglect, How Schools Can Combat Child Abuse and Neglect, The Educator's Role in Child Abuse and Neglect, Secret Scars: A Guide for Survivors of Child Sexual Abuse, Homeless Students,* and *Exploring Child Welfare: A Practice Perspective*. In addition, she has authored a monograph on *Designing and Implementing a School Reporting Protocol: A How-to-Manual for Massachusetts Teachers* for the Children's Trust Fund in Boston. Dr. Crosson-Tower consults to various schools and social agencies and maintains a private practice, Harvest Counseling and Consultation, specializing in the treatment of survivors of abuse and perpetrators of sexual abuse as well as the supervision of other professionals. She offers workshops and training both nationally and internationally for educators and other human service professionals.

Roger Delgado is Professor of Social Work at the California State University, Los Angeles. He received his M.S.W. from the University of Texas at Austin, and his Ph.D. in Social Work from the University of Southern California. In addition to teaching a variety of social work courses, Dr. Delgado is a licensed clinical social worker, is a part-time psychotherapist, and provides consultation and training to a variety of agencies and organizations which provide services to children and families and has received numerous awards for his services. He is currently director of the BASW program at CSULA.

Joselyn Geaga-Rosenthal (formerly Joselyn Yap), a California licensed clinical social worker since 1973, has practiced in various fields including child protective services, mental health, medical social work, and substance abuse treatment and prevention. She received her M.S.W. from the University of Southern California in 1971 and is currently a Children's Services Administrator with the County of Los Angeles Department of Children and Family Services.

Rita Ledesma, Ph.D., LCSW is an Assistant Professor of Social Work at California State University Los Angeles in the Department of Social Work. She received her M.S.W. and Ph.D. in Social Welfare from the University of California at Los Angeles. She has extensive direct practice experience working in the Latino and American Indian communities around child and family focused issues. Her research interests include American Indian and Latino children and families, health and child welfare, and bicultural and cross-cultural social work practice.

Amy Iwasaki Mass is Professor Emeritus in the Department of Sociology/ Anthropology and Social Work at Whittier College. She received her M.S.W. from the University of Southern California and her D.S.W. from the University of California at Los Angeles. In addition to her scholarly research in the area of cross-cultural socialization and interracial families, Dr. Mass is a clinical social worker in private practice, specializing in Asian-American families.

Gwendolyn Spencer Prater is Dean and Professor of Social Work at Jackson State University in Jackson, Mississippi. She received her M.S.W. from Ohio State University, and her D.S.W. from the University of Southern California. In addition to her teaching and research, Dr. Prater has been the recipient of numerous grants, including two from the U.S. Department of Health and Human Services; one for multidisciplinary training in the area of child abuse and neglect, and one for in-service training for Mississippi child welfare workers and supervisors. She has also received funding for M.S.W. student training through Title IV-E and served as Project Coordinator for the Mississippi Families for Kids Planning Project, focused on adoption placement of children lingering in foster care, funded by the Kellogg Foundation.

Carlos M. Sosa, M.S.W., is a former Deputy Director of the Department Of Children and Family Services for Los Angeles County, California. He earned his M.S.W. in Social Welfare from the University of California at Los Angeles. He is an adjunct faculty member at the California State University, Los Angeles, Department of Social Work and at the University of Southern California School of Social Work. His 30 years of professional social work have been in the field of public child welfare.

Paula Starr is an enrolled member of the Cheyenne and Arapaho Tribes of Oklahoma. Paula has a B.A. from the University of California, Irvine and attended graduate school at California State University, Long Beach. Currently, she is the Executive Director for Southern California Indian Center, Inc. (one of the largest Indian organizations in the United States), a local board member of FEMA in Los Angeles County and an Alternate Board Member of Orange County Community Development Council. She is a Senior Partner with Drew Child Development Center's Inter Ethnic Children's Committee.

1 Child Welfare: A Generalist Perspective

NEIL A. COHEN

California State University, Los Angeles

Child welfare is a field of service within the profession of social work that, in principle, concerns itself with all children, youth, and families. It consists of policies, programs, and human services that are designed to provide children and their families with the opportunity to experience, at the least, a minimum standard of living. Ideally, the field of child welfare tries to help them to achieve a quality of life that meets all the basic human needs (i.e., food, safety, clothing, shelter) and provides security, good health, and equitable educational and occupational opportunities and outcomes.

Child welfare, similar to other fields of human service such as health, mental health, public welfare, etc., in practice primarily concerns itself with the victims of social problems. How these social problems are defined, by whom, and how they are addressed are important issues that need to be understood in learning about the nature of the policies, programs, and services developed within child welfare.

This book will address these issues in an attempt to provide the reader with a critical perspective with which she or he can better understand the *whys, hows,* and *whats* of child welfare. This book will also endeavor to provide the student with the requisite knowledge, skills, values, and multi-cultural and multi-racial sensitivity to be able to work more effectively with people and organizations within the child welfare system.

Since the 1980s there has been a plethora of books devoted to the topic of child welfare. Tower (1998), Petr (1998), Downs, et al. (1996), Lindsey (1994), Kadushin (1980), McGowan and Meezan (1983), Stein (1981), and Zuckerman (1983) have provided excellent contributions to the conceptualization and historic description of child welfare policies, programs, and practice in the United States. Yet, to this writer, with the exception of Deutsch (1983), there is a discernible absence of child welfare texts directed to the undergraduate learner/practitioner interested in developing a working knowledge of the field of child welfare. In particular, a generalist, practice-oriented approach is needed that not only examines the historical antecedents of child welfare policy and practice in this country, but also provides the student with knowledge and skills in working with multi-racial and multi-cultural clients.

Stemming from this writer's experience as a child welfare practitioner in a large, racially and culturally diverse, urban public-sector setting, in addition to many years of teaching child welfare to undergraduate students in an inner-city, public university, the need for a different type of child welfare text has become apparent.

This book is intended, therefore, to meet this need by presenting a realistic overview of the field of child welfare as it exists today, examining why child welfare policies, programs, and services exist in their present form, and making recommendations for improvement, based on a generalist practice theory primarily for the undergraduate student.

The book will incorporate a multi-cultural and multi-racial perspective and emphasize the roles that economic, legal, racial, and sexual inequality have played in generating the need for child welfare services in the United States.

It will contain a normative focus, advocating those elements that quality child welfare policies, programs, and services should encompass. It also will describe the actual status of child welfare in the United States today, in terms of both policies and child welfare practice on the "front lines." Throughout, attention will be addressed to providing the reader with a framework that encourages the development of a spirit of inquiry—to develop an analytical perspective concerning child welfare directed toward providing a basis for contributing to needed improvements in this critical field of service.

The reader will be exposed to a contemporary blend of child welfare concepts, including rights of children; prevention, assessment, and intervention; quality of out-of-home care; managed care, permanency planning; deinstitutionalization; continuity of care; and normalization. The book will present child welfare case examples to illustrate and facilitate student "hands-on" generalist practice skills.

Child welfare, according to Kadushin (1980), involves providing social services to children and young people whose parents are unable to fulfill their child-rearing responsibilities, or whose communities fail to provide the resources and protection that children and families require. Child welfare services (1) are designed to reinforce, supplement, or substitute for the functions that parents have difficulty in performing and to improve conditions for children and their families by modifying existing social institutions or organizing new ones.

Child welfare is part of the larger social welfare institution, which in turn is only one of the many societal institutions that interact, influence each other, and give meaning to the nature of our society. The other societal institutions include the family, religious, educational, politico-legal, and economic (marketplace) systems.

To understand child welfare policies and practices in the United States, one must first develop an understanding of these various societal institutions and how they interact and complement each other. Equally important for analytic purposes is to understand how all of the institutions are perceived with regard to contributing to the on-going functioning of society.

An incisive discussion and analysis of societal institutions has been posited by Gilbert and Specht (2), who maintain that social welfare historically has been relegated to secondary status as an institution in this country. It serves a residual function (3) and operates only *after* there is a breakdown in the functioning of the primary, first-line institutions (i.e., family, religion, marketplace) that serve to transmit socialization skills, values, and appropriate behavior modes and to provide for people's economic, legal, social, and spiritual needs. That is, social welfare is said to provide for mutual support, if and when there is a breakdown in the primary need-meeting institutions in society.

This residual philosophic stance toward social welfare was put into operation by the previous federal administration and President Reagan, under what was quaintly described as the "safety net" approach. This approach was maintained by the present administration and former President Bush during this last decade of the twentieth century. According to this view, social welfare policies, programs, and services, including child welfare, should be reserved for the "truly needy," and used only when the primary institutions could not provide for basic human needs.

Unfortunately, basic human needs are not being met for millions of children, youth, and families by these primary institutions, nor are their needs being sufficiently met through the institution of social welfare. Some of the consequences have particular relevance for students of child welfare: increases in the number of latch-key children; rise in the number of homeless families; increases in the number of child abuse cases (and other forms of family violence); growing numbers of children and youth who are troubled and who are in trouble; including those diagnosed as severely emotionally disturbed (S.E.D.); increasing numbers of infants born with cocaine addiction ("crack babies"), HIV/AIDS and fetal alcohol syndrome (FAS) babies; increasing numbers of truants and school drop-outs; rise in illiteracy among school-age children and youth; an alarming increase in street violence among youth gangs. These are but some of the challenges that confront the field of child welfare at the present time.

Added to this challenge is the need for students of child welfare to be knowledgeable about the impact that racism, sexism, and other forms of inequality have on the nature and scope of policies and services provided to children and their families in the United States. Thus, this book also will devote particular attention to providing a working knowledge of women's issues, multi-cultural and multi-racial theories and concepts, and those requisite helping skills proved useful for working with culturally and racially diverse client groups.

Background

The following section will present a brief overview of the rise and impact of poverty and inadequate housing on children, youth, and their families.

Growing up in the United States during this last quarter of the twentieth century has been an exciting, challenging prospect, filled with optimism and dreams of achieving an improved quality of life. Yet, it is a prospect that is simultaneously tempered by the dread of nuclear confrontation, terrorism, violence at home and abroad, and anxiety concerning one's future economic chances in a period beset by a tremendous federal budget deficit. Not since the 1920s has this country been so divided between the doctrine of free enterprise, laissez-faire, and rugged individualism, found most often in the political right, and the values of dignity and worth of person/family/community and the philosophy of equity, equality, and moral justice, held by those endorsing a stronger commitment to humanitarianism and mutual support.

Poverty

Unlike the early 1960s, when there was the "rediscovery" of poverty in the United States (4), when we believed that hunger could be ended in this country, when there was optimism that this country could provide for the basic needs of its least-fortunate citizens and that the war on poverty could be won, it now appears that as we move into the twenty-first century, we are dividing ourselves into two countries. One, which is shrinking in size, can afford to live decently—and even well. The other, growing in size, struggles to provide for minimal needs—food, housing, and health. Since 1989, the poorest fifth (bottom 20 percent) of families have lost $587 each and the richest 5 percent have gained $29,533 each. Put another way, since 1989, these richest 5 percent have received a larger share of the nation's income than the poorest 40 percent (5).

In 1979, approximately 11.6 percent of the population in the United States lived in poverty. In 1993, 22.7 (15.7 million) percent did. According to the U.S. government, in 1996 a family of four was categorized as poor if its income was below $16,000.

The problems of the poor, and particularly the children—the most vulnerable and poorest group of Americans—living in poverty have reached almost crisis proportions.

1. In 1993, there were approximately 15.7 million children living in poverty, about 22.7 percent of all children (6).
2. In 1996, nearly one out of three children under the age of six (5.87 million) lived in poverty. There was a 24 percent increase in poor young children in California, for example, between 1983 and 1996 (7).
3. In 1989, nearly 40 percent of all black children lived in poverty. So did more than 32 percent of Hispanic children, 38.8 percent of Native American children, and 17 percent of Asian or Pacific Islander children (8).
4. More than one-sixth of the poor children—some 2.5 million of them—are in families where at least one person holds a full-time job, shattering the notion that a full-time job prevents poverty.
5. In 1996, 15.1 percent of children and youth under 18 lacked health insurance.
6. Presently, 20 percent of children live in a family receiving food stamps.

Poverty is considered the highest risk factor for children and families seen as an antecedent of adolescent crime, school failure, and early childbearing. According to Schorr (9), "risk factors leading to later damage occur more frequently among children in families that are poor . . . more frequently among families persistently poor and living in areas of concentrated poverty."

Is it any wonder that child welfare services are required most by poor families for whom the close association between poverty and risk holds for every component of risk—"from premature birth to poor health and nutrition, from failure to develop warm, secure, trusting relationships early in life to child abuse, from family stress and chaos to failure to master school skills" (10).

Housing

In 1936, at the height of the greatest depression ever experienced in the United States, the federal government pledged itself to the goal of decent housing for all Americans. But today, large numbers of men, women, and children are without adequate housing. They sleep in the streets, in train stations, under freeways, in cars, in shelters. Only a guess can be made concerning the real number of homeless in America. The Reagan Administration estimated in May 1984 that the number was 250,000 to 350,000. Advocates for the homeless today estimate between two and three million. Few dispute that the number is appalling and growing every day.

In most of the cities reporting to the Conference of Mayors, emergency shelters have had to turn people away. And merely "sheltering" the homeless cannot be the goal. Until recently, *shelters* meant places for animals, or places to wait for a bus or to protect oneself from a military attack. Shelters may be a way to avoid freezing temperatures (or falling bomb fragments), but they are not a way for human beings to live. Today, women and their children represent the fastest growing group of homeless including the rise of their numbers in the shelters of the central city.

In short, while many Americans have done well, others—millions of others—have done unacceptably poorly. While policymakers now focus on defense expenditures, tax cuts, and the deficit, the nation is without substantive policies to help provide food for the hungry, decent-paying jobs for the unemployed, housing for the homeless, and equal opportunity for youth of all colors.

Values

How can we begin to understand why a country as wealthy as the United States, replete with sophisticated micro-chip technology capable of placing people on the moon, struggles with the increasing problems of widespread poverty, destitution, homelessness, violence (including child, spouse, and elder abuse), structural unemployment, and an astronomic federal budget deficit. Not only do we not have solutions for these social problems; worse, they are being compounded by a seemingly increasing mood of meanspiritedness toward those suffering from these problems.

Lest we forget, the victims of these social problems invariably are the women, children, and youth of our society, with disproportionate numbers involving people of color. It is the children of society who suffer in the greatest numbers from hunger, homelessness, abuse, limited educational and employment opportunities. It is also the children and youth of society, particularly those of color, who are denied equal legal rights automatically ascribed to adults.

It is not enough to suggest that the social problems extant in this country are due to the absence of requisite technology, expertise, resources, or experience. Rather, analysis of the myriad of problems, especially those impacting on children and youth, must include consideration of values, power, and political will.

Although articulated very well by many observers and writers of the human condition in the United States, I believe Irving Sarnoff (11) speaks most saliently about how the conflict of values inextricably contributes to the absence of coherent commitment and consensus regarding national social welfare policy.

Sarnoff distinguishes two modal clusters of values as being operative simultaneously in the United States: values of aggrandizement, and values of humanitarianism. Aggrandizing values include competition, rugged individualism, material security, power, status, prestige, wealth, technological know-how, ambition—a melange of individualistic-oriented preferences. Contrasting with these are humanitarian values: equality, social and moral justice, freedom, liberty, human dignity, beauty, love-nurturing, developmental—collective-oriented preferences.

Sarnoff posits that the major values exhibited and operationalized are those of aggrandizement. The values of humanitarianism are secondary. Because both sets of values operate simultaneously, there is inevitable conflict, resulting in the patchwork quilt of incrementalist social welfare policies, programs, and services, including those within the field of child welfare. Until there is a reordering of those values that drive the kinds of decisions we make concerning the quality of life in this country for all people, we can expect that there will be a continuing retrenchment and defunding of human service programs—including those that focus on children, youth, and families. Ironically, the present reduction in social program funding will more than likely end up costing society even more money and resources in the long run.

As indicated earlier, child welfare today can be characterized as being primarily residual in nature. That is, its policies, programs, and services are basically reactive in nature. The primary emphasis is placed on changing the behaviors, attitudes, coping skills, and values of those children, youth, and families who come to the attention of child welfare programs. The locus of responsibility for experiencing social problems, be it child abuse, unemployment, dependency, delinquency, et al., is seen as residing within the individual. The primary approach toward change or treatment is to change ethnocentrically individual or family systems toward middle-class Anglo values, behaviors, and attitudes.

Within this nation's basically residual philosophical orientation toward child welfare, there are, nonetheless, several key concepts that are providing a framework for the current status of child welfare programs and services. Knowledge of these concepts should help the student better understand the current trends in child welfare.

Permanency Planning

Empirical longitudinal research efforts tracing the outcomes of children placed out-of-the-home into foster care arrangements have consistently demonstrated that children and youth, once placed, tend to languish for years in the foster care system (12). Although it usually was believed that foster care would be a short-term situation, the evidence has revealed that it is easier to "remove" children from their own homes than it is to return them to their home of origin.

More study and thought was needed in making the appropriate professional decision at the outset. Too often, children were "put" into foster care as a decision of short-term expedience and short-range problem solving. Once in foster care, too many children tend to become forgotten or, in the words of Maas and Engler (13), become "the orphans of the living." Biological parents may move away, die, become incarcerated, become more abusive, or disabled, and the original plan to return the child or children to their own home is no longer workable.

As a result of these empirical findings, coupled with the increased number of children coming to the attention of child welfare agencies and the local juvenile courts, present federal and state child welfare bodies are linking funding with the capability of local public child welfare agencies to develop permanency plans for *all* children within their caseloads. Permanency plans, in short, are directed toward establishing permanent homes for children, with their biological parents, or other permanent parents through adoption, guardianship, or planned long-term foster care. The goal is to move toward foster care arrangements that are more of an acute, short-term nature.

Deinstitutionalization

Recent discoveries of abuse and neglect in residential institutions for disturbed and delinquent youth, coupled with the impetus of the Community Mental Health Centers Act of 1963, wherein there was emphasis in returning patients from large closed state mental institutions back to the community, has led to the deinstitutionalization movement in the juvenile justice system within the field of child welfare.

Yet, although Lerman's (14) comparative analysis of the "youth-in-trouble system" in the 1920s and 1970s shows a significant decline in the institutionalization of dependent and neglected children, at the same time there was a marked increase in juvenile correctional and mental health institutionalization, especially in short-term and private facilities. There does appear to this date, deinstitutionalization rhetoric to the contrary, a societal predilection toward placing large numbers of youth in closed residential programs—and, it should be added, out of the view and consciousness of the public.

Normalization

The concept of normalization originated from practices and laws in the Scandinavian countries, particularly Denmark and Sweden (15). Early statements about normalization emphasized the need for dysfunctional children, especially the mentally retarded, to be treated as much like "normal" children as possible (16).

Wolfensberger (17) redefined normalization for use in the United States as being the "utilization of means in order to establish and/or maintain personal behaviors and characteristics which are as culturally normative as possible." Wolfensberger believes that the means used to provide services for the developmentally dysfunctional should be similar to those for other people, and that service goals should produce behaviors as similar to normal as possible ("mainstreaming"). According to Wolfensberger (18), the provision of culturally normative services is not sufficient; providers must demonstrate that services lead to desirable outcomes.

Attention to the provision of "normalized" services for exceptional individuals remains the most critical application of the normalization principle (19). According to this principle, all people, whether "deviant" or not, should be integrated to the maximum extent possible into the service delivery system.

This principle is closely related to those principles of deinstitutionalization (residential integration) and mainstreaming (educational integration).

Least Restrictive Environment

Historically, child welfare services have tended to supplant rather than to supplement parental care. According to Ziefert (20), operating from an "all or nothing" position, the tendency has been either to neglect families totally, on the grounds that government should not interfere in family life, or to respond to troubled situations by placing children out of the home, often for long periods of time. In recent years, the principle that care should be given in the least restrictive environment has become the cornerstone for policy, program, and service development in child welfare. In brief, this principle dictates that the maintenance of the biological family is the preferred option in the care and protection of children.

Family Preservation

Linked closely to the principle of least restrictive environment is the current increased emphasis on family preservation and family support services. These services exemplify a philosophy that emphasizes the importance of the family—that they should be kept together, and that intensive, focused and comprehensive efforts will mobilize family strengths. Legislative support for family preservation is to be found in the Indian Child Welfare Act of 1978, P.L. 95-6098, the Adoption Assistance and Child Welfare Act of 1980 (mandating that reasonable efforts be made to keep families together), and culminating in The Family Preservation and Support Services in the Omnibus Budget Reconciliation Act of 1993.

The emphasis on the biological family and the importance of family life for all children and youth (least restrictive environment and family preservation) have joined with the movement toward deinstitutionalization, normalization, and permanency planning as important planks in the present-day platform of child welfare policies, programs, and services.

Managed Care

Managed care, a growing trend originating in the health care system, has since begun to spread to child welfare. Managed care, in its brief version, tries to exert control over and manage three aspects of care: cost, quality, and access (21). There is emphasis on results, measuring outcome, prevention, cost containment, and time limitations.

At the core of managed care is some form of *capitation* system to finance the care. Capitation is a form of compensation in which fixed dollar amounts are paid to providers for a population of people in advance of the delivery of services (22). This prepaid pool of money must finance the provision of all contracted services and must be *managed* so that it is not exhausted and depleted by expensive procedures or services.

In child welfare governmental agencies, managed care principles extend to the way child welfare services are organized and funded. Through the use of purchase of service contracting (POSC), with private agencies for large programs, such as for family preservation services, the state/county child welfare agency computes what it has to spend to provide service to an average client. It then contracts with a private agency to provide the same services for a capitated fee. In sum, the private agency receives a set amount of dollars per family referred rather than reimbursement for specific services rendered (23). It is in the agency's interest to manage these monies most efficiently to maximize their care coverage, and through privatization mechanisms, to maximize their profits.

Generalist Practice

This book will endeavor to provide the reader with a generalist practice framework with which to link relevant child welfare theory, principles, policies, and services into child welfare practice. The human service generalist at the baccalaureate level can be described as a person with a broad systems view who can look at an entire social situation, analyze the interdependent interactions between people in all the resource systems connected to that situation, intervene in those interactions, determine which specialists are needed from a variety of disciplines, and coordinate and mobilize the knowledge and skill of many disciplines.

Emphasis will be placed on educating the reader to view children, youth, and families holistically, i.e., to focus on the whole person—body, spirit, and mind—and on the interdependence of each of the major dimensions of the person. In addition, primacy will be devoted to preparing the reader to view children, youth, and families not in isolation, but within their life–space milieu, i.e., their physical, intellectual, social, emotional, spiritual, and environmental setting. Providing knowledge and information about family, cultural and racial diversity, physical surroundings, and the society of the individual will be an essential part of this book's generalist practice framework.

As we examine the myriad issues extant in the field of child welfare today, these concepts or principles guiding the present practice of services to children, youth and families will be seen to be sorely tested. This is due, in large part, to a residual philosophy which has become manifest through a lack of resources, lack of federal, state, and local administrative support. It is further exacerbated by an increasingly individualistic orientation in society that militates against significant strides being made for children and their families who are seen as troubled and troublesome.

Within this context, this book will seek to provide the reader with a working knowledge of the history of child welfare in this country, as well as depicting and analyzing the current issues, policies, practices, and trends within the field. Particular attention will be given to multicultural and multiracial generalist practice perspectives.

Experts in various aspects of child welfare have written new material for this book specific to the issues addressed above. Chapters Two and Three have been written by Neil Cohen and will address the historical antecedents and current issues and prospects for child welfare (Two); and societal responses to the needs of children and families—the continuum of services (Three). The third chapter examines in some depth policies and services for children, youth, and families. An in-depth discussion of foster family care, group homes, residential treatment facilities and institutions is provided. Attention is focused on trying to find the best "mix" among meeting the needs of children, youth, and families; the reality of available resources and public support; and the current professional knowledge and skills extant in child welfare.

Stemming from an analysis of values and their concomitant manifestation into child welfare policies, Chapter Three provides an analytic framework with which to examine the *whys*, *hows*, and *whats* of current child welfare policies, programs, and services.

The second section of this book devotes itself to an in-depth presentation and examination of multicultural and multiracial programs and services as well as generalist practice perspectives in child welfare. In Chapter Four, Gwen Prater addresses child welfare and the African-American family. In Chapter Five, Rita Ledesma and Paula Starr examine child welfare and the Native American child, youth, and family. In Chapter Six, Amy Iwasaki Mass and Joselyn Yap address child welfare and the Asian-Pacific family. In Chapter Seven, Roger Delgado discusses child welfare and the Hispanic child, youth, and family.

Section Three consists of a discussion and analysis of family violence in this country. Cynthia Crosson Tower examines the issue of child maltreatment, including neglect, and physical, emotional, and sexual abuse in Chapter Eight.

An often overlooked aspect of child welfare is that of children, youth, and families residing in rural America. In Chapter Nine of Section Four, Charles Baker examines the child welfare policies, programs, and practice issues which involve and impact the millions of people in this country who live outside our large urban centers and devotes considerable attention to the distinctions between poverty and child neglect.

Neil Cohen, with Carlos Sosa, provide an integrative summary of the preceding chapters and discusses prospects and future directions into the twenty-first century for child welfare in Chapter Ten. Particular emphasis has been placed on providing a descriptive, normative perspective, and an analytic framework with which to further understand the progress already made in the field of child welfare as well as those dilemmas and issues which remain to be resolved.

Endnotes

1. Alfred Kadushin, *Child Welfare Services*, 3rd ed., p. 5.
2. Neil Gilbert and Harry Specht, *Dimensions of Social Welfare Policy*, 2nd ed.
3. Harold Wilensky and Charles Lebeaux, *Industrial Society and Social Welfare*, 2nd ed.
4. Michael Harrington, *The Other America*.
5. Children's Defense Fund, *The State of America's Children*.
6. Ibid.
7. Columbia University Study, July 1998. *Young Children in Poverty*.
8. U.S. Dept. of Commerce, Bureau of Census.
9. Lisbeth Schorr, *Within Our Reach*.
10. Ibid.
11. Irving Sarnoff, *Society of Tears*.
12. Charles Gershenson, *Child Welfare Population Characteristics and Flow Analysis: FY 1982*.
13. Henry Maas and Richard Engler, *Children in Need of Parents*.
14. P. Lerman, *Deinstitutionalization and the Welfare State*.
15. N. E. Bank-Mikkelsen, "A Metropolitan Area in Denmark: Copenhagen," in R. B. Kugel and W. Wolfensberger, eds. *Changing Patterns in Residential Services for the Mentally Retarded*.
16. B. Nirje, "The Normalization Principle and Its Management Implications," Ibid.

17. Wolf Wolfensberger, *Normalization.*
18. Ibid.
19. Francine Deutsch, *Child Welfare Services on Behalf of Children.*
20. Marjorie Ziefert, "Homemaker and Day-Care Services," in Joan Laird and Ann Hartman, eds. *A Handbook of Child Welfare* pp. 417–438.
21. P. R. Kongstvedt, *Essentials of Managed Care.*
22. V. H. Jackson, ed., *Managed Care Resource Guide for Social Workers in Agency Settings.*
23. Christopher Petr, *Social Work with Children and Their Families.*

Bibliography

Bank-Mikkelsen, N. E. "A Metropolitan Area in Denmark: Copenhagen." In R. B. Kugel and W. Wolfensberger, eds. *Changing Patterns in Residential Services for the Mentally Retarded.* Washington, D.C.: President's Committee on Mental Retardation, 1969.

Children's Defense Fund, *The State of America's Children, Yearbook 1998,* Children's Defense Fund, 1998.

Columbia University, *Young Children in Poverty,* July 1998, Columbia University.

Deutsch, Francine. *Child Welfare Services on Behalf of Children.* Monterey, CA: Brooks/Cole Publishing, 1983.

Downs, Susan Whitelaw, et al., *Child Welfare and Family Services,* 5th ed. White Plains, NY: Longman Publishers, 1996.

Gershenson, Charles. *Child Welfare Population Characteristics and Flow Analysis: FY 1982.* Washington, D.C.: Administration for Children, Youth, and Families, Children's Bureau, 1983.

Gilbert, Neil, and Specht, Harry. *Dimensions of Social Welfare Policy.* 2nd ed. Itasca, IL: F. E. Peacock Publishers, 1981.

Harrington, Michael. *The Other America.* New York: Macmillan, 1963.

Jackson, V. H., ed., *Managed Care Resource Guide for Social Workers in Agency Settings.* Washington, D.C.: National Association of Social Workers, 1995.

Kadushin, Alfred. *Child Welfare Services.* 3rd ed. New York: Macmillan, 1980.

Kongstvedt, P. R., *Essentials of Managed Care.* Gaithersburg, MD: Aspen Publishers, 1995.

Lerman, P. *Deinstitutionalization and the Welfare State.* New Brunswick, NJ: Rutgers University Press, 1982.

Lindsey, Duncan, *The Welfare of Children,* NY: Oxford University Press, 1994.

Maas, Henry, and Engler, Richard. *Children in Need of Parents.* New York: Columbia University Press, 1959.

McGowan, Brenda, and Meezan, William. *Child Welfare: Current Dilemmas, Future Directions.* Itasca, IL: F. E. Peacock Publishing Co., 1983.

Nirje, B. "The Normalization Principle and Its Management Implications." In R. B. Kugel and W. Wolfensberger, eds., *Changing Patterns for the Mentally Retarded.* Washington, D.C.: President's Committee on Mental Retardation, 1969.

Petr, Christopher G., *Social Work with Children and Their Families.* New York: Oxford University Press, 1998.

Sarnoff, Irving. *Society of Tears.* New York: Citadel Press, 1966.

Schorr, Lisbeth, *Within Our Reach: Breaking the Cycle of Disadvantage.* New York: Doubleday/Anchor, 1988.

Stein, Theodore. *Social Work Practice in Child Welfare.* Englewood Cliffs, NJ: Prentice-Hall, 1981.

Tower, Cynthia Crosson, *Exploring Child Welfare: A Practice Perspective*. Boston, MA: Allyn and Bacon, 1998.

U.S. Department of Commerce, Bureau of Census, 1990.

Wilensky, Harold, and Lebeaux, Charles. *Industrial Society and Social Welfare*. 2nd ed. New York: Russell Sage Foundation, 1965.

Wolfensberger, Wolf. *Normalization*. New York: National Institute on Mental Retardation, 1972.

Ziefert, Marjorie. "Homemaker and Day-Care Services." In Joan Laird and Ann Hartman, eds. *A Handbook of Child Welfare*. New York: Free Press, 1985.

Zuckerman, Erva. *Child Welfare*. New York: Free Press, 1983.

CHAPTER

2 Child Welfare History in the United States

NEIL A. COHEN
California State University, Los Angeles

This chapter is designed to provide a framework whereby the reader, new to the field of child welfare, will be helped to develop an understanding of child welfare history in the United States and of those present-day forces leading to the myriad of child welfare policies, programs, and services that have been established over time. These have been developed at the national, state, and local level with the intent to promote healthy development of children and their families.

The field of child welfare, which is a significant component of social welfare overall, may be defined as "the broad range of activities designed to benefit children, promote their well-being, and strengthen or assure provision for meeting their physical, social, emotional, educational, and moral needs" (1). Child welfare *services* are more specifically defined as those social services designed to "ensure that children will have the care, protection, and treatment they need when their parents, for any of a variety of reasons, are not able to provide these essentials" (2). This excludes health, nutritional, educational, and recreational services that also contribute to the welfare of children but do not focus on "the problems of the child that result when the needs which parents are ordinarily expected to meet are either unmet or inadequately met" (3).

A review of the history of child welfare in this country will help frame the conditions and antecedents which have given rise to the nature, form, and scope of child welfare today.

The Child-Saving Movement: 1600–1700s

The origins of the Child-Saving Movement can be traced to colonial days, when poverty was a sin and work the way to salvation. Except in relation to a few "worthy poor," poverty was believed to be caused by inherent habits or instincts of the individual. The early child savers relied upon two principal sources of authority: the power of the township overseer of the poor, and the power to intervene in the parent–child relationship under the laws of guardianship and the doctrine of *parens patriae* (the state's obligation and right to protect the young, the helpless, and the incompetent; i.e., to do what is best for the interest of the child).

The early immigrants to the United States came from many walks of life. A mixture of small tradesmen, wealthy businessmen, farmers, criminals, paupers, adventurers, and explorers, they were on the whole a socially mobile group seeking something different from the life they had known. Some came pushed by despair or anger, hoping to escape the control, hopelessness, and frustration of their lives. Some came pulled by individual dreams and looking forward eagerly to making those dreams become reality. Some came simply because they were challenged by the risks of the unknown and to find out what the excitement was all about. But few of those who came had any concept at all of what awaited them in the unexplored vastness of America. One of the factors basic to the understanding of American life is that it began to flourish even before it was known and perhaps because it was not yet known in even the roughest outlines (4).

The first colonists lived in the constant belief that something better might turn up—and probably would, if they could just keep things changing and moving. This orientation toward change, this belief that solutions to human problems may lie in the new, the different, and the unexpected, is an important part of American life and institutions (5).

When the colonies were first settled, among the greatest problems that the settlers faced were a lack of equipment and technical knowledge to deal with the forces of weather and climate, the vast geographic spaces, the wilderness that surrounded them, and the need for the unremitting labor of all members of the community (6).

Another important force for change was the scarcity of labor. The sparseness of the colonial population was in marked contrast to the heavily settled industrial areas of England from which most of the settlers came. Until the first quarter of the nineteenth century, only a relatively small number of people were dependent on wages from employment.

The American settlers did not see themselves as wage earners. They were small businessmen, artisans, craftsmen, and farmers. There was always the fresh opportunity of the frontier (7). The influence of the early scarcity and mobility of labor on social thinking had profound effects on the development of social welfare programs. Instead of passing laws to confine the poor and unemployed to a geographic area, the colonies became convinced that it was the obligation of the unemployed to move on to areas where work was available and that such areas could always be found.

Indenture

To augment a scarce labor supply, colonial families turned to three sources of labor outside the family: the Indian, the Negro slave, and the indentured servant. The settlers quickly found that the Indians were not easily domesticated. Although Indian slavery survived for a long time—as late as 1708 there are records of natives in bondage—it was not a dependable supply of labor. Thus, in the history of the economic development of America, the immigrants may have utilized and exploited the land of the Indian, but they were unable to exploit the Indian's labor (8).

One important source of labor, at least until the seventeenth century, was the indentured white servant. In order to secure transportation to America, men and women would bind themselves by a written contract, called an indenture, to serve some individual (any individual) who would pay the costs of transportation. They served for a specified period of time, usually four to seven years, for the food, clothing, and shelter necessary to maintain life.

It is estimated that more than 250,000 persons were indentured during the colonial period. In 1683 there were 12,000 indentured servants in Virginia (one-sixth of the population), while in Pennsylvania at that time, they made up two-thirds of the immigrants (9). Indenture seemed to have advantages for everyone involved: The colonists got the labor they needed; England rid itself of the "idle," the "wretched," and the criminal and relieved itself of their support; the indentured were given transportation to what many of them viewed as a world of opportunity; and the shipping trade had a good source of income (10).

Slavery

The terrible story of Negro slavery forms an especially inhuman chapter in the history of American life and social welfare. The horror that was slavery in the colonies began in August 1619 with the landing at Jamestown, Virginia, of "twenty negars" (11). However, blacks had come to America long before this as servants, explorers and slaves. The history of slavery is usually thought of in connection with the South, but there were slaves in New England. And the shipping industry in New England was deeply involved in the transportation of slaves from Africa to America. Thus, the slave trade was as economically important to New England as it was to the South. In fact, Massachusetts in 1641 became the first colony to give statutory recognition to slavery, followed by Connecticut in 1650 (12). Like indenture, slavery grew out of the growing labor requirements of the colonies. In the face of those requirements, white indenture and native labor were inadequate, particularly in the South. Furthermore, the cost of indentured servants was relatively high compared to the cost of black slaves. It is estimated that during the century from 1686 to 1786 approximately two million Africans were spirited away from their homes; 250,000 of them ended up in the American colonies (13). That which was cruel and inhuman regarding the indenture system could be multiplied many times over in describing that "peculiar institution," slave trade and slavery.

Child Labor

Children, like women, were an integral part of the colonial labor system. In colonial life, the labor of children was a social fact and a social necessity, not a social problem. In 1641 the General Court of Massachusetts ordered: "All masters of families should see that their children and servants should be industriously applied" (14). If necessity justified the labor of young children, religion sanctified it. From an early age children were warned that idleness destroyed the soul and undermined the social system. It was not uncommon in New England for well-to-do parents to bind their children to other households to serve as servants so that they would experience and profit from the discipline of work. Family, church, and government had a part in keeping everyone employed (15).

In addition to expecting their own children, or the children of their neighbors, to be employed and taught a trade, the colonists imported poor and orphan children from England and Holland to America to be bound out as laborers. In one example, the superintendents of the almshouses in London were directed to "take from the almshouses or orphan asylums 300 to 400 boys and girls of ten, twelve to fifteen years of age" for transport to America (16).

In 1654 the burgomasters of Amsterdam sent a cargo of poor children to Peter Stuyvesant at Fort New Amsterdam. The following letter accompanied the children to the New World:

> *Being informed by the governors of the almshouses of the vast number of poor people where with they are burdened and charged, we have concluded to relieve them and so do the Company a service, by sending some of them to New Netherland. We have therefore, sent over in the ship belonging to the bearer hereof, twenty-seven or twenty-eight boys and girls, requesting you, in a friendly manner, to extend to them your kind advice and assistance, and to advance them if possible; so that they, according to their fitness, may earn their board. If*

you consider that the populations of that country could be advanced by sending over such persons, we shall, on being informed, lose no time to have some more forwarded. Meanwhile, we shall be much obliged by the aid and assistance you will extend in this instance (17).

One can clearly see the social welfare implications involved. It relieves the mother country of the responsibility of caring for the orphans at the same time that it gives the orphans an opportunity to work out their own destiny (18).

Orphans

In March 1642, the first of many colonial laws relating to orphans was enacted in Virginia. The guardians and overseers of orphans were ordered to furnish an annual account of the handling of the estates of the orphans to the commissioners of the county court. They were also ordered to educate and instruct their charges "according to their best endeavors in Christian religion and in rudiments of learning" (19). The legislation stated that orphans whose estate was not large enough to provide for their education and care were to be apprenticed until 21 to learn a trade. An act of 1705 added that every orphan should be taught to read and write while so apprenticed (20).

The first public orphanage was established in the city of Charleston, South Carolina, in 1790. The institution was to care for and educate both orphan children and children whose parents were destitute and unable to maintain them (21). Mention should also be made of the orphanage that the Ursuline nuns founded in New Orleans in 1729. It was the first private children's institution in the country. As a result of an attack by a band of Natchez Indians on Fort Rosalie, New Orleans, on November 28, 1729, wherein every man in the post was killed, the Ursulines took in the orphans and provided them with shelter in their charity hospital.

Removal of Children from Their Parents

From the beginning, in all the colonies, children could not be removed from their parents without a court order. It is important to note, also, the reasons for which children could be removed. There is very little evidence that the community was interested in protecting children from hard labor or abusive treatment. Children were removed when the parents seemed unable to bring them up so as to give promise that the children would become independent citizens. In particular, fatherless children and illegitimate children were often removed from their mothers on the ground that the mothers could not care for them. And children of the poor were removed so that they might be placed in a situation in which they would learn a trade. Children were usually seen as little adults, and there was little concern about depriving them of opportunities for play and self-development activities. As pointed out earlier, child labor was a necessity, not a social problem. Thus, the right of the state to interfere between parent and child was established.

During colonial times, however, that right was exercised only when parents were poor or when the failure to educate was the result of the child's own delinquency (22).

The Child Rescue Movement: 1800–1850

In contrast to the religious motives and charitable impulses of the Child-Saving Movement, persons active in child rescue relied more upon legal concepts and efforts to advance the rights of children through the application of the law.

During the first half of the 1800s, the legal relationships between children and parents were beginning to change. Judges' decisions as to the needs of the child in particular cases began to override the rights of parents, particularly fathers, and even the rights of the community. This trend toward concern for the protection of the child was to accelerate in the last half of the nineteenth century, particularly in 1869 in re Fletcher et al. v. Illinois. The Illinois court ruled that even though the law gave parents a wide discretion in matters of discipline, parental authority "must be exercised within the bounds of reason and humanity." In 1884 in re State v. Jones, a North Carolina court ruled that "permanent injury or malice" was the test of excessive punishment.

As discussed earlier, during the colonial and early national periods children were largely cared for and educated through "binding out" and apprenticeship. However, as industry moved out of the home, as slavery grew, and as the tasks of the frontier no longer demanded the unskilled hands of every available person, taking young children into one's home became more a burden than an aid. As a result, by the 1800s, hundred of children in large cities were housed in almshouses, with or without their families (23).

By 1830, several events were pushing society toward the rapid development of special institutional care for children: (1) the number of orphans and dependent children was growing; (2) there were graphic reports by respected persons of the terrible conditions of life in the almshouses; (3) an increasing number of women were becoming active in benevolent activities, with a special interest in the welfare of children, particularly girls.

Foster Care

The concept of placing children in the West, as family members rather than indentured servants, is usually thought to have originated with Charles Loring Brace, reformer of the mid-nineteenth century. Brace, a minister, worked with prisoners and the poor in New York City. His work exposed him to the problems of thousands of vagrant children who were without any homes at all. He came to believe that most of the preventable causes of poverty could be avoided by getting such children out of the city and into a rural environment in the Midwest as members of a rural family.

The Children's Aid Society was established in 1853 under Brace's leadership. It was different in purpose in that it intended to employ paid agents to work with children. Brace's concept of foster home placement also differed from the earlier use of indenture and apprenticeship in putting a certain emphasis on healthy family life and family interaction, rather than work, discipline, and training, as the means for achieving rehabilitation. His approach began the movement toward the foster home programs that we know today (24).

African-American Children

Until after 1865, slavery was the major child welfare institution for African-American children. In a peculiar way, slavery as an institution performed many of the functions that the social welfare institution performs in a free society; that is, slaves "must be supported in some fashion when they were too old to work; they must have attention in sickness for they represent capital; and they could never be among the unemployed" (25). Thus, in the South there was no identified need for a separate system of child care. As well, the African-American child was almost equally ignored in the North. African-American children were found in alms-houses, but they were excluded as a matter of policy from most of the orphanages before the Civil War.

The Quakers, who were among the leaders in the abolitionist movement, became concerned about the care of African-American children. In 1822 they established the Philadelphia Association for the Care of Colored Children. This association developed and supported the first orphanage for black children. Several other institutions were established in Providence (1835) and New York (1836). However, despite the efforts of the founders to divorce the care of these children from the conflict of the times, white mobs burned the shelter for colored orphans in Philadelphia in 1838, and the Colored Orphan Asylum in New York was broken into and set afire by 500 white men and women during the Draft Riot of 1863 (26).

Inception of Youth-Serving Agencies: 1860–1900

Youth Agencies

Many of the youth-serving agencies that we know today began their work in the mid-1800s. The first of these was the Young Men's Christian Association. It was founded in 1851 in Boston by George Williams, a retired sea captain, who modeled it after the London society. It sought to improve the conditions of young men who came to the city to seek work. In addition, the Ys sought to protect new urban citizens from the dangers of irreligion, intemperance, and immorality (27).

The first Young Women's Christian Association was founded in Boston in 1866, followed by one in New York in 1867. The YWCAs followed the pattern that had been established by the YMCAs.

In 1860 the first Boys' Club was founded in Hartford, Connecticut, by a church women's group for the purpose of giving boys an opportunity to participate in various sport and social activities in a Christian atmosphere. The concept of this type of club took hold, and Boys' Clubs quickly spread over the country. The Jewish movement traces its roots back to the 1840s, when groups of Jewish young people began to establish literary societies. Jewish Centers served both boys and girls.

The Needs and Rights of Children

Up to the middle of the nineteenth century, there was little consideration of childhood as a special time of growth and development. Instead, children were treated as small adults, though without adult rights. The father was considered to have an absolute right to their custody and control. Not only dependent children, but most children, were sent to work very early, with little concern about childhood as a special stage of human development. The Census of 1870 reported that over 700,000 children between the ages of 10 and 15 were engaged in gainful occupations and that nearly one-sixth of these children were employed in industry (28).

However, in the late 1800s, the rights of children began to receive increasing attention as a result of three forces: (1) the proportion of children in the population began to decrease, so that more adults were available, both to do the work of society and to care for children; (2) more knowledge about the needs of children as a special group became available through the infant sciences of psychology and human learning; and (3) there was a general growth of concern for the rights of all persons and for the reform of situations that oppressed people (29).

Thus, toward the end of the nineteenth century we find two movements developing in child welfare: (1) a growing concern with the needs of childhood as a special period of life, and (2) an enlargement of the rights of children in relation to parents or to persons standing in the place of parents. In these movements the tendency has been for society as *parens patriae* to intervene so that the "presumably fair and uniform treatment" at the hands of professional authorities and agencies can be substituted for the "ignorance, neglect, and exploitation of some parents." This transfer of responsibilities required the development of administrative, judicial, and professional techniques of investigation, decision, supervision, and care (30).

As a result, from the late nineteenth century to the present, there has been an increasing substitution of public norms for the appropriate care, custody, control, and behavior of children in place of the private standards of the family in such matters. The rights of children that began to be of concern to the public were: (1) the right to an education; (2) the right to protection against being sent to work too early or in certain types of industries; (3) the right to protection against immoral influences; (4) the right to adequate food, clothing, shelter, and medical care; and (5) the right to protection against physical (and later emotional) abuse (31).

National Awareness of Children's Needs: 1900–1930

The White House Conference on Child Welfare

The historic White House Conference on Child Welfare is credited with first bringing the subject of dependent children before the entire nation. In an effort to gain support for a national bureau to protect the nation's children, President Theodore Roosevelt called the White House Conference on Child Welfare in late January 1909. The report of this conference, unanimously adopted by nearly 200 men and women in attendance, was to have far-reaching effects on the welfare of families and children throughout the nation.

The report stated: "Home life is the highest and finest product of civilization . . . children should not be deprived of it except for urgent and compelling reasons." It continued by saying that for children "who for sufficient reasons must be removed from their own homes, or who have no homes . . . it is desirable that they should be cared for in families whenever practicable. The carefully selected foster home is for the normal child the best substitute for the natural home" (32).

This recommendation became critical to the movement to establish programs for assisting mothers to care for their children in their own homes, to efforts to keep delinquent and dependent children in their own homes, to the development of adoption as a method for providing homes for homeless children, to the increased use of the foster home rather than the institution for the care of children, and to the development of a "cottage" type of institution for children, instead of the large, congregate type of institution.

An important outcome of this conference was the precedent it established. Every ten years since 1909, there has been a White House conference on children's problems and needs. And each conference in turn has had important effects on the concepts of child care and on progressive child welfare programs. The most recent White House conference was held in 1990 under the Administration of President George Bush.

However, the most important achievement of the first White House conference was its support for the creation of the Children's Bureau and the inauguration of programs to assist mothers. In April 1912, the bill creating the Children's Bureau, originally introduced by Senator William Borah of Idaho, was signed into law by President William Howard Taft.

The creation of the U.S. Children's Bureau was the first occasion in which the federal government entered the field of social services as distinguished from public health and education. Originally the bureau was located within the Department of Commerce and Labor. A year later it was transferred to the newly created Department of Labor, and in 1953 it was moved again to another newly created department—the Department of Health, Education, and Welfare. In 1967 the Children's Bureau became a part of the General Sciences Administration, where it is located today.

Services to Children

As the nineteenth century ended, the first juvenile court was established, and the early years of the 1900s saw a rapid expansion of these courts throughout the country. The resolution of the first White House Conference that no child should be removed from its home for reasons of poverty alone was a major landmark in social welfare. Throughout the country there began to develop programs of mothers' aid to support women who were left alone with their children, so that fewer children would need placement because of poverty alone. States began to adopt children's codes and to assume increasing responsibility for the regulation of services to children. Increasingly, the agencies concerned with children separated from their own parents utilized, supervised, and paid foster homes rather institutions. Increasingly, the states and counties were assuming responsibility for foster care of children (33).

The Child Welfare League of America

The delegates at the first White House Conference had discussed the need for a national organization concerned with the welfare of children. In 1915 Carl Christian presented a paper setting out the need to develop standards for work with children. This paper provided the framework for the development of the Bureau for the Exchange of Information among Child Helping Agencies. The BEI, with a grant of $25,000 in 1920, organized its 65 members into a new national agency to be called the Child Welfare League of America.

The league (CWLA) exists today as the strongest organized voice for children. It publishes the monthly periodical *Child Welfare*, and it circulates other literature relating to the problems of children. Adoption and foster care have been its primary concerns, but it has also been active in the areas of children's day care and homemaker service and, more recently, child abuse and neglect. The league has set standards for the operation of agencies in the above areas, has done significant research on child care, and has played an important role in the development of federal legislation in the interests of children (34).

The Child Guidance Movement

The beginnings of the child guidance clinics arose from the efforts of leaders such as Florence Kelley, Jane Addams, and Edith and Grace Abbott. They were active in the settlement movement and child welfare administration, served on school boards and supported educational changes, fought for child labor laws and the rights of women, served as probation officers, started public health clinics, and struggled with the establishment of juvenile courts (35). The child guidance clinics brought together all of those concerns.

In 1921 the Commonwealth Fund launched the child guidance clinics as a program that was meant to be a vital force in the community, closely related to other agencies and to the schools and designed to influence those agencies and the schools toward preventive service supporting mental health in children. Today such programs would be called community mental health programs. Once established, the clinics adopted their modern form, changing from agencies to provide preventive services and lead efforts for community reform to agencies that dealt with individual children and their mothers who came seeking "treatment."

Essentially, the child guidance clinics were privately supported; were staffed by teams of social workers, psychologists, and psychiatrists; and served as important training centers for the professionals they employed. Although these clinics were originally established as part of a program to prevent juvenile delinquency, by enabling other agencies to handle the problems of children more effectively, the clinics moved in the direction of providing treatment services almost exclusively. The population they served, as a result, changed from a predominantly lower-class population to a predominantly middle-class population (36).

The Great Depression: 1930–1940

The 1930s marked the near collapse of the American economy known as the Great Depression. Space does not permit a thorough discussion of the many factors surrounding the grievous economic problems extant and the New Deal programs designed to deal with these problems, initiated during Franklin Delano Roosevelt's presidency from 1933 to 1940 (37).

However, the reader should note that while speculation and fraud in the stock market investments were widespread before the stock market crash in October 1929, there were other indicators of trouble with the economy. A Brookings Institution study found that in 1929 a family required $2,000 to supply itself with only basic necessities and that an income of $2,500 would supply a family with only a moderate standard of living. Yet at the time 60 percent of all families had incomes below $1,000 and spent more than they earned. Forty percent of all families had no savings. It is easy to understand the heavy use of credit by these families. The welfare and security of such families were completely dependent on regular employment (38). Before President Hoover left office in 1932, unemployment in major cities approached 40 percent.

When President Roosevelt took office in 1933, he introduced a number of emergency programs designed to salvage and rebuild the economy. In addition, it was part of Roosevelt's plan to develop long-term federal involvement in public assistance. The principles which guided his thinking in this matter were: (1) federal assistance should focus primarily on the long-neglected problems of the able-bodied, leaving to the states, as in the past, the burden of caring for the impotent poor; and (2) this federal assistance should be work related in some fashion.

Social Security Act of 1935

In June 1934, Roosevelt appointed a Committee on Economic Security and named Frances Perkins, a social worker, as chairperson. The committee met through the summer and fall of 1934 and fashioned "a grand design" for economic security (39). With some important changes, this plan resulted in the Social Security Act of 1935, which is the foundation of our social welfare policy of today and intimately affects every one of us.

Although the Social Security Act, as finally introduced, represented the single most important piece of legislation in the development of the social welfare institution in the United States to date, it also accommodated to, and supported, many of the implicit social welfare principles of the past: reliance on the marketplace, the categorization of the poor, federal sharing but local control, and attachment to the work force (40).

The Social Security Act provided for the following programs: (1) unemployment insurance (UIB) which is completely financed by employer contributions; (2) old age and survivors' insurance (OASI), more popularly known as social security, and supported entirely by taxes on the employee and the employer; and (3) public assistance, designed to provide assistance payments to certain population groups that are normally considered as outside the work force: the aged, dependent children, and the blind.

With the enactment of the Social Security Act we had in place the foundation of our present income maintenance program. Far from a comprehensive, integrated program of income maintenance, it is a work-enforcing insurance system that provides retirement and temporary unemployment protection only to those actively attached to the work force and selected dependents, as well as a series of unconnected cash assistance provisions offering limited benefits to selected groups of the dependent poor on terms decided by each state (41).

Many of the original concerns regarding social security and public assistance continue to this day in regular challenges from the political left and right regarding the efficacy, scope, design, and purpose of these programs.

Child Welfare Services

Title V of the Social Security Act made provision for several grants to the states through the Children's Bureau for the purpose of establishing, extending, and strengthening public personal social services for children, particularly in rural areas. The services provided for were the protection and care of homeless, dependent, and neglected children, as well as children in danger of becoming delinquent.

The programs were to be established in all 48 states, the District of Columbia, Alaska, Hawaii, Puerto Rico, and the Virgin Islands, and they were usually lodged in the county welfare agencies. Each state was to receive a flat grant of $40,000 annually and to share in the balance of the appropriated funds on the basis of the proportion of its rural population under 18 years of age to the total rural population under that age.

The Growth of Public Child Welfare Services: 1940–1967

The *Encyclopedia of Social Work* (42) outlines the nature of child welfare services during the 1950s and the 1960s as directed toward solving problems connected with dependence, neglect, delinquency, physical and mental handicaps, and emotional disturbances. As discussed earlier, these services developed from the complete separation of children from their parents, to casework with parents to help them to maintain children in their own homes, to the provision of concrete resources that parents might use to supplement their own resources for the care of children, such as public assistance, day care, and homemaker services. The one important change in child welfare during this period was the growth of public child welfare services that provided many of the services mentioned above, and were responsible for the welfare and safety of children. Established originally to meet the needs of rural children, public child welfare services were steadily expanded to serve urban children also (43).

Foster Family Care

During the years that followed the Depression (post 1940), the methods of offering substitute care changed. The use of foster care increased, and the institutionalization of children decreased. The number of children placed by voluntary agencies decreased, while the number placed by public agencies increased. It was generally agreed by those working in foster care that at the end of this period (1967), more children were coming into foster homes from disturbed and disorganized homes. Also, as one would suspect, the children placed in foster homes were themselves more disturbed. As a result, children were tending to stay in foster care longer. In fact, a greater percentage of the children tended to live out their entire childhood in foster care once they entered the system.

Adoptions

Increasingly, adoption has grown as an acceptable way of providing parents for children rather than providing children for parents (44). In the ten-year period from 1957 to 1967, there was a continuous increase in adoptions, though the increase began to level off toward the end. An increasing number of the children placed for adoption had been born out of wedlock. From 1958 to 1968, the ratio between the number of applicants and the number of children declined steadily. For each 100 children, there were 158 applicants in 1958, and 104 applicants in 1967. Also, there was a steady trend away from assessing and evaluating adoptive applicants to helping them qualify as adoptive parents (45).

Today, there are far fewer babies (i.e., children aged 18 months or less) available for adoption, particularly healthy white infants. Yet the demand for these babies continues to be strong. Most families interested in adoption want a healthy white infant. These families often have to wait for years to go through an agency adoption for a young infant.

On the other hand, there are many children awaiting adoption placement for whom there is not much demand. These children are healthy white children over the age of ten, minority children of all ages, children with special needs, i.e., physical, emotional, mental or learning disabilities, and children who are members of a sibling group who want to remain together.

Institutions and Residential Treatment Centers

There were approximately 306,000 children living in institutions on any given day during the 1960s. Twenty-three percent of these children were there as neglected and dependent children; 33.1 percent were in some kind of correctional institution; 25.6 percent were in homes and schools for the mentally handicapped; 7.2 percent were in mental hospitals or residential treatment centers; and 9.3 percent were institutionalized because of physical disabilities.

The special institutions for children gave way to widespread use of adoption and foster homes. However, adoption or foster homes could not meet the special needs of certain children. From 1946 to 1967, the children's institutions that were developed were intended to serve emotionally disturbed, psychiatrically ill, and delinquent children. In 1965, private sources supported almost all of the maternity homes, the residential treatment centers for disturbed children, the institutions for dependent and neglected children, and the homes for the mentally retarded. Public funds largely supported juvenile correctional institutions, hospitals for mentally retarded and physically handicapped children, and psychiatric inpatient facilities (46). Presently, public monies, through the use of purchase-of-service agreements, support a significant portion (approximately 30–60%) of the costs of private, not-for-profit residential care for children who come from either public welfare or juvenile probation programs.

The Social Service Decade: 1960s

Particular attention should be given to the 1960–1970 decade, since it represented a watershed period for social welfare reform and expansion. With President Kennedy's election in 1960, the country began to reinvest its considerable energy toward bringing about reforms in social justice, poverty, and the quality of and access to affordable health care. Poverty was "rediscovered" (47) in the midst of affluence, and the federal government instituted a number of measures to combat it. While President Kennedy's untimely death in November 1963 prevented him from seeing the results of his social programs efforts, his successor, President Lyndon B. Johnson, signed into law a myriad of social programs in his quest to create a "Great Society."

The following pieces of federal legislation were signed into law during the 1960s:

1961   *Food Stamp Program*   focused on providing the eligible poor with authorization to purchase food at discounted prices through the use of stamps.

1961   *Area Redevelopment Act*   focused on problems of region-wide unemployment.

1962   *Manpower Development Training Act (MDTA)*   emphasized job training of the structurally unemployed.

1962   *Social Service Amendment to Social Security Act*   emphasized provision of social services within public welfare as a key strategy in reducing welfare dependency. The federal government would reimburse the states for 75 percent of the costs of the social service given to public assistance clients.

1963 *Community Mental Health Act* provided funds for the establishment and staffing of community mental health centers (CMHCs) throughout the nation; today there are over 781 CMHCs in the United States.

1964 *Civil Rights Act* enacted landmark legislation to prohibit discrimination in employment and established the Employment Equal Opportunity Commission (EEOC).

1964 *Economic Opportunity Act (EOA)* established the Office of Economic Opportunity (OEO); authorized a number of social programs as economic opportunities for the poor, by the provision of in-kind programs.

- *Job Corps Training Centers* provided education, skills, and work experiences for minority and low-income young people.
- *Neighborhood Youth Corps* provided for employment of young people still in school in various governmental and private, nonprofit service activities.
- *Work–Study Program* enabled young people to continue their education in secondary schools, colleges, and universities.
- *Volunteers in Service to America (VISTA)* established a corps of adult volunteers who would help with the rehabilitation and improvement of slums and other impoverished areas.
- *Urban and Rural Community Action Programs (CAP)* the best known and most controversial aspect of EOA; locally developed programs, operated by private, nonprofit, or public community action organizations, that promised progress toward the elimination of poverty and provided for the "maximum feasible participation" of residents of poverty areas.
- *Head Start* provided a preparatory educational program for preschool, low-income children.
- *Upward Bound* established an educational program designed to prevent school dropouts.
- *Day-Care Centers/Neighborhood Recreational Centers/Health Centers* were designed to compensate the children and youth involved for the failures of parental upbringing and the social effects of poverty and discrimination.

1965 *Voting Rights Act* enacted legislation to ensure that minorities are provided the same opportunities to vote as whites.

1965 *Medicare* (Title XVIII of the Social Security Act) provides prepaid hospital insurance for the aged under Social Security and low-cost voluntary medical insurance for the aged, directly under the federal administration.

1965 *Medicaid* (Title XIX of the Social Security Act) the federal government's largest single welfare program for the poor; provides an in-kind public assistance program designed for needy persons requiring health care.

1965 *Older Americans Act (OAA)* designed to recognize more social service needs of the elderly; created an "aging network" to express the concerns of the elderly—the Administration on Aging (AoA) at the federal level, ten regional offices, and 600 Area Agencies on Aging (AAAs) at the local level.

1967   *Work Incentive Now (WIN)*   established programs designed to train public welfare recipients for work and to help them locate employment.

1967   *Separation of Payments and Services in Public Welfare*   recognized that not all poor families are necessarily in need of social services, since poverty may be attributable to a variety of causes.

1968   *Fair Housing Act*   (particularly Section 235) amended the Housing Act of 1949 in order to prohibit discrimination in the sale and rental of property through the federal subsidization housing program.

The "Social Service Decade" coincided with the escalation of the Vietnam War and the conflicts within the United States about the conduct of the war, which "undermined the country's sense of integration, mutuality of purpose, and moral authority" (48). Social welfare programs were attacked by the far Left on one side and the far Right on the other. These factors led to the curtailment of programs for the poor during the late 1960s and the 1970s.

Children's Rights: 1960s to the Present

Against this backdrop of social program expansion and retrenchment during the 1960s and 1970s, at least eight major trends affected child welfare services that have continued up to the present: (1) an increasing concern with the rights of children; (2) a rapid increase in teenage pregnancies and in the number of teenagers who kept their children; (3) controversy over abortion; (4) a rediscovery of, and increased concern about, the problem of child abuse, particularly sexual abuse; (5) an increase in the number of working mothers; (6) the increasing number of single-parent, female-headed households, due to the increasing incidence of teenage parenthood, high divorce rates, and single adult women who choose to have a baby on their own; (7) emphasis on family preservation and family support, and (8) the increased efforts to enforce child support.

Legal Rights of Children

In the late 1960s and continuing into the 1970s, there was an increasing emphasis on the law as the protector of children's rights and on due process as an instrument for the reform of services to children. The following section briefly summarizes the major court decisions concerning children and youth during the 1960s and through the 1980s.

Major Court Decisions

1961   *Unreasonable Search and Seizure—Mapp v. Ohio, 367 U.S. 643*
This decision affected the juvenile court significantly by requiring state courts to abide by Fourth Amendment protections against unreasonable search and seizure.

1966 *Due Process in Waiver of Jurisdiction—Kent v. United States, 383 U.S. 541*   This decision was the first Supreme Court case to deal specifically with the juvenile court since its establishment. It ruled that a juvenile was by statute entitled to certain procedures and benefits as a consequence of his statutory right to the "exclusive" jurisdiction of the Juvenile Court. Waiver hearings "must measure up to the essentials of due process and fair treatment, 383 U.S. at 562" (49).

1967 *Due Process in Adjudication Hearings—Application of Gault, 387 U.S. 1*   Application of Gault became the landmark due-process case. The Supreme Court held that due process requires adequate, timely, written notice of the allegations against a juvenile, allowing sufficient time for preparation of a response. "In all cases involving the danger of loss of liberty, the juvenile must be accorded the right to counsel, privilege against self-incrimination, and the right to confront and cross-examine opposing witnesses under oath" (Application of Gault). The court was careful to limit Gault to the adjudication hearing in a delinquency action.

1970 *Standard of Proof—In re Winship, 397 U.S. 358*   This decision established the principle of proof beyond reasonable doubt as requirement in the adjudicatory stage of a delinquency proceeding. This standard is specifically inapplicable to the dispositional hearing and need not be extended to cases involving children in need of supervision.

1971 *No Mandatory Trial by Jury—McKeiver v. Pennsylvania, 403 U.S. 528*   This decision set a major limitation to legal rights by holding that a juvenile is not constitutionally entitled to the right of trial by jury. Fairness is the applicable due process standard for juvenile proceedings. A jury was considered an unnecessary component of accurate fact finding.

1975 *No Double Jeopardy—Breed v. Jones, 421 U.S. 519*   The Supreme Court ruled that once a person was processed through the adjudicatory hearing in the juvenile court, jeopardy was attached, and a minor could not be retried as an adult or a juvenile "absent some exception to the double jeopardy prohibition" (497 F.2d, at 1168).

1984 *Schall v. Martin, 467 U.S. 253,263*   Martin departed radically from Gault and eliminated most federal court challenges to unnecessary incarceration of youths in juvenile detention centers. The Martin Court diminished children's rights by exalting the state's interest in acting as parens patriae to protect the community and to protect juveniles from themselves.

The watershed in the legal rights of children that occurred from the mid-1960s to the mid-1970s, and which were set back by the Martin decision in 1984, involved a shift in direction from an emphasis on due process to one on juvenile diversion programs—that is, programs addressed to preventing youth from becoming ensnared in the juvenile justice system. Experience and research clearly demonstrated that once into the system, youth tended to remain in the system. Diversion efforts strive to keep youth in the community, connect them to social, recreational, employment, and educational opportunities, and divert them from a young lifetime of escalating juvenile offenses and concomitant escalating forms of incarceration. Yet, partly as a result of the Martin decision, between 1982 and 1989 national admissions to detention centers increased by 30 percent (501). Today, juvenile justice can be characterized as focusing on increased punishment (criminalization) and statutory considerations, on a state by state basis, on the death penalty for juveniles who commit serious, violent crimes.

Title XX Amendments to the Social Security Act (1975)

The 1962 Social Service Amendments to the Social Security Act, wherein the federal government reimbursed the states for 75 percent of the costs of social services, led to an open-ended authorization. Because this was perceived by President Nixon and Congress to lead significant abuse and runaway, spiraling costs (social service costs went from $282 million in 1967 to $1.7 billion in 1973) (51), Congress decided to take action to curb spending. In 1975, Title XX was added to the Social Security Act to place a ceiling on expenditures (a $2.5 billion limit on what could be spent for social services), to close the open-ended 75-percent match, to insure that the majority of federally funded social services went to the poor, and to require that the states assume the primary responsibility for planning and developing social services.

The Title XX federal guidelines stated that the social services must be directed toward at least one of the following goals: (1) achieving economic self-support or reducing dependence; (2) achieving or maintaining self-sufficiency; (3) preventing or remedying the neglect, abuse, or exploitation of children and adults unable to protect their own interests, or preserving, rehabilitating, and reuniting families; (4) preventing or reducing inappropriate institutional care by providing for community-based, home-based, or other forms of less intensive care; and (5) securing referral or admission for institutional care when other forms are not appropriate and providing services for individuals in institutions.

There was an attempt to make these services available to a broader population than public assistance recipients. Individuals and families that do not receive assistance, but have a family income of less than 115 percent of the state's median income for a family of similar size, are eligible for service.

What resulted was that a ceiling was placed on costs at the same time that the states were expected to provide personal social services for an increased pool of beneficiaries. In short, states were expected to serve more people while being provided with less federal funding.

Omnibus Reconciliation Act of 1981—Block Grants

In 1981, under strong lobbying from the Reagan Administration, Congress passed the Omnibus Reconciliation Act, which again reorganized the social services program created by Title XX. Under this new act, funding for some programs, including some child welfare programs, was consolidated into block grants with annual reductions in funding. These grants consolidate many service programs into a single source of funding, as opposed to funding each program (categorical grant funding).

Under block grants, many single services have received less funding, including: AFDC, Medicaid, child nutrition programs, school lunch programs, and others. Traditional child welfare programs, such as protective services, foster care, or adoption, appeared to be holding their own in 1983 (52).

New Federalism: Returning Programs to States

Reagan's New Federalism (1980s) represented a reversal from societal responsibility to societal disregard for the poor (including children) and became the guideline for the Republican-dominated Congress of 1994–1998, with its excessively punitive "Contract with America" (53).

Privatization and corporatization, two of the corner-stones of New Federalism, have led to competition which has often eliminated services to the poor as well as resulting in federal cuts to OBRA in 1981, the Tax Equity and Fiscal Responsibility Act of 1982, the Deficit Reduction Act of 1984, the Gramm-Rudman-Hollings Act (GRH) of 1986, and the Family Support Act (FSA) of 1988 (54). Of all the programs devastated by Reaganomics, children's programs were hit hardest. All told, Reaganomics brought about cutbacks in domestic spending for human resources by $101.1 billion, of which $65.4 billion came from programs that provided care or in-kind benefits to families (55).

But today even these programs appear to be at serious risk, given the epidemic of crack and cocaine. This phenomenon has resulted in increased demands on the foster care system, as parents are not able to make use of drug treatment programs. More children are entering this system and the juvenile court system, with even more severe problems to be addressed.

Other problems which continue to plague the foster care system include caseloads too large to manage effectively so that the worker can monitor the progress of the written service agreement, treatment plans, and the care provided in the foster home; inadequate selection, training, and monitoring of foster parents; inadequate efforts to reunite families; and inadequate protection provided to children in foster care against child abuse.

Adoption Assistance and Child Welfare Act of 1980

The formulation and eventual passage of Public Law 96-272, the Adoption Assistance and Child Welfare Act of 1980, drew heavily from the advent of the increasing attention to the legal rights of children and youth in the 1960s and 1970s, strong pressure from "parents' rights" groups, the emphasis of youth diversion, the increasing awareness of the scope and nature of child abuse, and the high cost and perceived improper use of foster care and institutional care. There was, most importantly, the realization that large numbers of children remained in care for unnecessarily long periods and suffered because they had no permanent future (56), and the perceptions by the government that family reunification efforts would be significantly cheaper than out-of-home care.

The primary intent of P.L. 96-272 was to reunify families and to provide pre-placement preventive services:

> *The state agency shall develop and implement policies and procedures to insure that in each case reasonable efforts shall be made to provide the services described in the law to prevent or eliminate the need for removal of a child from his or her own home, and to provide the services to make it possible for each child in foster care to return to his or her own home (57).*

In addition, the act required that the state agency must develop and implement a case system that ensured the following three conditions: development of a case plan; periodic reviews; and procedural safeguards.

Thus, provisions of this act encouraged the use of preventive home-based services, mandated documented use of such services prior to placement, and limited the extent of placement in non-permanent substitute care settings whenever possible (58). Allen and Knitzer (59) describe this act as using a "carrot-and-stick" approach to redirect funds away from the perceived inappropriate, often costly, out-of-home care and toward alternatives to placement.

A critical thrust of this act was the importance placed on permanency planning—"the systematic process of carrying out, within the brief time-limited period, a set of goal-directed activities designed to help children live in families that offer continuity of relationships with nurturing parents or caretakers and the opportunity to establish lifetime relationships" (60).

To provide a permanent future for children, P.L. 96-272 mandates several necessary services, home-based services, including preventive, remedial, and reunification services, adoption services, and foster-care and institutional services.

The Family Support Act of 1988

The FSA of 1988 constituted a shift from the welfare thinking of the past. The law was intended to strengthen the family by making AFDC available for two-parent families and to increase family self-sufficiency through the guarantee of child care and Medicaid. It provided funding for family preservation and community-based family support services. It also incorporated the principle of parental responsibility for the support of children by strengthening the child support enforcement provisions and emphasizing work and employment training for parents. States were to provide one of the following: Job Opportunity and Basic Skills (JOBS) programs, the Community Work Experience Program (CWEP), or on-the-job training (OJT).

While it has been argued (61) that FSA 1988 "embodied the sexual morality and work ethic values of the Religious Right . . . by changing recipient behaviors and by intensifying pressure on clients, their families, and state/local agencies to get off the welfare rolls into work," it did put pressure on states to increase child care resources, improved standards for child support, and established AFDC-UP (public assistance for two parent families) for intact families.

Family Preservation and Support Services Act of 1993—as part of the Omnibus Budget Reconciliation Act (OBRA)

This act, which is also the Amendment to Title IV-B or the Social Security Act, has three major purposes: (1) to prevent out-of-home placement for children; (2) to promote family strengths, enhance parenting, and protect children and youth; and (3) to reduce risk of abuse and/or neglect. This legislation provides financial appropriations for family preservation and support services offered through state child welfare agencies, and to encourage states to establish a continuum of coordinated, accessible, continuous, and integrated, culturally relevant, family-focused services for children and families (62).

Family preservation services, while linked to family support services, differ in that they are designed specifically to alleviate crises and to maintain the family unit to avoid the need for placing its children in foster care and to promote reunification after foster care. Family support services, on the other hand, are available to all families in the community on a voluntary basis and are primarily community-based preventive activities designed to alleviate stress and promote parental competencies and behaviors.

Personal Responsibility and Work Opportunity Reconciliation Act of 1996—P.L. 104–193

This bill, signed into law by President Clinton on August 22, 1996, eliminates the Aid to Families with Dependent Children (AFDC) program which has been in existence since the passage of the Social Security Act of 1935. It also makes deep funding cuts in basic programs for low-income children, families, the elderly, people with disabilities, and immigrants. This law replaces the JOBS program (along with AFDC and emergency assistance), with the Temporary Assistance for Needy Families (TANF) Block Grant.

While space does not permit a thorough discussion of this major piece of welfare reform, TANF does end public welfare as it has been known for the past 60 plus years by placing a cap on the length of time benefits can be received, by drastically increasing the work requirements, and by no longer guaranteeing aid for all those who may qualify. In addition, even though changes to child welfare programs and services are quite narrow under TANF, the presumed consequences of more people being pushed into poverty could place child welfare programs under greater stress as demand for its services increases.

Adoption and Safe Families Act of 1997— P.L. 105–89

This new law improves the protection and care of the nation's abused and neglected children, increases adoptions and other permanent homes for children who need them, and supports families. It amends the Adoption Assistance and

Child Welfare Act of 1980. With an emphasis on safety, the new law clarifies that children's health and safety are paramount concerns in deciding to remove or reunify them with their families. In addition, the law requires states to provide health insurance for any child with special needs for whom there is an adoption assistance agreement. Finally, this law reauthorizes and expands Family Preservation and Support Services (Title IV-B) and renamed the program "Promoting Safe and Stable Families."

Summary

This chapter began with a description of the origins of child welfare in the United States, the "Child-Saving Movement" during colonial times. Poverty was viewed as sin and work as the way to salvation. Children were seen as an important adjunct to the labor pool, working along with their parents, for others as apprentices, and in the case of dependency, bound out as indentured servants. Child labor was a social fact, not a social problem. The "Child Rescue Movement" of the early to mid-nineteenth century, in contrast to the religious motives and charity impulses of the "Child-Saving Movement" of the seventeenth and eighteenth centuries, relied more upon legal concepts and efforts to advance the rights of children through the application of the law. The needs of children were being increasingly recognized, and the heretofore seemingly inviolate rights of parents to raise children as they wished were being challenged more and more by the courts.

The foster care movement, under the leadership of Charles Loring Brace and Charles Birtwell, was initiated in the mid-1800s and gave rise to the rudiments of the out-of-home care system for children that still is in place today.

The Social Security Act of 1935 was described as the single most important piece of legislation in the development of the social welfare institution in the United States to date. Title V of the Social Security Act was specifically earmarked for child welfare services and provided modest amounts of monies in all 48 states for the protection and care of homeless, dependent, and neglected children, as well as children in danger of becoming delinquent.

The 1960s were noted for the expansion of social welfare reform and accordingly were described as "the Social Service Decade." Programs of particular relevance to the growth of child welfare services included the inception of: (1) the Economic Opportunity Act (EOA) of 1964, which gave rise to Head Start, the Job Corps, the Neighborhood Youth Corps, the Work–Study Program, Upward Bound, and day-care centers for children; (2) the Civil Rights Act of 1964; (3) the Social Service Amendment to the Social Security Act (1962); and (4) the Community Mental Health Act of 1963.

The 1970s were characterized as emphasizing the law as the protector of children's rights, with due process as an instrument for the reform of services to children. Attention, not detention, was the buzzword of the time, and community-based diversion programs were established to reduce the need for incarceration or other forms of institutionalization for youth.

With the passage of Public Law 96-272, the Adoption Assistance and Child Welfare Act of 1980, permanency planning, family reunification and maintenance, and least restrictive environment have become the operationalized child welfare policies of the 1980s. Increasing focus has been placed on prevention, with out-of-home care services for children and youth being viewed as the decision of last resort. The Family Support Act of 1988, The Family Preservation Act of 1993, and the Adoption and Safe Families Act of 1997 have all placed increased emphasis on the importance of preventive and alleviative services, directed toward preserving the family whenever it is safe for the child and in her/his best interest.

We have come a long way since colonial times with regard to our understanding of the needs and rights of children. no longer do we perceive children as adults, except smaller in stature. No longer do we view children as chattel, the exclusive property of parents, to be treated entirely as their parents (especially their fathers) see fit. Yet, in spite of these substantial inroads, there continues to be unmet needs for many of this nation's children and youth. If the future of the United States is to be determined, at least in part, by the quality of life experienced by all of its children, the need for ongoing, quality, child welfare services is a necessity, not a luxury.

Welfare reform, as portrayed in TANF of 1996, speaks volumes about the legacy of Reaganomics, privatization, the New Federalism, and the dramatic changes in our view of the role of the federal government as it impacts on children, youth, and families.

Endnotes

1. Alfred Kadushin, "Child Welfare Strategy in the Coming Years," in *Child Welfare Strategy in the Coming Years*, p. 4.
2. Ann W. Shyne, *Child Welfare Perspectives: Selected Papers of Joseph Reid*, p. 15.
3. W. T. Hagan, *American Indians*, 1.
4. Daniel J. Boorstin, *The Americans: The National Experience*, p. 1.
5. Ibid., p. 1.
6. Beulah R. Compton, *Introduction to Social Welfare and Social Work*, p. 172.
7. James Beard, 1931, p. 42.
8. Compton, *Social Welfare*, p. 187.
9. M. W. Jernegan, *Laboring and Dependent Classes in Colonial America, 1607–1783*, p. 145.
10. Compton, *Social Welfare*, p. 188.
11. Ibid., p. 188.
12. Ibid., p. 189.
13. Sidney Lens, *Poverty: America's Enduring Paradox*, p. 27.
14. R. H. Bremner, ed. *Children and Youth in America: A Documentary History*, vol. 1., p. 322.
15. Ibid., pp. 103–104.
16. Ibid., p. 23.

17. Ibid., p. 23.

18. Compton, *Social Welfare,* p. 200.

19. Jernegan, *Laboring and Dependent Classes,* pp. 143–144.

20. Ibid., p. 145.

21. Grace Abbott, *The Child and the State,* 2 vols.; vol. 1, pp. 29–31.

22. Compton, *Social Welfare,* p. 208.

23. Bremner, *Children and Youth,* p. 266.

24. Compton, *Social Welfare,* p. 241.

25. Andrew Billingsley and Jeanne M. Giovannoni, *Children of the Storm: Black Children and American Child Welfare,* pp. 28–30.

26. Ibid., pp. 28–30.

27. Compton, *Social Welfare,* p. 287.

28. Jernegan, *Laboring and Dependent Classes,* pp. 429–480.

29. Compton, *Social Welfare,* p. 292.

30. Bremner, *Children and Youth,* p. 117.

31. Compton, *Social Welfare,* p. 292.

32. Walter Trattner, *From Poor Law to Welfare State: A History of Social Welfare in America,* p. 181.

33. Compton, *Social Welfare,* pp. 402–403.

34. P. Romanofsky, ed. *Social Service Organizations,* 2 vols., pp. 224–230.

35. Compton, *Social Welfare,* p. 408.

36. M. Levine and A. Levine, *A Social History of the Helping Services,* pp. 231*ff.*

37. See Clark A. Chambers, *New Deal at Home and Abroad,* for an excellent overview of this period.

38. M. Levine, H. G. Moulton, and C. Warburton, *America's Capacity to Consume* (Washington, D.C.: Brookings Institution, 1934).

39. Compton, *Social Welfare,* p. 419.

40. Ibid., p. 421.

41. L. M. Salamon, *Welfare: The Elusive Consensus,* pp. 78–80.

42. David Fanshel, in Robert Morris, ed. *Encyclopedia of Social Work,* p. 99.

43. Compton, *Social Welfare,* p. 471.

44. Ibid., p. 473.

45. Alfred Kadushin, in Robert Morris, ed. *Encyclopedia of Social Work,* pp. 103–111.

46. J. Matushima, "Child Welfare: Institutions for Children," in Robert Morris, ed. *Encyclopedia of Social Work,* pp. 120–128.

47. See particularly Michael Harrington, *The Other America,* and Dwight MacDonald, "Our Invisible Poor," *New Yorker,* January 19, 1963, pp. 82–132.

48. Compton, *Social Welfare,* p. 485.

49. Donald Brieland and John Lemmon, *Social Work and the Law,* p. 152.

50. U.S. Department of Health, Education, and Welfare, *First Annual Report to Congress on Title XX of the Social Security Act,* p. 1.

51. National Center for Juvenile Justice, "National Estimates of Juvenile Delinquency Cases."

52. Louise Johnson and Charles L. Schwartz, *Social Welfare: A Response to Human Need,* p. 148.

53. Phyllis Day, *A New History of Social Welfare,* 2nd ed., p. 376.

54. Ibid., p. 377.

55. James Fendrich, Mamie Miller, and Tim Nichel, "It's the Budget Stupid: A Policy Analysis of Clinton's First Budget," *Journal of Sociology and Social Welfare,* Vol. xxi, no. 4 (Dec. 1994), p. 7.

56. See in particular the following: Anthony Maluccio, et al., "Beyond Permanency Planning," *Child Welfare* 59 (November 1980): 515–529, and Malcolm Bush and Andrew C. Gordon, "The Case for Involving Children in Child Welfare Decisions," *Social Work* 27 (July 1982): 309–314.
57. Statutes at Large, "Public Law 96-272, Adoption Assistance and Child Welfare Act, June 17, 1980," 94 STAT 517, 42 USC1397b.
58. Alfred Kadushin and Judith Martin, *Child Welfare Services*, 4th ed., p. 90.
59. Mary Lee Allen and Jane Knitzer, "Child Welfare: Examining the Policy Framework," in Brenda McGowan and William Meezan, eds. *Child Welfare: Current Dilemmas, Future Directions*, p. 120.
60. Anthony Maluccio and Edith Fein, "Permanency Planning Revisited," in Martha Cox and Roger Cox, eds. *Foster Care: Current Issues, Policies, and Practices*, pp. 113–133.
61. Day, *A New History of Social Welfare*, 2nd ed., p. 387.
62. Susan Whitelaw Downs, Lela B. Costin, and Emily Jean McFadden, *Child Welfare and Family Services*, 5th ed., p. 65.

Bibliography

Abbott, Grace, *The Child and the State*. 2 vols. Chicago: University of Chicago Press, 1938.

Allen, Mary Lee, and Knitzer, Jane. "Child Welfare: Examining the Policy Framework." In *Child Welfare: Current Dilemmas, Future Directions*, edited by McGowan, Brenda, and Meezan, William, p. 120. Itasca, ILL.: Peacock Publishing, 1983.

Billingsley, Andrew, and Giovannoni, Jeanne M. *Children of the Storm: Black Children and American Child Welfare*. New York: Harcourt Brace Jovanovich, 1972.

Boorstin, Daniel J. *The Americans: the National Experience*. New York: Vintage Books, 1965.

Bremner, R. H., ed. *Children and Youth in America: A Documentary History*. vol. 1. Cambridge: Harvard University Press, 1970.

Brieland, Donald, and Lemmon, John. *Social Work and the Law*. St. Paul, Minn.: West Publishing, 1977.

Bush, Malcolm, and Gordon, Andrew, C. "The Case for Involving Children in Child Welfare Decisions." *Social Work* 27 (July 1982): 309–314.

Chambers, Clark A. *New Deal at Home and Abroad*. New York: Free Press, 1965.

Compton, Beulah R. *Introduction to Social Welfare and Social Work*. Homewood, ILL.: The Dorsey Press, 1980.

Day, Phyllis, *A New History of Social Welfare*, 2nd ed., Boston, MA: Allyn and Bacon, 1997.

Downs, Susan Whitelaw, Costin, Lela, and McFadden, Emily Jean, *Child Welfare and Family Services*. 5th ed. White Plains, NY: Longman Publishers USA, 1996.

Fanshel, David. "Child Welfare," in *Encyclopedia of Social Work*, edited by Robert Morris, p. 91. New York: National Association of Social Workers, 1971.

Fendrich, James M., Miller, Mamie, and Nichel, Tim, "It's the Budget Stupid: A Policy Analysis of Clinton's First Budget," *Journal of Sociology and Social Welfare*, Vol. xxi, no. 4 (Dec. 1994).

Hagan, W. T., *American Indians*, Chicago: University of Chicago Press, 1961.

Harrington, Michael. *The Other America*. Baltimore: Penguin Books, 1963.

Johnson, Louise, and Schwartz, Charles L. *Social Welfare: A Response to Human Need*. Newton, Mass.: Allyn and Bacon, 1988.

Kadushin, Alfred, and Martin, Judith. *Child Welfare Services*. 4th ed. New York: Macmillan, 1988.

_____, "Child Welfare Strategy in the Coming Years." In *Child Welfare Strategy in the Coming Years*. Washington, D.C.: U.S. Department of Health, Education, and Welfare, 1978.

_____. In *Encyclopedia of Social Work*, edited by Robert Morris, pp. 103–111. New York: National Association of Social Workers, 1971.

Lens, Sidney. *Poverty: America's Enduring Paradox*. New York: Thomas Y. Crowell, 1969.

Levine, M., and Levine, A. *A Social History of the Helping Services*. New York: Appleton-Century-Crofts, 1970.

MacDonald, Dwight. "Our Invisible Poor." *New Yorker* (January 19, 1963): 82–132.

Maluccio, Anthony, and Fein, Edith. "Permanency Planning Revisited." In *Foster Care: Current Issues, Policies, and Practices*, edited by Martha Cox and Roger Cox. Norwood, N.J.: Ablex Publishing, 1985.

_____, et al. "Beyond Permanency Planning." *Child Welfare* 59 (November 1980): 515–529.

Matushima, John. "Child Welfare: Institutions for Children." In *Encyclopedia of Social Work*, edited by Robert Morris, pp. 120–128. New York: National Association of Social Workers, 1971.

National Center for Juvenile Justice, "National Estimates of Juvenile Delinquency Cases," 1989.

Romanofsky, P., ed. *Social Service Organizations*. 2 vols. Westport, Conn.: Greenwood Press, 1978.

Salamon, L. M. *Welfare: The Elusive Consensus*. New York: Praeger, 1978.

Shyne, Ann W. *Child Welfare Perspectives: Selected Papers of Joseph H. Reid*. New York: Child Welfare League of America, 1979.

Statutes at Large, "Public Law 96-272, Adoption Assistance and Child Welfare Act, June 17, 1980," 94 STAT 517, 42 USC1397b.

Trattner, Walter. *From Poor Law to Welfare State: A History of Social Welfare in America*. New York: Appleton-Century-Crofts, 1970.

U.S. Department of Health, Education, and Welfare. *First Annual Report to Congress on Title XX of the Social Security Act*. Washington, D.C.: Government Printing Office, 1977.

3 The Continuum of Child Welfare Services

NEIL A. COHEN

California State University, Los Angeles

This chapter will describe the nature and extent of problems impacting on children and families in the United States today. Emphasis will be placed on tracing the changes in family structure, the increased role of women in the workforce, and the consequences of these changes.

The continuum of child welfare services—supportive, supplemental, and substitute services—will be examined in detail. These services often are provided in response to those very problems that have resulted from the transformation of the family structure, with the attendant agonies of transition. "Instead of being liberated, families suffer from over-choice, and are wounded, embittered, plunged into a sorrow and loneliness intensified by the multiplicity of their choices and options" (1).

These types of families, along with the ones subjected to the broader social problems of inequality, poverty, unemployment, underemployment, family violence, and lack of adequate education, health, housing, and mental health, suffer from lack of stability and varying degrees of social disorganization. These are the families and children which most often become targets of child welfare policy, programs, and services.

Why Are Child Welfare Services Necessary?

Contrary to the conventional wisdom that child welfare services are required because of child- and youth-related problems, in actuality they are most often needed because of some form of problem in parental role functioning, A parent (or both parents) may be deceased, absent, unemployed, incarcerated, prone to physical, emotional, or sexual violence, or a substance abuser. One or both parents may be suffering from emotional, mental, physical, or marital problems or may be in some other way unable or unwilling to adequately fulfill the role of parent. Without the backbone of a stable childhood environment and the opportunity to bond with responsible adults, children of these families are at a great risk of becoming child welfare statistics. As a result, the quality of care provided to the child or children suffers. Depending on the degree, scope, and duration of the parental problems, some form of child welfare intervention is required.

On the other hand, there are some situations where the problems are child-focused, wherein the child suffers from some form of mental, emotional, or physical problem. Behavioral disorders, developmental disability and delay, HIV/AIDs, childhood schizophrenia, attention deficit disorder, hyperactivity, dyslexia, muscular dystrophy, blindness, and deafness are but a few types of child-related problems that could require the intervention of child welfare services.

Another factor that can cause the need for child welfare services is a lack of adequate community supports and resources that a family can utilize to prevent the onset of problems relating to child welfare. A society characterized, in part, by problems of: (1) inequality; (2) poverty; (3) a lack of available, decent-paying steady employment; (4) lack of adequate, affordable housing; (5) absence of quality, affordable, and accessible children's day care; (6) deteriorating quality of public education; (7) lack of affordable and acceptable recreational outlets; and (8) increasing crime, drug dealing, and violence in one's neighborhood, adds to the problems of inadequate social functioning for an otherwise well organized, integrated family system.

The following conditions impact children and their families in the United States at the present time:

1. Twenty-five percent of all children are born poor; 1 in 5 is poor now, totaling nearly 14.5 million; 40.3 percent of Hispanic children, 39.9 percent of African-American children and 16.3 percent of white children were poor in 1996.

2. Approximately 10 million women and children received AFDC/TANF benefits in 1997, down 29.2 percent from 14.11 million in 1993.
3. One in four children lives with only one parent.
4. In 1995, an estimated 2.7 million households with children experienced "worst-case" problems of overcrowding, deteriorated housing conditions, or heavy rent burdens (more than 50 percent of income on rent and utilities) (2).
5. There are approximately 100,000 homeless children; in 1997, families with children represented 36 percent of those in homeless shelters (3).
6. Among young families (headed by a parent under 30), median income plunged 33 percent between 1973 and 1994, and the child poverty rate doubled from 20 to 41 percent.
7. While teen pregnancies have declined over the past three years, the rate is still almost three times its level since the early 1960s.
8. About 11.3 million children (1 in 7) are without health insurance.
9. One out of eight children never graduate from high school.
10. Sixty-five percent of women with children under age 6 are in the labor force.
11. 13 million children—including 6 million infants and toddlers—are in child care.
12. The food stamp program will be cut by $20 billion over six years. This has already resulted in adult and children recipients declining from 27.1 million in 1994 to 20.9 million recipients in 1997.
13. Every day in this country:
    a. 443 babies are born to mothers who had late or no prenatal care
    b. 781 babies are born at low birthweight
    c. 1,403 babies are born to teen mothers
    d. 3,436 babies are born to unmarried mothers (4)

Why does our society allow these conditions to exist? Why, in a society as affluent, rich in natural resources, and technologically sophisticated as the United States, do we find child- and family-related social problems on the rise? The inquiring student is asked to thoroughly examine his or her own values and to consider the social conflicts inherent between the values of aggrandizement and those of humanitarianism. There is little agreement about solutions among the forces vying for political leadership in this country. Yet it is clear to this writer that at the root of the issue is **not** that poverty is too costly to eradicate or substantially diminish. Rather, our society does not yet value all children and families enough to allocate resources sufficient to provide adequate benefits, goods, and services.

If we acknowledge that our capitalist economy is driven by three variables: land, capital, and labor, we can better begin to understand how and where children and families fit into this model. They don't! (5) It appears that for children and families to receive adequate community resources through the social welfare system, it must be proved that these transfers are cost effective. Expenditures for social welfare programs have to answer to the following question: Will the program contribute to the economy or be a drag on it? Until this calculation is reformulated or reconceptualized, it doesn't appear that there will be significant qualitative change in the policies, programs, and services available to all families and children in this nation.

And when we do erect an array of child welfare institutions and programs, we find, according to Weissbourd, that "this system of care . . . is too splintered and complex to administer effectively, and it does little to prevent problems. . . . The system fails to stem problems at early stages, and it deals inadequately with many children and families once their problems become serious" (6).

Changes in Family Structure

The erosion of the traditional support systems, the nuclear and extended families, compounds the demands and pressures faced by present-day families. The popular conception of a family in the United States as consisting of mother and father and their children has undergone wrenching transformation. According to Alvin Toffler, "If we define the nuclear family as a working husband, housekeeping wife, and two children, and ask how many Americans actually still live in this type of family, the answer is astonishing: 7 percent of the total United States population" (7).

There was a time when extended families, often consisting of three or four generations of blood relatives living with others in the same household, were a dominant family form in America. Toffler refers to this historical period as "The First Wave" (8).

At the turn of the century, most children in America were raised in nuclear families. Nuclear families consisted of households with two or more children and two parents, a stay-at-home mother and a go-to-work father, who remained together throughout their lives. This domestic arrangement was well adapted to the needs of America's industrial manufacturing economy, creating an ample supply of male factory workers (9). Toffler refers to the period when the nuclear family was the social norm as "The Second Wave."

Today, the industrial manufacturing economy has been transformed into an industrial information-and-service economy that has employed nearly two-thirds of the workforce (10). In addition, America's families have shifted away from the two-parent, multi-child, male-wage-earner family toward alternative forms of domestic and sexual arrangements (11). Toffler refers to the diversification of American family relationships as the beginning of what he calls "The Third Wave."

"Serial monogamy now is competing with lifelong same-partner monogamy as a marital norm for American couples. Whether one out of three marriages ends in divorce, as some experts claim, or whether only one in eight marriages dissolves, as others contend, the old promise, 'till death do us part' does not carry the same weight as it once did" (12). In any event, it seems that about one-fifth of all marriages now are remarriages (13).

Further, more and more children are being raised in the fastest growing family form in America—80 percent more common in the 1990s than in the 1960s—the one-parent, usually female-headed family (14). Between 1959 and 1984, the number of female-headed families with children increased by 168 percent. In 1984, one of every five families with children under 18 was headed by a woman (15). This included 16 percent of all white families, 25 percent of all Spanish-surname families, and 52 percent of all black families. In 1959, only one in every eleven families with children was headed by a woman. By 1995, one of every four children under 10 lives in a family headed by a single woman (16).

The shrinking of the extended family has been reported by social scientists over the past twenty years. Quest for independence, job mobility, and movement to the suburbs have been offered as reasons for the continuing reduction of the extended family. Blood relatives now find themselves on both coasts of the United States, or in other countries, or separated by miles of freeways and turnpikes. No longer is it common for many families to be able to rely on neighborhood relatives for child care or other family assistance. Nor are most families able to rely on other neighbors for emergency child care or other forms of help. Many neighborhoods are without parents during the day, as increasing numbers of mothers are entering the work force.

Women in the Workforce

Between 1960 and the present, the number of women participating in the work force has increased by more than 106 percent. Women presently make up over 46 percent of the total U.S. work force, and nine out of ten women will work at some time in their lives. Women's labor force participation has grown from 37.7 percent in 1960 to 60.2 percent presently (17).

Not only are more women in the work force, but the marital status of women currently working has also changed. In 1940, 64 percent of all employed women were single, widowed, or divorced. By 1982, single, divorced, and widowed women were even more likely to be in the work force, but married women had increased their participation rate to the extent that they comprised 59 percent of all working women. Since 1980 there have been more families in the United States with both husband and wife working than families with only the husband working (18).

Increased employment rates have been greatest for women with children. In 1950, only about 20 percent of all women with children were in the labor force, but by 1996, 60 percent of mothers with children under eighteen were working. Also in 1997, 65 percent of mothers with children under the age of six were in the labor force, up from 39 percent in 1975 and 58 percent as recently as 1990 (19).

Paradoxically, at the same time that increasing numbers of women are entering the work force, greater numbers of women and their children are finding themselves victims of poverty. For the nearly eight million in 1996 of female-headed households, the poverty rate was 49.3 percent, a rate five times that for married-couple families (20). The poverty rate for white female-headed families was 27.1 percent, for African-American female-headed families, 51.7 percent, and for Spanish-surname families headed by women, 53.4 percent. Fully two out of every three poor adults are women, and the economic status of families headed by women is declining (21).

In 1995, while the median income of all family households was $40,611, that of female-headed households was only $19,691 with over 25 percent of these households having incomes under $10,000 (22).

The trends depicted by all of these data point to a future where, unless there are substantive social welfare policy reforms, there will be an increased "feminization of poverty," especially involving women of color. Associated with this projection is the probability of greater numbers of children residing in female-headed households, households where the mother is not home during the day but at the work place, usually earning 70 percent of wages that men receive for doing comparable or equivalent work.

It is for these reasons in main that child welfare policies, programs, and services continue to be vitally necessary today. The following section will consider the nature of child welfare services and the issues and challenges contained therein.

Continuum of Care

Although there is no standard typology of child welfare services, will utilize levels of intervention (supportive, supplementary, or substitute care) as our organizing framework. We believe that this approach offers the reader the most understandable and comprehensive system with which to examine the continuum of child welfare services.

The practice philosophy of child welfare services today is the preservation and upgrading of the quality of family life. "Our perceptions of families—their strengths and weaknesses in coping with problems that create risks to family stability—shape the content of child welfare programs" (23). The emphasis of child welfare services has been shifting slowly but steadily from protecting children by placing them in foster care to protecting them in their own homes; this practice philosophy is reflected in new terms, such as "family preservation," "wrap-around services," "family reunification," "family support," "permanency planning," and "the family asset model." Although not always attainable, the goal always is to ensure the well-being of children by maintaining or restoring adequate parental care and family stability.

Types of Child Welfare Services

According to the Child Welfare League of America (24), child welfare services include adoption, day-care services, foster-family care service, group home service, homemaker service, institutional care for children, maternity homes, protective service for neglected children, shelter care for children in emergencies, social services to children in their own homes, social services to families, children, and individuals under stress, and social services for unmarried parents.

Auspices and Sources of Funding

Child welfare services are provided by a diverse array of agencies that cut across the public and private sectors. Child welfare agencies can be further categorized by their auspices and sources of funding (25).

1. Public agencies under federal, sate, or county auspices are supported by public tax funds.
2. Voluntary not-for-profit agencies are generally supported by community-donated funds and are further subdivided as under either denominational

(sectarian) auspices—for example, Buddhist, Catholic, Jewish, or Protestant—or nondenominational (non-sectarian) auspices. Since voluntary agencies currently receive a large measure of support from public funds purchase-of-service agreements, they can legitimately be regarded as quasi-public agencies.

3. Private for-profit agencies are under proprietary auspices and supported by client fees. These include proprietary day-care centers, homemaker services, group homes, and residential treatment centers.

4. Industrially affiliated agencies, such as factory day-care centers, are part of employee assistance programs.

Levels of Intervention

The principle of *Least Restrictive Environment* presently governs decisions concerning the appropriate level of intervention by child welfare services. This principle advocates that the maintenance of the biological family is the preferred option in the care and protection of children. To the extent possible, it is preferable to provide whatever services are necessary to help the child within the context of his or her biological family and to keep the family intact. In many instances, problems that the child is experiencing are directly related to problems of one or both parents and the family as a whole. Operationally, the child's home is considered the least restrictive environment, and a locked institution is considered the most restrictive environment.

The focus of intervention therefore should be on the family system: its communication patterns; its economic role performance; its form of socialization, including its transmission of values, standards of behavior, and moral conduct; its discipline patterns; the parent–child, parent–parent, and child–child relationships; its problem-solving skills; and its interrelationship skills with larger systems. Helping the child or children without helping the family system too often results in temporary, short-term problem reduction (the symptoms), without dealing with the underlying problems of the family system (the causes).

Child welfare programs and services can be organized on a continuum ranging from the least restrictive environment for the child to the most restrictive environment: (1) supportive services; (2) supplemental services; and (3) substitute services. These services are not mutually exclusive and often are used in combination with one another (26).

Supportive Services

Supportive services are intended to "support, reinforce, and strengthen the ability of parents and children to meet the responsibilities of their respective statuses" (27). Supportive services are designed for children living in their own homes and are usually associated with the term, "home-based care." These services for lower-income, blue-collar and lower-middle-class parents and their children are regularly provided by child guidance clinics, family service agency programs, community health and community mental health centers, regional centers (for the developmentally disabled), school counselors, and protective service agencies. Other family support services, especially since the passage of the Family Support Act of 1988, include: information/referral; prenatal care; basic health care; family life education; quality child care; parks/recreation; and parenting education.

Self-help groups such as Parents Anonymous, Parents United, Alcoholics Anonymous, Al-Anon, and Al-Ateen provide a growing sector of supportive services. Community centers, "Ys," Boy and Girl Scout programs, and city parks and recreation programs provide important recreational and socialization opportunities. Private psychotherapists, including social workers, psychologists, pastoral counselors, mental health nurses, marriage and family counselors, psychiatrists, and psychoanalysts provide many of the supportive services for children and families of the middle and upper classes and others able to afford private sector for-profit fees.

Supportive services are the "first line of defense" in dealing with actual or incipient problems in child welfare, "when the family and the parent–child relationship system are structurally intact but subject to stress" (28). These services tend to be the most preventative and presently are receiving the greatest priority, in that they are the least restrictive and can prevent the need for removing children from the home. Supportive services are designed to use the family's own strength (asset model) to work toward a reduction of strain in the parent–child relationship system (29). In fiscal terms, also, they are often the most cost-effective services, in that they can minimize the need for more expensive supplemental services and the highly expensive substitute services where and when they are not appropriate.

Case Example: The Jones Family

The Jones family, consisting of mother who works full-time as a legal secretary; father, employed as a sales representative; and three children, Tommy, 11, Susan, 9, and Eric, 4, has experienced parent–child relationship problems. Tommy is beginning to associate with some of the neighborhood youth who are into petty theft, school truancy, and overall pre-delinquent behavior. He has become increasingly difficult to communicate with and to discipline. His schoolwork has suffered and he seems continually defiant and rebellious. The Joneses were referred by their pastor to the Excelsior Family Service Agency for family counselling.

Case Notes. As a Bachelor of Social Work, generalist, child welfare worker employed by the Excelsior Family Service Agency, some of your tasks and responsibilities could include the following:

1. *As an intake worker:* taking a family social history, including information about the precipitating problem and pertinent health, education, social, and psychological information regarding Tommy and other family members; obtaining information regarding parental disciplining patterns, family member role performance, nature of relationships between family members, including communication patterns, activities, and problem-solving patterns; obtaining data regarding family economic situation.

2. *As the generalist social worker assigned to the Jones family:* if you determine that the Jones family has a presenting problem that is appropriate for your agency, referral of this family to an Excelsior counseling specialist to provide a diagnostic assessment and determine the nature of the treatment. The counselling specialist (clinician, therapist) most often will be an M.S.W., but the agency might also have clinical Ph.D. psychologists or M.A. counselors (such as MFCC-licensed Marriage, Family, Child Counselors in California) for ongoing treatment.

3. *As case manager:* obtaining any additional information concerning the family (e.g., from schools or from other social agencies the Joneses might have contacted), and coordinating the activities and information concerning the family.

Supplemental Services

Supplemental services include income maintenance programs such as public welfare (TANF, formerly AFDC), food stamps, Women, Infant, and Children (WIC) food program, and social insurance programs such as Social Security (Old Age Security Disability and Health Insurance), Workers' Compensation, and Unemployment Insurance. These programs serve *in loco parentis* (in place of parents) concerning the income-producing responsibilities of the parents. Other forms of supplemental services include Big Brother and Big Sister programs. Homemaker (or homechore) programs, and child day-care programs as they are designed to supplement the mother or father's enactment of child-care functions.

To this list of services should be added family preservation services, formalized with the passage of the Family Preservation and Support Services Program of the Omnibus Budget Reconciliation Act of 1993. Family preservation services are called into play for families facing serious challenges, including: major health/mental health problems; temporary income loss; emotional/personal crisis; drug/alcohol abuse; school failure; illegal activity; isolation; general neglect; and other compounded problems. Family preservation services include: family/agency joint case management; family assessment; services plan; care-taker; in-home service/treatment; and other prevention services.

Supplemental services are called upon when a "parent–child relationship is seriously impaired because a significant aspect of the parental role is inadequately covered but the family configuration is such that, with supplementation, the child can continue to live at home without the probability of harm" (30).

Case Example: The Lopez Family

The Lopez family consists of Mrs. Lopez, 35, unemployed and receiving Aid to Families with Dependent Children (AFDC/TANF), Araceli, 12, Sara, 10, Hector, 5, and Carlos, 3. Mrs. Lopez has chronic hypertension, leaving her bedridden on occasion and in need of regular medical treatment. As a result, the children do not receive adequate parental supervision and the case has been referred to the county department of children's services.

Case Notes.   As a children's services worker with a B.A. degree in human services, you function as a generalist child welfare worker; that is, you are responsible for "assessing the situation with the client and deciding which system, i.e., individual, family, small-group, an agency or organization, or a community, is the appropriate unit of attention, or focus of the work, for the change effort" (31). In this situation, both Mrs. Lopez (individual) and the Lopez children (family) constitute the focus of your attention. The presenting problem is the "lack of adequate parental supervision." Your responsibility is to determine the needs of the Lopez family, its strengths and weaknesses, and, under the guidelines of P.L. 96-272, the Adoption Assistance and Child Welfare Act of 1980, whether there is the presumption of child abuse and/or neglect.

Based on your study of the family, you have determined that no neglect and/or abuse exists. Rather, the children are in need of supplemental services due to the relative incapacity of the mother in her parenting role. Using the principle of the "least restrictive environment," that is, endeavoring to maintain as natural a family situation as possible, you have ruled out the desirability of out-of-home care (substitute services) at this time. Rather, you have worked on locating any relatives in the area who might be able to provide assistance. You discover that the Lopez family has recently immigrated from Mexico and they have no relatives in this country.

As a middle-class, anglo social worker, you need to be sensitive to the differences in culture, traditions, and language that characterize the Lopez family. Rather than imposing your own values and class/ethnic standards, you need to "start where the client is" in terms of their own goals, expectations, cultural traditions, and experiences. You are sensitive to the strong family orientation typical in the Hispanic culture, and the reluctance to seek help from "outsiders." You approach this situation with ethno-cultural sensitivity and have been able to secure the trust and respect of Mrs. Lopez through your demonstrated concern and willingness to understand the problem situation from her perspective.

With Mrs. Lopez's understanding and concurrence, you have successfully contracted for the services of a homemaker (homechore worker) who comes into the Lopez home five days per week and helps the mother with her child-care responsibilities; in addition, because there is an absent father and no adult male role model for the boys in the family, efforts have been made to match Hector and Carlos with a Hispanic volunteer Big Brother. You have been successful, and Mrs. Lopez was recently notified that a Big Brother has become available and has agreed to work with the boys on an ongoing basis.

Substitute Services

Substitute services include temporary shelter care, foster family care, adoptive homes, group homes, residential treatment facilities, and institutions. The provision of substitute care for dependent, neglected, or abused children has long been the primary and indeed, until recently, almost the exclusive function of the child

welfare system. Although attention and resources are now shifting to the maintenance of children in their own homes, placement services continue to be an
important part of the child welfare system (32).

Substitute services constitute the most restrictive environments and are used
when the "situation is so damaging as to require either a temporary or a permanent dissolution of the parent–child relationship system" (33). In all substitute
family care arrangements, the biological parent or parents yield almost total
responsibility to someone else for the performance of the parental role in relation
to their child. Because substitute services constitute the most restrictive, and often
the most substantially disruptive, of "normal" ongoing parent–child relationships,
very serious consideration needs to be given as to whether this form of child welfare services intervention is appropriate.

Optimally, supportive services and supplemental services, including family
support and family preservation services, would have been offered to the family
prior to the consideration of substitute services. Yet, there are circumstances, particularly in instances of (1) chronic neglect and/or abuse, (2) the absence of parents, and (3) the child's or youth's serious emotional or behavioral problems,
where substitute services (out-of-home care) may be necessary and appropriate.

For some children, accordingly, substitute services are indicated and often
can be the most beneficial. Whittaker argues very persuasively that:

> *Our goal should be to develop an integrated continuum of care that provides a
> full range of home-based and residential options and contains an easily acti-
> vated set of linkages between the various service programs and the other major
> systems in which the child participates: family, peer group, school, church, and
> community.*
>
> *[The issue, according to Whittaker, is not the relative merits of residential
> versus community treatment or, for that matter, supportive versus supplemental
> versus substitute services—ed.]; rather, it is how best to translate the most use-
> ful knowledge from clinical research and practice wisdom to a total continuum
> of services, ranging from programs that provide help while the child remains in
> his own home, through smaller, open, community-based residential and day
> programs to larger, more secure residential facilities for those few children who
> need them (34).*

Ideally, the key element in developing a service plan for any particular child
would not center on whether he or she remained at home or was placed out; it
would focus instead on how the elements in the "total ecosystem could be so
mobilized as to constitute a 'powerful environment' for positive change" (35).

In American society, there is the strong belief that birth parents are the best
parents for a child and the home of origin is the best setting for child rearing. This
belief is particularly strong today among child welfare policy and practice experts.
They continuously stress the importance of family maintenance programs, family
preservation services, family reunification efforts, and family-based services. Yet,
every year thousands of children are removed from their natural homes into sub-

stitute care, some to stay until they reach their 18th or, in rare exceptions, their 21st birthday.

Estimates of the number of children in substitute care (out-of-home placement) were placed at 502,000 at the end of 1996, nearly double the 276,000 children at the end of 1985 and 25 percent more than in 1990 (36). Yet, in the first edition of this book, we celebrated the reduction from 500,000 children in placement in 1977 to the 276,000 in 1985.

We endeavored to explain the reduction in the number of children in out-of-home care during the 1980s as being attributed to a number of factors, including: (1) the impact of P.L. 96-272, the Adoption Assistance and Child Welfare Act, which has placed emphasis on permanency planning, family maintenance, and family reunification; (2) the increased emphasis on supportive and supplemental services, intended to prevent unnecessary out-of-home placements; (3) fewer young unmarried mothers relinquishing their babies for adoption; (4) the then conventional wisdom that supported the retention of children at home, even in situations of child abuse and neglect when they had proven to be idiosyncratic and *not* a threat to the safety and well-being of the child; and (5) the diminishing supply of foster-home resources, as increasing numbers of women enter the labor force.

While the children entering the out-of-home care system were older on average, and more seriously troubled and troublesome in the 1980s, these problems have compounded in the 1990s. The children who enter the child welfare system today bring more acute problems. According to the US DHHS, 1997 *National Study* (37), "a sizable percentage come from families with substance abuse problems, many are believed to be victims of or witnesses to domestic violence, and AIDS affects the families of a considerable number. Further, the percent of child welfare cases involving allegations of abuse and neglect have increased from 45 percent in 1977 to 80 percent in 1994." In addition, increasing numbers of children coming into foster care suffer severe emotional/behavioral problems, including attention deficit disorders and other learning disabilities, and are substance abusers. Even more tragically, increasing numbers of babies who are coming into placement are the victims of AIDS, cocaine addiction ("crack babies") or alcoholism (fetal alcoholism syndrome [FAS]) passed on to them by their birth mothers.

Foster Family Care

Foster family care can be defined as the 24-hour out-of-home care provided to children and youth by foster parent(s) not related to the child (*note:* foster care payments are now made to relatives in some instances through kinship care). Most often, the precipitating factors necessitating out-of-home placement, particularly into foster family care, are parent centered. That is, a dependency factor arises, whether due to the absence of incapacity of one or both parents, to neglect and/or child abuse.

Stein and Rzepnicki (38) provide a highly useful and succinct set of guidelines concerning out-of-home placement decision-making. It should be noted that many of their guidelines coincide with, and are discussed in depth by, Cynthia

Tower in her chapter on child abuse in this book. Stein and Rzepnicki advance that out-of-home placement is appropriate if:

1. There is no adult willing to care for a child, or the child refuses to stay in the home.
2. There is medical evidence that physical abuse or nutritional neglect is so severe as to be life threatening.
3. There was intent to kill the child, even if injury is not severe. Medical evidence should support a hypothesis of deliberate poisoning, or marks on the child's body should indicate assault with a deadly weapon or repeated beating with a heavy object.
4. There is medical or psychological evidence of abuse that, without intervention, may threaten the child's life, and the parent refuses help.
5. Medical evidence of repeated abuse exists. This reference is to previous untreated injuries generally identified through X-rays, where the location or type of injury suggests prior maltreatment.
6. Severe abuse or neglect recurs after services were offered.
7. There is evidence to suggest emotional neglect or abuse. Behavioral correlates include severe emotional disturbances or withdrawal by the child and parental rejection of the child.
8. Medical or psychological evidence suggests that the parent is incompetent to provide minimum child care, and there are no resources (e.g., family, friends, or community services) to help in the home while assessment is under way.
9. A child has been raped by a related adult or a non-related adult known to the parent, and the parent did not attempt to protect the child (39).

The vast majority of children and youth coming into out-of-home care, in particular, and public child welfare services, in general, are children of impoverished families. According to Edelman (40), "children are poor because our nation has lost its moral bearings." Presently, our nation is immersed in a politico-economic philosophy that increasingly has turned its back on the needy. The deconstruction of AFDC into TANF and the severe cutbacks in food stamps, public health care, mental health care, housing, government-supported job training programs, school lunch programs, Medicaid—the litany of government retrenchment on social programs beginning in the 1980s and through the 1990s is endless—have contributed immeasurably to the development of a two-tier society: the haves and the have-nots.

In brief, children are poor because of "decreasing government support at a time of increasing need, which has resulted from economic recession, unemployment, low wages, and increased taxes on the poor" (41). Poor children become doubly jeopardized in being victims of poverty which is highly correlated with family instability, including violence, substance abuse and disorganization, which further places these children at risk for substitute care consideration. (It is not the purpose of this chapter to critically discuss the "chicken-egg" debate waging among poverty experts, i.e., whether poverty leads to family disorganization, or whether family disorganization leads to poverty; more probably, they are interactive) (42).

The reader should be reminded that it is not only the children of poverty, or the children of color, who come from disorganized, unstable families. Nor is it correct to assume that only poor minority children and youth suffer from health, mental health, and/or socio-behavioral problems. Yet, families with more financial resources at their disposal are able to purchase those goods and services which can often help them prevent or alleviate their family or child-centered problems. They are not as subject to the scrutiny of public agency investigations as poor families and are not as likely to become part of our national statistics regarding child abuse and/or neglect, juvenile delinquency, etc.

More affluent families are not immune to problems of social functioning. However, through purchased psycho-social services, private and timely medical care, hiring of family helpers (nurses, babysitters, maids, governesses, au pairs), through use of private boarding and military schools for children with real or imagined behavioral problems, or through high-cost substance abuse recovery programs (often picked up by private health insurance), upper-middle-class and rich families engage in private actions to cope with their private problems. A disproportionate number of poor people and their children see their private problems become public issues.

There are 8.86 million children under age 18 who live in California—13 percent of the children in the United States (43). Latino and Asian children comprise 40 percent of the population—30.5 percent and 9.7 percent respectively; by the year 2000, nearly 60 percent of California's children will be "people of color": Latino (36 percent); Asian (13 percent); and African-American (9 percent).

Subsequent chapters in this book by Delgado (Hispanic families), Prater (African-American families), and Mass and Yap (Asian/Pacific families) and Ledesma and Starr (Native American families) will provide a detailed discussion of child welfare as it relates to children of color.

More than one out of four (26.4 percent) children—roughly 2.33 million—now live below the poverty level in California. According to a recent study by the National Center for Children in Poverty, the poverty rate for children under six in California is now 29 percent up a full 24 percent since 1983 (44). To provide a more graphic image of the enormity of the number of poor children in California: If there were a city of California's poor youngsters under age 18, it would be the third largest in the state, ranking behind only Los Angeles and San Diego!

These are the children at risk who constitute the bulk of attention for already overburdened child welfare and juvenile justice resources. Simply put, poverty and inequality are inextricably linked to the demand for child welfare resources. Yet, at the time of this writing, the demand for services far surpasses the resources available to adequately meet this demand. Family foster care is one of these resources that is being stretched dangerously thin.

The vast majority of foster family placements are typically provided by any one of three different types of public-sector (governmental) agencies: (1) children's services (providing the largest number of placements)—for situations of dependency, neglect, and/or abuse; (2) juvenile probation—for children and youth in trouble with the law who do not require a more restrictive environment, such as probation camp or a residential treatment facility; and (3) adoptions— where children are awaiting adoption proceedings. While there are differences among the states, increasing numbers of children who go into foster family care are wards of the court. Child petitions are submitted to the juvenile dependency court wherein the child is legally assigned the protection and supervision of the court while in placement.

Problems in Foster Care

Current policies directed at dependent and neglected children and their families have received criticism from many quarters (45). Criticisms have focused on several major problems, perhaps ominously summarized by the John D. Rockefeller-led National Commission on Children: "If the nation had deliberately designed a system that would frustrate the professionals who staff it, anger the public who finance it and abandon the children who depend on it, it could not have done a better job than the present child welfare system" (46).

Child welfare practice, as opposed to policy, is a history of removal of children from lower-class parents who have been deemed unfit: "The major service of child welfare agencies traditionally has been foster care placement" (47).

1. Children are removed from homes more frequently than is necessary.
2. When removed from natural homes, children are placed in inappropriate, unstable, and unnecessarily restrictive settings.
3. Too little effort is made to keep natural families involved, to provide services to solve problems in natural families, and to facilitate reunification.
4. There is inadequate monitoring of the foster care system in terms of quality of care, appropriateness of placement, and knowledge of the characteristics of children in foster care (48).

Children too often have been removed from their homes without sufficient reason. Cox and Cox (49) suggest that several factors have probably contributed to this condition. "When family problems have arisen, out-of-home care often has been the only solution offered by welfare departments, primarily because state and federal funding was almost exclusively for out-of-home care." Were there to be services such as emergency housing, emergency shelters, day care, emergency cash assistance, homemakers, and intensive therapy aimed at the prevention of out-of-home placement, far fewer children would be removed from their homes. Unfortunately, even when funds have been made available for those services through family preservation and where they have existed to some extent in the past, recent social program cutbacks throughout the country have significantly reduced their availability.

Other conditions leading to unnecessary placement may be the relative lack of experience of child placement workers, the very high caseloads per worker, the high turnover of staff, the lack of cross-cultural sensitivity, and the bureaucratic pressures to err on the side of child placement. Ostensibly, placement is to be in the best interests of the child, but, more often, it is to avoid the possibility of harm befalling children in their own homes—homes that are too often not provided with necessary and timely preservation and support services.

According to Mech (50), Native American children, along with other minorities, are overrepresented in substitute care, and tend to stay in care far longer. The placement rate of American Indian children is considerably higher than that of white children, and most have been placed in Caucasian homes. According to Hideki Ishisaka, "Social agencies don't have a clear appreciation of American Indian parenting patterns and involvement of siblings in care of younger children. This lack of understanding leads them to perceive need for intervention and placement where it is not valid" (51).

The Indian Child Welfare Act of 1978 (P.L. 95-608) was developed in response to the fact that 25 to 35 percent of all Native American children were placed in substitute care, and interracial adoption was rationalized although there was lack of effective adoption-home–finding programs for these children. The Act, therefore, was based on the principle that Native American children who must have substitute care are not to be disconnected from their own tribe and its distinct cultural heritage except under unusual conditions.

While space and the focus of this chapter do not permit a comprehensive, detailed examination of the many other issues and factors surrounding foster family care, the reader is advised to refer to a number of excellent in-depth studies of this subject (52).

Foster family care, when deemed necessary, is particularly appropriate for younger children who are able to derive benefit from a family atmosphere, who are not threatened by normal family relationships, who can identify positively with surrogate parent figures, and who do not possess serious emotional, mental, behavioral, or physical problems which require specialized treatment or care.

Foster Parents

Who are foster parents? Often, people such as yourself who possess love and caring for children, have room in their lives for one or more unrelated children, have good parenting skills, are flexible, and have the desire and ability to provide short-term care for children in need of respect, love, consistency, security, nurturing, and positive role models.

In addition, foster parents need to pass a rigorous physical examination, to clear background checks for any criminal violations (especially child abuse or maltreatment), to demonstrate that they are financially stable (not rich—but with a source of income separate from foster care payments), and to have a residence that will adequately accommodate one to six foster children in a hazard-free, safe, and secure environment.

In California and other states it is possible to be licensed as foster parents if you live in an apartment, mobile home, or other residence apart from owning your own home. You can also be licensed for foster care if you are a single parent and meet the other requirements.

Foster parents typically come from working-class, lower-middle-class backgrounds. They are usually from large families, have often had to help raise a number of their own brothers and sisters, and enjoy the hustle and bustle of a number of children in their midst. Quality foster parents are usually other-oriented and family-centered, and enjoy doing things with their children, biological and foster children alike. They usually possess very good people skills, exhibit good judgment, and are willing to work closely with the placement agency and the biological parent(s). They are also able to "let go" of the foster child(ren) when the time comes. They understand that their role is helping to provide foster children with a temporary home until they are able to return to their own family or have other plans made that will enhance the child's stability and opportunity to grow and thrive.

Kinship Care

A particular form of foster care is kinship care, which, in its many forms is generally viewed as a form of family preservation. This form of foster care is growing and today, over 50 percent of children placed in Los Angeles County are in some form of kinship care arrangement. According to the Child Welfare League of America, "the kinship support system may be composed of nuclear family, extended family, blended family, foster family, or adoptive family members, or members of tribes or clans. Its intent is to stabilize family situations, ensure the protection of children, and prevent the need to separate children from their families" (53).

In formal kinship care, the child is placed by the court in the legal custody of the child welfare agency; financial support for the care of children is often made through foster care payments; kinship homes are expected to meeting licensing standards.

In *Miller v. Yoakim*, a case appealed to the U.S. Supreme Court, the principle was established that states cannot discriminate against caregivers under the federal foster care program. Foster care payments are to be made to kinship providers when specific conditions are met, including being eligible for Title IV-E assistance, and there is judicial determination of abuse and neglect.

The positives of kinship care is that it can maintain the child's emotional ties while maintaining the child's family identity. A negative could be trapping the child in the middle of negative family dynamics, including maltreatment patterns and undetected substance abuse which could compromise the child's safety (54).

Case Example: The S. Family

The S. family has recently been beset with a host of social problems. Mr. S. was recently incarcerated for a variety of crimes, including the theft of an automobile. He has been sentenced to three to five years in the state prison. Mrs. S. has had a history of emotional problems and has required hospitalization in the past. Presently, she is on medication and receiving outpatient psychiatric care at a local county mental health clinic. There are two children: Lillian, 8, and Ray-mond, 3. The S. family has been helped to apply for AFDC, as Mrs. S. is unem-ployable and there is no income due to the recent incarceration of Mr. S.

The county department of children's services (DCS) has been contacted, as Mrs. S. is having difficulty in providing adequate care and supervision for her chil-dren. As the child welfare worker assigned to the S. family, what is your case plan?

Case Notes.   Child welfare services today place heavy emphasis on the first line of defense: supportive services. Empirical evidence has clearly indicated that once children are removed from their own homes, however temporarily, it is much more difficult to return them home. Too many children wander through the maze of out-of-home placements, often moving from foster home to foster home to group homes, until many of them become 18 years old.

The Adoption Assistance and Child Welfare Act of 1980 (P.L. 96-272), was formulated largely to counteract this problem. It contained provisions for pre-placement preventive services, reunifying families, and adoption assistance, and it required state agencies to develop and implement a case review system that ensures the following three conditions: development of a case plan; periodic reviews; and procedural safeguards.

Given all the above, as a generalist child welfare worker assigned to this fam-ily, how would you intervene in this family situation? What would be your child welfare goals? What resources and services would be indicated? What would be in the best interests of the children?

To proceed as professionally as possible, coping with the pressures caused by the bureaucracy and scarcity of resources of the public child welfare agency, it is essential for the child welfare worker to prepare a rigorous assessment of the fam-ily situation.

Assessment helps workers identify family problems in need of resolution and facilitates the selection of problem-solving strategies. Faulty or non-rigorous assessment can increase the dangers to children. The problems creating the great-est risks may be overlooked, or clients may receive services that are inappropriate, or even unnecessary, if family strengths are not correctly identified.

Assessment strategies would include: client self-reports (these include inter-views, inventories, and self-monitoring); direct observation by trained staff; and information stored in agency records and that which is provided by collateral resources who have worked with or are currently working with clients (55). The reader is directed to Stein and Rzepnicki's *Decision Making at Child Welfare Intake: A Handbook for Practitioners* (56) for further in-depth discussion of assessment and subsequent decision making.

Group Homes, Residential Facilities, Institutions

Foster family care is not appropriate for all children for whom out-of-home place-ment is required. For those children who cannot tolerate close family living situations, and/or who are troubled or troublesome and suffer from significant emotional, mental, physical, or behavioral problems, some form of group home, residential treatment facility, or institutional setting may be required.

Group Homes

Group homes represent a mixture of some of the qualities of children's institutions and foster homes. They have emerged as a compromise between institutional care for troubled adolescents and foster care for dependent and neglected youth (57).

There is much ambiguity and confusion surrounding what is precisely meant by the term "group home." According to Title XXII of the California Administrative Code, group homes are defined as settings in which "children are cared for on a 24-hour basis by hired staff members who reside elsewhere" (58). Group homes can range in size from seven residents to an open-ended upper limit. In a study conducted by the author, group homes containing over 100 youths were not uncommon (59).

According to Kadushin and Martin (60), a group home may be "viewed as a large foster family unit or a small institution. It is a living facility within the normal community simulating a family for a small group of unrelated children." The Child Welfare League of America's Group Home Standards Statement (61) suggests that group homes "should not be used for fewer than five children or more than twelve. A group of six to eight children is optimum. . . ."

In brief, group homes include small "Mom-and-Pop" settings of seven to twelve youngsters supervised by houseparents, often established in a residential community and indistinguishable from neighboring units. These homes are actually run similarly to foster homes but are required to have a social service consultant who provides contracted services, sometimes not more than four to eight hours per week. This type of group home is selected for "emotionally detached youngsters who are either too fearful to risk exposure of their feelings in close relationships or simply do not know how to find their way in close relationships but who can operate without difficulty in the normal community" (62).

Group homes also include those single homes or apartments owned or rented by a social service agency and/or larger residential treatment center and staffed by "foster parents" who are employed by the agency and who work around the clock. These homes (usually four to six youths) are often used as part of the continuum of services provided by the agency and offer more independent living opportunities for youthful residents, especially teenagers, who are being helped to return to the community. The agency continues to provide necessary services to these residents, and the residents are able to utilize the resources of the larger residential treatment facility.

Group homes also include those larger settings in which there may be 15 to over 125 youth in residence. According to the Child Welfare League of America (63), a children's institution is defined as a 24-hour residential facility in which a group of unrelated children live together in the care of unrelated adults. These are referred to as residential centers.

Very large residential centers for youth are also commonly referred to as institutions. Functionally speaking, they are institutions. Yet, technically speaking, institutions should be viewed as those large, governmentally operated facilities which had their antecedents in the almshouse movement during earlier times in this country.

The original residents of almshouses—the "lame and halt," the "impotent poor," the "blind, deaf and dumb," the old, the "insane," and women and young children—were subsequently placed in specialized institutions. Today, there are state-run hospitals (institutions) for children, youth, and adults who are developmentally disabled, severely emotionally disturbed (state psychiatric hospitals), or severely emotionally disturbed criminal offenders, as well as specialized institutions for the physically disabled, including the blind and deaf.

Having viewed the numerous definitions and descriptions of "group homes" above, the reader should now more fully understand why there is ambiguity and confusion regarding a precise definition of group homes, residential centers, residential treatment centers, and institutions. Too often, these terms are used interchangeably or are applied to settings where the scope, nature, and quality of care can vary dramatically.

Placement Criteria.   For what children and youth does group home placement appear to be appropriate? According to Sundel (64), there seem to be two basic criteria by which the choice of a group care placement is determined:

1. The child's need for control that cannot be provided in a family living situation
2. The child's need for an array of services that can only be provided effectively in a group setting

The need for control stems from the child's own inability to control impulsive behavior and/or from impaired reality perception that makes the child a danger to him- or herself or others. The child's need for services that can only be met in a group care setting may stem from a reality perception so impaired that the child would find it difficult, if not impossible, to make use of these services in anything but a group setting (65).

The factors most often described as indicating the desirability of a group care placement include:

- the severity of the child's emotional disturbance
- the amount and severity of the child's acting-out behavior
- the severity of the child's physiological impairment and/or impairment of intellectual functioning
- the child's age
- the child's ability to tolerate group life
- the child's need for an emotionally diluted environment
- the need for further diagnostic study of the child
- the child's choice of placement
- the parents' choice of placement

The most comprehensive system for matching child to facility currently available appears to be the one developed by Sister Mary Paul for the New York State Board of Social Welfare (66). Sister Paul's system is presented in Table 3.1.

Many of the larger "group homes" are more precisely known as residential treatment centers, particularly if there is a major emphasis on psycho-social services and/or psychiatric treatment. In these centers are to be found an eclectic mix of human service professionals: social workers (M.S.W.s), clinical psychologists, marriage, family, and child counselors (M.F.C.C.s), psychiatrists, child care workers (sometimes referred to as house or cottage parents or group supervisors), recreational therapists, occupational therapists, special education teachers, nurses, nutritionists, administrators, and residence and program directors. Some of the larger and better endowed facilities also have doctors, dentists, optometrists, et al. on a fee-for-service contractual basis.

In brief, well-staffed, quality treatment program group homes, a.k.a. residential treatment centers, are indicated for those children and youth who need substitute services (out-of-home placement) and who can benefit from:

1. A diluted emotional atmosphere
2. Structure, found in the program, the rules and regulations, and the daily routine and activities; as well as continuity and consistency of care
3. Group living experience, where children and youth learn to develop responsibility to the group and to develop and improve relational skills and behavior and where peer pressure can have a positive impact
4. A variety of positive adult role models—often referred to as "milieu therapy"—where the setting and the diverse personnel serve in the treatment process
5. Specialized services—treatment, education, recreation, occupation, physical and mental rehabilitation

The following summarizes the attributes of a comprehensive residential treatment center's program for children and youth:

1. Intensive Counseling
   a. group
   b. individual
   c. substance-abuse counseling
2. Social Development
   a. problem-solving techniques
   b. coping skills
   c. sensitivity to others
   d. acceptance of authority
3. Physical Development
   a. good sportsmanship
   b. teamwork
   c. promotion of growth in self-esteem
4. Educational Growth

TABLE 3.1 Sister Mary Paul's Typology: Criteria for Choosing Group Care Placement

	Group Home	Group Residence	General Institution*	Residential Treatment Center Type A	Residential Treatment Center Type B
Emotional Disturbance	cannot tolerate close emotional ties emotional disturbance which needs on-site professional observation and evaluation	mild or residual, e.g. returning from a psychiatric facility need to clarify complex personality, familial or environmental conflicts and/or need to clarify choice of long term placement, e.g. degree of structure, therapy, etc. needed		moderately disturbed, not psychotic	severe disturbance, needs 24 hour supervision thought or affect disorder severely withdrawn severe anorexia weakened ego boundaries so as to be severely accident prone
Acting Out Behavior	sufficient impulse control to maintain curfews and generally assure his safety in an open setting mildly acting out but child needs separation from controlling peer group and needs positive pressure	sufficient impulse control to maintain curfews and generally assure his safety in an open setting has been a drug or alchohol abuser child needs professionally toned relationship with authority figure child needs neutral environment to test out freedom and hetero-sexual relationships.		serious acting out drug or alcohol abuse	self or other destructive bizarre sexual behavior fire setter

Age	6 or older, or younger if part of a sibling group	6 or older	6 or older	no age specified, perhaps younger than six if any emotional disturbance or acting out characteristics make child undeniably dangerous to self or others
I.Q.	normal to mildly retarded	normal to mildly retarded	normal to moderately retarded	normal to mildly retarded
Need for Structure	needs some structure	needs some structure	needs considerable amount of structure, a wide range of supportive services and special program	needs considerable amount of structure, a wide range of supportive services and special program
Support Service	needs more professional help than is available in a foster home	needs some on-site services and specialized program		
Participation in Community	attends community schools / uses community recreation facilities	attends community schools / uses community recreation facilities	little or no community participation	no participation
Able to Participate in Group Life	Yes	Yes	Yes	not specified but likely to be little participation

M. Paul, *Criteria for Foster Placement and Alternatives to Foster Care* (Albany: New York State Board of Social Welfare, 1975), pp. 56–57.

*NOT AN APPROPRIATE RESOURCE FOR CHILDREN OF ANY DESCRIPTION. THESE INSITUTIONS OFFER TOO MUCH TO THE NORMAL CHILD, NOT ENOUGH TO THE EMOTIONALLY DISTURBED CHILD.

5. Moral and Spiritual Awareness
6. Structured Group Living Situation
7. Family Involvement
   a. family counseling
   b. family reunification
8. Vocational Training
9. Play, Occupational, Recreational Therapy
10. Emancipation Program
   a. independent living skills
   b. preparation for future schooling, jobs

In sum, residential treatment centers:

1. Have some theory or technique to deal with children's maladaptive behavior
2. Deal with children who are defined as deviant by some behavioral or psychiatric criterion
3. Select children using some diagnostic procedure
4. Select children for the purpose of treatment
5. Purposefully integrate a variety of program activities into daily life
6. Pay attention to individual needs (67)

To what extent are group homes for children and youth accomplishing their mission? Are group homes facilitating normalization, providing opportunities for peer interaction and peer group counseling, and aggressively using community resources?

In a study of thirty-three group homes in the Los Angeles area in which the author participated, it was discovered that the group homes provided good basic care; that is, food, clothing, education, recreational activities, and interventive medical care (68). Yet, it was revealed that the larger group homes (fifteen or more youths), by their very design, violated the principles of normalization and deinstitutionalization. "They are more similar to what we traditionally view as institutions than they are to homes with family-like living experiences and opportunities. . . . Normalization was low and institutionalization was high in the larger group homes" (69).

Another critical aspect of group homes is the need for continuity of care. Too often, important service providers such as the child care workers have a high job turnover rate because of low salaries and the demands of the job. This exposes the children to a continuing array of care givers and militates against a sense of structure and the continuity of care that is so important to children and youth who have often come from chaotic home situations.

A further aspect of poor continuity of care is the group homes' lack of (or inability to provide) follow-up of their residents after they have completed the program. It is not uncommon for children and youths to have made significant improvement in their functioning at the group home and then to return to the same environment that engendered many of their problems. To "change" the child, without impacting on the family and societal context, is a continuing problem and the wrong thing to do.

Independent Living (Emancipated Minors). For many other youth who have no homes to which to return, and/or who have turned 18 while in foster care, independent living is a critical issue. All adolescents approaching adulthood are faced with adjustment issues and the foster adolescent is no exception. According to Cook, "Typically, foster youths experience repeated emotional and physical separations from their biological and foster families that complicate the socialization and attachment process" (70). Foster care youths have had many people making decisions that impacted their lives. As a result, they have diminished control over decision making and have less opportunity to successfully strive for independence and establish their identity—tasks intrinsic to the period of adolescent development.

"Preparing youths for independent living and self-support has not been a cardinal aim of the foster care system. For young people in placement, bread-and-butter goals like education, employment, and career preparation have somehow taken a back seat," Barth finds (71). Barth (72) concludes that "educational and employment deficits are apparently the most troublesome problems for foster children to deal with as adults."

Studies have consistently pointed out that foster youths require specific preparation for independent living, leading the Child Welfare League of America to refer to this situation as a "national crisis in foster care." Issues of neglect, family violence, drugs, and multiple foster placements have placed these emancipated youth at-risk where fully 56 percent were non-high school graduates, and 17 percent of the girls were found to be pregnant. This need for independent living preparation has been emphasized by the implementation in 1985 of an amendment to Title IV-E, Section 477 of the Social Security Act that was included in the Consolidated Omnibus Reconciliation Act of 1985 (P.L. 99-272, Sec. 2307; codified at 42 U.S.C. Sec. 677), entitled "Transitional Independent-Living Program for Older Foster Children," that permits states to provide transitional-living services for youth aged 16 and older. The 1985 amendment linked closely with the national goals associated with Title XX (Social Services Block Grant Program, SSA) which referred quite clearly to self-support and self-sufficiency as aims for personal social services.

The Omnibus Reconciliation Act of 1993 (OBRA) increased the funding for these ILPs (Independent Living Programs) from $45 million to $70 million. The act authorized ILPs to provide benefits including: high school education, vocational training, career planning, education, employment, and training in daily living skills. These services and activities are designed to:

1. enable participants to seek a high school diploma or its equivalent or to take part in appropriate vocational training;
2. provide training in daily living skills, budgeting, locating and maintaining housing, and career planning;
3. provide for individual and group counseling; integrate and coordinate services otherwise to participants;
4. provide for the establishment of outreach programs to attract youths who are eligible to participate in the program; and

5. provide each participant with a written transitional independent living plan based on an assessment of his or her needs and incorporated into his or her case plan.

In addition, these program elements were found to be central to successful ILPs: accepting responsibilities, medical care/basic health, decision-making, and developing a support system (73).

While these programs have been helpful, and the additional monies are sorely needed, the plight of emancipated minors continues to be a serious problem in the child welfare system. Some recommendations which may assist with ILPs include: developing a comprehensive information system, collecting outcome data of emancipated minors, utilizing follow-up, developing a clearinghouse for resources, and including and emphasizing kinship ties.

In sum, it needs to be emphasized that for some children and youth, group homes or institutional care is both necessary and appropriate. Group homes can, and in many instances do, provide useful programs and services for a sizable number of children and youths. The utility of a group home is enhanced when an appropriate professional placement is made—i.e., one that utilizes an in-depth assessment of the child's needs, functioning level, motivation and capacity; that targets short- and long-range goals; that actively involves the family system to the extent possible; and that selects the group home that provides relevant, individualized quality of care. If placing the right child in the right group home for the right reason is accomplished, group homes can be an effective form of substitute care for children and youths who require this form of care.

Too often, however, demand for quality group home care exceeds supply. Group homes are often under-financed, faced with the dilemma of "filling beds," while at the same time screening applicants to determine their appropriateness for the program. Requests have also increased to accept children who are more troubled and troublesome than they have been in the past, thus requiring more specialized programs, staff, and services. As programs increase in size and scope, they become more institutionalized and are in jeopardy of providing less individualization, less normalizing experiences, and a more restrictive environment. On the other hand, efforts by group homes to include families in the treatment plan, to actively involve their program in family reunification efforts, and to provide independent living programs for older teenagers have added to the quality of care provided to children and youths in this type of out-of-home child welfare service.

Adoption

What of those children who are in need of a "forever home"? For children who are orphaned, abandoned, born out of wedlock to teenage or older parents who are not able or willing to care for them, victims of chronic neglect and/or child abuse, and who are removed from parental custody by court order, adoption is most often in their best interests. According to Kadushin (74), adoption is the most desirable form of permanent substitute care where this is the necessary alternative to the child's own family. It is a more securely permanent arrangement than the foster family home. It is more likely to provide the necessary long-term stability and continuity of affectionate, intimate care by the same parent than either the foster family home or an institution.

Adoption, according to McGowan and Meezan, "is a legal process through which a family unit is created by severing the ties between a child and his or her biological parents and legally establishing a new parent–child relationship between persons not related by blood" (75). The primary purpose of adoption is a permanent family for children who cannot be cared for by their own biological parents. Therefore, the child's welfare, needs, and interests are the basic determinants of good adoption practice. Homes should be selected for children, rather than children selected for homes.

American adoption was not created to solve the stigma and burden of an out-of-wedlock pregnancy. Nor was it intended to ease the pain of infertility by providing children for infertile couples. "That adoption practices did both was merely a fortuitous side effect of the primary purpose of adoption: to provide children with nurturant environments in the care of legally recognized parents whose custody, control, responsibilities, and rights were assured" (76).

We hold the belief that our future is inextricably linked to the well-being of our children. One way to produce adequate adults is to provide for their good development as children. While it is typically expected that birth parents will provide nurturance in a stable family environment, one which provides continuity of care, not all parents are willing or able to perform their functions and responsibilities. Other capable adults are willing to take and nurture children not born to them. "Adoption, therefore, became the legally sanctioned transaction for transferring parenting rights and responsibilities" (77).

Note how closely the modern Child Welfare League of America's adoption standards parallel these values:

1. All children regardless of their age, sex, race, physical, intellectual or emotional status are entitled to a continuous nurturant environment.
2. For most children, the biological family, in its broadest definition, provides the best environment for this nurturance.
3. When a child's birth family is not willing or able to nurture him or her, the child is entitled to timely placement with a family who will.
4. For most children, adoption provides this family better than any other type of substitute parenting.
5. Adoption is a means of finding families for children, not finding children for families. The emphasis is on the child's needs (78).

The history of adoption practice in this country has frequently differed from these idealized CWLA standards. Too often, adoption practice revolved primarily around finding healthy, white babies for couples. These couples were required to be young, physically healthy, white, middle-class, infertile, childless, active in church, financially stable, and in their first marriages.

Adoption programs and practice have undergone radical change since the late 1970s. This is particularly true for Native American children as a result of the Indian Child Welfare Act of 1978. Since its passage, several tribes have set up child welfare programs to blend traditional cultural strengths with formal helping methods, including adoptions.

Today, adoption is a program that seeks permanent homes for every child. As part of the permanency movement written into the Adoption Assistance and Child Welfare Act of 1980 (P.L. 96-272), the position was taken that *every* child is entitled to a permanent home. The first choice is with biological parents or other kin and the second, if that placement is impossible, is adoption.

The Multiethnic Placement Act of 1994, which will be discussed elsewhere, and the Adoption and Safe Families Act of 1997 add to the intent for children to have permanent homes and loving parents. The Adoption and Safe Families Act of 1997 is intended to improve the protection and care of the nation's abused and neglected children, increase adoptions and other permanent homes for children who need them, and support families. With an emphasis on safety, the new law:

- clarifies that children's health and safety are paramount concerns in deciding about removing them from or reunifying them with their families
- specifies situations in which reasonable efforts to keep children with their families are not required
- requires states to check prospective foster and adoptive parents for criminal backgrounds, although states may opt out of this.

A significant provision of the act requires states to provide health insurance for any child with special needs for whom there is an adoption assistance agreement and if the state determines that the child could not be placed for adoption without medical assistance.

Another particularly important provision to expedite permanency is the provision of incentive payments to states of $4,000 for each foster child adopted and $6,000 each for special needs children who are eligible for Title IV-E adoptions assistance.

Parents Who Place Voluntarily

A mix of societal forces has changed the nature of the availability of children for adoption. According to Cole, "until the 1960s adoption was represented by society as the ideal solution for an out-of-wedlock (illegitimate) pregnancy, when the option of marriage for the parents was not possible" (79). Abortion was a legally limited option and had minimal public acceptance. Thus, it was these babies, born out of wedlock primarily to white, middle-class women, who became the principal source of children available for adoption through voluntary termination of parental rights. Yet, it should be pointed out that the majority of single parents never placed their children for adoption: It has never been the parents' preferred option (80).

Since the 1960s, the shifts in sexual mores and access to contraceptives and abortion have been the principal factors in the decreased number of white, non-handicapped infants available for adoption. With expanding women's rights, increased mobility and access to the job market, and the availability of welfare benefits, fewer unmarried mothers are giving up their babies for adoption. The stigma of being an unmarried parent has lessened as more and more children are being raised by divorced parents, especially single-parent, female-headed households. The single unmarried parent does not stand out in today's community as once was the case.

Unmarried teenage mothers today are increasingly deciding not to give up their child voluntarily, viewing this giving up as "unnatural" (81). This is seen as particularly true in those cultural groups where there is a tradition of strong kinship networks helping raise and support the nuclear family (African Americans, Native Americans, some Hispanics).

Involuntary Termination of Parental Rights

Cases of involuntary termination of parental rights cases may be divided into two types—contested and uncontested. Uncontested cases are those in which an agency or individual brings a termination or guardianship transfer action where parents have consented, or are incapable of consent (those who are grossly retarded, psychotic, or in a comatose state).

Contested cases generally hinge on a determination of parental fitness based on expert testimony. Many times these cases involve poor, often uneducated parents who cannot afford private counsel or who are not represented by a guardian *ad litem* who would protect their interests.

Most termination cases are contested and commonly involve charges against the parent of abuse or neglect, desertion or abandonment, or a combination of these (82). In California, under provisions of Senate Bill 14, parents of dependent, neglected and/or abused children are required to appear in court every six months to attest to the efforts and progress they are making in rehabilitating the family situation. If demonstrable steps have not been made, the family's legal rights regarding their children made be terminated.

Questions have been raised about the vagueness of the termination statutes and their possible unconstitutionality. Specific problems have to do with the definition of such conditions as "neglect" or "deprivation," especially among bicultural families. Parents' right to treatment and right to legal representation are factors that often cloud the clarity and objectivity of involuntary termination procedures.

In brief, children available for adoption come from the following sources: out-of-wedlock newborns (principal source); abandoned, neglected, abused children; orphans; children voluntarily surrendered by parents for adoption; and foreign-born children. There is an increasing scarcity of newborn white infants (the supply) while the demand for these youngsters by prospective adoptive parents has not lessened. Thus, it is not uncommon for some white adoptive parent applicants going through an adoption agency placement to have to wait more than three years before they are matched with a young white infant. For those applicants who are even more selective and want children born to parents of the same religious background, the wait can be even longer.

On the other hand, there is a large group of children who await adoption and who may not be adopted—the "hard-to-place" children. These include minority children, those youngsters deemed "older," including healthy white children 10 and above, children who are members of sibling groups, and those children classified as disabled or with special needs (physically, including babies born addicted to drugs, HIV/AIDs, and fetal alcohol syndrome infants; emotionally; mentally; or some combination thereof). These groups of youngsters today constitute the majority of children whom public adoption placement agencies have available for a "forever home" and who are the hardest to place.

Adoption Rates and Composition of the Children

Current adoption figures in the United States are not available as this aspect of child welfare continues to be underdocumented. The most recent figures gathered from the National Council of Adoptions in 1992 reported that there were 51,157 unrelated domestic adoptions, with approximately another 50,000 related adoptions per year. It is estimated that 1 million children in the United States live with adopted parents, and between 2–4 percent of all American families include an adopted child (83).

While there is virtually no current national data on the composition of children awaiting adoption, Meezan (84), however, comments that in 1978:

> *Projections from the* National Survey of Public Social Services for Children and Their Families *estimate that there are 102,000 children legally free for adoption services. Of the 97,000 on whom data is available, 62 percent are white, 28 percent are black, 3 percent are Hispanic, and 7 percent belong to other ethnic groups including Native Americans and Asian. The median age of these children is over 7 years. Nine percent are under 1 year old, while 31 percent are between 1 and 6 years old. Fully 40 percent are over the age of 11.*

The number of children adopted increased from 57,000 in 1957 to 175,000 in 1970, the high water mark of adoptions in America. While there were 89,200 unrelated adoptions and 85,800 related adoptions in 1970, the National Committee for Adoption's state-by-state study conducted in 1982 (85) revealed that there were only 50,720 unrelated adoptions. Since 1970, there has been a slow, consistent decline in adoptions.

African-American, Hispanic, and Native-American children, as indicated earlier, are overrepresented among those available for adoption. Yet, it is not because African-American and other minority families are not adopting at about the same rate as white families. Rather, it is because there are more minority children in substitute placement awaiting adoptive placement compared to white children, relative to their numbers in the overall population. Thus, while African-American children comprise 14 percent of the child population, they are 25 percent of the foster care population, 33 percent of the children free for adoption, and 37 percent of those free who are not in an adoptive placement (86).

The Adoption Process

Adoption is rooted in civil law. It can be defined as the social and legal process by which the relationship of parent and child is established between persons not so related by nature. Broadly speaking, adoption is the process, legal and social, by which a child is transplanted from his or her own family into a new family.

There are two distinct types of adoptive placements. The first is *independent placement*: one where a child is placed in the adoptive home by parents, friends, relatives, physicians, lawyers, or others *without* the aid of a child-placing agency. This category includes related adoption as well as what is referred to as "the gray market"—where a doctor or lawyer may act as an intermediary and arrange for the adoption placement, often for a large fee to be paid by the adopting couple. Included also within this category is what is known as "black market" adoption. This is actually a business transaction where a black marketeer/entrepreneur undertakes to sell a baby to a couple eager to adopt. This last form of independent adoption is a high-risk proposition, without any safeguards for the biological mother, the child, or the adopting couple.

The second form of adoption placement is termed *agency placement*: here, a child is relinquished by her or his own biological parent(s) to a licensed child-placing agency, with the agency assuming responsibility for the child's interim care and for the selection of the child's new and permanent legal family. The agency can be a tax-supported public (governmental) adoption agency, such as the Los Angeles County Bureau of Adoptions, or can be a private (voluntary) sector, usually not-for-profit, agency such as the Children's Home Society, the Florence Crittendon Association, Catholic Charities, etc.

This form of adoption placement provides the most safeguards for the biological parent(s), the child, the adopting couple, and society in general. The following discussion will focus on agency placement practices and procedures only. Agency placement adoption service includes:

1. the preadoptive study of adoptive applicants and of children for whom adoption placement has been requested;
2. selection of a home suitable for a particular child and implementation of placement plans;
3. preadoptive supervision in the adoptive home;
4. participation in the legal process required to complete adoption; and
5. postadoptive supervision, usually for a period of six months following placement.

Following the pattern established by Massachusetts, which enacted the first state adoption law in 1851, adoption placement agencies adhere to the following principles in the adoption process:

A. *Protect the child* from unnecessary separation from his or her birth parents; from adoption by unfit parents; and from interference by his or her birth parents after a successful adoption has been arranged.

B. *Protect the birth parents*, particularly the unmarried mother, from unwise decisions made under emotional stress or economic pressure, which they might regret later.

C. *Protect the adopting parents* from taking a permanent responsibility for children whose health, heredity, or physical and mental capacities might lead to their disappointment, and also protect them from any disturbance of their relationship with the adopted child by threats or blackmail from the birth parents.

Steps in the Adoption Process

1. Identification of Suitable Children.   The first step in the process is to ensure that every child who needs an adoptive family is identified. If a child has no long-term home and is legally free of parental ties (or could become so), society bears responsibility for action in his or her behalf. In most instances such homeless children should be provided with family life which can give them affection, security, continuity in relationships, positive adult role models, and other kinds of care and guidance (87).

Until the 1960s, few children other than problem-free white infants or toddlers were classified as adoptable. Public attitudes toward adoption have never been entirely positive (88). Illegitimacy and a fear of bringing "bad blood" into the family caused doubts about the benefits of adoption. The belief that defective parents breed defective children particularly militates against older children and minority children being considered for adoption.

The adoptive parent and children's rights advocacy movement of the late 1960s and 1970s began to challenge agencies. They contended that no child was unadoptable, which eventually led to changing the professional norm to consider older children and minority children as adoptable. Yet, while this norm is acknowledged, present adoption practice reveals that the majority of adoptable children awaiting placement continue to be the older children and children of color.

2. Freeing for Placement.   This step has two aspects: helping children separate from former parents or parent figures and attach to new parents; legally terminating parental rights (relinquishment) so that they can be vested in another parent or parents.

Separate representation for children in termination cases is a very important concept which has evolved since the mid-1960s. Historically, parents or any agency acting in loco parentis were presumed always to speak in the child's interest. This is not always the case, and children appearing in court today may now have their own counsel and/or separate guardian *ad litem*. A central issue is whether or not children should consent to their own adoption, and if so, at what age? The appropriate age for children's consent varies among states between 10 and 14 years of age. Children's opinions should be solicited in every case, but because of the gravity of the decision, it appears wisest that their opinion be non-binding (89). It should be factored in with all the other facts and recommendations when the court makes its decision.

3. Selection of Adoptive Parents. As mentioned earlier in this section, there is an imbalance in the supply–demand equation surrounding adoption. A surplus of prospective adoptive parents exists for healthy infants and preschool children (especially white children). It has been estimated that some adoption placement agencies have or are able to obtain fifteen to twenty families for each white infant available. When agencies view their major goal as finding babies for childless couples, their major problem will be defined as one where demand exceeds supply. On the other hand, there are far more older, disabled, and/or minority children awaiting adoption than there are adoption parent applicants. Thus, if agencies view their major goal as finding adoption homes for all available children, their major problem will be defined as one where supply exceeds demand.

The following are some of the basic requirements of adoptive parenthood closely examined and investigated by adoption placement agencies: age (usually below 45); physical health; marital status; infertility; religion; financial stability; emotional health; capacity for parenthood; adjustment to sterility; quality of marital relationship; motives for adoption; and attitudes toward illegitimacy. Some of these requirements can be assessed objectively. Others are determined by subjective perceptions on the part of professionally trained adoption workers (most possess the M.S.W. degree) often based on white, middle-class values and expectations of what constitutes "good" parents.

In a study of social workers' perceptions of adoptive applicants, Bradley (90) identified two major conceptual dimensions, or models, of approved prospective adopters—positive psychological appraisal and suitability for a deviant child. Some of the items relating highly to positive psychological appraisal include: positive marital interaction; flexibility; non-neurotic motivation for adoption; absence of difficulty in early socialization. These attributes were applied to couples rated as good adoptive prospects, especially for babies. Yet, these couples were ruled out by social workers for the non-normal child.

Some of the items highly related to suitability of an adoptive couple for a non-normal child included: identification with the underdog; risk with respect to health; difficulties in early socialization; nonassertive personality on the part of the husband; demanding/controlling attitude toward children on the part of the wife; in short, attributes considered to be associated with the more marginal couples. Social workers saw these couples as more suitable for the "different" (read *hard-to-place*) child, and the "better" type of couple as suitable for the "better child."

What appears evident, and supported in other studies (91), is that dual standards exist: Those adoptive applicants manifesting acceptable middle-class values, behaviors, and income and are more often assessed as qualified for the more "normal" child awaiting adoption; those adoptive applicants assessed as more marginal (lower SES, different behaviors and attitudes) are deemed more appropriate for the hard-to-place (read *older, disabled,* or *minority*) child.

A significant practice issue in this regard is to identify worker attitudes about which children are or are not adoptable and correct them through training, especially ethno-sensitive training, and supervision. According to Cole, "the challenge of the coming years is to keep focus of children with special needs for attention and action" (92). Yet adoption agency practice does not exist in a vacuum. Communities wanting adequate adoption services need to provide adequate resources, not only for those programs serving infants, but also for those programs serving children with special needs.

Today the practice of selecting adoptive parents has seen some liberalization. Single parents, foster parents, parent(s) of below-average income, and in some instances gay or lesbian couples who demonstrate the ability to love, nurture, and provide care and security to a child, are being considered as adoptive parents, particularly in the instance of special-needs children.

The concluding steps in the adoption process include:

4. Placement with Adoptive Family.

5. Postplacement Services.

6. Legal Finalization of the Adoption.

7. Postadoption Services to the Adoptee.   Once an appropriate adoptive couple has been selected and the child has been placed, the placement agency will provide postplacement services, usually for at least six months. During this time, although the child is living with the adoptive couple, the adoption agency maintains legal rights to the child. If the adoptive bonding appears satisfactory, legal rights to the child are transferred to the adoptive couple through a court procedure, legally finalizing the adoption.

Factors Associated with Adoption Outcome

Generally speaking, those factors related to adoption success include attitudes of the parents toward the child and the nature of the relationship with the child. Where there is acceptance of and satisfaction in adoptive parenthood, plus warmth toward and acceptance of the child, the likelihood of adoption success is high. The key factor associated with adoption difficulty revolves around parental rejection of the child.

Adoptive parents face difficulties beyond the requisite bonding with their adopted child. Society has held a generally negative attitude toward adoption and accords ambivalence to adoptive parents due to their unique status: members of a minority group who have achieved parenthood in a special way. Pre- and postadoption services can play a very positive part in helping adoptive parents succeed in their new role. Support groups of adoptive parents are a particularly meaningful resource.

It is suggested that adoption workers should move from role of evaluator to that of educator. They should develop a partnership with adoption applicants so that applicants can decide for themselves whether this type of adoption is good for them.

Special Issues in Adoption

Transracial Adoption. Transracial adoption refers to the placement of children across racial lines and most often involves placement of a minority child with a white adoptive couple. It also refers to a family constellation involving a child with mixed racial background (usually a child with one white parent and one Asian, Native-American, African-American, or Hispanic parent) adopted by a white couple.

It should be noted that transracial adoptions began with the conclusion of World War II, involving children with mixed racial background from Europe and Asia. It has continued up to the present with Korean-American children due to the Korean War and the current stationing of American troops in Korea. As well, transracial adoptions continue with Vietnamese-American children born as a result of the Vietnam conflict. Finding adoptive homes for Native-American children followed. Contrary to what is generally assumed, the movement to place African-American children with white families is the most recent. It has also stirred the most controversy, however, and will be the focus of the discussion that follows.

Since adoption under any circumstances is a challenging and sometimes difficult process, one can readily understand that transracial adoption poses additional challenges, obstacles, and difficulties. As such, many transracial adopters who were concerned about minority children in need of permanent homes sought to develop organizations that promoted transracial adoptions. In addition, these organizations served as self-help groups which met to discuss common problems and share solutions, as well as to share common experiences and provide social and emotional support to each other. The Open Door Society in Montreal was the first such organization. There are now Open Door Societies in several midwestern states as well as other organizations including The East–West Society; the Council on Adoptable Children in Ann Arbor Mich.; Families for Interracial Adoption in Boston; the Interracial Family Association; and Transracial Adoptive Parents in Chicago.

In 1970, more than one-third of the black children adopted were placed in white homes (93). Criticism soon arose. In 1972 the National Association of Black Social Workers (NABSW) issued a statement opposing transracial adoption because of "fears of cultural 'genocide' on the one hand and concern for the child's identity on the other hand" (94). A black social worker called transracial adoption another expression of white colonialism—a "diabolical trick" and a "lethal incursion on the black family" (95). NABSW and individual black professionals expressed belief that black children in white homes would fail to develop positive identities, would not learn the "survival skills" necessary in a racist society, and would be deprived of the cultural and linguistic attributes crucial to functioning effectively in the black community (96).

In a seminal work on the place of black children in America, Billingsley and Giovannoni (97) posited that ". . . when agencies were unable to place black children as fast as white children, . . . the children and families were defined as 'prob-lems.' . . . The children were 'hard to place'; the families were 'hard to reach.'"

Similar positions were taken by other minority groups during this period of time. Native Americans were particularly critical and angered by the placement of Indian children in non-Indian homes. Many tribes took formal legal action to pro-scribe off-reservation placement.

In response to such protests, the 1978 Indian Child Welfare Act (P.L. 95-608) requires that in an adoption situation preference be given first to the child's extended family, then to other members of the child's tribe, and then to other Indian families. Only after all these possibilities have been exhausted may an Indian child be placed in a non-Indian home.

The opposition from minority professionals was effective in reducing the number of transracial adoptions. The transracial adoptions of black children declined from 35.3 percent of all adoptions involving blacks in 1970 to 19.6 per-cent in 1974. Yet from 1974 the trend reversed, and by 1976, about 25 percent of the adoptions of black children were biracial.

NABSW has argued that the child welfare system did not give African-Amer-icans equal access to African-American children (98). African-American families are often said to be discouraged, discriminated against, or "screened out" of the adoption process because of cultural misunderstandings, racist attitudes, and eth-nocentrism on the part of staff, as well as economic factors, such as high fees, and low income (99).

As such, African Americans established adoption agencies to increase the adoption placement of black children into black adoption homes. According to a study by the North American Council on Adoptable Children (100), they have been successful in 94 percent of their efforts. Among others, the success of the Association of Black Social Workers' Child Adoption, Counseling and Referral Service (New York Chapter), Homes for Black Children (Detroit), the Institute for Black Parents (Los Angeles), Roots, Inc. (Georgia), and the One Church One Child Program (nationwide), have dispelled the myth that black families do not adopt.

What was the position of the Child Welfare League of America during this controversy? The 1968 revised CWLA *Standards for Adoption Service* stated: "Racial background in itself should not determine the selection of the home for a child. It should not be assumed . . . that difficulties will necessarily arise if adoptive parents are of different racial origin" (101).

In 1972, the standard was amended to "it is preferable to place children in families of their own racial background." The CWLA's 1978 *Standards for Adoption Services* takes the position that adoptive parents selected for a child should ordi-narily be of a similar racial background, but children should not have adoption denied or significantly delayed when adoptive parents of other races are available.

Notwithstanding all of the controversy surrounding transracial adoptions and that "as historically practiced, transracial adoptions can be viewed in large part as an expression of racism" (102), every child should have the right to a perma-nent home and loving parents. In most instances, it is in the best interests of the minority child to be placed in a transracial adoptive home when minority adoptive homes are not available. This position as elaborated above is in disagreement with some black social work professionals, who hold that institutional care or long-term foster care is preferable to transracial adoption.

Congressman Howard Metzenbaum (Ohio) introduced legislation which became the Multiethnic Placement Act (MEPA) of 1994, out of his concern for the number of children available for adoption languishing in foster care, especially minority infants and youth (17,500 in 1991). The purpose of MEPA is the promotion of the best interests of children by:

1. Decreasing the length of time children wait to be adopted
2. Preventing discrimination in the placement of children on the basis of race, color, or national origin
3. Facilitating the identification of foster and adoptive families that can meet children's needs

The Multiethnic Placement Act of 1994 represents a compromise among the various constituencies of transracial adoption, including NABSW and the Child Welfare League of America (CWLA). "It mandates faster placements, but also calls on agencies to recruit homes from communities of color and allows agencies to consider race and culture when placing children in foster and adoptive homes" (103).

To enhance the success of transracial adoptions (for all minority children, including Asians, Hispanics, Native-Americans, and African Americans), it is essential to afford the minority child racial identity, survival skills and cultural and linguistic attributes. A minority child should have a clear image of himself or herself as a minority person. The child must learn the skills that minority persons learn to cope with racism and must learn the cultural and linguistic attributes of his or her specific ethnic community (104).

An important factor, then, is the ability of the adoptive parents to provide a bicultural socialization. The parents must be aware of and accepting of racial/cultural differences; they should possess the ability to provide support when the child is hurt by racism; and the transracial adopters should possess a willingness to make a commitment to a lifestyle that will maximize socialization opportunities for the child.

Openness in Adoption

"Telling."   Should the adopted child be told that she or he is adopted, and if so, at what age? Adoption experts are in accord that adoptive parents must tell their adopted child, not for purposes of threatening or confusing the child, but because it helps to build the parent–child relationship on a foundation of integrity, honesty, and trust. Children have a right to know about their history, and "telling" can help adopted children in their quest for identity. Experts suggest that adoptive parents use their judgment about when the child is ready to be told; they believe the best time is usually when the child is between six and twelve years old.

Open vs. Closed Birth Records.   A second issue that is receiving increasing attention in adoptions practice is the growing debate among adoptees, adoptive parents, birth parents, social workers, and family attorneys over opening sealed adoption records. Current law in this country is that birth records be sealed and that they can only be opened through court order. Nine states (California, Colorado, Florida, Louisiana, Michigan, Nevada, New York, Oregon, and Texas) have passed voluntary-consent registry laws whereby adoptees and birth parents can register their desire for contact or anonymity.

The prevailing viewpoint supporting sealed birth records has been that normal, well adjusted individuals would not, and should not, need to know any parents other than those who raised them. Some of the main arguments against an open-records law are that it would: (a) help to unravel the adoptive family unit by shifting focus away from the adoptive family to a preoccupation with biological family members (105); (b) enhance and transform into reality the adoptive parents' fear that they might lose their children (106); (c) lead to a totally open adoption system where children would be raised by their adoptive parents, but have frequent visits by birth parents (107).

Advocates for an open-records law point to research that indicates that adopted children may have problems in their search for identity because they do not receive adequate information about their biological parents. According to Sorosky, the lack of adoption and background information may lead to "genealogical bewilderment" for the child (108). Studies of characteristics of adult adoptees who have sought to discover their birth parents reveal that most of the searches are predicated upon a lack of needed information: parents' medical histories; personality characteristics, physical descriptions, names, ethnic backgrounds; own early medical history; why they were placed for adoption; and their birth parents' personal interests, occupations, educations, and marital status (109).

Others argue that adult adoptees should have access to their birth records as a matter of right. This idea dates back to 1971 with founding of the Adoptees' Liberty Movement Association (ALMA). Founded by Florence Anna Fisher, ALMA now has 60 chapters and has connected more than a million adult adoptees with their birth parents. Other organizations pursuing this same goal include Adoptees in Search and the North American Council on Adoptable Children (NACAC).

Special Needs Children.   A major problem of concern to adoption agencies today revolves around the decline of young, healthy white children surrendered for adoption and the increased need of placements for special-needs children—the minority-group child, the older child, and the disabled child. Disabilities range from physical, emotional, mental, or social, and increasingly include attention deficit disorders (ADD and ADHD), HIV/AIDS, substance abuse, and severely emotionally disturbed (s.e.d.) children.

Efforts to counteract this problem have included the use of various publicity techniques to inform the local community of special-needs children available for adoption. In addition, Adoption Resource Exchanges have been developed on regional and national levels to increase the pool of potential adopters. In 1967 the

Child Welfare League of America established a National Adoption Resource Exchange that included Canada and was known as ARENA (Adoption Resource Exchange of North America). The Adoption Reform Act of 1978 provided for updated computer technology to match parents and children available for adoption and provided funding for NAIES (National Adoption Information Exchange System) to supersede ARENA.

The Model Act of 1981 was the first comprehensive adoption law for children with special needs. It focused on eliminating barriers to adoption of children with special needs which existed in the law and practice. The Adoption Assistance and Child Welfare Act of 1980 was designed to promote special needs adoption by providing not only cash but medical assistance, and social services to adoptive families of these children. And finally, the Adoption and Safe Families Act of 1997 provides Medicaid or state-funded health insurance to children if determined to have special needs. In addition, it provides incentive payments to states of $6,000 each for special needs children who are eligible for Title IV-E adoptions assistance.

Despite these efforts, exchanges have succeeded in placing only fairly small numbers of children. The strategy that has had a greater impact on placing special-needs children has been that of adoption maintenance subsidy. The 1980 Adoption Assistance and Child Welfare Act assured uniformity in subsidy legislation. It provided that all states must have in place provisions for subsidy for children with "special needs."

The act stipulates that the amount of subsidy should be determined prior to placement of the child in the adoptive home. The amount of subsidy cannot exceed current foster care payment levels, and subsidies can be continued until the child reaches 18 or, in the case of severe handicap, until the child is 21. Subsidies are to continue even if the family moves away from the state (110).

Subsidizing adoption payments has been instrumental in enabling otherwise qualified adoptive parents to adopt special-needs children. Heretofore they could not, or were unwilling to, take on the added financial burden of an adopted child, when that child had physical, mental, and/or emotional disabilities.

This is particularly germane with regard to foster parents who have been receiving board and care payments for a foster child in their care. Previously, if they adopted the child, all financial support would cease. Under the 1980 act, if the child qualifies as a special-needs child, and the foster parents qualify as approved adoptive parents for that particular child, they will receive an adoption subsidy. This ensures fulfillment of the goal of permanency planning, removes the child from "foster care drift," and provides a "forever home."

Summary

This chapter has discussed and examined the nature of personal problems and public issues that have particular relevance to families and children in this country. These problems and issues impact with disproportionate severity on the poor, minorities, and women.

Throughout, we have emphasized the need to develop a holistic view of the interactions taking place within and among families and the other institutions in society. We have examined the changing nature of the family, the increased role of women in the workplace, and the involvement of child welfare programs and services.

Particular attention has been placed on elaborating the continuum of child welfare: supportive, supplemental, and substitute services. Foster family care, group home services, and the many issues involved with adoptions were discussed in detail. Case examples were presented which called for generalist skills and professional sensitivity in working with people of color.

The following four chapters will focus specifically on child welfare policy and practice and Asian/Pacific, African-American, Native-American and Hispanic families.

Endnotes

1. Alvin Toffler, *The Third Wave*, p. 240.
2. Children's Defense Fund, *The State of America's Children*, p. 16.
3. Ibid., p. 16.
4. Ibid.
5. Scott Briar, Child Welfare League of America Western Regional Conference, Pasadena, Calif., April 1988.
6. Richard Weissbourd, *The Vulnerable Child*, p. 129.
7. Toffler, *The Third Wave*, pp. 227–228.
8. Ibid., p. 44.
9. Marvin Harris, "Growing Convervatism? Not in Family Patterns." *Los Angeles Times*, December 23, 1981.
10. Ibid.
11. Ibid.
12. *The Phillip Morris Family Survey*, April 1987.
13. Ibid.
14. Harris, "Growing Conservatism?"
15. U.S. Bureau of the Census. "Money, Income and Poverty Status of Families and Persons in the United States, 1984," *Current Population Reports*, series P-60, no. 146, 1984.
16. Select Committee on Children, Youth and Families 1983, iv and 27, 1983.
17. U.S. Department of Labor, *Bureau of Labor Statistics, 1998.*
18. U.S. Bureau of the Census, p. 415, 1985.
19. U.S. Department of Labor, *Bureau of Labor Statistics, 1997.*
20. U.S. Department of Labor, *Bureau of Labor Statistics, 1996.*
21. Ruth Sidel, *Women & Children Last: The Plight of Poor Women in Affluent America*, p. 3.
22. *Statistical Abstracts, 1997.*
23. Theodore J. Stein, *Social Work Practice in Child Welfare*, p. 3.
24. Child Welfare League of America, *Directory of Member Agencies*, 1985.
25. Alfred Kadushin and Judith A. Martin, *Child Welfare Services*, 4th ed., p. 30.
26. Ibid., pp. 27ff.
27. Ibid., p. 83.

28. Alfred Kadushin, *Child Welfare Services,* 3rd ed., p. 25.

29. Ibid., p. 25.

30. Ibid., p. 27.

31. Louise C. Johnson, *Social Work Practice,* 3rd ed., p. 1.

32. Joan Laird and Ann Hartman, eds., *A Handbook of Child Welfare,* p. 561.

33. Alfred Kadushin, *Child Welfare Services,* p. 27.

34. James K. Whittaker, *Caring for Troubled Children,* p. 6.

35. Martin Wolins, ed., *Successful Group Care: Explorations in the Powerful Environment.*

36. Children's Defense Fund, *The State of America's Children,* p. 65.

37. U.S. Dept. of HHS, *National Study, 1997.*

38. Theodore J. Stein and Tina L. Rzepnicki, *Decision Making at Child Welfare Intake,* p. 60.

39. Ibid., pp. 60–61.

40. Marian Wright Edelman, *Families in Peril, An Agenda for Social Change,* p. 35.

41. Ibid., p. 40.

42. See particularly the following: Greg J. Duncan and Jeanne Brooks-Gunn, eds. *Consequences of Growing Up Poor;* P. Lindsay Chase-Lansdale and Jeanne Brooks-Gunn, eds. *Escape from Poverty;* and Jill Berrick, *Faces of Poverty.*

43. Children's Defense Fund, *The State of America's Children.*

44. National Center for Children in Poverty, 1998.

45. See for example: Renny Golden. *Disposable Children: America's Child Welfare System;* John M. Hagedorn, *Forsaking Our Children: Bureaucracy and Reform in the Child Welfare System;* and Duncan Lindsey, *The Welfare of Children.*

46. Laura M. Markowitz, "Making House Calls: Family Preservation Goes Beyond Office-bound Therapy," *Networker,* July/Aug 1992, p. 29.

47. Lerdy Pelton, *For Reasons of Poverty,* 1989, p. 19.

48. Martha J. Cox and Roger D. Cox, eds., *Foster Care: Current Issues, Policies, and Practices,* p. xi.

49. Ibid., p. xi.

50. Edmund Mech, "Out-of-Home Placement Rates," *Social Service Review* 57, 4 (December 1983): 659–667.

51. Hideki Ishisaka, "American Indians and Foster Care: Cultural Factors & Separation," *Child Welfare* 57, 5 (May 1978): 299–307.

52. See particularly the following: Anthony Maluccio and Paula Sinanoglu, eds., *The Challenge of Partnership: Working with Parents of Children in Foster Care;* William Meezan and Joan F. Shireman, *Care and Commitment: Foster Parent Adoption Decisions;* David Fanshel and E. Shinn, *Children in Foster Care: A Longitudinal Investigation;* Alan R. Gruber, *Children in Foster Care—Destitute, Neglected, Betrayed;* Henry Maas and R. E. Engler, *Children in Need of Parents;* T. J. Stein, E. Gambrill and K. T. Wiltse, *Children in Foster Homes—Achieving Continuity of Care.*

53. Child Welfare League of America, p. 1.

54. Susan Whitelaw Downs, Lela B. Costin, and Emily Jean McFadden, *Child Welfare and Family Services,* 5th ed., p. 300.

55. Stein and Rzepnicki, *Child Welfare Intake,* p. 73.

56. Ibid.

57. Neil A. Cohen, "Quality of Care for Youths in Group Homes," *Child Welfare* V. LXV, no. 5 (Sept./Oct 1986): 482.

58. Department of Social Services. *Title XXII: Residential Facilities for Children and Adults.* State of California, 1980, Division 6, chapters 1–3.

59. Neil A Cohen, "Quality of Care for Youths."

60. Alfred Kadushin and Judith A. Martin, *Child Welfare Services*, pp. 670–671.

61. Child Welfare League of America, *Standards for Group Home Service for Children*, 1978, p. 27.

62. Miriam Schwartz and Isadore Kaplan, "Small Homes—Placement Choice for Adolescents," *Child Welfare* 40 (November 1961): 10.

63. Child Welfare League of America, *CWLA Standards for Residential Centers for Children*, 1982.

64. Martin Sundel, *The Local Child Welfare Services Self-Assessment Manual: Resources*, VII-12.

65. Ibid.

66. Sister Mary Paul, *Criteria for Foster Placement and Alternatives for Foster Care*.

67. G. H. Weber & B. J. Haberlein, Residential Treatment of Emotionally Disturbed Children.

68. Neil A. Cohen, "Quality of Care for Youths," pp. 490–491.

69. Ibid., p. 492.

70. Ronna Cook, "Trends and Needs in Programming for Independent Living," *Child Welfare* v. LXVII, no. 6 (Nov./Dec. 1988): 499.

71. Edmund Mech, "Special Issue: Independent Living, *Child Welfare* v. LXVII, n. 6 (Nov./Dec. 1988): 490.

72. R. Barth, "Emancipation Services for Adolescents in Foster Care," *Social Work* (May/June 1986): pp. 165–171.

73. H. D. Stone, Ready, Set, Go: An Agency Guide to Independent Living.

74. Alfred Kadushin and Judith A. Martin, *Child Welfare Services*, p. 533.

75. Brenda G. McGowan and William Meezan, *Child Welfare: Current Dilemmas, Future Directions*, p. 425.

76. Elizabeth Cole, "Adoption—History, Policy, and Program," in Joan Laird and Ann Hartman, eds., *A Handbook of Child Welfare*, p. 640.

77. Ibid.

78. Child Welfare League of America, *CWLA Standards for Adoption Service*.

79. Elizabeth Cole, "Adoption History," p. 650.

80. Alfred Kadushin, *Child Welfare Services*, 3rd ed., p. 441.

81. Elizabeth Cole, "Adoption History," p. 651.

82. Ibid., p. 655.

83. K. S. Stolley, "Statistics on Adoption in the U.S.," *The Future of Children*, 3(1), pp. 26–42.

84. William Meezan, *Adoption Services in the States*, p. 5.

85. National Committee for Adoption, *Adoption Fact Book: United States Data Issues, Regulations and Resources*.

86. Penelope Maza, *Child Welfare Research Note 2*, p. 20.

87. Lela B. Costin and Charles A. Rapp, *Child Welfare, Policies and Practices*, p. 395.

88. David Kirk, *Shared Fate*, 1964.

89. Elizabeth Cole, "Adoption History," p. 646.

90. Trudy Bradley, *An Exploration of Caseworkers' Perceptions of Adoptive Applicants*.

91. Henry Maas, "The Successful Adoptive Parent Applicant," *Social Work* v. 5, no. 1 (January 1960): 14–20; and Alfred Kadushin, "A Study of Adoptive Parents of Hard-to-Place Children," *Social Casework* v. 53, no. 5 (May 1962): 227–233.

92. Elizabeth Cole, "Adoption History," p. 645.

93. Rita J. Simon and Howard Altstein, *Transracial Adoption*, p. 44.

94. Leon Chestang, "The Dilemma of Biracial Adoption," *Social Work* XVII, 3 (May 1972): 103.

95. Edmond D. Jones, "On Transracial Adoption of Black Children," *Social Work* LI, 3 (March 1972): 38.

96. Charles E. Jones and John F. Else, "Racial and Cultural Issues in Adoption," *Child Welfare* LVIII, 6 (June 1979): 374.

97. Andrew Billingsley and Jeanne Giovannoni, *Children of the Storm: Black Children and American Child Welfare*, p. 55.

98. Leora Neal and A. Stumph, *Transracial Adoptive Parenting: A Black/White Community Issue*.

99. Leora Neal, "Focal Point."

100. T. Gilles and J. Kroll, North American Council on Adoptable Children.

101. Child Welfare League of America, *Standards for Adoption Services*, rev. ed., p. 34.

102. Charles Jones and John Else, "Racial and Cultural Issues," p. 375.

103. Susan Whitelaw Downs, Lela B. Costin, and Emily Jean McFadden, *Child Welfare and Family Services*, 5th ed., p. 361.

104. Ibid., p. 378.

105. D. D. Broadhurst and E. J. Schwartz, "The Right to Know," *Public Welfare* 37, 3 (1979): 5–8.

106. S. Geissinger, "Adoptive Parents' Attitudes Toward Open Birth Records," *Family Relations* 33 (1984): 579–585.

107. A. Foster, "Who Has the 'Right' to Know?" *Public Welfare* 37, 3 (1979): 34–37.

108. A. D. Sorosky, et al., *The Adoption Triangle*.

109. Ruth McRoy, et al., *Openness in Adoption: New Practices, New Issues*, pp. 6–7.

110. Gloria Waldinger, "Subsidized Adoption: How Paid Parents View It," *Social Work* 27, 6 (November 1982): 516–521.

Bibliography

Balcerzak, Edward, ed. *Group Care of Children: Toward the Year 2000*. Washington, D.C.: Child Welfare League of America, 1989.

Barth, R. "Emancipation Services for Adolescents in Foster Care," *Social Work* (May-June 1986): 165–171.

Berrick, Jill. *Faces of Poverty: Portraits of Women and Children on Welfare*, NY: Oxford University Press, 1995.

Billingsley, Andrew, and Giovannoni, Jeanne. *Children of the Storm: Black Children and American Child Welfare*. N. Y.: Harcourt Brace Jovanovich, 1972.

Bradley, Trudy, *An Explanation of Caseworkers' Perceptions of Adoptive Applicants*. N. Y.: Child Welfare League of America, 1967.

Briar, Scott. Presentation, Child Welfare League of America Western Regional Conference, Pasadena, Calif., April 1988.

Broadhurst, D. D., and Schwartz, E. J. "The Right to Know," *Public Welfare* 37, 3 (1979): 5–8.

Chase-Lansdale, P. Lindsay, and Brooks-Gunn Jeanne, eds. *Escape from Poverty: What Makes a Difference for Children*. NY: Cambridge University Press, 1995.

Chestang, Leon. "The Dilemma of Biracial Adoption." *Social Work* XVII, 3 (May 1972): 103.

Child Welfare League of America, *CWLA Standards for Adoption Service*. N.Y.: Child Welfare League of America, 1978.

Child Welfare League of America. *CWLA Standards for Residential Centers for Children*. N.Y.: Child Welfare League of America, 1982.

———. *Directory of Member Agencies*. NY: Child Welfare League of America, 1985.

———. *Standards for Group Home Service for Children*. N.Y.: Child Welfare League of America, 1978.

Child Welfare League of America, *Kinship Care*. NY: Child Welfare League of America, 1994.

Children's Defense Fund. *The State of America's Children: Yearbook 1998*. Washington, D.C.: Children's Defense Fund. 1998.

Cohen, Neil A. "Quality of Care for Youths in Group Homes." *Child Welfare* LXV, 5 (Sept.–Oct. 1986): 481–494.

Cole, Elizabeth. "Adoption—History, Policy, and Program," in *A Handbook of Child Welfare*, edited by Laird, Joan, and Hartman, Ann, 638–666. N.Y.: The Free Press, 1985.

Cook, Ronna. "Trends and Needs in Programming for Independent Living." *Child Welfare* LXVII, 6 (Nov.—Dec. 1988): 497–515.

Costin, Lela B., and Rapp, Charles A. *Child Welfare, Policies and Practices*. 3rd ed. N.Y.: McGraw-Hill, 1984.

Cox, Martha J., and Cox, Roger D., eds. *Foster Care: Current Issues, Policies, and Practices*, Norwood, N.Y.: Ablex Publishing, 1985.

Department of Labor, Bureau of Labor Statistics, Washington, D.C., 1998.

———, Bureau of Labor Statistics, Washington, D.C., 1997.

———, Bureau of Labor Statistics, Washington, D.C., 1996.

Department of Social Services, *Title XXII: Residential Facilities for Children and Adults*, "Quality of Care for Youths," State of California, 1980.

Downs, Susan Whitelaw, Costin, Lela B., and McFadden, Emily Jean, *Child Welfare and Family Services*, 5th ed.: White Plains, NY: Longman Publishing, USA, 1996.

Duncan, Greg J., and Brooks-Gunn, Jeanne, eds., *Consequences of Growing Up Poor*, NY: Russell Sage Foundation, 1997.

Edelman, Marian Wright. *Families in Peril: An Agenda for Social Change*. Cambridge: Harvard University Press, 1987.

Fanshel, David, and Shinn, E. *Children in Foster Care: A Longitudinal Investigation*. N.Y.: Child Welfare League of America, 1978.

Foster, A. "Who Has the 'Right' to Know?" *Public Welfare* 37, 3 (1979): 34–37.

Geissinger, S. "Adoptive Parents' Attitudes Toward Open Birth Records," *Family Relations* 33 (1984): 579–585.

Gilles, T. and Kroll, J. *North American Council on Adoptable Children*, n.d.

Gruber, Alan. *Children in Foster Care—Destitute, Neglected, Betrayed*. N.Y.: Human Sciences Press, 1978.

Golden, Renny. *Disposable Children: America's Welfare System*. Belmont, CA: Wadsworth Publishing Company, 1997.

Hagedorn, John M. *Forsaking Our Children: Bureaucracy and Reform in the Child Welfare System*. Chicago, IL: Lake View Press, 1995.

Harris, Marvin, "Growing Conservatism? Not in Family Patterns." *Los Angeles Times*, December 23, 1981.

Hubbell, R. *Foster Care and Families: Conflicting Values and Policies*. Philadelphia: Temple University Press, 1981.

Ishisaka, Hideki. "American Indians and Foster Care: Cultural Factors and Separation." *Child Welfare* 57, 5 (May 1978): 299–307.

Johnson, Louise C. *Social Work Practice*. 3rd ed. Boston: Allyn and Bacon, 1989.

Jones, Charles E., and Else, John F. "Racial and Cultural Issues in Adoption," *Child Welfare* LVIII, 6 (June 1979): 373–382.

Jones, Edmond D. "On Transracial Adoption of Black Children," *Social Work*, LI, 3 (March 1972): 38.

Kadushin, Alfred. *Child Welfare Services.* 3rd ed. New York: Macmillan, 1980.

——. "A Study of Adoptive Parents of Hard-to-Place Children." *Social Casework* 53, 5 (May 1962): 227–233.

——, and Martin, Judith A. *Child Welfare Services.* 4th ed. NY: Macmillan, 1988.

Laird, Joan, and Hartman, Ann, eds. *A Handbook of Child Welfare.* New York: The Free Press, 1985.

Lindsey, Duncan. *The Welfare of Children.* NY: Oxford University Press, 1994.

Maas, Henry. "The Successful Adoptive Parent Applicant." *Social Work* 5, 1 (January 1960): 14–20.

——, and Engler, R. E. *Children in Need of Parents.* New York: Columbia University Press, 1959.

Maluccio, Anthony, and Sinanoglu, Paula, eds. *The Challenge of Partnership: Working with Parents of Children in Foster Care.* NY: Child Welfare League of America, 1981.

Markowitz, Laura M. "Making House Calls: Family Preservation Goes Beyond Office-Bound Therapy," *Networker.* July/August 1992, p. 29.

Maza, Penelope. *Child Welfare Research Note 2.* Washington, D.C.: Administration for Children, Youth and Families, December 1983.

Mech, Edmund, ed. "Special Issue: Independent Living." *Child Welfare* LXVII, 6 (Nov.–Dec. 1988): 490.

——, "Out-of-Home Placement Rates," *Social Service Review* 57, 4 (December 1983): 659–667.

Meezan, William. *Adoption Services in the States.* U.S. Department of Health and Human Services, Office of Human Development Services, Administration for Children, Youth and Families, Washington, D.C.: Children's Bureau, 1980.

——, and Shireman, Joan F. *Care and Commitment: Foster Parent Adoption Decisions.* Albany: State University of New York Press, 1985.

McGowan, Brenda G., and Meezan, William. *Child Welfare: Current Dilemmas, Future Directions.* Itasca, ILL: F. E. Peacock Publishers, 1983.

McRoy, Ruth G., Grotevant, Harold D., and White, Kerry, L. *Openness in Adoption: New Practices, New Issues.* New York: Praeger, 1988.

National Center for Children in Poverty, 1998.

National Committee for Adoption, *Adoption Fact Book: United States Data Issues, Regulations, and Resources.* Washington, D.C.: National Committee for Adoption, 1985.

Neal, Leora. "Focal Point," Regional Research Institute for Human Services, NY. 1996.

—— and Stumph, A. *Transracial Adoptive Parenting: A Black/White Community Issue.* Bronx, NY: Haskett-Heal Publications, 1993.

Nybell, Lynn, compiler. *A Sourcebook in Child Welfare: Serving American Indian Families and Children.* Ann Arbor: National Child Welfare Training Center, 1984.

Paul, Sister Mary. *Criteria for Foster Placement and Alternatives for Foster Care.* New York: New York State Board of Social Welfare, 1975.

Phillip Morris Family Survey, April 1987.

Schwartz, Miriam, and Kaplan, Isadore. "Small Homes—Placement Choice for Adolescents." *Child Welfare* 40, (Nov. 1961): 10.

Select Committee on Children, Youth and Families. *Children, Youth, and Families, 1983—A Year-End Report.* U.S. House of Representatives, Ninety-Eighth Congress, 2nd Session, Washington, D.C.: Government Printing Office, 1984.

Sidel, Ruth. *Women & Children Last: The Plight of Poor Women in Affluent America.* New York: Penguin Books, 1986.

Simon, Rita J., and Altstein, Howard. *Transracial Adoption.* New York: Wiley, 1977.

Sorosky, Arthur D.; Baran, Annette; and Pannor, Reuben. *The Adoption Triangle—The Effects of the Sealed Record on Adoptees, Birth Parents, and Adoptive Parents*. New York: Anchor Press/Doubleday, 1978.

Statistical Abstracts, 1997.

Stein, Theodore J. *Social Work Practice in Child Welfare*. Englewood Cliffs, .N.J.: Prentice-Hall, 1981.

———; Gambrill, Eileen; and Wiltse, Kermit T. *Children in Foster Homes—Achieving Continuity of Care*. New York: Praeger, 1978.

———, and Rzepnicki, Tina L. *Decision Making at Child Welfare Intake*. New York: Child Welfare League of America, 1983.

Stolley, K. S. "Statistics on Adoption in the United States," *The Future of Children*, 3 (1), A Publication of the Center for the Future of Children, The David and Lucille Packard Foundation, 1993, pp. 26–42.

Stone, H. D. *Ready, Set, Go: An Agency Guide to Independent Living*, Washington, D.C.: Child Welfare League of America, 1987.

Sundel, Martin. *The Local Child Welfare Services Self-Assessment Manual: Resources*, Washington, D.C.: The Urban Institute, 1978.

Toffler, Alvin, *The Third Wave*. New York: Morrow, 1980.

U.S. Bureau of the Census. "Money, Income and Poverty Status of Families and Persons in the United States, 1984," *Current Population Reports*, series P-60, n. 146, 1984.

Waldinger, Gloria. "Subsidized Adoption: How Paid Parents View It." *Social Work* 27, 6 (Nov. 1982): 516–521.

Weber, G. H., and Haberlein, B. J. *Residential Treatment of Emotionally Disturbed Children*. NY: Behavioral Publications, 1972.

Whittaker, James K. *Caring for Troubled Children*. San Francisco: Jossey-Bass Publishers, 1979.

Wolins, Martin, ed. *Successful Group Care: Explorations in the Powerful Environment*. Chicago: Aldine, 1974.

4 Child Welfare and African-American Families

BY GWEN PRATER
Jackson State University

The everchanging nature of U.S. families poses a continuing challenge to the profession of social work. Child welfare services for these families and children must be responsive to the families' social realities. In particular, if social workers are to meet the challenge of appropriately serving African-American children and families, they must understand the dynamics of both individual and institutional racism and its deleterious effects on African-American families. Child welfare workers must become aware of these families' culture—their history, family structure, dynamics, religion, language, and communication style; in essence, their life experiences—if they are to provide effective services. Further, this cultural knowledge must be integrated into all levels of service provided to African-American families from assessment to termination.

The history of African-American families in the United States includes the dehumanizing experience of slavery. Yet, remarkably, it also includes positive African retentions, such as a cooperative spirit and a continual emphasis on the critical importance, even primacy, of children (1). Early formalized U.S. child welfare services were built upon the philosophical foundation of the English Poor Laws of 1601. Some free African-American children and families were limited participants in the indenture system and in the almshouses, but they were excluded from most pre-Civil War orphanages. As a result of philanthropy, government intervention, and the efforts of the African-American community itself, orphanages, free foster homes, and other community supports for African-American families developed after the Civil War (2). Informal adoption, an African retention, also continued to meet the needs of children without homes. The Freedmen's Bureau was established by Congress in 1865 and lasted until 1871. The Bureau was an early significant government-sponsored child welfare service which positively impacted African-American families. It provided land, work, and direct relief to poor children within their families. It was a revolutionary development in child welfare service since it was financed by the federal government and provided in-home services to African-American children and families. Its demise came as a result of inadequate financial support and the belief that the Freedmen's Bureau work encouraged the "natural slothfulness of the Black race" (3). Other late 1800s community efforts by early African-American organizations, such as lodges (e.g., the Masons, the Odd Fellows, and Knights of Pythias), women's clubs (e.g., The National Association of Colored Women), and educational institutions were instrumental in meeting the needs of African-American families and children.

The early and mid-1900s continued the exclusion of African-American children and families from the formalized child welfare service system. Other national community organizations, such as the National Urban League and the National Association for the Advancement of Colored People (NAACP), struggled for economic opportunity and other civil rights for African-American families. Since that time, African-American families have become more visible in the child welfare service system; however, adequately meeting African-American families' and children's service needs in the current system of service delivery remains problematic.

The past half-century has also witnessed broad societal changes which influence the status of African-American families, such as the civil rights movement, urban unrest, political discontent, the War on Poverty programs, school busing to achieve integration, the Voting Rights Act, affirmative action, the affront to affirmative action, and an employment-focused welfare system. Society has also experienced the numerical predominance of African Americans in some U. S. cities, the expansion of the African-American middle class and stable working class, the achievement of an annual one million-plus enrollment of Black youth in higher education, and the exponential increase in the number of African-American elected officials. Yet, the African-American community itself has faced significant problems. For example, although African-American teenagers have been having fewer children since the 1970s, the percentage of births to unmarried teens has soared. This phenomenon accounts, in large part, for the rise in out-of-wedlock pregnancies and subsequently for an increase in single parents (4).

During the 1990s, African-Americans continued to experience a growing "underclass," high rates of unemployment and underemployment, and a high rate of school dropouts. Thus, clearly, the African-American community continues its transition. African-American families, however, are retaining their strength to "make it against all odds." It is due to the complexity of problems encountered by African-American families that a workable system of child welfare services for this minority group must proceed with a generalist practice perspective.

A generalist approach requires that the child welfare social worker assesses the situation with the client and together they determine which system or combination of systems should be the appropriate unit(s) for the change effort. The unit of attention may be the family, the school, the neighborhood, an administrative interpretation of policy, or a social policy which impacts children and families. African-American families have indicated that the one-sided emphasis of social work on finding the source of problems in the individual psyche and in the dysfunctional family alone, while helping clients to adapt to white social institutions, is no longer acceptable (5). Child welfare generalist practice with African-American families must incorporate and consciously operationalize the dual focus of the social work profession. Practice must emphasize both positive social functioning of the family as a unit and of its individual members, and the provision of a supportive social environment.

This two-pronged approach to child welfare practice requires ongoing attention to the problems of individuals and families, which are referred to as intrapsychic or intrafamilial, respectively. These problems, which are viewed as originating within the individual or family, frequently occupy the whole attention of child welfare workers. Generalist child welfare practice, however, implies a broader perspective. It suggests a system analysis of those situations that impact the lives of African-American children and families, and, therefore, their functioning. These include, for example, assessing the need-meeting functions of external systems such as the marketplace (economic system) or the school (education system) as well as the family system.

The provision of child welfare services to African-American families requires knowledge of intervention strategies that can be skillfully utilized at various levels of the helping process—micro (change sought in the individual, family, and/or small group), mezzo (intervention at the neighborhood or community levels), and macro (intervention aimed at social policy change) levels. Cultural knowledge of African-American families is not *sufficient* to adequately meet the service needs of children and families. However, this cultural knowledge is *necessary* and must be integrated into all aspects of service provided to African-American families from the assessment phase to the termination phase at all levels of practice. It is important information that must be consciously utilized, along with other *appropriate* social work practice knowledge, skills, and values and ethics, if competent social work practice with African-American children and families is to be achieved.

Current Child Welfare Issues

Socioeconomic Status of African Americans

African Americans are the largest minority group in the United States, comprising approximately 12 percent of the population in 1995. There were just under 226 million people in the nation in 1994. Over 10 million of the 33 million African-Americans were living in poverty. In contrast, of the 193 million whites, 18 million were living in poverty. Thus, one-third of African Americans and less than one-tenth of whites were living in poverty in 1994. Although the African-American population comprised only 15 percent of the white population, its share of the poverty population was almost 40 percent (6). Between 1970 and 1992, the proportion of African-American households with incomes over $50,000 expanded by 56.9 percent, from 10 percent in 1970, to 16 percent in 1992, while whites' share at that income level rose by 45.7 percent, from 25 percent in 1970 to 38 percent in 1992 (7). However, labor market disparities remain between black and white Americans. For example, for more than 30 years the African-American unemployment rate has been twice that of whites, and it has not dropped below 10 percent since the 1970s; and the rate of poverty among blacks is three times that of whites (8). The absolute gap between African-American and white median family income was $14,586 in 1978, higher than at any point during the 1970s.

The proportion of African-American families with very low income increased during the 1980s. For example, the proportion of African-American families with incomes under $5,000 increased from 8.1 percent in 1978 to 11.9 percent in 1988 (9). In 1988, the per capita net worth of African-American households was $9,359, less than 21 percent of the per capita of $44,980 for whites. Thus, during the Reagan-Bush years, the relative inequality and lack of economic parity between whites and blacks remained about constant, although the absolute gap increased significantly. At the other end of the distribution, in 1991, the proportion of African-American families with incomes in the top five percent bracket had mean incomes of $95,201 compared to mean incomes of $152,297 for the top five percent of whites (10). In 1997, the nation's African-American population consisted of 12.109 million households of whom 3.85 million were married couples, 3.94 million were headed by women, and 657,000 were led by men. Furthermore, also in 1997, African-American families with children under 18 were comprised of 1.97 million married couple families, 2.59 million female-headed families, and 1.70 million were headed by males. Among the African-American families, which consisted of families with children under 18, 58 percent were headed by females who had no spouse present and had never been married, as compared with 41 percent of mother-child family groups in the total population. The number of families headed by African-American women and women in the general population has increased dramatically over the past several decades. For example, in 1970, approximately 30 percent of African-American families were female-headed; by 1987, the figure was 42 percent. In 1997, all married couples with children under 18 had declined to 25 percent, down from 40 percent in 1970 (11).

Both African-American males and females are more likely than whites to be employed in lower-paying occupations and also to receive lower wages within many occupations. In 1984, for example, the African-American community lost about $15.2 billion in income due to high rates of unemployment which resulted in zero earnings for a significant number of African-American individuals and families. African-American males and teenagers were the hardest hit by unemployment (12).

To understand and appreciate the economic difficulties of African-American families, four social and economic disadvantages that have plagued the African-American community must be realized. First, African-Americans own or control few businesses or other economic enhancement or job-creating institutions. Second, African-Americans have had little accumulated wealth. Third, they have historically experienced racial discrimination in gaining equal access to education and employment opportunities controlled by whites. Finally, African-Americans have traditionally had lower levels of formal training and education than their white counterparts. The impact of deleterious economic circumstances on family functioning is negative. The primary functions of the family are to provide for the basic physical needs of its members and to nurture its members. Adequate income is required to fulfill the provider role which, if accomplished, raises the self-esteem of parents and consequently supports the ability to nurture their children. As job opportunities decline and unemployment gains momentum, we tend to find a simultaneous decrease in two-parent families, growth of out-of-wedlock births, and increase in an underclass of families in poverty.

Scope of Services

As we move further into the description of African-American children and families who are likely to be serviced by the child welfare system, it is imperative to remember that each child is not faceless, but has his or her own personality with feelings and needs that include both hope and fear. The field of child welfare is principally concerned with the well-being of children and families. Traditionally, the family is viewed as the system appointed to ensure children's welfare. It is charged with meeting the physical, social, educational, and healthcare needs of its members. The larger system, frequently through the auspices of child welfare agencies, tends to become involved only after families have been judged by society to be incapable of guaranteeing the child's welfare. This is referred to as the *residual approach* to service delivery as contrasted with an *institutional approach*. The latter approach, on the other hand, avails itself to children and families through institutional arrangements on the premise that any family and its children may benefit from services to families and children at some point during the family life cycle. It is based upon the belief that all families face normal and natural problems while rearing children. These problems may derive from an array of causes, such as developmental difficulties, financial and economic pressures, and dysfunctional educational systems. Most children and family welfare services in the United States, however, are residual in nature, rather than institutional. The institutional approach is based upon the assumption that children and families can be functionally maintained and strengthened through institutional supports. The institutional approach is undergirded by a preventive philosophy, while the residual approach is ameliorative or restorative in function and purpose.

The three primary forms of services historically offered by child welfare agencies are *supportive services, supplemental services,* and *substitute services.* These services are generally mandated at the micro level while utilizing a residual approach to service delivery. Supportive services, such as child care and counseling, provide help to families that are carrying out the basic caretaking role and providing for the needs of their members. Supplemental services are made available to families by the child welfare system to aid them in fulfilling the basic family functions of feeding, clothing, housing, and ensuring the provision of adequate healthcare services for their members. These services include, for example, Medicaid, the Food Stamp Act of 1997, and the Temporary Assistance for Needy Families (TANF) program created by the Personal Responsibility and Work Opportunity Reconciliation Act of 1996 with the implementation deadline of July 1, 1997 (PRWORA: P.L. 104-193). The latter replaces the former Aid to Families with Dependent Children (AFDC) program, the Job Opportunities and Basic Skills Training (JOBS) program, and the Emergency Assistance program.

Both supportive and supplemental services are usually provided to families in their own homes. Moreover, there is increased overlap of supportive and supplemental services as the federal laws and guidelines for states link supportive services such as child care with economic assistance such as TANF. The final primary service category is substitute services. These are generally out-of-home services provided to children and families, when, for a myriad of reasons, families are unable to provide for the basic needs of their members. Examples of these child welfare services are foster care, group homes, and other institutional settings, and adoption and permanency planning. A significant number of African-American children and families interface with the child welfare system in the supportive, supplemental, and substitute service arenas.

The child care provisions of the new law (PRWORA: P.L. 14-193) are intended to support the goal of promoting self-sufficiency through work. They are also designed to streamline the federal government's role in child care services, reduce the number of programs, and increase flexibility to states. Thus, the Child Care and Development Block Grant (CCDBG) is expanded to become the primary child care subsidy program operated by the federal government. The federal government has been involved in child care at least since the New Deal of the 1930s.

Under the CCDBG, entitlement and discretionary funds are provided for child care in the potential available total amount of $20 billion during fiscal years 1997–2002. Discretionary funds are one billion per year, while entitlement funds began at two billion in fiscal year (FY) 1997 and increase to $2.7 billion in FY 2002. States have the authority to use funds to provide child care services on a sliding fee scale basis to families with incomes no higher than 85 percent of the state median. At a minimum, 70 percent of the entitlement funds must be used for welfare families and for non-welfare families who would be at risk of welfare dependence without subsidized care. States are also required to use significant portions of their remaining monies for other low-income, non-welfare families. At least 4 percent of state funds must be used for activities to improve the quality of child care.

Implementation issues that disproportionately affect African Americans include the extent to which child care resources will be adequate to meet the needs of eligible low-income families, including those who receive welfare and those who do not. Important factors for analysis and assessment are the specific work requirements developed by the states for welfare recipients, whether states are complying with federal work requirements, the amount of non-federal resources committed to child care, and whether states will use all child care funds potentially available from the federal government (13). Other federal program initiatives that also impact child care include the Social Services Block Grants, Head Start, Child and Adult Care Food program, and the Child and Dependent Care Tax Credit. Child care is especially important for African-American low-income and poverty-stricken families, since the key to an economically self-sufficient and stable family in the African-American community is usually comprised of both parents working in two-parent families. Further, it is critical for a low-income female-headed family to maintain a job or participate in education and training for meaningful employment in order to approach economic self-sufficiency. Therefore, available, affordable, quality child care is necessary if this quest for self-sufficiency and family stability is to be mastered.

The number of children in need of protective services is spiraling. In 1996, child protective services agencies investigated more than 2 million reports alleging maltreatment of more than 3 million children. The national rate of children who were reported was 44 per 1,000 children, while the national rate of victims was 15 per 1,000 children in the population. Of the 41 states reporting race and ethnicity data, more than half (52 percent) of all victims suffered neglect, almost a quarter suffered physical abuse, and about 12 percent of the victims were sexually abused. Children suffering medical neglect and emotional maltreatment accounted for 3 percent and 6 percent of all victims, respectively. More than half (53 percent) of all victims were white. African-American children represented the second largest group of victims (27 percent). The percentages of African-American victims were disproportionately high, almost twice their representation in the national child population (14). Additional analysis of maltreated children in 11 states indicated that, while white victims represented a disproportionately low percentage of medical neglect victims and a high level (65 percent) of sexual abuse victims, African-American children were disproportionately represented by a low percentage of sexual abuse and emotional maltreatment victims. African-American children, however, accounted for 44 percent of all medical neglect victims (15). However, there is a strong need to understand that various factors relate to substantiated abuse. Of significance is the interaction in decision-making of race and ethnicity, family and environmental strengths and risks among both mandated service providers and community reporters, and the entire nature of the child welfare system (16).

Neglect, in protective services, can be defined as deleterious acts of omission rather than commission. Neglect is consistently the largest single discrete category of children documented to be in need of protective services, comprising approximately 55 percent of the total number of abused and neglected children in 1986 and 52 percent in 1996 (17). Consistent with some analysis of child abuse and neglect reporting and substantiated data, it can be reasonably postulated that, since many African-American families in the child welfare system are poor, neglect is one significant factor, at least, to account for a sizable number of African-American children in protective services. A comparable analysis of neglectful women showed that loneliness was experienced to a greater extent among women who were urban, African-American, had very low income, and were living without a partner. Conversely, women who were from rural areas, white, had somewhat higher incomes, and lived with a partner were less likely to be described as neglectful (18).

Further studies have indicated that some African-American families who abuse their children suffer from poverty, social isolation, depression, and stressful relationships. Suggestions to strengthen these families include financial support, professional assessment, treatment, and support groups. These helping efforts are to occur while ensuring that the child is protected and the family kept together whenever it is feasible (19). It has been suggested that the responsibility for child abuse in the African-American community resides as much in the wider society as in the relationships among the family members and that it should be conceptualized as a symptom rather than as a disease (20). Neglect is frequently spurred by inadequate parenting knowledge and skills and insufficient financial resources to provide for the safety and well-being of children. Studies have provided evidence that the etiology of much chronic neglect can be found in extreme poverty. Interventions needed include affordable quality child care, increased education and employment opportunities, increased supply of adequate low-income housing, and large-scale drug prevention and treatment initiatives (21). The latter broad-based intervention approach is necessary to prevent further deterioration of the fabric of cities and the continued infiltration of rural and suburban areas. In addition, informal and familial sources of support, cornerstones in the African-American community, need to be consciously and deliberately utilized by protective services and other social service agencies. Thus, it is suggested that an institutional approach designed to provide effective parenting knowledge and skills combined with sufficient income for families to care for their children could effect a downward trend in neglect cases.

Until Congress passed and President Bill Clinton signed the Personal Responsibility and Work Opportunity Reconciliation Act in August, 1996, the Aid to Families with Dependent Children program was a primary supplemental child welfare service in the United States, and the program long identified with the term "welfare." From 1965 to 1996, the average case size fell by one-third, from 4.17 to 2.78 recipients per case. The number of children per case fell by over 40 percent from its peak of 3.28 children per case in 1967 to the 1996 average of 1.91 children per case. The average number of adults per case remained within a range of .89 to 1.00 between 1973 and 1994. The 1995 average of .86 adults per case is the lowest number since 1970 (22). Since the early 1970s, the recipient rate has been constant at between 5 and 7 percent of the population under age 65. Fluctuations in the rate mirror the changes in the nation's economic conditions with increases during times of recession and unemployment and decreases during times of growth and high employment (23). In 1996, the average monthly number of cases participating in the AFDC program was 4.55 million families. This represents a decrease of nearly 10 percent from the average of 5.05 million families in 1994. By the end of August 1996, the number of cases had declined to 4.41 million (24).

The average annual benefits paid to a mother and two children in 1996 dollars was $4,569 (25). Over the period between 1983 and 1995, roughly equal proportions of cases had either African-American or white parents—in 1983, African-Americans made up 38.3 percent of the cases compared to 36.5 percent for Whites and, in 1996, the percentages were 37.2 percent and 35.9 percent, respectively (26). These figures indicate that African-American families do not comprise the majority of AFDC families. It is imperative to understand that most African-American families are not "on welfare" but rather function autonomously. Under the TANF Act, individuals will be unable to receive more than five years of federally funded assistance. The vast majority of former recipients of AFDC did not receive payments for more than five years. However, of the approximately 25 percent of families who did remain longer, most tended to be comprised of individuals who have greater barriers to employment, which confirms the need for close study of the impact of TANF on the well-being of needy children and families.

Other supplemental services important for the well-being of and health status of African-American children include the Women, Infants and Children's (WIC) program and the Head Start program. A healthy start for children requires early maternal, prenatal, and postnatal health care. An African-American infant is more than twice as likely as a white infant to die before its first birthday. Infant mortality is particularly responsive to primary prevention approaches such as early prenatal care, good maternal nutrition to prevent low birthweight, and adequate infant nutrition. Yet, the nation was surpassed on this one indicator of good public health by 22 major industrialized countries. If African-American infant mortality rates were used, the nation would have ranked fortieth (27). Using the Healthy People 2000 goal, black infant mortality would be reduced to no more than 11 per 1,000, which remains higher than the 1992 white infant mortality rate of 6.9 percent. For black infants, AIDS and sudden infant death syndrome (SIDS) are major contributors to early death. Other factors more prevalent in African-American infant deaths than in the general population are respiratory distress syndrome, infections, and injuries. Of significance is infant low birthweight (defined as below 2,500 grams or 5 pounds, 8 ounces) as a health risk factor. The Healthy People 2000 project's goal is to reduce low-birthweight births among African-American babies to nine percent, using 1987 baseline data of 12.7 percent. Risk factors of poverty, environmental toxins, poor nutrition, low-educational status, in utero exposure to drugs such as alcohol, nicotine, heroin, cocaine, and methadone, and lack of early and continuous quality prenatal care all contribute to both low-birthweight births and infant mortality (28).

In this country, one in two African-American children is poor and one in four is uninsured. According to a report by the Children's Defense Fund (CDF), Medicaid works. During the ten years following the establishment of the Medicaid program, African-American infant mortality was reduced by 50 percent. However, in 1987, Medicaid was determined to serve fewer than 50 percent of the eligible poor (29). Medicaid continues to be a major insurer of children and families beset by poverty. In FY 1995, there were 23,408,114 children under age 21 enrolled in Medicaid. In August 1997, the Federal Balanced Budget Act was passed and contained provisions to enact the Children's Health Insurance Program. Children eligible for this program must be under 19, at or below 200 percent of the federal poverty level, and not eligible for Medicaid. This program is to be coordinated with other health insurance programs in the states (30). In the mid-1980s, over 40 percent of non-white infants were not fully immunized against polio. Nine childhood diseases are preventable with proper immunization: Diphtheria, pertussis, tetanus, measles, mumps, rubella, *Haemophilus influenzae* type B, and hepatitis B. Immunization is a proven cost-effective public health preventive. Outbreaks of measles in young children and college students, with an overrepresentation of black children in poor neighborhoods, occurred during the 1990s. Yet, financial cutbacks at both federal and state levels have weakened the infrastructures of health departments while the policy of less government has politicized the debate on immunization as children remain in need (31). Every dollar invested in immunization saves at least ten dollars in costs for medical care and lifelong disability.

Another alarming and devastating childhood disease that is a deadly and growing threat to African-American children is Acquired Immune Deficiency Syndrome (AIDS). Between 1992 and 1996, the number of perinatal AIDS incidents dropped among all racial and ethnic groups, but despite these declines, the majority of perinatally acquired AIDS cases continue to occur among African-American and Hispanic children. This indicates the need for intensified efforts to prevent infection among women in these groups and to reach women who are infected with early prenatal care and preventive treatment. AIDS incidence increased among all races through 1994, with the most significant increases seen among African-Americans, who, by 1996, accounted for more AIDS diagnoses annually than whites. In 1996, an estimated 6,750 African-American women and 17,250 African-American men were diagnosed with AIDS. Among the women, most (53 percent) were infected heterosexually, and 43 percent were attributed to injection drug use (IDU). Transmission among African-American men differed. Forty percent was transmitted through men who have sex with men (MSM), injection drug use accounted for 38 percent, and heterosexual contact accounted for 13 percent (32).

Moreover, of additional significant concern for the future of African-American families is the rise in HIV infection among adolescents and young adults. It is the leading cause of death for African-Americans between the ages of 25 and 44.

Many of these young adults contracted the disease as teenagers. It is estimated that half of all new HIV infections in the United States are among people under age 25, and the majority are infected sexually. The magnitude of HIV/AIDS cases is explained by estimates that 650,000 to 900,000 Americans are now living with HIV, and at least 40,000 new infections occur each year. Because of the long and variable time between HIV infection and the onset of AIDS, surveying and reporting HIV infection provides a much clearer picture of the impact of the epidemic in young people than surveillance of AIDS cases. The CDC recently announced results from a study of 25 states that had integrated HIV and AIDS reporting systems for the period January 1994 and June 1997. In these states, young people (aged 13–24) accounted for a much greater proportion of HIV than AIDS cases (14 percent versus 3 percent), with at least 2,000 diagnosed with HIV every year. Nearly half (44 percent) of the HIV infections were reported to be young females, and well over half (63 percent) were among African-Americans. Further, the study indicated that although there has been a declining trend in AIDS diagnosis, HIV diagnosis remained stable, and a higher proportion of HIV than AIDS cases were among women and minorities (33).

The reasons for the disproportionate prevalence of HIV/AIDS in the African-American community are numerous and complex. One reason for the high incidence of AIDS in the African-American community might be the high poverty rate and the concomitant felt need to temporarily escape it via drug usage. It has been suggested that for prevention efforts to be successful, the dangerous intersection of drug-related and sexual risk must be addressed. Healthy behavior and avoiding risk-focused behavior are prerequisites for HIV/AIDS prevention. Prevention programs which are ongoing and targeted specifically to African-American young people and women are required. All groups that exert influence over young people, such as families, schools, peers, social organizations, youth-serving agencies, and religious groups must be involved. School, community, and church-based programs with culturally sensitive and culturally competent provision of both prevention and treatment services are necessary to result in a critically needed downward trend in HIV/AIDS cases among African Americans. Health education for parents and children is important to reverse this decline in the health status of African-American children, young people, women, and men, all of whom ultimately comprise families. At the same time, analysts and advocates for children have noted that the single greatest barrier to improved health care for African-American children and families is financial. A lack of available adequate financial resources to maintain self-sufficiency, for example, is likely to contribute to dangerous or risky behavior.

The final primary child welfare service category is substitute services. Adoption as a substitute service for African-American children has been a subject of long-term debate and discussion among African-American individuals, as well as professional, community, and advocacy groups. The debate has concentrated on the issue of transracial adoption. The National Association of Black Social Workers (NABSW) has taken a consistent stand over the years *against* adoption of black children by non-blacks. In 1994, NABSW's position statement on transracial adoption stressed keeping families together and children safe through family reunification, relative placement, adoption within the same race, and transracial adoption, only after clearly documented evidence of unsuccessful same-race adoption. The National Association of Social Workers' policy statement purports the position that an effort to maintain a child's identity and ethnic heritage should prevail in services and placements involving children in foster care and adoption programs.

Furthermore, with regard to adoption, it notes, "The recruitment of and placement with adoptive parents from each relevant ethnic or racial group should be available to meet the needs of children" (34). Scholars and researchers, on the other hand, have held differing positions on the relative benefit and/or detriment to African-American children of growing up in homes where their adoptive parents are of a different race from their own. However, most agree that it is preferable to place a child in an adoptive home with parents of the same race. The controversy centers on whether African-American children can develop a positive racial identity in white homes. One view holds that as long as African-American children are growing up without permanent homes, transracial adoption offers a valuable resource by providing a strong support system. Another view is that African-American children lose the continuity of their culture and racial identity if they grow up in a home comprised of racially different parents (35). It has been postulated that as a child becomes assimilated into the transracial family and into that family's lifestyle, race becomes less of a factor; thus, the child's racial identity stops growing, whereas in a same-race adoptive home, racial identity continues to develop.

Other practitioners, including program developers and advocacy organizations, have elected to concentrate on disseminating viable approaches, focused on community development strategies and techniques, to garner African-American families for African-American children waiting for permanent homes. The "One Church, One Child" strategy (in which one member of each African-American church adopts an African-American child) initiated by Father George Clements of Holy Angels Church in Chicago when he adopted his first child is one such approach (36). Other community involvement innovations have incorporated education and media campaigns to inform the public of waiting children in their communities. Many successful adoption efforts include coalition activities with established organizations in the community, such as the Urban League, or through the formation of support groups for African-American children such as "Friends of Black Children," established in North Carolina (37). Furthermore, in the mid-1990s, The Kellogg Foundation mounted an initiative in a number of states (19 initially) which focused on developing a coalition of stakeholders such as legislators, judges, child welfare administrators, adoptive parents, foster parents, and birth parents. The goal of the initiative was to increase the number of children placed in permanent homes through adoption, including African-American children and other children of color, by progressive system change as developed by the proponent stakeholders in the communities. An often underutilized resource for advocating for African-American children without permanent homes is the successful African-American adoptive parents. In a recent report on racial characteristics of children served by the child welfare system, African-American children comprised 40.4 percent of children in care, 42.8 percent awaiting adoptive placements, and 29.2 percent of children in finalized adoption (38). However, African-American adoptive families may not be inclined to talk about their adoption to people they do not know. Child welfare workers are cautioned to adhere to the agreement of confidentiality unless permission to use adoptive parents as role models of adoption success has been granted (39).

Another issue in same-race versus transracial adoption relates to the definition of kinship care and the related concept of a permanency plan and description of the term "availability for adoption." The passage of the Adoption Assistance and Child Welfare Act of 1980 (P.L. 96-272) allowed adoption subsidies to families that choose to adopt "special needs" children, who may include African-American children and promoted kinship family foster care. The enactment of the Multiethnic Placement Act of 1994 prohibited agencies receiving federal funds from denying any person the opportunity to become an adoptive parent based solely on the basis of race, color, or national origin of the foster or adoptive parent or the child. Moreover, in August, 1996, additional legislation, as part of the Small Business and Job Protection Law, was passed and enacted into law that modified the Multiethnic Placement Act. First, it allowed a tax credit to adoptive families with incomes not exceeding $75,000 of up to $5,000 ($6,000 in the case of children classified as special needs) annually for qualified adoption expenses. Second, it removed the qualification of same-race protection policies of the 1994 Act which permitted consideration of race, culture, and ethnicity in the placement of children. This change was accomplished by preventing any entities that receive federal assistance from denying any person the opportunity to provide foster care or adopt a child or delay or deny the placement of a child based of the criteria of race, color, or national origin of the foster or adoptive parent or the child. Some researchers have indicated that kinship foster placements among African-Americans frequently do not result in formal adoption, and are often perceived as permanency failures (40). These placements are noted to be primarily with grandparents, or great-aunts or uncles.

Due to the cultural definition of family in the African-American community, many foster parents considered themselves and the foster child to be a part of the same family and thought that it was unnecessary to adopt. Others believed adoption would interfere with their relationship with the biological parents (41). Of importance is the issue of whether or not long-term or permanent kinship placements of African-American children are considered permanent placements, as an option for adoption, will impact the number of reported African-American children listed as "waiting for adoption." The number of African-American children in the child welfare system without permanent homes is also related to the method child welfare agencies use to determine which children are actually available for adoption versus the agencies having a permanency plan for the child. Children available for adoption are those children whose parental rights have been legally terminated. However, an agency's worker may have a plan for permanency including adoption that has not yet reached the stage of parental rights being terminated.

Finally, five themes regarding transracial adoption of various professional organizations, regarding transracial adoption, have been thus summarized by Hollingsworth (42).

1. That ethnic heritage is important
2. That children be raised preferably by their biological parents or, when not possible, by other biological relatives
3. That economic need alone is not an acceptable reason for children to be deprived of their biological parents
4. That efforts should be made to ensure that adoptive parents of the same race as the child are available and systemic barriers should not interfere
5. That placement with parents of a different race is acceptable and even preferable when the alternative means a child is deprived of a permanent home and family.

It is important that social work organizations publicize their positions to their members and advocate for public policies that facilitate these themes.

In summary, it is well-known that the younger the child entering the foster care system, the greater the likelihood of adoption. Thus, it is important to work with families who wish to regain custody of their children as expediently and as competently as possible. Research has indicated that family preservation services may result in fewer placements for families of color compared to white families. Ergo, intensive services and resources to families at risk of termination of parental rights may prove useful in reunification whenever possible, while ensuring the safety of the child. There remains a need to recruit African-American adoptive families for those children who are unable to remain with their biological families or to be reunited with them in reasonable time periods. The younger the child, the greater chance of adoption, and the longer the child remains in the foster care system, the less likely that he or she will be adopted. Thus, there is a serious call to action of the black community to ensure permanent homes for its children.

Child Welfare Practice

Cultural Diversity

One of the most important characteristics of African-American children and families is their heterogeneity. There is *not* one African-American family, but many, running the gamut from the traditional two-parent family structure to various combinations of blended families, as well as single-parent families. The children from these families tend to have the same hopes and dreams for the "American successful life" as children from other races. Their everyday realities, on the other hand, influence their aspirations and the accomplishments which they believe are actually possible for themselves, both in the present and in the future. Black children are poor, wealthy, and middle-income. However, because a disproportionate number of them are poor, they may be more likely to be consumers of residual child welfare services. Since social work is the profession traditionally charged with the delivery of such social services, practitioners must be aware of the various kinds and specific characteristics of the culture of African-American families, particularly as they affect help-seeking behavior. Some typical characteristics include single- versus dual-parent families, socioeconomic status, and varying family size.

As in all helping relationships, one of the tasks of the helper is to identify and work with the strengths of the client. Hill has operationally defined family strengths as "those traits which facilitate the ability of the family to meet the needs of its members and the demands made upon it by systems outside the family unit" (43). Common features of African-American families that have been described as strengths include strong kinship bonds going beyond blood ties, strong work orientation, adaptability of family roles, high achievement orientation, and religious orientation.

As part of the assessment process, it is important to understand family structures and dynamics from the cultural perspective of the client. Cultural stereotypes of African-American adults as "lazy," youth as "violent," children as "non-verbal and aggressive," and the community as a whole as "culturally deprived" or "culturally disadvantaged," present "helping stumbling blocks" to the social worker. This prevents effective intervention with African-American children and their families. The conceptualization of troubled African-American families as "overwhelmed," for example, rather than "multiproblem or vulnerable," has been described as presenting concerns and issues of African-American families in a non-judgmental and, therefore, more acceptable manner (44). African-American families have a rich culture that is most likely a compound of elements from traditional African culture and from slavery in the United States, reconstruction, and subsequent experiences with racism and discrimination, as well as the impact of the majority white American culture (45). Thus, black children live in two worlds—the African-American community and a predominantly white society. This dual exposure necessitates strength and adaptability for coping with a bicultural lifestyle.

Although some view differences between African-American families and white families as due primarily to socioeconomic conditions, rather than to cultural differences, other studies have documented cultural similarities among African-American families across social class lines (46). There are certain aspects of African-American family functioning that appear to be characteristic, regardless of socioeconomic factors. The strong extended family bonds, for example, have traditionally provided African-American families with mutual aid beyond the nuclear family structure. The concept of strong kinship bonds extends to the "family" of friends and neighbors. This "Harambee spirit" of togetherness, love, brotherhood, and sisterhood promoted with self-help initiatives in African-American communities is a significant characteristic of African-American families. These mutual-aid community efforts are viewed as African retentions. They were reinforced by slavery and subsequent racism and discrimination in the United States, which forced black families, for the most part, to depend on their own communities for mutual aid and support (47). This attitude of African-American families can be used to empower them. Self-determination and self-help efforts are consistent with values of the social work profession and should be consciously utilized in child welfare practice.

Further, since both parents tend to work in both working-class and middle-class African-American families, the expressive (nurturing) and instrumental (providing) family roles tend to be shared by both men and women. Researchers have pointed out over the years that children have special significance in the lives of African-American parents (48). This advantageous phenomenon is rooted in the African heritage, where children have traditionally held special value since they represent the continuity of life. In traditional Africa, children are perceived as required for a complete family life experience (49).

The desire to achieve through hard work and education has been a desired goal for African-American families. Education is believed by parents to be the primary means for their offspring to be economically successful in this country. However, when parents and children interact with the educational system, sometimes there are conflicts. These problems are more likely to occur when the ways of the home and those of the school are different. For example, African-American children are frequently taught to be independent and assertive at an early age. These values, however, sometimes conflict with those of the school. Oftentimes, a history of institutionalized racism and unresponsiveness to cultural difference is demonstrated by the educational system's inability or lack of creative effort to provide a quality education to the majority of its students, particularly in large urban school systems. In instances like these, the African-American student who worked hard and thought he or she was a good student in high school, too often, finds himself or herself ill-equipped to readily compete with students with stronger educational foundations when he or she matriculates at a college or university.

Religion has also been a hallmark of African-American family stability. Religious consciousness has been referred to as "deliberate attempts by blacks to live according to religious beliefs that require acts of charity and brotherliness and neighborliness toward one another as a means of coming closer to God and of carrying out God's will" (50). Thus, God is never an abstraction not linked to the here and now (51). The answer to family crises is frequently viewed as coming about as a result of prayer. The church has also acted for the African-American community as a service organization in the struggles for civil equality and economic parity. For example, Dr. Martin Luther King, Jr.'s work in the civil rights movement began in the church, as did Reverend Leon Sullivan's job and skill training program, which developed into the Opportunities Industrialization Centers across the country. Dr. Sullivan's leadership in the establishment of the biennial African and African-American Summit, begun in 1991, has further promoted economic self-sufficiency and partnerships among African peoples living in both the diaspora and on the African continent. The church has also provided families with the hope and courage they need to sustain hard times, whether due to limited financial resources or any other form of racially based prejudice and oppression. The African-American religious experience has also provided outlets for emotional expressions and opportunities for recreation that were affordable and accessible. This is particularly valuable as a way of managing stress.

When positive self-esteem emanates from African-American families and communities, it cushions children from the inevitable bruises they will undoubtedly encounter in the sometimes hostile outside environment. Thus, the African-American family is the only place where African-American children can be assured of unconditional love and acceptance. It is, therefore, important in disciplining a child to disapprove of his or her unacceptable act or behaviors, while retaining approval and acceptance of the child.

Child Welfare Intervention

During the early decades of the development of professional social work practice, little attention was given to the role of culture in African-American families. However, when African-American culture was recognized, it was generally perceived as interfering with effective social work intervention. Discrimination was perceived as having influenced the development of negative cultural attitudes and behaviors, such as immediate gratification and lack of commitment to family, particularly from African-American males. Further, as late as the 1950s and 1960s, these cultural characteristics led to the labeling of African-American families as "multiproblem" or "hard-to-reach"; this then led to the perception that they were, therefore, difficult to engage in the child welfare service delivery process. Problems were often viewed as generated from within the family system. Some attention was given to the issues of the effect of the race of the worker on the African-American family-worker relationship. Little attention, however, was paid to macro-level problems, such as limited access to jobs, training, and educational opportunities for African-American parents to function as adequate adults.

The 1970s began the quest for social work practice that would incorporate knowledge of an African-American perspective when working with African-American children and their families. In practice, it is important to incorporate the knowledge that a sense of belonging is only felt by African-American families when the rights of parents are protected and obstacles are not placed in the way of earning a living for one's family. This sense of belonging—a oneness with society—is denied to African Americans as a result of racist attitudes and actions (52). Negative valuations by a more powerful white society, when internalized, produce negative self-images in African-American children and families that lead to a sense of powerlessness. In contrast, the opportunity to adequately fill valued social roles such as worker and parent instill positive feelings about self.

Although most African-American families, at some time during the life course, will encounter negative valuations by systems external to their families, many do not internalize these negative images of themselves and their communities. The positive environment of their families and communities shield them. A positive self-image begins its formulation in the family. It is crucial for children to have good affectional relations with people that are significant to them, namely, their family and group (53). Children then develop a sense of their own worth which leads to feelings of self-confidence and capability. When this foundation is laid in the protective environment of the home and community, the positive self-esteem that has germinated is likely to survive the inevitable bruises it will undoubtedly encounter in the sometimes hostile outside environment. When this foundation has not maintained itself, however, the process of empowering the client family is necessary. Empowerment has been defined as a process where the practitioner engages in activities with the client to reduce the powerlessness that has resulted from membership in a stigmatized group that has been valued negatively (54).

Social workers can utilize the natural support networks in the African-American community, together with basic social work knowledge and skills, to help families develop a sense of control and power over their lives through increased effectiveness in the performance of valued social roles, thereby empowering the client system. The following case examples demonstrate this approach, incorporating a generalist child welfare practice framework:

Case Example: John R.

Mr. John R., aged 45, lost his job as a line worker due to the closing of the Shabutu Automobile Plant in Centreville, Tenn., after he had worked for the company for three years. After six months of unemployment, Mr. R. is still looking for another job. His wife, Brenda, 38, works two days a week at a local dry cleaners. They have four children: Aisha and Kwesi, twins, aged 4, Bianca, who is 6, and Christopher, 8.

The R. family was reported to Protective Services by Christopher's teacher, Mrs. Janice Banks, a second-grade teacher at Malcolm X Elementary School. Christopher has been acting out in school—bullying both boys and girls in the classroom and at recess. This behavior has been occurring for the past month. Before that time, Christopher had no behavioral difficulties, performed academically at slightly above the average range, and got along well with his peers. During the past several weeks, however, Christopher has been involved in several fights, was sullen in school, and his grades had dropped to somewhat below average.

The teacher had a private conference with Christopher and questioned him about his recent changes in behavior and academic performance. Christopher finally admitted, through tears, that things were not going well at home and that he was angry with his father, who seemed to take everything out on Christopher. Further discussion led to Christopher's revelation that his father had lost his job, that recently the father had begun to blame Christopher for "everything," and that his father was frequently "hollering" at him for "no reason at all." Last week the father whipped Christopher "for the first time in his life." Christopher said that last night his father "beat" him and proceeded to show his teacher several welts on his legs from "Daddy's belt." Before these two *incidents, Christopher had usually been punished by his mother and father by withdrawal of privileges, and only occasionally by "spankings" which were described by Christopher as "not really hurting at all."*

The teacher reported Christopher's case as suspected child abuse. Ms. Mitchell, newly graduated professional social worker, is assigned to the case.

Case Notes The social worker's initial assessment of the family's situation is that the family is malfunctioning primarily as a result of economic pressures brought about by the loss of the father's income. The family was functioning adequately before the crisis of job loss. Although the loss of job by the father is through no direct fault of his own, he now is suffering from decreased self-esteem as a result of his inability to provide for his family. The small income from unemployment insurance has also run out. The father is assessed as having displaced anger at the oldest child, a son, because he views the son as sure to have problems, such as he himself is now having, as an African-American male in this society suffering from the "last-hired and first-fired" syndrome. The father began to inappropriately prepare his son for later mistreatment by "the system" by toughening the son now, which led to the unusually harsh physical punishment by the father.

The worker's first task is to protect the child. Upon investigating, the worker finds that the family has indeed been under unusual stress in recent months. The father admitted, with regret and remorse, that he had punished his son too harshly. The father apologized to his son in the worker's presence and openly demonstrated affection for his child by hugging him. The family agreed to continued home visits by the social worker for a period of six weeks to "work on alternative solutions" to some of the family's "stressors," including exploring job possibilities for Mr. R. The worker served as an advocate for the client system by assisting the client with job applications commensurate with his training and experience. Mr. R. was able to find night work with a janitorial service within two weeks through a referral from the worker. The next week he was also able to get a part-time day job with a landscaping company, something he always enjoyed as a hobby. With the worker's support, he and his wife decided to explore technical training programs at the local junior college, after which Mr. R. decided to pursue a horticulture program on a part-time basis.

Mr. R.'s self-image has improved significantly because he is again able to meet his family's basic needs and begin a new career program. Mrs. R. also decided to enroll in a typing class in the morning, while the twins were in the Head Start program. They stated that maybe Mr. R.'s ". . . job loss was a blessing in disguise." "This may be God's way of leading us to a better life," Mr. R. said. He and Christopher are again involved in basketball scrimmages, and Christopher is functioning well in school again and has joined the school soccer team. In six weeks, there have been no further indications of child abuse, and the family is functioning well as a unit. Therefore, there seems to be no need for further weekly involvement by the agency. However, the family and the worker agreed to follow-up monthly contact for three months as a stabilizing and supporting effort. After this time the case will be closed, if there are no further indications of a need for protective services.

In this case example, the social worker used her generalist social work practice framework to assess the client's behavior and its origins. She did not limit herself to an intrapsychic analysis of the father's or the son's difficulties nor to an intrafamilial malfunction, exclusively. Rather, the worker examined external systemic factors that impacted upon the family's functioning as well, i.e., the job market. Further, the worker was able to help the family explore more appropriate means of ridding itself of stress, such as exercise (e.g., basketball scrimmages), rather than hitting. The worker also served as an advocate for the family in alleviating the precipitating factor in the family crisis, i.e., the lack of a job and income for the husband and father. This change effort occurred through the pursuit of employment and new training opportunities.

The worker recognized the cultural milieu in which the family was living and consciously utilized this knowledge in working with the family. The worker built upon the strong family bonds in the family and helped the family to use them effectively. The strong religious and achievement orientations of the family were recognized and used by the worker. The worker explored helping avenues at the family, individual, and community levels. She used the professional value of the dignity and worth of the individual as an underlying principle. She was nonjudgmental in her investigation and development of a treatment plan. The worker consciously used her knowledge of human behavior and crisis theory in targeting the problem area. She used her interviewing skills to explore, reflect, confront, and listen to the family members. The worker exhibited a genuine sense of caring and positive regard for the family. She also used the sanction of the agency and the profession to ensure the health and safety of the primary client of the protective service agency—the child. The policy implications of the case example include the requirement that child welfare workers also support the goals of full-employment policies to protect displaced workers, and legislative agendas that promote equal access to adequate education and job training skills for every American.

A second case example involves a professional social worker in a community-based agency setting.

Case Example: Kenda M.

Seven-year-old Kenda M. complained about headaches and stomachaches every Sunday at Sunday school for the past six to eight weeks. The Sunday-school teacher became concerned and talked with the mother about the child's complaints. The mother, Mrs. M., is a 28-year-old single parent who worked as a registered nurse at a hospital, had already taken her daughter to the doctor, since she had been complaining of headaches and stomachaches to her mother also. Medical examination and tests showed no organic reason for the complaints. The Sunday-school teacher suggested to Mrs. M. that maybe Kenda has some concerns that she might like to discuss with the social worker, Mrs. Jamer-

son, at the community center. Mrs. Jamerson had a reputation of being able to "reach" the children in the neighborhood when they were having problems.

Mrs. M. agreed to allow Kenda to talk with Mrs. Jamerson at the community center. After several sessions with Mrs. Jamerson and after engaging in such extracurricular activities at the center as Saturday-morning skating trips, Kenda told the social worker how much she missed her mother in the evenings now that her mother had finished nursing school and was working the 3:00 P.M. to 11:00 P.M. shift at the hospital. Kenda has to stay with the sitter while her mother works and is awakened three to five nights a week after 11:00 P.M. to be taken home. Kenda's onset of stomachaches and headaches began shortly after her mother began working this shift three months ago.

Case Notes The social worker, having developed a positive working relationship with Kenda, facilitated a meeting with Kenda and her mother. With the worker's support and presence, Kenda was able to express her feelings to her mother. The young, eager, enthusiastic registered nurse had not realized the impact her change of schedule had on her 7-year-old daughter. Mrs. M. decided that the disruption was too much for her daughter and opted to change jobs and work at the local health center, where the work schedule was 8:00 a.m. to 5:00 p.m., Monday through Friday. Kenda was able to stay at the community center after school until her mother got off work. She was able to ride the school bus to the center.

The mother, however, still desired to have some experience of working with more severe forms of illness than the community health center was equipped to handle. She has worked in the emergency room at the local hospital since completing her training three months ago. Mrs. M. and her daughter, with the worker's assistance, explored possible options. They were able to agree to an "on-call" schedule for Mrs. M. one weekend day per month at the local general hospital. This was the same hospital where she had been employed since graduating from nursing school and where she had developed very positive working relationships. An aunt, with whom Kenda had a good relationship, agreed to care for Kenda on these days. Thus, Mrs. M. felt relieved that she could better fulfill her parenting responsibilities as well as continue her career development in two different health-care settings. Both Mrs. M. and her daughter were satisfied with this compromise arrangement. Kenda's stomachaches and headaches ceased. She continued both her interest in Sunday-school class and her social interactions with classmates and Mrs. Jamerson, without further somatic problems.

The child welfare community worker began her work with Kenda by relationship building. A positive, trusting relationship is critical for work with children. This case demonstrates the beneficial partnerships that can develop between natural community supports, such as the church and the extended family, and formalized external community organizations, like the community center. Referral, cooperation, and collaboration among the natural and formalized helping networks were elements of a case management approach that worked appropriately with this African-American family. At all times during the process, the client system actively participated in the decision-making process. The social worker's knowledge of human behavior helped to identify the precipitating event which led to the onset of Kenda's somatic complaints. The worker's sanction came from the profession, the agency, and the African-American community's own informal helping network. One policy implication, in this particular case, is that services housed in and near the communities of the people targeted for services are important to facilitate service delivery. Case management is a crucial process in service delivery. As a system, it provides a single accountable individual to perform activities in the service of the client, to ensure to the maximum extent possible that the client system has access to and receives all the resources and services that can help the client reach an optimal level of functioning. In the case above, the worker facilitated a positive outcome for the client family with an integrated approach that found solutions through the job market, the extended family, the nuclear family, the school system, the community agency, and the church.

In all aspects of service delivery, the child welfare social worker must be engaged in evaluating the process and outcome of the service provided. Accurate recordkeeping and evaluation of tasks accomplished and goals attained are relevant aspects of evaluation that must be attended to by the professional social worker in child welfare practice. Another issue significant to the evaluation process is adherence to the ethical dictates of professional practice at all times. This includes adhering to client confidentiality and showing respect for the dignity and worth of all individuals, regardless of race, ethnicity, religion, age, handicapping conditions, or socioeconomic status.

Future Issues and Trends

Race as a factor in child welfare services is likely to continue to be an important consideration in child welfare policy and practice. As long as many children in substitute care and children receiving supplemental services, as well as children engaged in supportive services are African-American, race cannot be ignored by child welfare workers.

The training of workers for more effective practice with African-Americans who can and will identify and understand cultural traits is needed. The use of the Africentric perspective, based upon an African world view and its accompanying values, is suggested as one way that this can be accomplished. This perspective acknowledges feelings and emotions equally with rational and logical ways of thinking and appreciates the richness of heritage and experiences of African Americans. The importance of cooperation and spirituality are also acknowledged (55). For example, when working with African-American families experiencing domestic violence, it has been suggested that the use of collective aid in the African-American family and community, such as the extended family and neighbors to provide advice, counseling, and shelter, has provided a positive effect (56). Such efforts can be incorporated into service delivery approaches that must focus primarily on the healthy survival of the victim of violence, yet remain, as much as possible, syntonic with the individual's culture or world view.

A second and related training approach includes didactic and experiential learning opportunities through awareness of cultural difference rather than deficit, developing cross-cultural counseling approaches, heightening awareness of self, and understanding social, political, and economic realities of African-American children and families. The cross-cultural learning by agency staff through direct experiences with African-American families and communities is crucial for successful intervention with this population group. Staff development, intercultural and multicultural experiences, with appropriate supervision and competent administrative oversight, are important as the experiential learning focuses not only on cultural awareness but also on actual utilization of knowledge and skills in practice (57). High-level administrators' involvement in the process is necessary in order to garner support and commitment for the incorporation of such multicultural perspectives in the agency's organizational culture.

Too often, economic status and membership in the majority racial group in this country determine access to needed services in order to have a quality life. This trend appears to be continuing. In addition to providing service, a concomitant role of the child welfare worker, then, is to be knowledgeable of and to support public social policy initiatives to improve the plight of all children and families. This can be done through support of progressive child and family legislative agendas through community organizations, professional organizations, and child advocacy organizations, for example. Support of African-American families and children can occur through encouraging and patronizing African-American economic development efforts. Economic development in the African-American community through such methods as support of African-American businesses, professionals, and educational institutions is paramount for the functional survival of black families. Recent information indicates that of the 24.7 million small businesses in the United States, only 2.9 million belonged to people of color. From 1985–1996, the number of national black business start-ups grew annually at 7.55 percent (58). Although diversity in color is expected to comprise the majority of the nation's population by 2050, the historical economic advantage of whites in terms of accumulated and inherited wealth is likely to remain steadfast. The need for financial and moral support of African Americans and all persons need for financial self-sufficiency and family security remained a significant need throughout the 1990s. It is anticipated to continue as a long-range goal in the new millennium. A strong community needs a positive value base, economic means for survival, and a strong family system. African-American families' common strengths, at this time, are still missing the economic component in their quest for parity. Child welfare workers must support the passage of bills designed to improve services to meet such basic needs for all families as health care, job training, adequate affordable child care, and safe housing.

Child welfare workers must serve as advocates for African-American families and children through the political and legislative process in order to continue to increase services for all families in need to provide the basic child welfare services of adequate food, clothing, housing, health care, and education. In addition, professional social workers and their organizations should support the society's moral responsibility to offer real opportunities for all groups to achieve economic self-sufficiency and financial security for their families. Generalist child welfare practice, utilizing a broad systems perspective, allows the social worker to address all levels of practice—the individual, family, community, organization, and social policy. This makes it an especially useful approach when working with African-American children and families.

Endnotes

1. Gwendolyn Spencer Prater, "The Essential Ingredients of a Stable Family," in *Readings on Black Children and Youth*, Lula A. Beatty, ed., pp. 49–72.

2. Andrew Billingsley and Jeanne M. Giovannoni, *Children of the Storm: Black Children and American Child Welfare*, pp. 38–59.

3. Ibid., p. 43.

4. Marion Wright Edelman, *Families in Peril: An Agenda for Social Change*, p. 4.

5. Barbara Bryant Solomon, "Social Work with African-Americans," in *Social Work: A Profession of Many Faces*, 8th ed., Armando Morales and Bradford W. Sheafor, eds., p. 242.

6. John M. Jeffries and Richard L. Schaeffer, "Changes in the Economy and Labor Market Status of Black Americans," in *The State of Black America 1996*, Audrey Rowe and John M. Jefferies, eds., p. 29.

7. Andrew Hacker, 1995, *Two Nations: Black and White, Separate, Hostile and Unequal*. New York: Ballantine Books.

8. John M. Jeffries and Richard L. Shaeffer, "Abstract," p. 13.

9. David Swinton, "The Economic Status of Black Americans During the 1980s: A Decade of Limited Progress," in *The State of Black America 1990*, Janet Dewart, ed., p. 28.

10. David Swinton, "The Economic Status of Black America 1993, p.162.

11. U.S. Bureau of the Census. *Current Population Reports: Household and Family Characteristics*, P20-509ER. March 1997. Washington, D.C.: U.S. Government Printing Office, 1998. Available: http://www.bls.census.gov/cps/pub/1997/int_race.htm; U.S. Bureau of the Census, *Current Population Reports Series: Household and Family Characteristics*, p. 20, No. 424. March 1987, Washington, D.C.: U.S. Government Printing Office, 1988, pp. 21–24; and *The State of Families 2: Work and Family*, Milwaukee: Family Service America, 1987, p. 42.

12. David Swinton, "The Economic Status of Blacks 1987," in The State of Black America 1987, Janet Dewart, ed., p. 70.

13. *Congressional Research Service Report for Congress: Child Care for Low-Income Families: Federal Programs and Welfare Reform* by Karen Spar, updated October 7, 1996, (Summary).

14. U.S. Department of Health and Human Services, National Center on Child Abuse and Neglect. *Child Maltreatment 1996: Reports from the States to the National Child Abuse and Neglect Data System*, Washington, D.C.: U.S. Government Printing Office, 1998, p. xi.

15. Ibid., pp. 2–11.

16. Michael R. Petit and Patrick A. Curtis, *Child Abuse and Neglect: A Look at the States 1997* CWLA Stat Book, Washington, D.C.: CWLA Press, 1997, p. 19.

17. *Highlights of Official Child Neglect and Abuse Reporting: 1986*, Denver: American Humane Association, 1988, pp. 10–21. See also *Study Findings: Study of National Incidence and Prevalence of Child Abuse and Neglect: 1988*, U.S. Department of Health and Human Services, Office

of Human Development Services, Administration for Children, Youth and Families, Children's Bureau, National Center on Child Abuse and Neglect, Washington, D.C. 1988; See also Child Welfare League of America, *Too Young to Run: The Status of Child Abuse in America* (Washington, D.C.: Child Welfare League of America, 1986); and National Center on Child Abuse and Neglect, *Child Maltreatment 1996: Reports from the States to the National Child Abuse and Neglect Data System.*

18. Norman Polansky, "Determinants of Loneliness Among Neglectful and Other Low-Income Mothers," *Social Service Review* 8 (Spring 1985): 1–12.

19. Jessica H. Daniel, Robert L. Hampton, and Eli H. Newberger, "Child Abuse and Accidents in Black Families: A Controlled Comparative Study," *American Journal of Orthopsychiatry* 53 (October 1983): 652–653. See also Norman A. Polansky, Paul W. Ammons, and James M. Gaudin, Jr. "Loneliness and Isolation in Child Neglect," *Social Casework* (January 1985): 38–47.

20. Jessica H. Daniel, et al., "Child Abuse and Accidents in Black Families: A Controlled Comparative Study," p. 653; Jeanne Giovannoni, and Andrew Billingsley (1970), "Child Neglect Among the Poor: A Study of Parental Adequacy in Families of Ethnic Groups," *Child Welfare 49* 196–204; and Kristine E. Nelson, Edward J. Saunders, and Miriam J. Landman, "Chronic Child Neglect in Perspective," *Social Work* 38 (November 1993): 661–671.

21. June Jackson Christmas, "The Health of African-Americans: Progress Toward Healthy People 2000," p. 106.

22. *Aid to Families with Dependent Children: The Baseline,* Office of Human Services Policy Office of the Assistant Secretary for Planning and Evaluation, U.S. Department of Health and Human Services, June, 1998, p. 45.

23. Ibid., p. 13.

24. Ibid., p. 14.

25. Ibid., p. 91.

26. Ibid., p. 57

27. June Jackson Christmas, "The Health of African-Americans: Progress Toward Healthy People 2000," p. 99.

28. Ibid., pp. 99–100.

29. Dana Hughes and Elizabeth Butler, *The Health of America's Black Children,* Marsha Meehan, ed., Washington, D.C.: Children's Defense Fund, 1988.

30. *Children in the States 1997,* Children's Defense Fund, p. 103; and *Mississippi Healthy Baby Update Newsletter 11* (June-July, 1998), Jackson, MS: Human Services Coalition.

31. June Jackson Christmas, "The Health of African-Americans: Progress Toward Healthy People 2000," p. 104.

32. *Trends in the HIV & AIDS Epidemic,* Atlanta, GA: Centers for Disease Control and Prevention, 1998, pp. 5–12.

33. Ibid., p. 2 and *Combating Complacency: HIV Prevention* "Young People at Risk—Epidemic Shifts Further Toward Young Women and Minorities," Geneva '98, pp. 1–5.

34. National Association of Social Workers, "Social Work Speaks: NASW Policy Statements," 4th ed. Washington, D.C.: NASW Press, 1997, p. 140.

35. Penny R. Johnson, Joan F. Shireman, and Kenneth W. Watson, "Transracial Adoption and the Development of Black Identity at Age Eight," *Child Welfare* LXVI (January–February 1987): 45–55 and *Report of the Child Welfare League of America National Task Force,* Washington, D.C.: Child Welfare League of America, 1987.

36. Anthony J. Veronico, "One Church, One Child: Placing Children with Special Needs," *Children Today* 12 (March–April 1983): 6–10.

37. Linda Dunn, "Finding Permanent Homes for Black Children: The California Inland Area Urban League Project," *Children Today* 10 (Sept–Oct 1981): 16–18; and Valora Wash-

ington, "Community Involvement in Recruiting Adoptive Homes for Black Children," *Child Welfare* LXVI (Jan–Feb 1987): 57–68.

38. Valora Washington, *Families for Kids of Color: A Special Report on Challenges and Opportunities*, Battle Creek, MI: Kellogg Foundation, 1995.

39. Gwendolyn Prater and Lula T. King, "Experiences of Black Families as Adoptive Parents," *Social Work* 33 (November/December 1988): 544.

40. J. L. Thornton, "Permanency Planning for Children in Kinship Foster Homes," *Child Welfare 70* (September/October 1991): 593–601; and Berrick, J. D., Barth, R. P., & Needell, B., "A Comparison of Kinship Foster Homes and Foster Family Homes: Implications for Kinship Care as Family Preservation," *Children and Youth Services Review* 16 (1994): 33–63.

41. J. L. Thornton, "Permanency Planning for Children in Kinship Foster Homes," *Child Welfare 70* (September/October 1991): 593–601.

42. Leslie Doty Hollingsworth, "Promoting Same-Race Adoption for Children of Color," *Social Work* 43 (March 1998): 113.

43. Robert Hill, *The Strengths of Black Families*, New York: National Urban League, 1972, p. 3.

44. Linda Anderson Smith and Shirley P. Thrasher, "A Practice Approach for Working with Overwhelmed African-American Families," *Black Caucus* (Spring 1993): 1.

45. Barbara Bryant Solomon and Helen A. Mendes, "Black Families from a Social Welfare Perspective" in *Changing Images of the Family*, Virginia Tufte and Barbara Myerhoff, eds., New Haven: Yale University Press, 1979, pp. 285–289.

46. Andrew Billingsley, *Black Families in White America*, New Jersey: Prentice-Hall, 1968; and Barbara Bryant Solomon, *Black Empowerment: Social Work in Oppressed Communities*, New York: Columbia University Press, 1976.

47. See Jomo Kenyatta, *Facing Mount Kenya: The Traditional Life of the Gikuyu*, Nairobi: Heinemann, 1978; and Wade Nobles, "Africanity: Its Role in Black Families," *The Black Scholar 5* (January/February 1975): 10–17.

48. Lee Rainwater, "Crucible of Identity: The Negro Lower Class Family," *Daedelus* 95 (Winter 1966): 72–215; Joyce Ladner, *Tomorrow's Tomorrow: The Black Woman*, New York: Doubleday, 1971; Gwendolyn Spencer Prater, "The Essential Ingredients of a Stable Family," pp. 49–72.

49. Mario Azevedo and Gwendolyn Prater, *Africa and Its People*, Dubuque: Kendall Hunt, 1982.

50. Joanne M. Martin and Elmer P. Martin, "The Helping Tradition in the Black Family and Community," Silver Spring, MD: National Association of Social Workers 1985, p. 5.

51. Solomon, "Social Work with African-Americans," pp. 548–549; and see also, Wendy L. Haight, "'Gathering the Spirit' at First Baptist Church: Spirituality as a Protective Factor in the Lives of African-American Children." *Social Work* 43 (May 1998): 213–221.

52. James P. Comer and Alvin F. Poussaint, *Black Child Care*. New York: Simon and Schuster, 1975.

53. Abraham Maslow, *Motivation and Personality*. New York: Harper and Row, 1970.

54. See Solomon, *Black Empowerment: Social Work in Oppressed Communities*, pp. 285–289.

55. Alfrieda Daly, Jeanette Jennings, Joyce O. Beckett, and Bogart R. Leashore, "Effective Coping Strategies of African-Americans," *Social Work* 40 (March 1995): 240–248.

56. Ibid., 243.

57. Ibid., pp. 3–10, and J. A. Alexelson, *Counseling and Development in a Multicultural Society*. 2nd ed. Pacific Grove, CA: Brooks/Cole, 1993.

58. David Judson, "Minorities Going for Business," *Clarion-Ledger*, Gannett News Service, September 6, 1998, Section H, p. 1.

Bibliography

Adoption Assistance and Child Welfare Act of 1980 (P.L. 96-272)42 U.S. C. 601, 94 Stat. 505, 1980.

Aid to Families with Dependent Children: The Baseline. Office of Human Services Policy Office of the Assistant Secretary for Planning and Evaluation. U.S. Department of Health and Human Services. June, 1998.

Alexelson, J. A. *Counseling and Development in a Multicultural Society*. 2nd ed. Pacific Grove, CA: Brooks/Cole, 1993.

Anthony, J. "One Church, One Child: Placing Children with Special Needs." *Children Today*. vol. 12, no. 2 (March/April, 1983): 6–10.

Azevedo, Mario, and Prater, Gwendolyn. *Africa and Its People,* Dubuque, IA: Kendall Hunt, 1982.

Berrick, J. D., Barth, R. P., & Needell, B., "A Comparison of Kinship Foster Homes and Foster Family Homes: Implications for Kinship Care as Family Preservation." *Children and Youth Services Review* 16 (1994): 33–63.

Billingsley, Andrew, *Black Families in White America*. New Jersey: Prentice-Hall, 1968.

_____ and Giovannoni, Jeanne M. *Children of the Storm: Black Children and American Child Welfare*. New York: Harcourt Brace Jovanovich, 1972.

Child Welfare League of America, *Too Young to Run: The Status of Child Abuse in America*. Washington, D.C.: 1996.

Children in the States 1997, Children's Defense Fund, p. 103; and *Mississippi Healthy Baby Update Newsletter 11* (June/July, 1998), Jackson, MS: Human Services Coalition.

Christmas, June Jackson. "The Health of African-Americans: Progress Toward Healthy People 2000," pp. 95–126 in *The State of Black America 1996*, New York: National Urban League, 1996.

Combating Complacency: HIV Prevention "Young People at Risk—Epidemic Shifts Further Toward Young Women and Minorities," Geneva, Switzerland, 1998. pp. 1–5.

Comer, James P. and Poussaint, Alvin F. *Black Child Care,* New York: Simon and Schuster, 1975.

Congressional Research Service Report for Congress: Child Care for Low-Income Families: Federal Programs and Welfare Reform. (Summary) by Karen Spar, Washington, D.C., updated October 7, 1996.

Daly, Alfrieda, Jeanette Jennings, Joyce O. Beckett, and Bogart R. Leashore. "Effective Coping Strategies of African-Americans." *Social Work* 40 (March 1995): 240–248.

Daniel, Jessica H.; Hampton, Robert L.; and Newberger, Eli H. "Child Abuse and Accidents in Black Families: A Controlled Comparative Study," *American Journal of Orthopsychiatry* 53 (October 1983): 645–653.

Dunn, Linda "Finding Permanent Homes for Black Children: The California Inland Area Urban League Project." *Children Today* 10 (September/October 1981): 16–18.

Edelman, Marion Wright. *Families in Peril: An Agenda for Social Change*. Cambridge: Harvard University Press, 1987.

Guidelines for Adoption Services to Black Families. Washington, D.C.: National Black Child Development Institute, 1987.

Hacker, Andrew. *Two Nations: Black and White, Separate, Hostile and Unequal*. New York: Ballatine Books, 1995.

Haight, Wendy L. "'Gathering the Spirit' at First Baptist Church: Spirituality as a Protective Factor in the Lives of African-American Children." *Social Work* 43 (May 1998): 213–221.

Highlights of Official Child Neglect and Abuse Reporting: 1986. Denver: American Humane Association, 1988.

Hill, Robert. *The Strengths of Black Families.* New York: National Urban League, 1972.

Hollingsworth, Leslie Doty. "Promoting Same-Race Adoption for Children of Color." *Social Work* 43 (March 1998): 104–116.

Hughes, Dana, and Butler, Elizabeth. *The Health of America's Black Children,* Marsha Meehan, ed. Washington, D.C.: Children's Defense Fund, 1988.

Jefferies, John M. and Schaffer, Richard L., "Changes in the Economy and Labor Market Status of Black Americans," pp. 12–77, Audrey Rowe and John M. Jefferies, eds., New York: National Urban League, 1996.

Johnson, Penny R., Shireman, Joan F., and Watson, Kenneth W. "Transracial Adoption and the Development of Black Identity at Age Eight. *Child Welfare* (January/February 1987): 45–55.

Judson, David. "Minorities Going For Business." *Clarion-Ledger.* Gannett News Service. September 6, 1998. Section H. p. 1.

Kenyatta, Jomo. *Facing Mount Kenya: The Traditional Life of the Gikuyu,* Nairobi: Heinemann, 1978.

Ladner, Joyce. *Tomorrow's Tomorrow: The Black Woman,* New York: Doubleday, 1971.

Martin, Joanne M., and Martin, Elmer P. *The Helping Tradition in the Black Family and Community.* Silver Spring, MD: National Association of Social Workers, 1987.

Maslow, Abraham. *Motivation and Personality,* New York: Harper and Row, 1970.

Multiethnic Placement Act of 1994, P.L. 103-382, 553, 108 Stat. 4057 (1995).

National Association of Social Workers, "Social Work Speaks: NASW Policy Statements," 4th ed., Washington, D.C.: NASW Press. 1997.

Nelson, Kristine E., Edward J. Saunders, and Miriam J. Landman. "Chronic Child Neglect in Perspective," *Social Work* 38 (November 1993): 661–671.

Nobles, Wade. "Africanity: Its Role in Black Families," *The Black Scholar* 5 (January/February 1975): 10–17.

Omnibus Budget Reconciliation Act of 1993, P.L. 103-66, 107 Stat. 312.

Personal Responsibility and Work Opportunity Reconciliation Act of 1996 (P.L. 104-193), 110 Stat. 2105 (1997).

Petit, Michael R. and Patrick A. Curtis. *Child Abuse and Neglect: A Look at the States 1997 CWLA Stat Book,* Washington, D.C.: CWLA Press, 1997.

Polansky, Norman. "Determinants of Loneliness Among Neglectful and Other Low-Income Mothers," *Social Service Review* (Spring 1985): 1–12.

Polansky, Norman A.; Ammons, Paul W.; and Gaudin, James W., Jr. "Loneliness and Isolation in Child Neglect," *Social Casework* (January 1985): 38–47.

Prater, Gwendolyn Spencer. "The Essential Ingredients of a Stable Family" in *Readings* on Black Children and Youth, Lula A. Beatty, ed., Washington, D.C.: Institute for Urban Affairs and Research, Howard University, 1986, pp. 49–72.

_____ and King, Lula T. "Experiences of Black Families as Adoptive Parents," *Social Work* 33 (November/December 1988): 543–545.

Rainwater, Lee. "Crucible of Identity: The Negro Lower-Class Family," *Daedelus* (Winter 1966): 172–215.

Report of the Child Welfare League of America National Task Force, Washington, D.C.: Child Welfare League of America, 1987.

Smith, Linda Anderson and Shirley P. Thrasher, "A Practice Approach for Working with Overwhelmed African-American Families," *Black Caucus* (Spring 1993): 1–10.

Solomon, Barbara Bryant. *Black Empowerment: Social Work in Oppressed Communities,* New York: Columbia University Press, 1976.

_____ and Helen A. Mendes, "Black Families from a Social Welfare Perspective," in *Changing Images of the Family,* Virginia Tufte and Barbara Myerhoff, eds., New Haven: Yale University Press, 1979, pp. 285–289.

_____. "Social Work with African Americans" in *Social Work: A Profession of Many Faces,* Armando Morales, and Bradford W. Sheafor, eds., Boston: Allyn and Bacon, 1998, pp. 541–561.

The State of Families 2: Work and Family. Milwaukee: Family Service America, 1987.

Study Findings: Study of National Incidence and Prevalence of Child Abuse Neglect: 1988. U.S. Department of Health and Human Services, Office of Human Development Services, Administration for Children, Youth and Families, Children's Bureau, National Center on Child Abuse and Neglect, Washington, D.C.: 1988.

Swinton, David. "The Economic Status of Blacks 1987," in *The State of Black America 1987,* Janet Dewart, eds., New York: National Urban League, 1987, pp. 49–73.

_____. "The Economic Status of Black Americans during the 1980s: A Decade of Limited Progress," *The State of Black America 1990,* Janet Dewart, eds., New York: National Urban League, 1990, pp. 25–52.

_____. "The Economic Status of African-Americans During the Reagan-Bush Era: Withered Opportunities, Limited Outcomes, and Uncertain Outlook," *The State of Black America 1993,* Billy J. Tidwell, ed., New York: National Urban League, 1993, pp. 135–201.

Thornton, J. L. "Permanency Planning for Children in Kinship Foster Homes," *Child Welfare* 70 (September/October 1991): 593–601.

Trends in the HIV & AIDS Epidemic. Centers for Disease Control and Prevention. Atlanta, GA. 1998.

U.S. Bureau of the Census. *Current Population Reports Series: Household and Family Characteristics.* P-20, No. 424. March 1987. Washington, D.C.: 1988: U.S. Government Printing Office.

U.S. Bureau of the Census. *Current Population Reports: Household and Family Characteristics.* March 1997. Washington, D.C., 1998: U.S. Government Printing Office.

U.S. Department of Health and Human Services, National Center on Child Abuse and Neglect. *Child Maltreatment 1996: Reports from the States to the National Child Abuse and Neglect Data System.* Washington, D.C., 1998: U.S. Government Printing Office.

Veronico, Anthony J. "One Church, One Child: Placing Children with Special Need," *Children Today* 12 (March–April 1983): 6–10.

Washington, Valora. "Community Involvement in Recruiting Adoptive Homes for Black Children." *Child Welfare* LXVI (January/February 1987): 57–68.

_____. *Families for Kids of Color: A Special Report on Challenges and Opportunities,* Battle Creek, MI: Kellogg Foundation, 1995.

5 Child Welfare and the American Indian Community

BY RITA LEDESMA
California State University, Los Angeles

AND PAULA STARR
Southern California Indian Center, Inc.

This chapter discusses issues associated with child welfare and the American Indian community. Child welfare is conceptualized broadly to include a range of issues that impact the growth and development of children and adolescents. Cultural values associated with this community emphasize a familial and collective orientation; therefore, analysis of issues focuses upon children in the context of family and community. For the purposes of this discussion, the authors will refer to members of the indigenous nations of this continent as American Indians and Alaska Natives. The term "native American" has become meaningless as a descriptor for communities with indigenous roots in the United States, because anyone born on the continents of North or South America can be labeled "native American." The issue about how to label the children, families, and communities that are the focus of this chapter reflects a long history of imprecision and misunderstanding that began when non-Natives first encountered the indigenous residents of this continent. The most accurate labels are those which describe the specific tribal affiliation of individuals, families, and nations. Readers are encouraged to recognize that great diversity characterizes "Indian country." However, shared cultural characteristics and socio-historical experiences buffer the differences between Indian nations and promote analysis of issues of concern to the Indian community.

Any examination of issues associated with this community must commence with a discussion of the social, political, and historical forces that influence the lives and opportunities of American Indian children and families. These forces fundamentally shape the course of life in American Indian and Alaska Native communities. American Indian and Alaska Native children experience many of the problems and issues which plague other poor children in this country, such as low educational attainment, limited employment opportunities, few community resources, adolescent pregnancy, substance abuse, poor health status, inadequate housing, and malnutrition. Their caregivers are frequently overwhelmed by a multitude of personal and environmental stressors that undermine capacities to cope and to parent. However, unique socio-historical and cultural conditions have influenced the development of problems and the identification of solutions. Historically, solutions to problems in Indian Country have been driven by policies established by the federal government. Socio-historical, political, and cultural variables are integrated in every facet of life in Indian Country. The development of knowledge about the child welfare issues impacting American Indian and Alaska Native children requires the examination of these issues.

Therefore, we will discuss contextual and demographic issues that influence individual and community development, cultural considerations, and a variety of issues significant for the health and well-being of American Indian children. These include: the Indian Child Welfare Act, health status, mental health, substance abuse and fetal alcohol syndrome, and educational status.

Contextual Issues

The American Indian experience differs from the experiences of all other minority groups within the United States. Examination of the contemporary experiences of American Indians and Alaska Natives cannot be disentangled from historical processes and forces, which are the consequences of contact with Europeans and Euro-Americans. The lives and opportunities of American Indians are fundamentally influenced by political and legal relationships that exist between Indian tribes as sovereign nations and federal and state governments (1). A report distributed by the Indian Health Service, which is an agency of the U.S. Public Health Service, Department of Health and Human Services, states: "This government-to-government relationship is based on Article I, section 8 of the United States Constitution, and has been given form and substance by numerous treaties, laws, Supreme Court decisions, and Executive Orders" (2). Indians are citizens of the United States and of a tribal nation. It wasn't until 1924, Congress granted American Indians U.S. citizenship. However, this action did not abrogate existing treaty rights (3). Treaties between Indian nations and the United States government identify and guarantee specific rights and obligations incurred by the United States in exchange for the appropriation of tribal land and resources. Reservations, established by the federal government as a means for confiscating and exploiting the traditional Indian land base, illustrate the government-to-government relationships and the sovereign nation status of American Indian tribes. However, Vine Deloria Jr. notes the contradictory nature of these relationship as follows: "The Indian tribal status is therefore a dubious blessing, conferring some benefits, but exacting a tremendous price in self-esteem and independence" (4). The contemporary problems found in "Indian Country" are rooted in the contradictory and ambivalent nature of these relationships. American Indians are members of "domestic dependent nations" (5) whose life opportunities have historically been influenced by the intrusion of non-natives into traditional life, by the federal government's willingness/unwillingness to honor treaty obligations and by the ambivalence nonnatives frequently demonstrate towards Indians. There is a tendency not to acknowledge three forms of government (federal, state, and tribal) within the United States.

The history of interactions between Indian nations and the U.S. government is marked by attempts to address the "Indian problem." These efforts have resulted in conflict, anguish, domination, accommodation, and adjustment. Federal policies have been established to address the "Indian problem." The "Indian problem" essentially relates to the difficulties non-Indians experienced in trying to identify how to co-exist with tribal communities and nations. Co-existence was complicated by differences in values, differences in the technologies available to assert power, and competition for natural resources. The federal policies of removal, reservation, relocation, and termination were attempts to address problems associated with co-existence and to deal with the "Indian problem."

The policy of removal formalized in the "Indian Removal Act of 1830" sought to assert authority over traditional American Indian land and resources through the forced exile of Indian communities and nations in the Eastern United States to areas east of the Mississippi. The notorious "Trail of Tears" which refers to the forced relocation of members of the Cherokee, Choctaw, Chickasaw, Creek, Seminole, Wyandotte, Ottawa, Peoria, Miami, Potawatomi, Sac, Fox, Delaware, and Seneca nations to the Oklahoma territories is an example of the relocation policy (6). Trafzer and Champagne note that this event "directly results in the death of four thousand to eight thousand people."

The reservation policy was designed to coerce the sale of American Indian lands to the U.S. government and to confine Indians to designated tracts of land.

This policy was implemented following the fierce resistance of many Indian nations who refused to accept the encroachment of non-natives into their land. Resolution of this conflict was not achieved through military strategies, despite the fact that military interventions resulted in war, battle, and the massacres of many Indian children and families.

According to Deloria, the reservation policy represented a shift in federal thinking about the "Indian problem" moving away from the notion that Indians and the "Indian problem" could be resolved by a geographical solution (7). Reservations offered the federal government the hope that Indians would adopt a sedentary lifestyle that non-Indian education could be provided to Indian children, and that assimilation could be promoted. Assimilation could be promoted, because life-sustaining traditional practices were forbidden, declared illegal and rendered difficult to realize given the nature of reservation life. The reservation policy also set the stage for assigning specific plots of land to Indian families and nations and for "freeing" huge tracts of land and resources for colonization by non-natives. This policy was imposed and implemented despite the reality that many Indians would not sign treaties nor accept the parcels of land offered by the federal government. Continued resistance on the Plains culminated in the Ghost Dance Movement and the Wounded Knee Massacre in 1890 in which more than three hundred men, women and children were killed by the Seventh Cavalry (8).

In the years between the implementation of the reservation and the relocation policies that followed World War II, critical developments occurred within Indian country. Education in boarding schools located off the reservation was mandated for Indian children as a mechanism for facilitating assimilation. The objective of the boarding schools was to destroy the fabric of cultural life for American Indian children by removing children from families and tribal communities, by forbidding children to speak native languages and by preventing the practice of traditional behaviors. The mission of the boarding schools remained relatively intact until the 1960s. Significant numbers of Indian children were raised in institutions relatively hostile to traditional life, away from family and community. The long-term impact of this practice had significant implications on the parenting capacities of those adults who were raised in these settings. As noted earlier, American Indians were declared citizens of the United States in 1924. In 1928, the Merriam Report cataloged the significant problems confronting American Indians. These included "deplorable" conditions on reservations, high rates of infant mortality and infectious disease, the failure of boarding schools to provide adequate living conditions and educational success, poverty, and malnutrition (9). In 1934, the "Indian Reorganization Act" mandated the development of tribal governments modeled after non-native structures and promoted economic development. During the Second World War, American Indian men made significant contributions to the war effort. Especially notable were the contributions of the Navajo and Comanche "Code Talkers" who developed a code (based on the Navajo and Comanche language) that allowed the U.S. military to communicate efficiently in the various theaters of the South Pacific.

The policy of relocation (Bureau of Indian Affairs Relocation Act), after World War II was implemented to promote assimilation by relocating Indians from reservations to urban communities. It was developed in response to the failure of reservations to assimilate American Indians into the fabric of the dominant culture. Relocation was an attempt by the Federal government to terminate responsibilities to Indians on reservations by encouraging movement to urban communities. It was believed that additional opportunities (jobs, housing, education) would be available to Indians in urban environments and that these opportunities would facilitate assimilation and end dependence upon the federal government.

As a result of these policies, approximately 160,000 Indians were relocated to major urban communities, such as Chicago, Los Angeles, Denver, New York, and Seattle. Some Indians floundered in the urban environment, because opportunities were not always accessible and because of the losses incurred in moving away from tribal communities. The separation from tribal and family support systems created profound loss that was difficult to manage in isolation. The cultural differences between Indians and non-Indians created distance and separation between people that was often difficult to bridge. Additionally, the strength and pull of cultural variables associated with tribal communities undermined the assimilationist goals of the policy. While some Indians adapted to life in urban communities, adaptation did not necessarily equal assimilation. Culturally based behaviors, beliefs, and practices did not disappear, because individuals were removed and separated from reservation communities. Many American Indians retained ties to "home" and recreated tribal organizations and support systems in the urban environment. These processes led to what has been identified as the urban "pan-Indian" experience wherein differences in tribal practices and productions are balanced by cultural values, beliefs, and behaviors held in common across tribes. The relocation and urban experience also gave birth to national organizations that focus on intertribal advocacy and leadership in Indian Country.

Termination was an attempt to end sovereign nation status and end federal responsibilities toward American Indians and Alaska Natives. This policy represented an effort to fundamentally contain and limit federal obligations to Indian people in spite of treaty guarantees. This era began in 1953 with the "Termination Resolution" when the federal government sought to abrogate treaties, alter the sovereign nation status of Indian communities, terminate Federal responsibilities with regard to the provision of services on reservations, and allow states to assume jurisdiction over elements of reservation life (10). Several tribes were decertified and lost federal recognition and the guarantee of federal services during this era. Indian organizations mobilized against these efforts to break the contract that existed between Indian nations and the federal government. They were joined by various state administrations who feared that the policy would create "higher state service costs to Indians" (11).

During the 1960s there was an infusion of funds to reservation communities as a result of the War on Poverty. These funds were released for the development of programs and activities that would address the pervasive poverty which marked "Indian Country." Conditions on many reservations were worse than conditions in the poorest communities of Mississippi and Appalachia. The most recent policy of self-determination, epitomized by the "Indian Self-Determination and Educational Assistance Act of 1975," sought to change the focus of policy from efforts to "civilize" the Indian and to change the role of the Bureau of Indian Affairs (12). This was accomplished by encouraging and promoting tribal leadership, decision-making, and control over resources. Tribal communities and Indian organizations were allowed to assume their rightful positions in determining the course of Indian life. However, the capacity to self-determine is related to the resources available to support decisions and the path charted. Indian Country confronted contractions in the exercise of self-determination, because many resources remained under federal jurisdiction and control. For example, American Indians and Alaska Natives are entitled to health care from the Indian Health Service. These services may be provided directly by IHS or a tribe may contract these services from IHS. However, many Indians living off the reservation and in urban communities are unable to access these services unless they are able to travel to locations where these services are provided, because federal monies for services do not always follow Indians off the reservation.

Contemporary conditions in Indian Country are the consequences of more than two hundred years of contact. Federal policies have directly and indirectly influenced the lives and opportunities available to Indian children and families. Litigation is a constant factor as American Indian and Alaska Native nations continue to seek redress for historical injustices and to secure guarantees that federally mandated obligations and agreements are implemented. The Indian Child Welfare Act (which will be discussed in greater detail later) is one example of the intersection of policy and litigation.

Tribal communities experienced disease, dependence, and political/cultural disorganization as a result of contact and federal policy. Disease and death were intentionally introduced to indigenous communities as a mechanism for gaining control over resources valued by non-natives (13). The health status of American Indians is compromised by the consequences of contact as American Indians and Alaska Natives were disenfranchised from a traditional life, which supported the health and well-being of the tribal community. Tribal nations' dependence emerged with the separation from life-sustaining environments and as traditional practices were declared illegal. Disorganization unfolded as an outcome of removal policies and the forced reorganization of traditional political infrastructures. Despite the brutal consequences of contact with non-Indians and the countless deaths of American Indian and Alaska Native children, men, and women, many American Indian communities were able to resist, accommodate, and survive. Many Indian families and tribal communities remain strong and vibrant, because the cultural system that supported daily life survived. Culture continues to exist as a resource for managing the multitude of adversities that permeate Indian Country. Despite all efforts to extinguish the "Indian problem," American Indians and Alaska Natives remain a valued resource to one another and to the dominant society, because their culture was not extinguished.

American Indians and Alaska Natives remain members of sovereign nations whose histories and cultures pre-date European contact. American Indian children who are growing up on reservations today are doing so, because years ago a policy was developed which mandated the creation of reservations. The struggles of American Indian and Alaska Native adults who confront problems with unemployment, alcohol, poverty, and parenting cannot be understood without understanding the socio-environmental conditions and the policy decisions that influenced the circumstances of their development. Such policy decisions continue to impact American Indians and Alaska Natives in profound and direct ways. Examination of current issues requires knowledge and understanding of historical processes and the relationship between past and present circumstances. We encourage students interested in working within this community to seek out additional information and material to supplement the introduction provided here.

Demographic Issues and Health Statistics

Despite similarities in cultural values, beliefs, practices, and productions and a shared history of contact with the Europeans and the United States government, there is much heterogeneity in Indian Country. Evidence of diversity is noted with regard to: tribal affiliation, language, landbase, social and political history and access to resources. Indian Country includes 554 federally recognized tribal groups, 304 federal reservations, and over 100 non-federally recognized groups. Each nation has its own history, cultural traditions, and practices. However, despite the heterogeneity found within Indian Country, similarities exist with regard to the fundamental belief systems associated with tribal communities.

Census data from 1990 indicates that 1,959,234 American Indians and Alaska Natives were identified (14). The following information is derived from data disseminated by the Indian Health Service (15). The majority of this population is concentrated in the western United States on reservations and in communities adjacent to reservations. A significant number, 65 percent of the 1990 Census of American Indians are living in urban communities; approximately 77,000 reside in the greater Los Angeles and Orange County communities of California. According to the Indian Health Service, American Indians and Alaska Natives are younger, less educated, and more impoverished than the U.S. all races population. Data from the IHS indicates that the birthrate and the infant mortality rate are higher than the U.S. all races rate. The death rate is 35 percent greater that the overall U.S. rate. Significant differences between Indian and overall U.S. rates are identified in the examination of specific causes of death. For example, the following causes of death occur at rates which are significantly greater than the overall U.S. rates:

Alcoholism—579 percent greater

Tuberculosis—475 percent greater

Diabetes mellitus—231 percent greater

Accidents—212 percent greater

Suicide—70 percent greater

Homicide—41 percent greater

Malignant neoplasms—15 percent less

Human Immunodeficiency virus (HIV) infection—72 percent less (16).

These findings indicate that some adult caregivers of American Indian and Alaska Native children are at great risk to die from preventable and treatable conditions which are associated with socio-economic and psychosocial conditions. The American Indian and Alaska Native population is notable for its youth, poverty, and the impact of the social environment upon life opportunities and individual, family, and community development. The capacity to appreciate the struggles and strengths of this community is strengthened as one develops knowledge about the social problems and issues plaguing the community.

Cultural Considerations

Cultural diversity is evident within Indian Country with regard to the beliefs, values, productions, and practices of specific tribal nations. Cultural values and belief systems are acted out in culturally based practices and productions. For example, the belief in a Creator and the value of giving thanks to the Creator can give rise to particular kinds of ceremony and specific types of songs wherein the belief and the value are actualized in behavior. It influences how individuals and communities experience daily life. It includes the beliefs, values, practices, and productions which belong to a community and forms a recognizable pattern that is transferred from elder to child, that is passed from generation to generation. This cultural system is transferred through culturally based religious, healing, linguistic, artistic, educational, and organizational activities. Culture influences world view, identity, social roles, rules, and rituals. In American Indian and Alaska Native communities, evidence of these processes can be seen in the cultural values, belief systems, oral histories, stories, dances, family/community traditions, relational styles, and communication patterns of members of the community.

Culture influences how people perceive the world and one another and how people interact with each other. For American Indians and Alaska Natives, beliefs, behaviors, relational styles, and communication patterns are grounded in cultural values that are shared across Indian Country. According to Blanchard, these values include cooperation, sharing, generosity, respect, harmony, spirituality, and veneration of elders (17). The importance of values such as respect, interdependence, and a collective orientation are illustrated in the concept of the "Seventh Generation" as discussed by Oren Lyons. He describes how reciprocity, interdependence, responsibility, and obligation characterize relationships between generations, when he notes that all actions and decisions made by the present generation must consider and protect the interests of the seventh generation to

follow in order that contemporary resources are available to succeeding generations (18). Culture also identifies what is important or unimportant to a community. Social workers, particularly in their work with children and families, must
strive to elicit information and interpret behavior from the point of view of the
client. This can only be done after one develops knowledge about the cultural values, beliefs, practices, and productions of a community. It is necessary to also
develop some knowledge about how culture is experienced in the lived reality of
an individual's or community's life and how competing cultural systems co-exist.

American Indian and Alaska Native communities have accommodated Western political, social, and cultural arrangements within traditional infrastructures.
This accommodation results in the process of biculturation wherein individuals,
families, and communities are exposed to the cultural expectations and skills necessary for functioning in traditional and non-traditional settings. An individual
becomes "bicultural" based on their acculturation rate when she/he has internalized expectations and developed the appropriate skills that promote movement
between both cultures and the ability to negotiate differences between the two cultures. However, biculturation is not an absolute, not everyone becomes bicultural
to the same degree and on the same schedule in a given community or family.

It is useful to think of individuals, families, and communities as located on a
cultural continuum that extends from the traditional to the non-traditional. This
continuum includes the values, beliefs, practices, and productions that are associated with both traditional and non-traditional cultures. Individuals, families, and
communities are usually not located in a static position; situational demands and
conditions influence where one sits on this continuum at any given time. Therefore, movement is possible along this continuum. Culturally based values and
behaviors can conceptually be identified along the cultural continuum. These
influence preferences, choices, relational styles, and communication patterns. Values and behaviors associated with the home culture may reflect more traditional
characteristics, while those associated with the work culture may reflect the non-
traditional culture. An example can be found in the choices an individual might
make with regard to work and family. Since family relationships and children are
highly valued within the traditional community, it is possible that these relationships would be paramount in an individual's life even at the expense of career
development. Thus, one's intimate life may be located on the more traditional side
of the cultural continuum, and one's work life may be located on the more non-
traditional side. The example also illustrates another issue associated with biculturation and the cultural continuum. Individuals, families, and communities can
experience cultural conflicts and cultural dissonance, wherein the traditional and
non-traditional cultures compete against or contradict one another. Cultural conflicts and cultural dissonance affect developmental processes, specifically those
associated with attachment, affiliation, and identity formation.

Another important issue concerns the viability of traditional culture. Many
assume that because the traditional life no longer exists intact as it did hundreds
of years ago, that cultural values, beliefs, practices, and productions no longer
exist. American Indians exhibit living cultures. Culture is woven into the social

and structural fabric of a people and continues to exist even as the social and structural fabric is changed. The manifestations of culture change to reflect the lived reality where the culture is situated, because culture is dynamic and ever evolving. However, traditional cultural systems can remain consistent and intact with core elements relatively unchanged even in changed circumstances and with the infusion and influence of non-traditional systems. Conversely, core elements of traditional culture can be lost, modified, and distorted given the influence of changed circumstance and competing cultural systems.

It is clear that a significant number of American Indian and Alaska Native cultures did not survive the assaults experienced at the hands of non-Indians. However, it is also clear that core elements of the cultures of many Indian nations have survived and accommodated in response to contact. Core elements of cultural systems have been renewed. Some elements were never lost, despite attempts to criminalize practices and to extinguish the cultural fabric of the people. There is ample evidence that Indian culture has endured and that similarities in American Indian and Alaska Native nations can be found in the fundamental belief systems, history, and consequences of contact with non-Indians and in the processes of cultural accommodation and survival (19). This allows examination and analysis of issues affecting American Indian and Alaska Native children and families from a cultural perspective. This is a significant development, because this promotes understanding of the role of culture as a resource and strength. Knowledge about the many facets of culture must be integrated in the assessment of strengths, in the identification of problems confronting Indian children and families, and in the design and development of services and interventions.

As noted previously, similarities exist in cultural systems across Indian Country. Several authors discuss cultural values and beliefs from an intertribal perspective that discusses the common themes found across the cultural systems of specific nations and communities (20). The core values and beliefs identified in this literature about American Indian and Alaska Native communities include the following concepts:

1. Humans are multi-dimensional, composed of spirit, mind and body.
2. Plants, animals and nature share equal status with humans.
3. A supreme "Creator" is acknowledged as a giver and sustainer of life. Additional spirit helpers exist who model appropriate relational styles and provide support and guidance.
4. Individuals are responsible for their behavior.
5. Harmony and balance are necessary for sustaining life.

These elements give rise to additional values: interdependence, a collective orientation, respect, equality, generosity, patience, autonomy, personal responsibility, cooperation, veneration of elders, mutuality, modesty, discipline, tranquility, orientation to the present, and allegiance to kin. These, in turn, influence interactions, relationships, and behaviors. Relational styles and culturally sanctioned behaviors include a preference for developing observational and listening skills, maintaining clearly delineated divisions of labor and social responsibilities, teaching through modeling and by example, and interactions characterized by sharing, caring, and non-interference.

This set of culturally based values, beliefs, and behaviors is rooted in a familial and collective orientation. It has been noted that "the extended family support system is of ultimate importance" and "to be really poor in the Indian world is to be without relatives" (21). Family is conceptualized as a core value, and family includes immediate, biological, and extended kin relationships, community, clan, tribe, and nation. Within the circle of family, children have a special, almost sacred, status. Children have long been conceptualized as "our most precious resource." Family attachments (through kin, clan, and tribal relationships) shape identity, identify responsibilities, offer support, sustenance and comfort, reduce isolation, and link the present and past. This attachment promotes a strong and healthy sense of self and affiliation with the tribal community. The creation stories of tribes promote the family and community orientation and offer guidance about how one can operationalize this orientation in daily life through caring and nurturing behaviors in respectful and reciprocal relationships.

The concepts of balance and harmony are also critical to the cultural systems of American Indians and Alaska Natives. Notions about "health" offer an example of this process in that health refers to a state of balance and harmony across all dimensions of life: mind, spirit, and body. Each is necessary to sustain life and wellness (22). Illness is present when mind, spirit, or body lack harmony and balance. Many of the issues currently creating "at-risk" status for American Indian and Alaska Native youth can be understood as caused by the absence of balance and harmony. Joe has described one method for addressing this: "notions of interrelatedness and harmony are illustrated in dances and healing ceremonies that seek to reaffirm the oneness with the universe and restore harmony as a part of treating illnesses and misfortune" (23). Certainly, the multiple adversities affecting Indian youth when conceptualized from a cultural perspective can be understood as "illnesses and misfortunes" and as evidence of a loss of harmony and balance. Therefore, culturally appropriate interventions designed to address the problems confronting American Indian youth should incorporate activities that restore balance and harmony and that maintain the natural order of life (24).

Families, balance, harmony, and the natural order of American Indian cultural systems have been assaulted by interactions with Europeans and Euro-Americans. There is a long historical record containing evidence that interactions between these two groups have resulted in the loss of traditional relationships, the life-sustaining land base, and in the deaths of countless people from disease, starvation, poverty and violence. Contemporary socio-economic conditions and problems impacting American Indian children and families are fundamentally related to the social, economic, and political consequences of contact and to ruptures in the cultural fabric of the people. The pressures of assimilation, acculturation, oppression, and isolation have undermined the productive expression of values. However, while cultural systems have been assaulted, they have not vanished nor have they been rendered powerless as a support for the people.

Indeed, cultural values are perceived by many within Indian Country as a vital resource for promoting the well-being of American Indian and Alaska Native children, families, and communities (25). The survival of Indian peoples in the last 400 years offers evidence of the viability of traditional cultural systems. Cultural values and expectations have survived and been passed down through countless generations in the oral traditions of the people. The creation stories document the group's history, identify values and behaviors necessary for a healthy life, provide moral prescriptions, and set guidelines for managing daily life. The creation stories identify the behaviors necessary for the growth and survival of the people. Contemporary Indian cultural values, beliefs, practices, and behaviors reflect the traditional and spiritual orientation of the creation stories. From this perspective, culture operates as a resource and strength in addressing the multitude of problems confronting Indian children and families. One American Indian service provider summarized these issues as follows:

> *The value of family, extended family, family gatherings, the closeness of your people is really important. The values of community and sharing, being generous with one another, the value of cooperation and the spiritual values of carrying on traditions are important. You see this in how people live and in how they treat one another, in giving thanks. These values are important, because they are very centered; they have carried on for many years. They are not values that are part of a cultural movement that exists just for the moment. They are values that offer comfort when they are practiced and lived. The values I've talked about are important to pass onto children, because that's how the culture continues, that's how you deal with daily life, through passing on the traditional values (26).*

The capacity to reflect upon the intersection of child welfare and the American Indian community requires knowledge of the social, historical, and cultural development of the community. One must become familiar with the role that policy continues to play in determining the life opportunities and the resources available to Indian children and families as they construct life on and off the reservation. Familiarity with the cultural life of Indians is critical in developing accurate assessments of strengths and problems and in the design of culturally based interventions.

Children's Issues

American Indian and Alaska Native communities are notable for high rates of poverty and an absence of opportunities. The most vulnerable members of the community bear the brunt of disadvantage and disenfranchisement that are the outcome of impoverishment. Examination of the issues confronting children in Indian Country is testament to this. This section will discuss several issues that affect the quality of life and the well-being of Indian children including educational issues, health status, mental health, substance abuse and Fetal Alcohol Syndrome, and the Indian Child Welfare Act.

Educational Issues

Prior to contact with Europeans and Euro-Americans, the education of Indian children occurred within a community context. Children learned the necessary skills for survival in their community through observing behavior modeled by adult caregivers. The creation stories of the people offered moral guidance and instructions for living through the oral tradition. Learning and education was a process that was integrated into daily activities. The history of the education of American Indian children after contact offers insights about how Indians were perceived by non-natives.

Post contact, responsibility for educating Indian children was assigned to religious organizations that had the mission of promoting civilization and Christianity to Indian nations. During the reservation era, formal education was provided through the day schools and the boarding school system. By 1868, there were 109 schools offering academic, religious, and practical instruction to more that 4,600 students. All students were expected to perform manual labor and in so doing to learn how to work in the manner of non-natives. Initially, day schools offered this instruction, but it soon became apparent that the assimilationist objectives of the educational system were undermined by the continued contact that children had with families and tribal communities.

Carlisle Indian School, founded in 1879, was the first off-reservation institution to execute the objective of isolating Indian children from their families and tribal communities and of restricting contact between children and their families. The model implemented at Carlisle emphasized religious instruction, academic training, and institutional labor was adopted by other boarding and mission schools in subsequent years. It was common that children would attend boarding school for many years. Luther Standing Bear, who was a student in the first class at Carlisle, offers his thoughts about the experience:

> At last at Carlisle the transforming, the 'civilizing' process began. It began with clothes. Never, no matter what our philosophy or spiritual quality, could we be civilized while wearing the moccasin and blanket . . . Almost immediately our names were changed to those in common use in the English language . . . I was told to take a pointer and select a name for myself . . . We were forbidden to speak our mother tongue, which is the rule in all boarding-schools. This rule is uncalled for, and today is not only robbing the Indian, but America of a rich heritage . . . Of all the changes we were forced to make, that of diet was doubtless the most injurious . . . But, the change in clothing, housing, food, and confinement combined with lonesomeness was too much, and in three years nearly one half of the children from the Plains were dead and through with all earthly school. In the graveyard at Carlisle most of the graves are those of little ones (27).

The off-reservation boarding school was the primary mechanism for offering education to Indian children until the 1920s.

However, the Merriam report documented the many failures and inadequacies of the off-reservation educational system. Therefore, reservation schools established by missionaries and the federal government provided both day and boarding school education. Despite offering children shelter, food, training, and education, boarding schools essentially remained agents of control in Indian Country. Poverty and a lack of transportation contributed to an increase in the number of students who attended boarding schools through the 1970s. Indian parents had few significant opportunities to voice concerns about the educational process or to become involved in the education of their children until passage of the Indian Education Act of 1972 and the Indian Self-Determination and Education Assistance Act of 1975.

Despite the development of public schools, the infusion of resources and greater tribal control over the educational process in the last 20 years, Indian children continue to experience low educational attainment and drop-out rates remain relatively high. Swisher notes that "Indian students continue to rank among the lowest of all demographic groups in terms of academic achievement and the highest of all groups for rates of leaving school . . . these issues involve a multitude of complex, sociocultural cause and effect relationships that are not easily sorted out and resolved" (28). Additionally, large numbers of children experience learning disabilities that impinge upon academic success. Educational deficits impact occupational success and socioeconomic development, while poverty status undermines educational success.

Until recently, the education of American Indian children was directed towards promoting assimilation and separating children from their culture. The Boarding School movement left a legacy of trauma, separation, and pain. This legacy has negatively impacted the caregiving capacities of adults who were raised in institutions. The contemporary movement that has allowed Indians to exert greater control over the education of Indian children has existed for only a relatively short period of time. This time span has been insufficient to remedy the legacy of an educational system that was fundamentally hostile to the culture and identity of Indian children.

However, we continue to find evidence of the strength, determination, and viability of American Indian culture and the American Indian community in this educational history. Indian children in boarding schools cared for one another; generations of children are bonded to their elders because each has experienced and survived the same trauma. The most recent educational initiatives integrate cultural knowledge in the academic arena and promote the development and success of the community in this process. President Clinton signed an Executive Order in 1998 to increase the funding for Indian Education. It is a hopeful attempt to raise the academic achievement for all American Indians in the education process.

Health Status

The literature indicates that American Indian children are at risk for infectious diseases and conditions that no longer pose threats for other children (29). For example, otitis media (infection of the middle ear) and gastrointestinal and upper respiratory infections are major problems on reservations. Otitis infections are associated with hearing loss, which ultimately affects developmental processes and school performance, particularly in adolescence (30). Fetal alcohol syndrome, death, and serious injury resulting from accidents, developmental delays and disabilities associated with poverty, and inadequate prenatal and well-baby care, depression, psychological difficulties, suicide, and substance and inhalant abuse are critical problems for Indian children (31). Diabetes and substance abuse create high-risk pregnancies and additional risks for developmental delay and disability (32). Indian Health Service (IHS) reports that the infant mortality rate in their service areas is 26 percent higher that the U.S. all races rate, and that the leading causes of infant death are sudden infant death syndrome, congenital anomalies, accidents and adverse effects, respiratory distress syndrome, and disorders related to prematurity and low birthweight (33). These conditions result in the premature death of Indian children; those children who survive infancy face an overall health status that is significantly lower than non-Indian children and that undermines development in early childhood and adolescence.

These findings indicate that the health status of American Indian and Alaska Native children is dramatically different from non-Indian children. This occurs despite entitlement to health services provided by the Indian Health Service. The health of a community and its children is related to social and demographic variables. When these variables exert a negative influence upon the community, they can be conceptualized as hazardous conditions, which are frequently associated with poverty and oppression. Hazards, such as poverty, low educational status, joblessness, substance abuse, poor nutrition and malnutrition, inadequate housing, economic underdevelopment, poor sanitation and water supply systems, and toxic environments adversely impact the health and well-being of Indian children and the future of American Indian communities.

The majority of Indian people are generally dependent upon the Indian Health Service for health care, cutbacks in funding pose specific threats to the community. Consumers of IHS health care must frequently travel great distances to health care sites on the reservation; individuals living off the reservation are not guaranteed easy access to health clinics or hospitals. These issues result in access barriers that further erode the health status of Indian children. This discussion of the health status of American Indian children has emphasized biomedical and physiological processes. Readers are reminded that from an American Indian cultural perspective, "health" refers to mind, spirit, and body and a state of balance and harmony across each. However, the biomedical issues, which undermine the physiological health of Indian children also, impact spiritual and emotional well-being. The health status of American Indian children must be understood in context. Analysis of issues must include attention to the influence of socio-environmental conditions upon the health status of the community. The role that policy plays as a causative factor or as a problem-solving mechanism must be acknowledged. Attention must be focused upon identifying issues from a cultural perspective and from the point of view of the community itself. Finally, strategies for resolving problems must build upon the strengths of the clients and the community and integrate cultural knowledge in the design and delivery of services.

Mental Health Status

One limitation in the discussion of the mental health status of this population is the paucity of empirical research focused on American Indian children and methodological problems associated with existing research. Many research designs have used instruments and protocols that are culturally biased. Research that examines the experiences of children living in non-reservation settings is very limited. Large national epidemiological studies that comprehensively investigate the mental health status of American Indian and Alaska Native children have not been initiated. However, data from IHS and review of the literature indicates that anxiety, depression, suicidal ideation, and suicide are significant mental health issues for Indian children; the literature has also noted increased rates of depression, anxiety, conduct disorders, delinquency, and suicide for Indian children as compared to non-Indian children (34). Testimony offered by the National Indian Child Welfare Association to the Senate Committee on Indian Affairs noted that "Indian adolescents have more serious mental health problems than all races' populations in the U.S. with respect to developmental disabilities, such as mental retardation and learning disabilities, depression, suicide, anxiety, alcohol and substance abuse, running away, and school drop-out (35).

Two significant variables implicated in each condition identified above are low self-esteem and low self-efficacy. Clinical practice indicates that individuals, across cultures, tend to experience depressed mood or anxiety when they are devalued by a dominant group and when they are unable to influence their environment. Depression and anxiety frequently mask frustration, sadness, and rage, and each emotion is associated with the experience of oppression. Children and adolescents who are raised in hostile and oppressive environments can also experience depression and anxiety; however, these emotions may manifest as internalized or externalized aggression. Conduct disorders and acting-out behaviors can be conceptualized as externalized aggression; substance abuse and suicide can be conceptualized as internalized aggression. Indian children are particularly vulnerable to emotional distress, because many are raised in impoverished environments or in hostile circumstances by caregivers whose adaptive capacities are compromised. The vulnerability of American Indian children is increased, because the larger society has been inattentive to their life circumstances and because federal policies are implicated as causative factors impacting their mental health status. The cumulative effect of these experiences negatively impacts self-esteem and self-efficacy and creates risk for depression, anxiety, acting out behaviors, substance abuse, and suicide.

As noted previously, definitions of health in Indian Country include attention to the mind, spirit, and body and the need for balance and harmony. Analysis of the mental health status of Indian children must attend to this definition if we are to promote appreciation of the perspective of those within the community. Research conducted with a select group of American Indian services providers in Los Angeles and Orange Counties examined these issues and found an association between culture and health, which indicated that "good health is associated with a positive sense of self and identity as an American Indian" (36). Identity formation is a developmental task and process associated with childhood and adolescence which takes place in a cultural environment. Therefore, the link between culture, health, and the development of a positive identity as an Indian is particularly critical in the examination of mental health issues affecting Indian children. The research cited above indicated that illness and poor health (including mental health) result when one "is out of kilter or lost the balance necessary for life," and one respondent stated:

> *There is an absolute connection between health and values, if your spiritual life is intact, then you will be healthy. If your mind is cluttered with unhappiness or confusion, if your life is out of balance, you will become sick. If your life is in harmony, if you are strong spiritually, you will be well. You can become sick physically or emotionally when you lose your values. The doctors might call this psychological. But, if you are separated from your family, if you are alone and away from people, life is very hard, because you lose support. Health and illness begin within, they have to do with how you feel inside, with your beliefs, with your choices. Some of our clients are so out of balance in these areas, they are always in crisis, always ill, and so, they give up (37).*

In this discussion, psychological and physical distress is associated with the loss of cultural supports and with the choices that individuals make when they are not affiliated with productive cultural systems. When these losses are experienced in childhood or early adolescence, a negative or unproductive identity may be adopted and poor life choices may result.

This research also indicated that the primary threats to the health and emotional well-being of Indian children are perceived as socioeconomic, environmental, and political. Poverty and the consequences of poverty, geographic isolation on reservations or in urban communities, and the politics of funding social policy undermine opportunities for Indians to affiliate with one another and to access needed services. However, poverty is associated with a multitude of experiences (such as joblessness, illiteracy, instability, substance abuse, violence, powerlessness, and shame) which undermine emotional well-being and create at-risk status for Indian children:

> *I truly believe that poverty is the greatest threat to the health of Indian people, and that is it is probably not so different for others. An infant or a young child may suffer, because the parents cannot appropriately meet their needs materially. Or they might suffer, because the parents are so distressed by what it takes to support the family that they can't give the child what it needs spiritually or emotionally. If the family remains in this condition, and if the family becomes isolated from a support system (which is frequently the case), then all kinds of other things can happen. The parent can behave abusively, against one another or the kids, they can use alcohol or drugs. This creates more stress and new complicated problems for the whole family. Even if none of this happens, at some point, the children and parents can begin to experience shame and humiliation about the way their life is, and by then the whole sys-*

tem is completely out of balance, and of course, their physical, emotional and spiritual health suffers. We just see this scenario all the time, yet many times there is still something that is holding them together (38).

American Indian children, who are poor or who have experienced generational poverty, are vulnerable to a host of interpersonal and social difficulties. These difficulties can manifest themselves as depression or aggression; they can negatively impact the process of identity formation; and they can promote risk of substance abuse or suicide. The eradication of poverty does not appear to be high on the social policy agenda, but the impact of poverty upon the mental health status of Indian children cannot be underestimated. However, providing Indian children and families with opportunities to affiliate with one another and to practice culturally based values and behaviors may neutralize some of the adversities associated with impoverishment. Appreciation for the mental health status of Indian children is promoted, when the analysis includes attention to contextual and cultural variables.

Strategies for addressing the mental health vulnerabilities and problems of American Indian children require commitment from federal and state agencies and the implementation of culturally based services. The testimony of the National Indian Child Welfare Association on this issue notes the dire need for additional resources given the incidence of depression, suicidality, poverty, child abuse, and substance abuse that plagues Indian Country. NICA cites a government report that indicates: "at least *397,000* children and adolescents were in Indian Health Service (IHS) service areas, yet IHS funded only *17* mental health providers trained to treat children and adolescents, a ratio of less than *one mental health provider to every 23,250 children and adolescents* (emphasis added) (39). This figure does not even include the resources available (or unavailable) to Indian children outside of IHS service locations. This gap in services is related to policy decisions that underfund vital resources that could be directed towards supporting and restoring the emotional, spiritual, and physical health of Indian children. The absence of a viable mental health service delivery system for American Indian children, on reservations and in urban communities, concretely undermines the health of Indian Country and creates risk that "the most precious resource" is denied the resources and opportunities necessary for growth and development.

Comprehensive, centralized, coordinated, and family-focused services, which are adequately staffed and funded and which integrate cultural values and practices, must be developed and implemented to address the overwhelming issues that impact the mental health status of Indian children. Resources are available within Indian country to ameliorate these problems. These include spirituality, ceremony, prayer, and operationalizing culturally based values and behaviors in daily life. There exist models for service delivery which integrate traditional healing practices and cultural knowledge with the prevailing treatment modalities in the mental health arena. These models can be replicated and evaluated to assess their utility in addressing the substantive problems that impinge upon the lives of Indian children.

An example of a model for a comprehensive service delivery system for Indian Child Welfare is located in Los Angeles County. One of the largest urban Indian

Centers in the nation, the Southern California Indian Center, Inc. (SCIC) has a myriad of services available to the Indian community. SCIC's Indian Child and Family Services, Education Component, Legal Assistance and the Advocates for American Indian Children network with Los Angeles County's Departments of Children and Family Services' American Indian Unit and the Indian Mental Health Program. It is vital to provide services designed to strengthen American Indian families and to keep Indian children in their own homes whenever possible. Networking and developing strong linkages in the area of policy making is crucial to the decisions that will affect the future of American Indian children. The cooperation of the Los Angeles County's Children and Family Services and Mental Health Program in working with a community-based Indian organization, SCIC, is an incubator for a healthier child. The success and support is greater when Indian organizations collaborate with county, state, and federal entities for what is truly in the best interest of the child.

Increased opportunities to exercise self-determination at the tribal and community level can help in the management of contradictions associated with politics and policy. Programs that offer opportunities for mentoring, modeling, and affiliation with other Indians can reduce social isolation and promote the acquisition of skills associated with productive functioning. While personal responsibility and accountability cannot be minimized, knowledge and resources are available within the cultural history and fabric of Indian communities to support the mental health of Indian children and the development of healthy identity.

Substance Abuse and Fetal Alcohol Syndrome

Substance abuse is frequently related to problems in living and psychosocial functioning. High rates of lifestyle diseases compromise the well-being of children and families in Indian Country. Alcoholism and diabetes are major health problems which result in developmental disability and delay and which shorten life expectancy. Indian Health Service data indicates that accidents, cirrhosis of the liver, suicide, and homicide (four of the top ten causes of death in Indian Country) are alcohol related (40). Some Indian children and adolescents have, unfortunately, followed the path of their caregivers; therefore, substance abuse data for Indian children indicates high rates of drug and alcohol use. The literature indicates that American Indian children begin use at an early age and that they abuse a variety of substances, including alcohol, drugs, hair spray, gasoline, spray paint, tobacco, and snuff (41). Their patterns of use differ from those of other children and the levels of abuse clearly represent a threat to physical, emotional, and spiritual well-being. The substances of choice for abuse, particularly inhalants, can cause irreversible organic damage. As this issue is analyzed, it is critical to be reminded of the multiple ways in which hazardous conditions (such as poverty, low educational status, ineffective caregivers, joblessness, inadequate housing, and lack of resources and opportunities) promote vulnerability for substance abuse in Indian children and adolescents.

The National Organization of Fetal Alcohol Syndrome defines fetal alcohol syndrome "as a series of mental and physical birth defects that can include mental retardation, growth deficiencies, central nervous system dysfunction, craniofacial abnormalities and behavioral maladjustments" and fetal alcohol effect as "a less severe set of the same symptoms" (42). FAS/FAE are the consequence of drinking during pregnancy, and they are implicated as a leading cause of the developmental delays and learning disabilities that compromise the life opportunities of Indian children. Dorris has stated that FAS is the leading cause of birth defects among Southwestern Plains groups, and he has indicated that alcohol abuse may be the most pressing problem affecting American Indians, impinging upon the development of future generations and pervasively affecting the development of afflicted children (43).

Unfortunately, the one area of American Indian life that has received attention from the dominant society in the popular press and the media is the high rate of alcohol abuse and the impact of FAS/FAE. While attention is needed to remediate substance abuse problems, substance abuse throughout the life course in Indian Country must be examined in context. Not every Indian child is born preexposed to alcohol or drugs; not every child experiments with substance abuse or becomes impaired and addicted. Despite the reality that it often seems that every family has been assaulted by alcohol, there are many caregivers of children who have not had or no longer have problems with substance abuse. The spotlight on the problem of Indian drinking has typically been understood as a symptom of individual pathology. Less attention has been focused upon analysis of the social and environmental circumstances that lead to substance abusing behaviors or the role of substance abuse as a functional, albeit unproductive and healthy, coping mechanism in a hostile environment.

There is an intersection of health, mental health, and substance abuse problems. Evidence of this is made visible in the examination of the causes of problems, the relationships between one problem and another, and in the design of interventions. Testimony offered by the National Organization for Indian Child Welfare supports this analysis in the following:

> There is a serious and persistent lack of funding for Indian children's mental health. No single system has assumed primary responsibility for this population. There is no equitable access by tribes for federal children's mental health and social funding. Native American children suffer a greater degree of environment and social stresses than mainstream culture children. Native American children appear to suffer from emotional disturbances as often as, if not more often that, mainstream culture children. Indian children suffer disproportionately from PTSD and fetal drug effects . . . Traditional healing practices are a vital and useful part of the mental health service delivery system that cannot currently be embraced as a part of the system of care due to mainstream cultural prohibitions and funding barriers. Traditional healing has the potential to be a dramatic resource in the successful treatment of Indian children (44).

Therefore, comprehensive and culturally based service delivery systems must be supported by policy and adequately funded if we are to improve the life opportunities for vulnerable Indian children.

The Indian Child Welfare Act

The Indian Child Welfare Act (ICWA) of 1978 was introduced into legislation after the American Indian Policy Review Commission made recommendations for Congressional changes for American Indians in the United States of America. The Task Force for the American Indian Policy Review Commission reported in 1976 the outline for ICWA. Prior to 1978, 1 out of 4 American Indian children were placed outside of their family and reservation. According to the Report, 25–35 percent of all Indian children were raised at some time by non-Indians in homes and institutions (45). The 1990 Census demographics for American Indian children (including Eskimo and Aleut) ages 0–20, indicate that 39 percent of the population was under 20 years old in 1990 compared with 29 percent of the Nation's total population.

The purpose of the ICWA is to determine "what is in the best interest of the child." When Congress passed the ICWA it stated, ". . . it is the policy of this Nation to protect the best interest of Indian children . . . by the establishment of minimum Federal standards for the removal of Indian children from their families and the placement of such children in foster or adoptive homes which will reflect the unique values of Indian culture . . ." (46). Unfortunately, according to Indian Health Services statistics in the 1980s, American Indian children who were raised out of the Indian culture and adopted by non-Indians had a higher rate of suicide. Physical genocide was the reason for the Indian wars during the 1700s and 1800s. Cultural genocide appears evident with the removal of Indian children placed into non-Indian homes and institutions. The hearings which preceded passage of ICWA, Congress found: (1) that Indian children are the most vital resource for the continued existence of Indian Tribes and therefore must be protected, (2) that an alarmingly high percentage of Indian families are broken up by the removal, often unwarranted, of children by public and private agencies and that an alarmingly high percentage of such children are then placed in non-Indian homes and institutions, and (3) that the States have failed to recognize the tribal social and cultural standards prevailing in Indian communities and families (47). Congress passed ICWA to correct the removal of Indian children.

In California, there are 39,579 Indian children under 21 years of age. One of every 26.3 or 1,507 of these Indian children have been adopted: 92.5 percent of these were adopted by non-Indian families. The adoption rate for non-Indian children is 1 out of every 219.8. There are therefore, by proportion, 8.4 times (840 percent) as many Indian children in adoptive homes as there are non-Indian children. There are 319 or 1 out of every 124 Indian children in foster care. The foster care rate for non-Indians is 1 out of every 366.6. There are therefore, by proportion 2.7 times (270 percent) as many Indian children in foster care as there are non-Indian children (48). Many other states have similar statistics reflecting the overwhelming amount of Indian children placed outside of the family and tribe.

The absence of specially designated court advocates for Indian families residing off reservation creates great risk for Indian families involved with the system. The lack of primary prevention services and activities, geographical distance and isolation, and poverty undermine the parenting capacities of Indian families. The attempts to erode the provisions of ICWA reflect the ambivalence that the federal government demonstrates when pressed to honor the sovereignty of Indian nations. The inability to secure funding and benefits from Title IV-E Foster Care and Adoption Assistance legislation limits the scope of child welfare services available to Indian children. The current preference for "fast-track" settlement of protective services cases can lead to premature termination of parental rights. ICWA offers guarantees that Indian nations can assert their authority in protecting the most vulnerable members of their communities.

ICWA is designed to promote changes with regard to how Indian children are protected and how Indian children are treated in the courts, adoption process, and foster care system. Ultimately, the desired goal is to keep Indian families intact whether it be through programs designed for family preservation, reunification, or what is truly in the best interest of the child. The American Indian relationship with the United States of America is unique. It is based on tribal sovereignty, the trust responsibility that lies in the Constitution, and Indian treaties. The Indian treaties were the first contracts with America, but somehow, over time, elected officials have forgotten. This chapter is a reminder to remember the Indian treaties, the U. S. Constitution, the Synder Act, the Indian Self-Determination Act, and Indian Child Welfare Act. American Indians are members of sovereign nations; only Indian tribes have the authority to determine who is a tribal member, not the states within the United States.

Despite the negative stories being told by the proponents of HR 3275, the ICWA is and has been successful in fulfilling Congress's intent, which was to halt the destruction of American Indian families, preserve and bring strength and stability to American Indian families. The Pryce amendment, if enacted, would turn back the clock on those efforts and result in numerous prolonged expensive lawsuits to the detriment of American Indian children and their families. No other cultural value is more important than the preservation of families.

Summary

This chapter has offered a brief introduction to the many issues which impact child welfare in the American Indian community. It is clear that Indian children and adolescents are stressed by a multitude of social and environmental conditions that threaten healthy growth and development. Indian children demonstrate great vulnerability on almost every demographic marker. Many of the vulnerabilities that Indian children confront are directly related to the losses experienced as a result of contact with non-natives, federal policy, relocation, and the boarding school legacy.

There is a need for more research that investigates the experiences of Indian children in reservation, rural, and urban communities. Yet, one cannot hope to accurately interpret these experiences without attention to the great diversity that characterizes Indian Country, without appreciation for the sovereign nation status of Indian communities, without knowledge of the role of federal policy, and without respect for the significance of culture. Therefore, students who wish to work in an Indian community are encouraged to undertake a course of study about the community. There are numerous books that discuss the Indian experience. There are wise teachers within each community who can offer knowledge about the specific history and issues associated with that community. There is a wealth of knowledge and expertise residing within each community.

Culture influences the social development of children and families and creates the context for life. Effective child welfare workers must develop the necessary skills for interpreting culture and evaluating its impact upon client functioning. Cultural knowledge must be integrated in the development of individual and family assessments and in the intervention/problem-solving process. The impact of socio-political history and the social environment upon the child and family's current circumstances must be examined. The design and development of comprehensive, family-focused, bicultural treatment and intervention approaches must be supported. Child welfare and social policies must strive to protect the legal and political rights of American Indians on and off the reservation; child welfare and social policies must acknowledge the role of culture, support the sovereign rights of Indian nations and the right to self-determination. Policy should ensure that resources available on the reservation are available to those members of the community who reside in urban or rural communities.

Children are acknowledged as "our most precious resource" within American Indian communities, although some children may not have needs appropriately met as a result of parental or social circumstance. Historically, children have been perceived as "sacred," treasured and vital members of the tribe and family. Children are a resource and an asset; they bridge the past and the future, and they are a symbol of hope and continuity. American Indian children should be treated as a valued resource to be nurtured and protected for the survival and future of the American Indian community.

> The hearts of little children are pure and therefore, the Great Spirit may show to them many things which older people miss. Black Elk, Oglala Lakota, C. 1949
>
> We do now crown you with the sacred emblem of the antlers, the sign of your lordship. You shall now become a mentor of the people of the Five Nations. The thickness of your skin will be seven spans, for you will be proof against anger, offensive action and criticism. With endless patience you shall carry out your duty, and your firmness shall be cast aside. You shall look and listen to the welfare of the whole people, and always in view, not only the present but the coming generations—the unborn of the future Nation. The Peace Maker, Iroquious Oral Tradition
>
> If today I had a young mind to direct, to start on the journey of life, and I was faced with the duty of choosing between the natural way of our forefathers and that of the present way of civilization, I would, for its welfare, unhesitatingly set that child's feet in the path of my forefathers. I would raise him to be an Indian! Luther Standing Bear, Lakota, 1933

Endnotes

1. J. Chaudhuri, "American Indian Policy: An Overview," pp. 15–34.

2. Indian Health Service, *Regional Differences in Indian Health*, p. 1.

3. C. Trafzor and D. Champagne, "Chronology" in *The Native North American Almanac*, p. 53.

4. Deloria, V. "The Evolution of Federal Indian Policy Making" in *American Indian Policy in the Twentieth Century*, p. 239.

5. Cherokee Nation v. Georgia, 30 U.S. (5 Pet.).1 (1931).

6. C. Trafzor and D. Champagne, "Chronology" in *The Native North American Almanac*, pp. 39–40.

7. Deloria, V. "The Evolution of Federal Indian Policy Making" in *American Indian Policy in the Twentieth Century*, p. 246.

8. C. Trafzor and D. Champagne, "Chronology" in *The Native North American Almanac*, p. 49.

9. Ibid., p. 52.

10. Ibid., p. 54.

11. Ibid., p. 54.

12. R. Nelson and J. Shelly, "Bureau of Indian Affairs Influence on Indian Self-determination" in *American Indian Policy in the Twentieth Century*, pp. 178–79.

13. L. Stiffarm and P. Lane, "The Demography of Native North America: A Question of American Indian Survival," pp. 23–54.

14. Bureau of the Census (1992) "1990 Census of Population: General Population Characteristics."

15. Indian Health Service, *Regional Differences in Indian Health*, pp. 1–5.

16. Ibid., p. 6.

17. E. Blanchard, "The Growth and Development of American Indian and Alaska Native Children" in *The Psychosocial Development of Minority Group Children*.

18. B. Moyers, *The Faithkeeper, A Conversation with Oren Lyons*.

19. E. Blanchard, "The Growth and Development of American Indian and Alaska Native Children" and J. Red Horse, "Indian Family Values and Experiences" in *The Psychosocial Development of Minority Group Children*.

20. E. Blanchard, "The Growth and Development of American Indian and Alaska Native Children" and J. Red Horse, "Indian Family Values and Experiences" in *The Psychosocial Development of Minority Group Children*; G. Guilmet and D. Whited, "The People Who Give More: Health and Mental Health Among the Contemporary Puyallup Indian Tribal Community" in *American Indian and Alaska Native Mental Health Research*; T. LaFromboise and D. Bigfoot, "Cultural and Cognitive Considerations in the Prevention of American Indian Suicide" *Journal of Adolescence*; C. Locust, "Wounding the Spirit: Discrimination and Traditional American Indian Belief Systems" in *Harvard Educational Review*; G. P. Sage, "Counseling American Indian Adults" in *Multicultural Issues in Counseling: New Approaches to Diversity*; T. Tafoya, "Circles and Cedar: Native Americans and Family Therapy" in *Journal of Psychotherapy and the Family*.

21. G. Guilmet and D. Whited, "The People Who Give More: Health and Mental Health Among the Contemporary Puyallup Indian Tribal Community," in *American Indian and Alaska Native Mental Health Research*.

22. C. Locust, "Wounding the Spirit: Discrimination and Traditional American Indian Belief Systems," in *Harvard Educational Review*.

23. J. Joe, "Health: Traditional Indian Health Practices and Cultural Views," in *Native American: Portrait of the Peoples*.

24. G. Guilmet and D. Whited, "The People Who Give More: Health and Mental Health Among the Contemporary Puyallup Indian Tribal Community," in *American Indian and Alaska Native Mental Health Research*; G. P. Sage, "Counseling American Indian Adults," in *Multicultural Issues in Counseling: New Approaches to Diversity*; T. Tafoya, "Circles and Cedar: Native Americans and Family Therapy," in *Journal of Psychotherapy and the Family*.

25. R. Ledesma, *Cultural Influences Upon Definitions of Health and Health Sustaining Practices for American Indian Children*.

26. Ibid., p. 102.

27. L. Standing Bear, *Land of the Spotted Eagle*, pp. 232–235.

28. K. Swisher, "Primary and Secondary U.S. Native Education," in *The Native North American Almanac*, p. 864.

29. P. May, "The Health Status of Indian Children; Problems and Prevention in Early Life," in *American Indian and Alaska Native Mental Health Research*.

30. C. Fleming, S. Manson, and L. Bergeisen, "American Indian Adolescent Health," in *Health Issues for Minority Adolescents*, p. 119.

31. B. Claymore and M. Taylor, "AIDS—Tribal Nations Face the Newest Communicable Disease: An Aberdeen Area Perspective," in *American Indian Culture and Research Journal*; M. Dorris, *The Broken Cord*; Indian Health Service, *Regional Differences in Indian Health*; T. LaFromboise and D. Bigfoot, "Cultural and Cognitive Considerations in the Prevention of American Indian Suicide," *Journal of Adolescence*; R. Ledesma, *Cultural Influences Upon Definitions of Health and Health Sustaining Practices for American Indian Children*; P. May, "The Health Status of Indian Children: Problems and Prevention in Early Life," in *American Indian and Alaska Native Mental Health Research*; D. McShane "An Analysis of Mental Health Research with American Indian Youth," *Journal of Adolescence*.

32. G. Campbell, "The Political Epidemiology of Infant Mortality," in *American Indian Culture and Research Journal*.

33. Indian Health Service, *Regional Differences in Indian Health*, pp. 33–36.

34. C. Fleming, S. Manson and L. Bergeisen, "American Indian Adolescent Health," in *Health Issues for Minority Adolescents*, pp. 120–130.

35. National Indian Child Welfare Association, "Testimony regarding the Mental Health Needs of Indian Children and Their Access to Mental Health and Related Services," p. 3.

36. R. Ledesma, *Cultural Influences Upon Definitions of Health and Health Sustaining Practices for American Indian Children*, pp. 134–146.

37. Ibid., p. 143.

38. Ibid., p. 149.

39. National Indian Child Welfare Association, "Testimony regarding the Mental Health Needs of Indian Children and Their Access to Mental Health and Related Services," p. 2.

40. Indian Health Service, *Regional Differences in Indian Health*.

41. C. Fleming, S. Manson and L. Bergeisen, "American Indian Adolescent Health," in *Health Issues for Minority Adolescents*, pp. 123–124; M. Dorris, *The Broken Cord*; Indian Health Service, *Regional Differences in Indian Health*; T. LaFromboise and D. Bigfoot, "Cultural and Cognitive Considerations in the Prevention of American Indian Suicide," *Journal of Adolescence*; R. Ledesma, *Cultural Influences Upon Definitions of Health and Health Sustaining Practices for American Indian Children*; P. May, "The Health Status of Indian Children: Problems and Prevention in Early Life," in *American Indian and Alaska Native Mental Health Research*; D. McShane, "An Analysis of Mental Health Research with American Indian Youth," *Journal of Adolescence*.

42. The National Organization on Fetal Alcohol Syndrome, "Fact Sheet."

43. M. Dorris, *The Broken Cord*.

44. National Indian Child Welfare Association, "Testimony regarding the Mental Health Needs of Indian Children and Their Access to Mental Health and Related Services," p. 11.
45. R. Orantia, "The Indian Child Welfare Handbook," p. 1
46. Ibid., p. 7
47. American Indian Policy Review Commission, Task Force Report, p. 7
48. R. Orantia, "The Indian Child Welfare Handbook," p. 2

Bibliography

American Indian Policy Review Commission, Task Force Report, 1976.

Blanchard, E. (1983). The Growth and Development of American Indian and Alaska Native Children in Powell, G. J. (ed.) *The Psychosocial Development of Minority Group Children*, New York: Brunner/Mazel, pp. 115–130.

Bureau of the Census (1992). *1990 Census of Population: General Population Characteristics*, Washington, D.C.: U.S. Government Printing Office.

Campbell, G. (1989). The Political Epidemiology of Infant Mortality. *American Indian Culture and Research Journal* 13:3–4.

Chaudhuri, J. (1985). American Indian Policy: An Overview, in Deloria, Vine Jr. (ed.), *American Indian Policy in the Twentieth Century*, Norman: University of Oklahoma, 15–34

Cherokee Nation *v.* Georgia, 30 U.S. 1 (5 Pet.) (1931).

Claymore, B., and M. Taylor (1989). AIDS—Tribal Nations Face the Newest Communicable Disease: An Aberdeen Area Perspective, *American Indian Culture and Research Journal*: 13:3–4.

Deloria, Vine Jr. (1985). The Evolution of Federal Indian Policy Making in Deloria, Vine Jr. (ed.) *American Indian Policy in the Twentieth Century*, Norman: University of Oklahoma.

Dorris, M. (1989). *The Broken Cord*. Harper and Row: New York.

Fleming, C., S. Manson, and L. Bergeisen (1996). American Indian Adolescent Health in Kagawa-Singer, M., P. Katz, D. Taylor, J. Vanderryn (eds.), *Health Issues for Minority Adolescents*, Lincoln: University of Nebraska Press.

Guilmet G., and D. Whited (1989). The People Who Give More: Health and Mental Health Among the Contemporary Puyallup Indian Tribal Community in *American Indian and Alaska Native Mental Health Research*. Monograph 2.

Indian Health Service, (1997) *Regional Differences in Indian Health*, U.S. Department of Health and Human Services, Washington, D.C.: U.S. Government Printing Office.

Joe, J. (1994) Health: Traditional Indian Health Practices and Cultural Views in Champagne D. (ed.) *Native American: Portrait of the Peoples*. Detroit, MI: Visible Ink Press, pp. 525–548.

LaFromboise T., and D. Bigfoot, (1988). "Cultural and Cognitive Considerations in the Prevention of American Indian Suicide," *Journal of Adolescence* 11, 139–153.

Ledesma, R. (1997) *Cultural Influences Upon Definitions of Health and Health Sustaining Practices for American Indian Children*. Ph.D. Dissertation: Los Angeles: University of California Los Angeles.

Locust, C. (1988). Wounding the Spirit: Discrimination and Traditional American Indian Belief Systems, *Harvard Educational Review* 58:3, 315–330.

May, P. (1988). The Health Status of Indian Children; Problems and Prevention in Early Life, *American Indian and Alaska Native Mental Health Research*. 1:244–289.

McShane, D. (1988). An Analysis of Mental Health Research with American Indian Youth, *Journal of Adolescence*. 11:87–116.

Moyers, B. (1991). *The Faithkeeper, A Conversation with Oren Lyons*, Public Broadcasting Service.

National Indian Child Welfare Association (1997). Testimony regarding the Mental Health Needs of Indian Children and Their Access to Mental Health and Related Services. Portland, Oregon.

The National Organization on Fetal Alcohol Syndrome (1998). *Fact Sheet.*

Nelson, R., and Shelly J. (1985) Bureau of Indian Affairs Influence on Indian Self-determination, in Deloria, Vine Jr. (ed.) *American Indian Policy in the Twentieth Century*, Norman: University of Oklahoma.

Orantia, Rose-Margaret (1991) *The Indian Child Welfare Act, A Handbook*, Sacramento: Bureau of Indian Affairs.

Red Horse, J. (1983). Indian Family Values and Experiences, in Powell, G. J. (Ed.) *The Psychosocial Development of Minority Group Children*, New York: Brunner/Mazel, pp. 258–271.

Sage, G. P. (1991). Counseling American Indian Adults, in Lee, C., and B. Richardson (eds.) *Multicultural Issues in Counseling: New Approaches to Diversity*, Needham, MA: Allyn and Bacon.

Standing Bear, L. (1978). *Land of the Spotted Eagle*, Lincoln: University of Nebraska Press.

Stiffarm L., and Lane P., (1992) The Demography of Native North America: A Question of American Indian Survival, in Jaimes, Annette (ed.), *The State of Native America: Genocide, Colonization and Resistance*, Boston: South End Press, pp. 23–54.

Swisher, K. (1994) "Primary and Secondary U.S. Native Education," in Champagne, D. (ed.), *The Native North American Almanac*, Detroit: Gale Research Inc.

Tafoya, T. (1989). Circles and Cedar: Native Americans and Family Therapy. *Journal of Psychotherapy and the Family* 6:71–98.

Trafzor, C., and Champagne, D. (1994), Chronology in Champagne, D. (ed.) *The Native North American Almanac*, Detroit: Gale Research Inc.

6

Child Welfare: Asian and Pacific Islander Families

BY AMY IWASAKI MASS
Whittier College, Emeriti

JOSELYN GEAGA-ROSENTHAL
Children's Service Administrator, Los Angeles

Because the cultural values and perspectives of Asians and Pacific Islanders are different from the Western democratic values and ideologies on which the child welfare system in the United States is based, some of the ways children are regarded are dissimilar from the U.S. norm, and differences in approaches to raising and nurturing children can be observed.

Most Asian immigrants, from the first Chinese who arrived in the United States in the 1840s to the more recent influx of Asian immigrants since the liberalized 1965 Immigration Laws, share traditional Asian perspectives on the centrality of the family unit. Traditional Asian families do not look upon their members as individuals, each with their own separate life and destiny. Instead, individuals are responsible to and for their family—in the past, the present, and the future. Values of group affiliation over individualism also characterize the perspectives of Pacific Islanders (1). Understanding such cultural differences is an important prerequisite to social work practice with Asian/Pacific families.

Gusukuma and McRoy (2) compare Asian-American and Anglo-American perspectives of children and family in Table 6.1:

TABLE 6.1   Asian Perspectives of Children and Family

Traditional Asian-American View	Anglo-American View
Children are extension of parents.	Children are individuals.
The family makes decisions for the child.	The child is given many choices.
Older children are responsible for their siblings' actions.	Each child is responsible for his or her own actions.
Children should submit to structure.	Children should think what's right for themselves.
Children should respond to and be sensitive to the environment.	The environment is sensitive and should respond to the child.
Young children do not have well-formed feelings or individual needs.	Young children have well-defined feelings and personalities.
Praise is not given for a job well done.	Praise and rewards are given for a job well done.
Children should not express anger, frustration or contempt.	It is better to vent anger and frustration then let it sit inside.
Punishment for discipline problems include shaming, withdrawing of love.	Punishment for discipline problem should have logical consequences, e.g., removing toys, cleaning up messes.
Questioning adults or asking why is not accepted.	Curiosity and individuation is encouraged.
Parents provide authority.	Parents provide guidance, support and explanations.

Diversity Among Asian Pacific Islanders

Reference to Asian/Pacific Americans as a single group is misleading, in that it conceals the enormous diversity and heterogeneity among the subgroups that comprise this ethnic category. A 1993 Public Policy Report (3) notes the growing population of Asian/Pacific Americans is made up of nearly 30 major ethnic groups. Table 6.2 shows the population of 10 of these Asian/Pacific ethnic categories in 1980 and 1990.

Americans of Asian/Pacific background represent a complex, pluralistic aggregate of national and cultural characteristics. They also represent a great diversity of nationalities, languages, and cultures. In addition, within each group they vary according to socioeconomic background and degree of Americanization or acculturation. There are differences between refugees and immigrants. There are differences in facility with the English language and adaptation to American life; differences by gender, age, education, and number of generations in the United States.

A Chinese American, for example, can be a college professor whose ancestors came to the United States over a century ago, or a non-English speaking widow who recently immigrated to the United States from Taiwan with her school-age children. A Filipino American can be an elderly, single, unskilled laborer who immigrated as a young man in the 1920s to fill the need for cheap, agricultural labor in the United States, or a highly skilled female physician who came to the United States in the late

TABLE 6.2 Asian/Pacific Americans Population by Ethnicity: 1980 and 1990

	1980	1990	Percent Growth
Total Asian/Pacific	3,726,440*	7,273,662	95%
Chinese	806,040	1,645,472	104%
Filipino	774,652	1,406,770	82%
Japanese	700,974	847,562	21%
Asian Indian	361,531	815,447	125%
Korean	354,593	798,849	125%
Vietnamese	261,729	614,547	135%
Hawaiian	166,814	211,014	26%
Samoan	41,948	62,964	50%
Guamanian	32,158	49,345	53%
Other Asian Pacific	226,001	821,692	264%

*The 1980 number for Asian/Pacific Americans in this table is slightly higher than that used in other published reports because it includes the count for "other" Asian/Pacific American groups. Other published census reports include only nine specific Asian/Pacific American groups for the 1980 count. Therefore, our calculation of percent growth is 95% which is lower than the published 108% growth +2.

1970s to escape the unstable political situation in her native country. A Southeast Asian refugee may be a refugee from Vietnam when it was taken over by the Communists in 1975, or a Cambodian-American gang member whose family survived the trauma of Pol Pot's "killing fields," managed a dangerous escape from his country by boat, and spent several years of his childhood in a refugee camp in the Philippines before finally resettling in the United States.

In spite of the widespread image of all Asian Americans as a model minority group who does well educationally and economically, adapts quietly to U.S. expectations and standards, and takes care of their own problems, there are other Asian Pacific families and children who are living in poverty, having difficulty obtaining decent jobs and housing, unable to communicate effectively in English, and struggling with physical and mental health problems.

Demographic Profile

The Asian/Pacific population is the fastest growing minority group in the United States. The Immigration Act of 1965 abolished racial quotas and emphasized family reunification and occupational skills. Since then, over one-third of all legal immigration to the United States has been made up of Asians and Pacific Islanders. The majority have entered under the family reunification category (4). The tremendous growth rate is expected to continue. In 1970, Asian/Pacific Americans constituted only 0.7 percent of the U.S. population. By 1998, they were an estimated 10.2 million Asians and Pacific Islanders in the United States, comprising 3.8 percent of the total population. It is projected that the total population for all Asian/Pacific ethnic groups will increase to 20.2 million by the year 2020 (5).

According to the 1990 Census (6), the largest proportions of Asian Americans were Chinese 24 percent; Filipino 20 percent; Japanese 12 percent; Asian Indian 11.8 percent; and Korean 11.6 percent. The newer immigrant groups are Vietnamese 8.9 percent, and Cambodian, Laotian, Thai, and Hmong each with less than 2 percent. Pacific Islanders include Hawaiian, Samoan, Guamanian, Tongans, and others. Fifty-four percent of Asian Americans live in five states— California, New York, Hawaii, Texas, and Illinois. The largest numbers are in California.

Asian Americans seem to be faring well financially, indeed, the median family income of Asians in 1990 was $42,250 compared to the median income for white families which was $36,920. However, more family members are in the work force than the national average, and the poverty rate for Asian/Pacific Americans was slightly higher than the national average of 13 percent. Several groups have a much higher rate of poverty; for example, Hmong 63.6 percent, Cambodian 42.6 percent, Lao 34.7 percent, and Vietnamese 25.7 percent (6).

Thus the successful image of all Asian Americans as highly educated, socioeconomic achievers is far from accurate. In reality, Asian Americans earn less than their white counterparts in spite of additional schooling, they have difficulty finding jobs commensurate to their education, and many find discrimination expressed in the glass ceiling phenomenon which keeps them from being promoted at the highest levels. The success image also results in their being excluded from the health, education, economic, and social service programs they need (7).

Cultural Variables

In Asia and the Pacific, there are two major cultural orientations: (1) Confucianism, which predominates in northern Asian countries such as China, Japan, Korea, and Vietnam, and (2) a combination of Hindu/Malayan/Polynesian cultures that predominate in the southern countries such as India, the Philippines, Indonesia, and Malaysia, as well as the Pacific Islands. The people of the first group are usually referred to as the "yellow races," while the people of the second group are referred to as the "brown races." This grouping also reflects the extent to which Chinese traders flourished in northern Asia and also coincides with the more obvious corollary of which countries or areas use chopsticks.

Another notable difference is the status of women in some countries. Although in many Asian countries, women's legal and political status is inferior to that of men, in the Philippines, women have had equal rights of property ownership and access to important roles in government and religion.

Generational Differences

An important feature in understanding the behavior of Asian/Pacific clientele is the concept of generational difference. This is particularly evident in three areas: (1) degree of acculturation, (2) reaction to oppression and racism, and (3) ethnic identity issues. The degree of ethnic identification of various family members, the family's adherence to traditional Asian/Pacific values, and its response to oppression and racism will differ depending on how many generations an Asian/Pacific family has been in America.

First-Generation Asian/Pacific Immigrants

It can be expected that first generation Asian/Pacific immigrants in this country will continue to be more strongly guided by Asian values than will later generations. Especially for those immigrants who live and work in the Koreatowns, Chinatowns, and Little Saigons of America, the neighborhood institutions—trading with Asian merchants, chatting with Asian/Pacific neighbors, attending recreational and religious functions with people from the same country of origin—will serve to reinforce traditional Asian/Pacific attitudes and values. In such situations there is not much need or motivation for individuals to change and incorporate American ways. Although they now live in the United States, they will continue to identify themselves as Chinese, Korean, etc., rather than seeing themselves as American.

Second-Generation Asian/Pacific Americans

Children of Asian/Pacific immigrants are exposed to American values through the media, the American school system, and the experience of growing up in America. To be an ethnic target of racist attitudes is difficult, and when one's identity has not yet been clearly established, it can be psychologically devastating.

Second-generation Asian/Pacifics experience the most conflict regarding their ethnic identity. They are not as clear in their Asian identity as their parents were. They have been raised to honor parental authority and revere Asian values, but they also learn new and sometimes conflicting values as they grow up in America. They feel torn between their loyalty to their parents' teachings versus the strong desire to be accepted as American. Second-generation Asian/Pacific Americans can experience a sense of inferiority and shame because they are different, especially when the majority culture views them as inferior or unacceptable. They may handle these feelings by rejecting Asian/Pacific ways and taking on the outward symbols of the American dream—a good income, nice homes, new cars, and the latest in household appliances and fashions. Or some of the youth rebel against the model minority image and their parents' values by running away from home or becoming involved in gangs and drugs.

Third-Generation Asian/Pacific Americans

Third-generation Asian/Pacific Americans have been raised by second-generation parents who want their children to fulfill their dreams of being fully accepted as Americans. The third generation is much more secure in their American identity. Because they were not raised by immigrants, they have not internalized old Asian/Pacific values in the same way that their parents did. Their more consistent internalization of American values and a strong sense of being American makes it possible for Asians of the third generation to assimilate more completely (e.g., as seen in more interracial marriages). It also allows them to reexamine their ethnic roots and outwardly affirm the positive aspects of this heritage more comfortably than their parents could.

Child-Rearing Practices

In working with Asian/Pacific families, we must continue to be mindful of the difference between current majority U.S. society's focus on the child as an individual to be cared for and protected, versus the more traditional focus on the family unit and the corollary assumption that the child is cared for properly if the family has its basic needs met. In the Asian/Pacific family, the preferred way to meet the needs of the child is to focus from the outset on the needs of the family. The following values guide family relationships and child-rearing practices in the Asian/Pacific community.

Filial Piety. A basic concept in Asian/Pacific family values is filial piety. Parents are respected, revered, and obeyed. Family hierarchy is based on age and sex. The oldest male has the highest rank in the family, and the youngest female has the lowest rank. (Note: because of the difference, mentioned earlier, between the Confucian-based cultures and the Southeast Asian countries, the status of women is higher in the latter countries.) The authority of the person of higher rank is deferred to unquestioningly. The ultimate importance in a relationship is to know one's role in relationship to others and to fulfill the appropriate obligation, duty, and loyalty owed to others.

One implication of this family value for child welfare practice is that workers need to recognize the status of fathers in Asian/Pacific families. Since the concept of egalitarian roles is unfamiliar to Asian families, the child welfare worker needs to be sensitive to how difficult it can be for the male head of the family if his wife can find a job more easily than he can, or his children can speak English and therefore are able to negotiate with public officials and service providers more effectively than he can. Wives and children may accept abusive behavior on the part of the father because they feel it is their duty to accept whatever punishment the father sets forth, and/or they may understand the frustration and sense of failure he is experiencing as the head of the family.

Family Attachment vs. Individual Autonomy

Traditional social work practice and theory reflect democratic values and uphold the autonomous rights of the individual. By contrast, traditional Asian families value hierarchical relationships and the sense of oneness and attachment to the family. One of the most important differences between the way an American and an Asian family influence individuals is the prominent role the family plays throughout an individual's life.

Although Americans begin life with parents and siblings, American child-rearing practices are geared toward eventual physical and psychological separation of the child from the family. For an American, an important measure of self-esteem is the degree of autonomy from the family, and closeness to siblings is voluntary rather than compulsory and essential. In Asian/Pacific families, on the contrary, members are not encouraged to separate from each other. The expectation is that one should always maintain strong ties with the family. For many Asians, self-esteem and a sense of psychic and interpersonal equilibrium and well-being are closely tied to their relationships with parents, siblings, and other relatives.

This issue is particularly critical when working with Asian/Pacific teenagers. At a time when Western society recognizes and supports the need for young people to become independent, Asian/Pacific parents may see autonomous behavior as a betrayal and rejection of traditional family values. If the child welfare worker automatically supports the independent behavior in the adolescent and evaluates the parents' stance as a pathological fostering of dependency, the opportunity to help each member of the family system understand the importance of the cultural conflicts will be missed. Awareness of Asian cultural values will allow more sensitive intervention in family interactions that can enhance understanding and growth rather than attack or destroy important family values.

Family Honor

Confucian principles state that stable families ensure a stable society (8). Therefore, the welfare of the family and family honor are considered to be of greater importance than the interests and goals of any of its individual members. For example, entrance into a prestigious university or graduating with honors is not an individual accomplishment but reflects on the honor of the family. Similarly, an adolescent who is arrested for drug use or a woman who is going through a divorce are not seen as individuals struggling with their own conflicts and problems; they bring shame and dishonor to their respective families.

In this sense, shame is a powerful method for controlling individual behavior. The possibility that outsiders would know of family problems or difficulties means losing face or bringing shame to the family. Sharing negative aspects of family life with outsiders would also be considered a betrayal of loyalty to other family members.

To work effectively with Asian/Pacific clients, child welfare workers need to recognize how self-conscious and self-condemning their clients are likely to be about the need for outside help. In initial contacts with clients, worker interventions should reflect recognition and credit for the positive step the client has taken in participating in such a difficult endeavor. The principle of confidentiality and respect for the clients' privacy needs to be carefully explained in the early meetings.

Harmony

The concept of harmony is another prominent aspect of the Confucian value system. The individual who subordinates his or her own needs for the sake of peace and harmony in the group is valued over one who is challenging or combative. Avoiding outward confrontation and using self-control and restraint are recognized as being indicative of maturity. Expressiveness is associated with the kind of spontaneity and lack of control children exhibit. Model adult behavior is that of emotional equanimity and composure.

Because the Western model of mental health encourages openness and expression of feelings, the emotional composure of Asians is often negatively interpreted as excessive emotional control, inscrutability, or evasiveness. Indiscriminate encouragement by the human service worker for the client to be assertive, open, and confrontive will be in direct conflict with the style in which Asian/Pacific families socialize their members to behave.

Self-Esteem

For most people from Asia and the Pacific Islands, self-esteem is primarily determined by others rather than oneself. Strong concern about self-esteem or self-respect are very much tied to how one is viewed by family members, how one's family is viewed by the community, and how the Asian/Pacific community is viewed by the majority culture. By trying to act in a way that brings honor to the family, by fitting into the norms of the group, and by avoiding conflict and confrontation, one is constantly aware of and sensitive to what others are thinking. Because being criticized or judged in a negative way is experienced as losing dignity, Asian/Pacific Americans become highly vulnerable to hurt feelings and develop a keen sensitivity to the attitudes and judgments of others. This sensitivity to evaluation by others makes Asian clientele especially vulnerable to narcissistic injury in the course of the helping process. Messages from the human services worker that give credit and enhance self-esteem will be useful in helping Asian/Pacific clients develop a positive relationship with the human services worker.

Education

Confucian philosophy holds education in the highest esteem. Teachers are honored and highly respected; Asian families will sacrifice any number of personal pleasures or gratifications to encourage and support the education of their children. Educational achievement is one of the most effective ways Asian children can bring honor to their families.

Racism

For minorities in America, a strong determinant of world views is racism and the subordinate position assigned to people of color by society (9). Each immigrant group has experienced common feelings of alienation and oppression. For child welfare workers to be effective in helping Asian/Pacific families, they must become aware of the values and world views of Asia and the Pacific that may be very different from the Western values upon which social work theories are based. They must also be aware of the reality of racism and how it affects families that come for help.

Strong anti-immigrant sentiment in the 1990s was reflected in repressive legislation and divisive state initiatives against immigrant populations. In California, three state initiatives, which drew national attention, reflected strong public sentiment against illegal immigrants, affirmative action programs, and bilingual education. The original version of the Welfare Reform Act of 1996 which cut SSI benefits and food stamps for legal immigrants resulted in physical and emotional hardship for immigrant families. The prevalent anti-immigrant feeling expressed in the elimination of basic subsistence benefits manifested itself in other more invasive ways. According to an audit of violence against Asian/Pacific Americans, there was a significant increase in the violence against Asians in 1995 compared to 1994 (10). The report linked severe anti-immigrant sentiment with the intolerance that fuels acts of violence.

Rising community tensions in the 1980s between African Americans and Korean immigrants, reflected a clash of cultures in poor, inner-city neighborhoods. Violence and confrontations between the two groups developed because of a lack of understanding of each other's historical and cultural experiences and from problems in language and communication styles. Increasingly conflictual interchanges took place in the context of the Korean immigrant as shopkeeper or liquor store owner vis-à-vis an African-American customer or patron. Escalating incidents of fatal exchanges occurred with one or the other side as victim. The problems, exacerbated by underlying economic problems and fueled by media images, came to a head in the devastating civil unrest in Los Angeles following the Rodney King decision on April 29, 1992. Many of the shops that were looted and burned were owned by Koreans. In the aftermath of the disturbance, all Asians were vulnerable to being perceived as Korean, in the same way that any Asian could be the victim of anti-Japanese sentiment during the period of Japan's economic power in the United States in the 1980s.

Child Welfare Issues

As we approach the end of the twentieth century, the field of child welfare is witnessing a crisis in child protective services nationwide. The dramatic rise in drug abuse during the late 1980s and through the 1990s, coupled with greater community awareness and exercise of mandatory child abuse reporting laws, have resulted in skyrocketing referrals to child welfare agencies. Nationally, the reports of child mistreatment from 1993 to 1998 increased by 16 percent to more than 3.1 million. In Los Angeles County, child abuse reports soared 63 percent in the same period (11).

In the latter half of the 1980s, a similar trend of increased child abuse reports emerged among new, immigrant, Asian/Pacific communities in Los Angeles. In 1989, the Los Angeles County Department of Children's Services established a centralized Asian/Pacific unit with bilingual, culturally sensitive competent workers. It provided child abuse prevention/education and treatment services in the native language of the target communities (Cambodian, Chinese, Japanese, Korean, Lao, Samoan, Tagalog, Tongan, Thai, and Vietnamese). From its inception in 1989 to January, 1997, a total of 12,650 children and families were served. Table 6.3 notes the intakes per community per year and their cumulative totals (12).

A survey of Children's Services Workers (CSWs) in the Asian/Pacific unit was conducted in 1997 (13). Respondents indicated at least 77.7 percent agreement on the following statements:

1. Child care is a major problem for families.
2. The "unaccompanied minor from Taiwan" phenomenon is no longer a problem.
3. Conflict between parents and their adolescent children is a major problem.
4. There is a serious lack of Asian/Pacific foster homes and adoptive homes.

Respondents were equally divided on the following:

1. Children were referred to Child Protective Services (CPS) because they were left alone or lived with other minor children.
2. Poverty of families has increased over the last five years. More families are receiving welfare.
3. There are more churches and private groups in the community helping poor families.

TABLE 6.3 Los Angeles County Department of Children and Family Services

Asian Pacific Project
Statistics on Intakes
1989–1996

Year	Cambodian	Chinese	Filipino/ Japanese	Korean	Lao/Thai	Samoan/ Tongan	Vietnamese	Total
1989	158	67	0	0	0	0	110	335
1990	546	298	0	74	0	0	318	1,236
1991	568	355	0	163	0	0	608	1,694
1992	511	306	23	223	84	9	539	1,695
1993	651	348	73	206	43	53	539	1,913
1994	559	414	99	230	89	41	508	1,940
1995	596	429	96	269	59	33	433	1,915
1996	514	466	111	253	104	40	434	1,922
ACCUM TOTAL	4,103	2,683	402	1,418	379	176	3,489	12,650

In terms of social work practice, CPS workers experienced some of the same dilemmas, and even more exaggerated situations, as workers in other communities. In addition, there were the twin challenges of acknowledging differences in child-rearing practices and explaining a concept alien to Asian/Pacific clientele— the practice of government curtailing parental sovereignty over their children. These are serious barriers that children's services workers need to bridge even before any discussion of the "transgression" and abuse can be dealt with. At the very least, these issues have to be dealt with simultaneously. This is an example of the sometimes conflicting bilateral function of Child Protective Services—investigation of charges as well as therapeutic intervention into a family system.

A study of child abuse/neglect in Los Angeles' Indochinese refugee population (14) indicates even though cultural factors were considered, once caseworkers determined allegations to be true, they took the conventional approach of removing children from the home and filing a petition in court. The overriding concern was child safety which meant "erring on the side of caution." Nonetheless, the placement rate of children in the Los Angeles County Asian/Pacific unit was 30 percent as compared with the departmental average of over 50 percent (15).

In Eastern cultures, children are viewed in the context of the family's long-term welfare and survival. The family is seen as the one important unit to care for each member's welfare from birth to death. Therefore, children are viewed as a means for survival, at the minimum, and at best, as affirming the viability of the family. For workers who serve Asians and Pacific Islanders, a core question becomes whether the double goals of protecting children and maintaining the integrity of the family, who has not yet adapted to mainstream society, can be achieved.

Practice Implications

The following cases illustrate working with Asian youth and families within a generalist practice framework. Clients are viewed in terms of their total psycho-socio-biological situation. Identifying information in the cases has been disguised to protect the confidentiality rights of the clients. Of particular significance in these cases are the values and issues pertinent to Asian/Pacific clients.

Case Example: Vinh Van T.

Vinh Van T., a 13-year-old ethnic Chinese student from Vietnam, and his parents were referred to the Asian/Pacific Family Center by the vice-principal of Vinh's middle school. The vice-principal had been trying to reach Vinh's parents for 8–10 weeks because of Vinh's frequent truancy, but because both parents worked long hours away from the home, he had not been able to reach them. Recently, there was a fight between two Asian and Latino gangs after school, and Vinh was picked up by the police. The parents had no idea that Vinh had been having trouble at school or that he was involved in gangs until they had to go after Vinh at the police station.

Vinh and his family had arrived in the United States four years ago, after spending several years in a refugee camp in the Philippines following a har-

rowing boat trip out of Vietnam. The parents spoke very little English and had trouble finding good jobs because of their language problem. The also had no understanding of the U.S. school system and were suspicious of the educational system; their experience in Vietnam with school was a government run "re-education" system. They were angry that Vinh had brought trouble and shame to the family and blamed permissive U.S. cultural norms for his problems.

The intake interview was conducted by a Vietnamese-speaking social worker who praised the parents for coming in to help their son. The worker recognized how hard it was to make a living in a strange country and to raise children where norms and expectations were so different from their home country. The worker also expressed support of Vinh and the challenges young people faced when they spent so much of their time at home alone and where there were no constructive after-school programs or activities for them. The worker explained the nature of counseling services as (1) providing support for the issues parents were dealing with and helping them to gain cultural competence in parenting tasks, and (2) providing support groups and positive role models for Vinh in the after-school programs at the Center.

Case Notes.   An important aspect of social work intervention in this case was the language competence and cultural sensitivity of the worker. Effective work with Asian refugee clients requires more than merely using an interpreter who can translate the words of the worker. This worker acted as a cultural broker who was tuned into the fear and alienation these parents experienced by talking to outsiders about their very personal family problems. The worker was also aware of how a lonely, young teen could be attracted to gangs of his own ethnic group when there was little else to connect with hopeful experiences at school or at home. Vinh had no consistent limit setting, discipline, or attention from his parents who were busy holding multiple jobs because they were so poorly paid. In addition to feeling neglected by his parents he was angry that they (and he) did not fit into the acceptable images of mainstream America. Because of his low self-image, Vinh spent most of his time with the young people he met at video parlors and pool halls who also felt cut off from positive experiences in their lives.

Case Example: Cora M.

Cora M., a 6-year-old Filipino girl, was referred from an inner-city public school to an Asian/Pacific outpatient child and youth facility because of fighting, hitting, and head-banging in her kindergarten classroom. Cora had been on medication for seizures since she was six months old. She lived with her unemployed, unmarried mother, her grandparents, an aunt, and two uncles. Her father's identity is unknown. Although she had one friend, most of her social interactions were with her aunt and uncles. At intake, Cora appeared anxious, disdainful, and at times quiet and sad.

The lifestyle of the family was chaotic, and there were psychological, economic, and social problems. The grandmother was alcoholic, she periodically brought boyfriends to the home to live, and her other children were by two different men. Cora's mother was erratic in her handling of Cora and did not always get Cora to school. The grandfather was unable to set limits and ended up, against his will, catering to the demands of his family.

Treatment approaches included individual work with Cora and work with the mother and the extended family, particularly with the grandfather, who seemed to provide the most stable point of reference for Cora. The increasing attachment of Cora to her grandfather, even to the point of her sleeping with him, was directly discussed with him in terms of Cora's psychosexual development. Cora was placed in a small school for children with special problems, where she received better instruction and more support. Bus transportation was provided to the school, and Cora's attendance improved as she no longer had to rely on her mother to get her to school. With more consistency and stability in her life, Cora became less hyperactive, no longer needed excessive attention, and advanced to placement in a class with children of her own age.

Work with Cora's mother focused on developing parenting skills and improving her own self-esteem. She was also referred to vocational rehabilitation for job training. The extended family was seen, as needed, to coordinate a consistent environment for Cora.

Case Notes. The systems framework is especially helpful in assessing appropriate intervention in this case. By viewing Cora and her problems in light of her entire social situation, a number of practice interventions could be considered. The worker analyzed the interdependent interactions between Cora and the many members of her family; he was sensitive to the special issues of Hiya (shame) and Amor propio (self-esteem) in Filipino families. This knowledge was useful in dealing with the family's feelings about the grandmother's alcoholism and extramarital liaisons. The worker established a positive, supportive alliance with Cora's mother; he understood the interrelationship between the mother's low self-esteem and her ineffectiveness as a parent and used the relationship to work on both issues. He also recognized the positive role the grandfather provided for Cora and involved the grandfather to play a healthier role in Cora's life. The worker also made creative use of resources in the community to find a more suitable school environment for Cora and job training for her mother.

Case Example: Reverend K.

Reverend K., a 52 year-old Korean minister, was referred for counseling. He had been charged with child abuse for beating his 17-year-old son and 15-year old daughter, whom he accused of lying and truancy. Rev. K. had left a well-established church in Korea in order to provide an American education for his children. In America, he led a small Protestant congregation, and his wife worked long hours as a beautician. Because the family sacrificed so much for the children, he expected them to do well in school and behave in an exemplary manner as children of a minister. He was angry that instead of being grateful, his children resented the fact that he was so controlling and restrictive. Rev. K.'s English-speaking ability was limited.

Because the Korean-speaking worker in this agency was a young woman, a mature, male worker was also enlisted to work with Rev. K. in a team approach. The goal of the treatment was not to undermine Rev. K.'s belief system, but to focus on negotiating a compromise. The work also involved educating Rev. K. to some of the realities of American life (e.g., beating children is considered a crime in America) and to differences between American and Korean social norms. The workers tried to help Rev. K. see that he could work toward his goal of providing a good education for his children by enlisting their participation in the process rather than giving orders from above.

Case Notes. This case illustrates the hierarchical nature of Asian family systems. As noted in the discussion of Asian values, the father is the ultimate authority in the Asian family. As a self-righteous minister and Korean father, Rev. K. had never considered the possibility that his ideas could be questioned. The concepts of negotiation and compromise within a family were very new to him. The agency staff was sensitive to the fact that Rev. K. would find it difficult to defer to a younger female, and arranged for an older, male worker to join the Korean-speaking young woman. The workers recognized Rev. K.'s basic concern for his children as an asset and used this concern to find ways to actualize his aims.

The Asian custom of unquestioned obedience to authority and loyalty to the family is in strong contradiction to U.S. values of egalitarianism and individualism. The normal generational conflicts between parents and children are heightened in immigrant families where the parents' Old-World values contrast so greatly with the New-World values the children are struggling to adopt. Children quickly become more proficient in English than their parents. This, coupled with the long hours most parents work away from the home, contributes to increasing distance and communication difficulties between the two generations.

Case Example: Brian H.

Brian H., an 11-year-old, third-generation Chinese-American boy, was referred to the child guidance clinic by his school. Brian had developed an involuntary facial tic that embarrassed him so much, he had been refusing to go to school. Brian was an excellent student, captain of the soccer team, and a leader among his classmates and friends. He was the second of two children; his brother was a freshman at a small private college. His father was an orthopedic surgeon and his mother worked part-time at his father's office. The family lived in a wealthy suburb where there were not many other Asian families.

Brian came with his mother for the intake interview. She was very anxious about Brian's tic; their pediatrician had said Brian was too pressured, and she had been telling Brian, "You just have to relax." She noted that it is important to her husband that their sons do well, and she devoted a great deal of her time to the boys at home, at school, and with their extracurricular activities. Brian had a "mod" haircut, was dressed in the latest fashion, and was quite articulate for an 11 year-old. In spite of an impressive exterior, Brian broke down during the individual interview and spoke of how upset he was that the facial tic made him look like a "weirdo." An exploration of family relationships revealed that currently there was a great deal of tension between the father and the older brother because Brian's brother was getting Bs an Cs in his first year of college instead of the straight As the father required of his sons. The father had told Brian's older brother that he would have to transfer to a community college because he was wasting the family's money at the private college.

The intake worker recommended family therapy as the treatment of choice for Brian's problems. This made the mother even more anxious, as her husband did not believe in "psychological therapy," and she knew he would be angry if he had to participate. The worker suggested that he could contact Dr. H. directly to invite him to participate.

Case Notes.   It was clear to the worker that Brian's symptoms were directly related to conflicts occurring in other parts of the family system. The family operated in terms of many traditional Confucian values—the importance of education, the hierarchical nature of the relationships, the importance of the gender roles, the need to keep harmony in the family (i.e., refrain from making the father angry), and concern about behavior that would cause shame to the family. It can be speculated that part of Dr. H.'s resistance to participate in therapy was that: (1) admitting anything was wrong with his family would bring dishonor to the family, and (2) the typical Asian attitude toward psychological problems is that they should be handled within the family by willpower rather than by talking to outsiders about intimate family matters. In this case, it would be easy for a worker with a Western orientation to judge Dr. H. as being rigid, autocratic, and unsympathetic to the feelings of his family. A recognition of Asian family values and styles enables social service workers to understand that what seems pathological in a Western context may not be so within an Asian cultural context.

By offering to call Dr. H. directly, the male intake worker may indeed be able to help Dr. H. see the need for family therapy, especially if the worker approaches Dr. H. as a partner who needs to be enlisted in working on problems for his son. It is important to keep in mind the need to respect psychological defenses and build self-esteem in all family members. In spite of Dr. H.'s status in the family and community, he, like most parents, is likely to be threatened by the idea that he failed in some way and will be sensitive about being blamed and attacked for not doing a good job as a parent. Because of this sensitivity and defensiveness, it may take longer to build a sense of trust and mutual respect before confronting or making interpretations with an Asian family. The family had obviously worked hard to fulfill the image of the successful, model minority. Unfortunately, the success image seen by Americans is often at great psychological cost to the individuals involved.

Case Example: Kim O.

This is the case of a three-generation, Korean-American family consisting of a maternal grandmother; her 35 year-old daughter, Kim O.; and the daughter's two children, ages 6 and 3. They lived in a large metropolitan area. Child Pro-

tective Services staff were called by neighbors because of screams and children crying. The investigation determined that the grandmother was inflicting physical and verbal abuse on Kim and the two grandchildren. The three were removed from the home and placed in a shelter for women and children. Other pertinent information was that grandmother was the sole support of the family and Kim, who had been diagnosed in the past as having a manic-depressive disorder and was not receiving treatment. Kim was initially described as hostile and belligerent, and the children were withdrawn and guarded.

The staff at the shelter filed for a restraining order preventing the grandmother from having contact with her daughter and grandchildren. Staff also helped Kim apply for SSI and low-cost housing and AFDC for her children. The family was referred to Family Preservation Services with bilingual Korean staff who placed Kim and the children in an apartment. The Multidisciplinary Case Planning Committee, which included Kim's participation, developed a case plan with mental health treatment for Kim, referral of the children to an early childhood education program, and most importantly, in-home counseling, in addition to the more traditional office visits with the bilingual mental health worker.

Case Notes.   The latter feature of in-home counseling, played a very important role in the treatment plan for the family. While all the other elements of the case-plan were critical and important, the in-home counseling consolidated all the gains of the various other interventions. While initially, Kim showed resistance to having the in-home counselor visit every week, she began to express a positive regard for this. Kim successfully worked through the conflictual and ambivalent relationship with her mother. Many issues of boundaries and reciprocity were clarified resulting in more mutually satisfying interactions among all four members of the family. Kim also expanded her social circle by becoming active in volunteer work in the community.

This case demonstrates the matriarchal role of the grandmother who carried heavy burdens and responsibilities as well as the culturally condoned authoritarian and controlling behaviors. Kim was paralyzed by fear of her mother, and the cultural arrangement had prevented her from establishing independence and gaining self-worth and self-pride.

Summary

Economic hardships, problems of adaptation, and lack of familiarity with social resources all contribute to difficulties for immigrant Asian/Pacific children and their families. Although second- and third-generation families are more acculturated and do not suffer the same kind of difficulties as immigrant families, cultural issues still affect interpersonal interactions with family members and with society.

Child welfare services to the Asian/Pacific population need to be culturally appropriate and provided by workers who are trained to be aware of the values and needs of this particular population. Because of the emphasis on family among

Asian/Pacifics, a two-pronged approach that combines work with the family with work with the individual child is especially important. This may call for an investment of time, energy, and commitment to advocacy and case management that goes beyond simply meeting bureaucratic requirements of client contact and numbers of home visits. An ecological systems approach to helping Asian/Pacific clients allows recognition of unique cultural characteristics and the interdependence of people and their resource systems. The child welfare worker with a generalist approach to helping is aware of this ecosystem perspective and intervenes at the beginning professional level by providing information, problem identification, screening, intake, case management, advocacy, community outreach, and referral.

Current Trends and Concerns for the Future

Because Asians and Pacific Islanders continue to be the fastest-growing racial group identified by the U.S. Census, the need for social workers to be aware of the characteristics and needs of this group will continue to grow. Within this diverse and heterogeneous group there are sharp contrasts between people who are very affluent and who are very poor; people who have been successful in moving up the educational and economic ladder, and others who are illiterate and part of the fastest-growing segment on welfare in California (15).

Many Asian/Pacific immigrant and refugee families need to be educated about American child-rearing practices, child abuse laws, and the underlying democratic philosophic foundation upon which these laws were erected. This is a challenging task requiring sensitivity and knowledge of the culture given the prevailing skepticism among traditional Asian/Pacific immigrants who perceive the permissiveness of Western culture as a corrupting influence responsible for delinquency, pregnancies, and drug abuse among the youth.

For traditional immigrant parents, the erosion of family ties translates into the erosion of the most dependable system that provides for the care and nurturance of the individual from birth to death. It is not uncommon for a parent to expect that his children will care for him in his old age. As the accelerated and dramatically different acculturation of their adolescent children develops, parents may despair and react in keeping with their fears. These fears are further reinforced by their seeing the institutionalized, nursing home care we give our elderly.

For Asian/Pacific adolescents, complex identity issues will continue to be a major challenge. Questions such as where they belong, whether they are American or Asian, needing to act more Asian at home if their parents are from the old country and to act more American while at school and with peers, lacking of a variety of positive role models, rejection and negative stereotypes of Asians and Pacific Islanders by the general public, and negative stereotypes of Americans by traditional Asian parents pose complicated struggles and choices for Asian/Pacific youth.

Concerns for the future include the need to improve relations with other races. Current tensions among some Asian groups and African Americans and Latinos, mirror the current tensions in the larger community and underscore the need for Asian Americans to become part of creating a paradigm of improved race relations in the United States. On the other hand, the increase in intermarriage rates and educational–economic assimilation, cause some Asian American leaders to fear a loss of community identity (15).

In conclusion, it is important to note that although cultural awareness is an important prerequisite for working effectively with Asian/Pacific families, it is very easy to cross the boundary from cultural sensitivity to cultural stereotyping (16). The generalizations about Asians and Pacific Islanders presented here should not be used as a prescriptive formula for how to work with this population. Instead, the intent of this chapter has been to increase cultural sensitivity and provide the kind of understanding and awareness that will help child welfare workers to be more comfortable and competent in their work with Asian/Pacific children and their families.

Endnotes

1. Patricia L. Ewalt and Noreen Mokuau, "Self-Determination from a Pacific Perspective," *Multicultural Issues in Social Work,* p. 258.

2. Isaac V. Gusukuma and Ruth G. McRoy, *Asian Americans: A Cultural Diversity Training Module,* p. 87

3. *The State of Asian Pacific America, A Public Policy Report: Policy Issues to the Year 2020* (Executive Summary).

4. Bill O. Hing and Ronald Lee, eds., *Reframing the Immigration Debate: The State of Asian Pacific America.*

5. U.S. Bureau of the Census. 1998. *U.S. Population* Estimates, Release PPL-91, from the Internet.

6. U.S. Bureau of the Census. 1992. *1990 Census of Population—General Population Characteristics.*

7. Pallassana R. Balgopal, "Asian Americans Overview," *Encyclopedia of Social Work, 19th Edition,* p. 234.

8. Akemi Kikumura and Harry H. L. Kitano, "Persistence and Change in the Japanese American Family," in *Ethnic Families in America,* 2nd ed.

9. Derald W. Sue, *Counseling the Culturally Different.*

10. National Asian Pacific American Legal Consortium. *1995 Audit of Violence Against Asian Pacific Americans.*

11. James Rainey and Sonia Nazario, "Child Abuse Reports Threaten to Overwhelm L. A. Protection System," *Los Angeles Times,* January 11, 1998, Section A, p. 1.

12. *Asian Pacific Project,* Unpublished report, County of Los Angeles, Department of Children and Family Services. January, 1997.

13. Frank Nguyen, Director, Asian/Pacific Project, Los Angeles County Department of Children and Family Services (workshop presentation at the Third Annual Conference presented by California State University, Los Angeles, and Los Angeles County Juvenile Court, Los Angeles Convention Center, October 17, 1997).

14. P. H. Nguyen and R. LaFarge, *Child Abuse/Neglect in Los Angeles' Indochinese Refugee Population: Cultural Implications for Child Protective Services Practitioners and Policy Makers.* Unpublished research project, UCLA School of Public Policy and Social Research, p. 74.

15. K. Connie Kang, "Reaching Critical Mass: Asian Americans in California," *Los Angeles Times,* July 12, 1998, Section A, p. 1.
16. Paul Pederson, et al., *Counseling Across Cultures,* p. 10.

Bibliography

Audit of Violence Against Asian Pacific Americans, National Asian Pacific American Legal Consortium, 1995.

Balgopal, Pallassana R., "Asian Americans Overview." In *Encyclopedia of Social Work, 19th Edition,* vol. 1, Washington D.C.: NASW Press, 1995, pp. 213–237.

Ewalt, Patricia L., and Noreen Mokuau, "Self-Determination from a Pacific Perspective." In *Multicultural Issues in Social Work.,* Ewalt, P. L., Freeman, E. M., Kirk, S. A. and Poole, D. L., eds. Washington, DC: NASW Press, 1996, pp. 255–268.

Gusukuma, Isaac V., and Ruth G. McRoy. *Asian Americans: A Cultural Diversity Training Module,* The University of Texas at Austin: Center for Social Work Research, 1997.

Hing, Bill O., and Ronald Lee, eds. *Reframing the Immigration Debate: The State of Asian Pacific America,* Los Angeles: LEAP Asian Pacific American Public Policy Institute and the UCLA Asian American Studies Center, 1996.

Kang, K. Connie. "Reaching Critical Mass: Asian Americans in California," *Los Angeles Times,* 12 July 1998, sec. A, p. 1.

Kikumura, Akemi and Harry L. Kitano. "Persistence and Change in the Japanese American Family." In Charles Mindel and Robert Habenstein, eds., *Ethnic Families in America,* 2nd ed., New York: Elsevier, 1981.

Nguyen, Frank, Workshop presentation at the Third Annual Conference presented by California State University, Los Angeles and Los Angeles County Juvenile Court, Los Angeles Convention Center, October 17, 1997.

Nguyen, P. H., and R. LaFarge. *Child Abuse/Neglect in Los Angeles' Indochinese Refugee Population: Cultural Implications for Child Protective Services Practitioners and Policy Makers,* Unpublished research project, UCLA School of Public Policy and Social Research.

Pederson, Paul, et al. *Counseling Across Cultures.* Honolulu, HW: University Press of Hawaii, 1976.

Rainey, James and Sonia Nazario, "Child Abuse Reports Threaten to Overwhelm L. A. Protection System," *Los Angeles Times,* 11 January 1998, Sec. A, p. 1.

The State of Asian Pacific America-A Public Policy Report: Policy Issues to the Year 2020 (Executive Summary), Los Angeles: LEAP Asian Pacific American Public Policy Institute and the UCLA Asian American Studies Center, 1994.

Sue, Derald W. *Counseling the Culturally Different,* New York: John Wiley & Sons, 1981.

U.S. Bureau of the Census. *1990 Census of Population—General Population Characteristics,* 1992.

U.S. Bureau of the Census. *U.S. Population Estimates,* 1998. Release PPL-91, from the Internet.

7 Generalist Child Welfare and Hispanic Families

ROGER DELGADO

California State University, Los Angeles

How best to address the child welfare needs of children and their families continues to be a challenge for disciplines with an interest in the healthy growth and development of children. The social work profession has historically been at the forefront of concerted, multifaceted efforts to enhance the psychosocial functioning of children and their families. Such efforts, while always important, have never been as timely as they are today. Harris (1), commenting on the relevance of an issue of *Social Work* to child welfare, states that:

Statistics show an increase in reports of child abuse and neglect, with many states also experiencing a rise in out-of-home placements for children. At the same time, public child welfare agencies are experiencing drastic budget cuts. This tragic picture becomes more compelling when the widespread abuse of alcohol and drugs, increased poverty among children, alarming number of high-school dropouts, and high rate of adolescent pregnancies are added.

Writing in the same issues of *Social Work*, Hogan and Siu (2) attest to the special needs of minority children in the child welfare system. They state that:

Current treatment of minority children continues to reflect racial bias: The system responds more slowly to crisis in minority families; such families have less access to support services such as day care and homemaker services; black and Hispanic children receive less comprehensive service plans; and parents of color have been viewed as less able to profit from support services. Thus, minority children are overrepresented in substitute services, and a greater discrepancy exists between recommended and delivered services for minority children than for non-minority.

Underscoring the significance of inadequate child welfare services to minority children is the demographic reality that, from 1970 to 1980, there was a 52 percent population growth for total minorities (3). Thus, the child welfare needs and problems of Hispanics, who tend to be younger than other population groups, will become even more pronounced during coming decades.

This chapter is designed to provide the reader with an overview of child welfare and the welfare of Hispanic children and their families. It will address the following areas: the demographic characteristics, child welfare needs, and problems of Hispanic children and their families; socio-cultural attributes and diversity; and the need for culturally relevant child welfare services to Hispanics.

Socio-Demographic Synopsis of Hispanics in the United States

One of the difficulties in writing about the child welfare needs and problems of Hispanic children and their families is the lack of written documentation regarding this group's experience with the child welfare system. We are thus left with the need to extrapolate from what information is available.

In 1977, 7 percent of the children involved with the child welfare system were Hispanic (4). A July 1989 Children's Defense Fund report (5) presents the following socio-demographic profile of Hispanic children:

Hispanic Population Growth

- Of the 30.8 million Hispanics in the United States as of 1998, more than 10.8 million were children younger than 18. From 1987 to 1998, the Hispanic population in the United States increased by 59 percent.

Distinct Ethnic Subgroups

- The Hispanic population includes various ethnic subgroups: Mexican-American, 62 percent; Puerto Rican, 13 percent; Central and South American, 12 percent; other Hispanic, 8 percent; Cuban, 5 percent.
- Two-thirds of all Hispanics in the United States live in California, Texas, or New York.

Poverty, Hispanic Families and Children

- About 25 percent of all Hispanic families are poor.
- About 28.6 percent of all Hispanic families are headed by a single woman; the poverty rate among female-headed families is about 51.8 percent.
- Two out of five Hispanic children (i.e., 39.3 percent) in the United States are poor. This compares to 15.0 percent for white children.

Education Status of Hispanic Children

- The school dropout rate in 1987 for Hispanic children was 44.7 percent. For white children, the dropout rate was 15.1 percent.

Teen Parenthood

- In 1986, of 389,048 babies born to Hispanic women in the United States, 63,816 or 16.4 percent of births were to Hispanic women younger than 20 years of age; half of these were unmarried.

Maternal and Child Health

- In 1995, only 70.8 percent of Hispanic babies were born to mothers who had received early prenatal care, up from 60.3 percent in 1986.
- Hispanic children 5 to 11 years old are twice as unlikely as white children to have visited a dentist.

Like most non-white groups, Hispanics have a higher birth rate and lower life expectancy than whites. Thus, when compared to whites, Hispanics have a larger proportion of children and fewer elderly.

Who Are the Hispanics?

Throughout this chapter, the term *Hispanic* is primarily used to include Mexican-American (or Chicanos), Puerto Ricans, mostly concentrated in New York and New Jersey; Cubans, for the most part living in Florida; and people from other Spanish-speaking countries of Latin America and Spain. Of these four groups, Mexican-Americans have lived in this country the longest; many are able to trace their ancestry back to the Spanish colonists and Indians who were the original inhabitants of the American Southwest (i.e., Arizona, California, Colorado, New Mexico, and Texas). Only since 1970 has information on Hispanics been collected in a more organized, consistent, and integrated manner. Thus, in past years the actual number of Hispanics living in the United States has been only moderately accurate at best.

According to the U.S. Bureau of the Census (6), in 1985 there were 16.9 million Hispanics in the United States. This was 6.4 percent of the total U.S. population of 226.5 million. Whereas years ago Hispanics, especially Mexican-Americans, lived in rural, agrarian areas, today the majority live in large metropolitan areas. However, 45 percent of Mexican-Americans continue to live in smaller urban or rural locales.

By 1990, there were 22.4 million Hispanics, a 53-percent increase from the 1980 census (7). It is estimated that by the year 2000, the number of Latinos will reach 30 to 35 million (8) and will constitute the largest U.S. minority group (9).

The Hispanic population is growing at a rate approximately seven times greater than that of the general population, due to higher rates of fertility and legal immigration (10). It is projected that by the year 2010, Hispanic children will be the largest minority among the child population (18 percent), and by 2040, will represent one in four of all children (11).

Families and Marital Status

One of the typical stereotypes of the Mexican-American family is that it is maritally intact, headed by the father as patriarch, and less vulnerable to divorce, perhaps because of strong religious ties to Catholicism. In actuality, Hispanics are less likely to be living in married-couple families that the general U.S. population (73.1 percent to 81.7 percent, respectively). Hispanics are also more likely to be living in single-parent families (for the most part, headed by the mother), than is the case for the general population (18.2 percent versus 10.4 percent, respectively; headed by Hispanic mother only, 16.3 percent, to 9.3 percent for the general population (12). From a Hispanic intra-group perspective, it is significant that Puerto Rican families are the most likely to be headed by a woman (i.e., 40 percent; 15 percent among Mexican-Americans; 17 percent among other Hispanics, including Cubans). Since Hispanic family households are larger than those in the general population (i.e., 3.9 persons, to 3.3 for all U.S. families), the economic and parenting challenges facing female heads of household are quite formidable.

Marital Status

One of the reasons for the larger percentage of female-headed households is that Hispanics are more likely to separate or divorce than persons in the general population. More specifically, in 1981, 14 percent of Hispanic women aged 15 and over were separated or divorced; this compared to 10 percent for all women in the United States 15 and over. Another way of looking at this phenomenon is that in the same year, the ratio of divorced Hispanic women was 146 out of 1,000 married and living with their husbands. This compared to 129 for all women in the United States (13). Also true about Hispanic marriages is that participants tend to marry younger. Thus, in 1981, 25 percent of Hispanic women 20 years or younger were or had been married; this compared to 15 percent for all women in the same age range. Since teen marriages have about a 50 percent chance of survival (14), this might partially explain the higher rates of separation and divorce among Hispanics.

Education

Although there are significant intra-group differences, Hispanics as a group still lag far behind whites and African-Americans in terms of average educational achievement. Since level of educational attainment is so closely associated with economic and occupational betterment, lower educational achievement levels by Hispanics represent a serious disadvantage with numerous negative implications for quality of life.

Nearly all Hispanics, African-Americans, and whites between the ages of 5 and 15 attend school. However, at the age of 16, when it is legal for students in most states to leave school, the rate of enrollment begins to reflect critical differences. For example, in 1981 the school enrollment among 16- and 17-year-old Hispanics was 83 percent. This compared to 91 percent for African-Americans and whites. However, at ages 18 and 19 only 38 percent of Hispanic students were still enrolled; this was in contrast to 50 percent for African-Americans and whites. For the same age range, 36 percent of Hispanics, 16 percent of whites, and 19 percent of African-Americans were not high-school graduates (15). There is also a high-school completion gap for Hispanics who live in cities versus non-city dwellers. Thus, in 1979, 35 percent of Hispanic adult men living in metropolitan areas had completed high school. This was less than the 44 percent for men living in non-metropolitan areas. Also discouraging is the decrease from 35.4 percent in 1975 to 29.9 percent in 1980 of Hispanics who went on to college. In 1981, Hispanics made up only 4.8 percent of total college enrollment in the United States.

In 1990, just under half (49.8 percent) of all Hispanics (age 25 and older) had a high school diploma and less than one in ten (9.4 percent has a bachelor's degree or higher compared to 77 percent and 21 percent of non-Hispanics, respectively (16).

Hispanics who do go on to college are more likely than other groups to drop out. Thus, 57 percent of Hispanic males and 54 percent of Hispanic females fail to graduate. This compares to 34 percent for all white males and females (17). Some educators believe that the poorer scholastic preparation of Hispanic high-school graduates puts them at a disadvantage once they get to college (18). Also, many Hispanics are the first in their families to go to college. Thus, the pressure to succeed can be tremendous. Yet, there is often a lack of Hispanic role models on campuses and few support services. Those available are primarily staffed by non-minority faculty.

According to one expert, the high dropout rate for Hispanics prior to graduating from high school is partly due to the fact that many are enrolled in grades below the average for their age, where they can be bored, feel out of place, and be labeled slow learners. Other reasons given for high dropout rates among Hispanics include early pregnancy and marriage, early entry into the labor force due to poverty, schools that are overcrowded and inadequately funded, and the diverse consequences of discrimination (19). Language problems and decreased funding for bilingual programs are also perceived as contributing factors to lower academic achievement among Hispanics, many of whom have recently immigrated to the United States (20).

Employment and Education

In earlier portrayals of the work patterns of Hispanics, the husband/father was typically the "breadwinner," while the wife/mother stayed home and "took care of the house and children." While this pattern may still exist in some Hispanic households, the modal U.S. labor force participation of Hispanics is markedly different. Among Hispanic men and women 20 years and over, 85 percent and 48.8 percent, respectively, were found to be working or seeking work in 1980. This compares to 79.4 percent and 51.3 percent for all men and women 20 years and over in the United States (21). In fact, between 1973 and 1981, the number of Hispanic women in the workforce increased by 82 percent. Unfortunately, when unemployment rates are examined, Hispanics find themselves without a job at a rate that is generally 40 to 50 percent higher than the overall unemployment rate for the United States. For example, in 1982, when unemployment rates were the highest since the Depression of the 1930s, 15.2 percent of Hispanic workers were out of work in comparison to an overall U.S. unemployment rate of 10.7 percent.

Another area of concern vis-á-vis the employment experience of Hispanics is their higher concentration in lower-paid, less-skilled occupations than the overall U.S. work force. In 1981, a total of 75.3 percent of all Hispanic women were clerical (31.9%), machine operators (22.0%), or service workers (21.4%) in comparison to 63.8 percent of all women. These occupations are consistently among the lowest paid. The rate for Hispanic men in low-paid occupations was 38.6 percent. This compared to 26.4 percent for all adult male U.S. workers.

In 1990, unemployment rates were higher for Hispanics (10.4 percent), compared to six percent for non-Hispanics. And, working Hispanics were only half (14 percent) as likely to be employed in managerial or professional occupations as non-Hispanics (27.4 percent), and almost twice as likely to work in service occupations, 19.2 and 11.5 percent, respectively (22).

Poverty and Income

In 1972, the median family income for Hispanics was $17,790; however, by 1981 it had decreased to $16,107. The corresponding median family income for whites was $25,107 in 1972 and $23,517 in 1982. In 1972, the median income for Hispanics was 71 percent of that for whites, and in 1981, it was 70 percent.

In 1990, the median family income of Hispanics was $25,064, compared to $36,028 for non-Hispanics. Hispanic families with children under 18 were almost twice as likely to live in poverty (27.4 percent) as non-Hispanic families, and over half (55 percent) of all Hispanic female-headed families with children were poor compared to 40.6 percent of non-Hispanics (23).

The higher percentage of youthful and lower-paid Hispanic wage earners has played a role in the lower median income for Hispanic families. Hispanic female-headed families fare even worse, with a median income of $7,586, 60 percent of the median income of $12,508 for white female-headed families. However, in 1981, the median Hispanic family income with both husband and wife working was $23,641, or 80 percent of the median income of $29,713 for white married couples when both spouses worked (24).

In 1981, when the average poverty threshold for a family of four was $9,287, almost one-fourth (24 percent; 800,000) of Hispanic families were defined as poor by the U.S. Census Bureau; this compared to a much lower, 8.8 percent of all white families.

In summary, there is a serious gap between the economic well-being of Hispanics and that of the general U.S. population.

The negative implications for the welfare of Hispanic children and families of higher divorce rates, especially among younger couples, lower educational achievement levels, under-employment, higher unemployment, lower median family incomes, and higher rates of poverty are multiple. At the very least, the latter circumstances dictate the need for more adequate supportive, supplemental, and substitute services.

Hispanic Socio-Cultural Diversity

One of the many dimensions of human nature is the need to make sense of our environment. Frequently, we strive to fulfill this need by placing people and things into pseudo-descriptive categories. We then operate from the subsequent illusion that we "understand" and have, once again, succeeded in making some sense of the complex environment that we live in. Thus, as one looks at earlier (i.e., pre-1970s) descriptions of Hispanics, especially by non-Hispanic psychologists and sociologists, one comes away with the impression that Hispanics are characteristically poor, unacculturated, and living in mostly non-metropolitan areas, especially throughout the southwestern United States, Miami, Florida, and in and around Chicago.

More currently, however, there is much popular and scholarly speculation about how time, trial events, and acculturation have affected Hispanics in the United States.

What follows is a summary of selected socio-cultural attributes relevant to the cultural experiences and adaptations of Hispanics in the United States. The content presented should be viewed from the perspective that Hispanics are a socio-culturally diverse group, constantly in a state of flux. To view Hispanics as a culturally static and homogeneous subgroup would detract from a more sensitive, accurate, and dynamic understanding that is so essential for human service providers.

Familialism

One of the major themes dominating the classical portrayal of the traditional Mexican family is the deep importance of the family to all its members (25, 26, 27). Murillo states that for the Mexican-American male, the family "... is usually at the core of his thinking and behavior and is the center from which his view of the rest of the world extends" (28). He further adds that the importance of the family primarily revolves around its ability to provide emotional support and material security (29).

While the nuclear family is generally believed to be of central importance in most cultures, both as a socializing agent and primary source of emotional and instrumental support, for Hispanics the family may take on special significance as a source of social support and as a vehicle for coping. According to Grebler et al., "The extended family may include one or more relatives, the wife's unmarried sister or widowed father, for instance, or even another nuclear family related to the head of the household" (30). Montiel (31) cautions, however, that to define an extended family in terms of a single household only is unnecessarily restrictive and inaccurate.

Utilizing samples of urban Mexican Americans in San Antonio (N = 603) and Los Angeles (N = 947), Grebler et al. found that few respondents were living in extended family structures (one household) (32). Nevertheless, other data collected by the researchers indicated that family members, both within and outside the nuclear family, were particularly sought out for advice regarding personal problems. Interestingly, higher-income Mexican Americans in both cities tended to follow this pattern more than did low-income Mexican Americans (33).

In a study by Keefe et al. (34) the researchers compared the emotional support systems of Anglos and Mexican-Americans and found that Anglos were, on the whole, more likely to seek help from friends, neighbors, co-workers, and other groups, whereas Mexican-Americans tended to turn to family and extended kin networks first and then to other resources. They point out, however, that the source to which a Mexican-American turns for help varies according to the problem being experienced (35). Thus, for marital (or boyfriend–girlfriend) or family (parent–child) problems, relatives and clergymen were consulted more than twice as often as any other source (i.e., doctor, friend, private therapist, mental health clinic, neighbor, co-worker, *curandero* (folk healer), community worker, etc.).

For the child welfare worker, acknowledging the importance of the Hispanic family unit, nuclear or extended, is very helpful. Capitalizing on the family's strengths and striving to enhance its functional viability will help to keep it intact. Thus, when providing supportive services to Hispanic families, the use of family interviews is especially appropriate. In this context, a major goal of supportive services might be to help the Hispanic family maintain or regain its functional equilibrium without undue culturally dystonic intrusive activities by the child welfare worker. In this sense, it is important for the worker to acknowledge and understand the Hispanic father's usual position of authority and respect afforded him by the children. Thus, for the worker to inappropriately challenge the father's position of authority in the family can further exacerbate the family's state of disequilibrium. This is not to say, however, that helping the father to learn more functional ways of exercising this authority should not be a goal for intervention. In Hispanic families, the mother is typically revered by the children. Thus, for the worker to be openly critical or disparaging towards her would constitute a therapeutic mistake. As Hispanics travel the road towards biculturalism, it is likely that child welfare workers will find themselves working with families whose members are at different stages of acculturation. This can create a great deal of culture conflict, especially between less acculturated parents and more acculturated children and adolescents. It is important for the child welfare worker to help family members understand the dynamics of acculturative stress and culture conflict, especially if the latter is at the core of the family's systemic disequilibrium. Culture conflict between Hispanic children and parents may acutely exacerbate typical conflicts regarding the child's performance of home chores, use of time, morals and manners, choice of friends, selection of clothes, dating practices, etc.

Effective family counseling sessions with Hispanic families might necessitate the use of interviews with the parents and children separately, as well as interviews with the family as a whole.

Compadrazgo

In the traditional Mexican-American family, the social support system of *compadrazgo* (godparents named in a religious ceremony, usually Catholic, who become co-parents to the child and *compadres* to the parents) was seen as a significant resource for mutual support, both expressive and instrumental.

In their exploration of *compadrazgo* in Los Angeles and San Antonio, Grebler et al. found that while *compadrazgo* remains a viable system for mutual support, it ". . . appears to be a minor feature of kinship and community social organization in the major urban centers" (36). Keefe et al. similarly point out that "*Compadres* who are not relatives do not appear to be an important additional source of emotional support for Mexican-Americans" (37). In their study, five percent of the Mexican-American respondents mentioned turning to *compadres* for help.

In the Grebler et al. study (38), it was primarily those respondents who had come to this country from Mexico who saw their own godparents as an important source of help (39).

It is reasonable to surmise that the reliance by Hispanics on the *compadrazgo* system will vary by level of acculturation and possibly by social class as well, although the Grebler et al. study (40) found that social mobility did not seem to make much difference in the strength of the bonds between *compadres*.

In a study of godparents in Puerto Rican families, Vidal explored the perceptions of Puerto Rican godparents (N = 71) in the New York City area (41). He found that 80 percent of the godparent respondents cited four major reasons for having been selected as godparents. The reasons were: (1) being perceived as a person who could maintain family values, norms, and traditions; (2) being respected by the child's parents; (3) being perceived as someone the godchild could look up to; and (4) being able to provide a home for the godchild if needed.

Other reasons, such as being a good friend, a provider of emotional support, a blood relation, and a member of the same community were also considered important by a majority of the godparents. Vidal's findings support the notion that child welfare workers need to consider the significance of the institution of godparenting and incorporate it into collaborative plans for service delivery. Godparents, when available, can be used as a culturally congruent resource in family crisis situations and as temporary, emergency foster care if appropriate. Since there is an acute shortage of Hispanic foster homes, the creative use of godparents, when available, can help to lessen the emotional trauma and structural disruptiveness experienced by Hispanic families in crisis.

The Church

While Catholicism remains the predominant religion for Mexican Americans, Grebler, et al. found that church attendance by Mexican Americans was irregular (42). For Mexican Americans in Los Angeles, there was a positive correlation between church attendance and education. And in San Antonio, the level of income seemed to make little difference to church attendance.

Acosta posits that, "Even if Catholicism is not practiced through regular church attendance, basic Christian beliefs and practices such as prayer may provide tremendous help to the Mexican American in time of need and emotional distress" (43).

Keefe et al., in exploring the use of the Catholic church as a source of emotional support, "used in the last year by Mexican Americans and Anglos," found a utilization rate of 16 percent and 9 percent respectively (44).

Klor de Alva, assessing the role of the Catholic church in Hispanic communities, notes that, "By the 1960s and 1970s, popular pressure forced the church to engage in social actions on behalf of poor Hispanics" (45). He adds, however, that since the beginning of this century, "Protestant sects have been far more active at proselytizing Hispanics, and since the 1960s they have been much more seriously involved in social action projects that support them, than has the Catholic church" (46). Reasons given for the dramatic growth of Hispanic Protestantism include: the high percentage of ministers who are Hispanic, the small and personal congregations, the familiarity of the ministers with Hispanic culture, and the congruence of folk-based spiritual and healing beliefs. The church, whether Catholic or Protestant, can be an important source of support in the child-rearing efforts of Hispanic parents. The church is thus one of the informal support systems that child welfare workers must consider incorporating in their efforts to enhance the psycho-social functioning of Hispanic children and their families. To do so, it is important for a child welfare worker to have positive working relationships with religious leaders in the Hispanic community. This can have two potential benefits. If there are a preexisting rapport and mutual trust, priests and ministers may feel more comfortable referring members of their church for supportive services. This can help alleviate the need for more restrictive child welfare services to the family. Conversely, a child welfare worker who is already working with a Hispanic family might be instrumental in encouraging the family's use of the church as a valuable source of support, especially during a crisis.

Hispanic families stand to gain when child welfare workers are able to effectively interact and collaborate with natural support systems in the community such as the church.

Machismo

One of the factors that has perhaps been a major obstacle to a more humanistic and culturally sensitive understanding of Hispanics, especially males, has been the distortion of the concept of *machismo*. In her extensive review of the literature on the subject of *machismo*, Ruiz found that the writings by Mexican and Latin American writers did not reflect the acknowledgment of cultural or social change, the impact of chronological chance, class differences and urban/rural differences (47, 48). According to Ruiz, these writers tended to interpret *machismo* as a form of psychological overcompensation for feelings of inferiority. Most of the attitudes attributed to the *macho* were defined in negative terms, with negative behavioral implications, e.g., dominance by the male over the female, never backing down from a fight, not opening up, not giving in, sexual promiscuity, etc.

Regarding the research and writings by Anglo authors on the subject of *machismo* and *hembrismo* (the female complementary role), Ruiz asserts that they are characterized by:

> *(1) the "face value" acceptance of the inferiority models posed by Latin writers Ramos, Paz, Bermudez, and Diaz-Guerrero as authentic behavior for all Mexicans both in Mexico and the U.S.; (2) the advancement and application of research and descriptive generalizations about the concepts which further stereotyped them; (3) the continuation of conceptual descriptions affirming machismo and hembrismo as peculiar to Mexicans (and therefore) also to Chicanos, culturally exotic, and behaviorally pathological; (4) the over-simplification of the operational value of these two concepts; and (5) popularization of machismo to the extent that it has been adopted as a commonly used word in the English language with equally popular behavior (49).*

Chicano writers (50), in recognizing the stereotyped manner in which *machismo* has been applied to Chicanos (e.g., pathological in character, genetically inferior, culturally deviant, etc.), and the way in which assumptions made regarding Mexicans from Mexico have been generalized to Chicanos from the United States, and assumptions made regarding rural Chicanos have been generalized to urban Chicanos, have called for a clarification of this state of affairs. Delgado, for example, asserts that:

> *A man who beats up his wife is not macho, but a coward and an* abuzon *(abuser). A man who steps out on his old lady and has extramarital affairs is not macho, but a* sinverguenza *(two-timing vato guy). A man who gets plastered, stoned or pulls a knife on his* compas *(compadres) for no reason at all, is not macho, but a drunk and a troublemaker. These and other attributes have been erroneously labeled as displays of machismo (51).*

Chicano authors suggest that *machismo*, more positively and accurately defined, is associated with a sense of honor, courageousness, and a strong sense of obligation and responsibility to one's family, both nuclear and extended kin.

Machismo is hardly a phenomenon that is unique to Hispanics. However, when negatively defined and generalized to Hispanics, the usual outcome is ethnocentric stereotyping. Such a practice creates social distance between child welfare workers and Hispanics; and, when such labeling is directed to Hispanic fathers, the likelihood of more effectively intervening with Hispanic family systems is greatly diminished. This might occur for two reasons. First of all, if the child welfare worker stereotypically associates negative attitudinal and behavioral attributes to the Hispanic male, the latter may be thought to be uninterested and inaccessible to intervention. In a sense, the worker gives up before he or she even begins. In contrast, a recent study found that 66.7 percent of Mexican-American males surveyed would turn to a professional counselor for help if they were having serious marital problems (52).

A second reason why negative stereotyping of Hispanic males might hamper the effective delivery of services is the child welfare worker's feelings of intimidation at the prospect of working with "such a difficult client." When there is inadequate rapport during initial helping efforts, the development of a viable worker/client relationship might be irreparably undermined.

On the other hand, child welfare workers may enhance their service delivery efforts by acknowledging and appealing to the Hispanic male's sense of honor, courageousness, and strong sense of obligation and responsibility to his family. The social worker must also be sensitive to the potential impact of low income, underemployment, and unemployment upon the Hispanic male's self-concept and self-esteem. Helping the Hispanic male and his family to achieve a stronger sense of empowerment may be a sound goal for intervention.

Folk Medicine

The utilization of folk medicine as a resource for coping by Hispanics, but particularly Mexican Americans, has received ample attention in the social science literature (53, 54, 55, 56).

Kiev, for example, states that *"Curanderismo* persists in the American Southwest because it works" (57). He then goes on to consider the factors that perhaps contribute to the stability of the traditional folk beliefs and practices of *curanderismo,* i.e., the authoritarian structure of the Mexican American family and social and religious life (58). From their study of Mexican-American women in a large Southwestern city in Texas, Martinez and Martin surmised that the use of folk healers continues to be widespread among urbanized Mexican Americans (59).

Ruiz and Langrod (60), in their paper dealing with the relationship between socio-cultural factors and psychopathology in Hispanic groups in a disadvantaged urban area, posit that folk healers are frequently preferred to psychiatrists because ". . . folk healers communicate in the same terminology that their clients use; psychiatrists do not, thus jeopardizing identification and development of a therapeutic alliance" (61). They add that communication problems also create serious difficulties with the non-Spanish-speaking mental health professional's ability to develop empathy toward the non-English-speaking patient. They add that, "Folk healers often understand their clients' frustrations better than psychiatrists do because the folk healers live in the same neighborhood and know it well" (62); because they are generally more available than mental health professionals, especially in economically oppressed communities; and because their services are considerably cheaper. As a result, folk healers are frequently in a strategic position to reach patients when they are in a state of crisis and most amenable to change. The effectiveness of folk healers is also linked by the authors to their ability and willingness ". . . to utilize cultural concepts that are vital in the Hispanic community, such as the extended family network of *ahijados* (godchildren) and *padrinos* (godparents)" (63).

Gonzales, in supporting the continued exploration of *curanderismo* as a viable resource for Chicanos, posits that ". . . the issue of who defines mental health and how it is defined must be examined from a Chicano's perspective" (64).

The extent to which folk healers are actually utilized by Mexican-Americans and other Hispanics is presently open to conjecture. While an appreciable number of writers infer a widespread use of *curanderismo,* others support the view that its importance has greatly diminished over the years (65).

Since adherence to traditional beliefs and practices has frequently been shown to change over time, one might speculate that less acculturated Hispanics might exhibit a higher reliance on folk healers as a resource for coping with psychological stress and problems in the family than more acculturated, middle-class Hispanics.

According to Le Vine and Padilla (66), "most modern-oriented, urban or middle-class Hispanics will not subscribe to faith beliefs." They suggest, however, that, "The therapist should look for a client's belief in folk medicine and faith healing" (67) as a possible adjunct to the helping relationship. Gibson posits that many studies that have linked Hispanics to the use of folk healers have not sufficiently considered Hispanics' limited access to adequate medical and other health services (68). Thus, under these circumstances, folk healers have served to fill a critical void or gap in services for Hispanic children and their families.

Biculturalism

If one is to more fully understand the range of potential psycho-social stresses facing Hispanic children and their families, it is important to consider their experiences with stress as related to a range of cultural adaptations such as biculturalism and the process of acculturation.

Padilla et al., in addressing the psycho-social stresses impacting on Hispanics, have stated that as a group they are only partially acculturated (69). The authors view with concern "... the very stressful problem of acculturation to a society which appears prejudicial, hostile and rejecting. "Biculturalism is a major form of cultural adaptation, whereby the Hispanic person both consciously and unconsciously retains major aspects of his own indigenous culture, but also borrows from that of the dominant majority culture. This may be viewed as a potentially positive acculturative adaptation, to the extent that it implies cultural synthesis, expansion, and flexibility, so that the person is able to concurrently function in two distinct cultural milieus: his, and that of the dominant majority culture. On the other hand, biculturalism may also be experienced as a source of psycho-socio-cultural stress, to the extent that the Hispanic individual finds it mentally, psychologically, and emotionally taxing and, thus, stressful to switch from functioning in one more or less distinct cultural milieu to another. However, optimal biculturalism is not achieved by all Hispanics. Szapocznik and Kurtines, for example, state that individuals living in bicultural contexts may become maladjusted when they remain, or become, mono-cultural (70). They add that individuals who live in a bicultural context, and who either under-acculturate (that is, fail to learn how to, or do not wish to interact with the Anglo-American context), or over-acculturate (that is, reject the skills necessary to interact with the Hispanic-American context), may not have the flexibility necessary to cope with their entire cultural milieu. This state of disequilibrium between the individuals and their context may lead to maladaptive psycho-social functioning.

The acculturative process may be a source of stress because change itself is stressful and because individuals in a given Hispanic family may acculturate at different rates; this may give rise to conflict within the family and between the family and other social institutions in the community, such as schools, social services agencies, etc.

In summary, cultural group membership for Hispanics may be perceived as occurring along a continuum. At one end of the continuum is the person with limited knowledge of the new cultural milieu, but who then gradually becomes more cognitively, socially, and behaviorally congruent with it. At the other end of the continuum is the individual who has become fully acculturated to the formerly new, but now familiar, cultural scenario. The midpoint between the two extremes of the continuum will then be occupied by the individual who has achieved a bicultural adaptation.

A dilemma for some Hispanic families is that family members often acculturate at different rates. According to Ramirez, children usually adapt to American values and norms more readily than their parents, often stimulating inter-generational acculturation conflicts (71). Within the parental dyad itself, there may be acculturation differences, often related to the degree of adherence to traditional family and sex roles, or to different ages at migration. For these reasons, the various complexities of acculturation within the family need to be carefully assessed.

Unfortunately, since there continues to be a shortage of bicultural, bilingual child welfare workers, it is not yet possible for agencies to generally achieve a more viable fit between culturally unique counseling needs of especially unacculturated Hispanic clients and staff available to serve them.

Hispanic Children, Families and Psycho-social Stress

Stress has been defined as something that disturbs a person's psychological or biological equilibrium (72). Another definition is offered by McGrath, who asserts that stress occurs when there is substantial imbalance between environmental demand and the response capability of the focal organism, which may be an individual, a group, or a large organization (73). In the view of Lazarus (74), an environmental demand can produce psychological or perceived stress only if the subject anticipates that he will not be able to cope with it, or cope with it adequately, or cope with it without endangering other goals. Thus, here the stress evolves from the threat experienced by the person through his anticipation that he will not be able to adequately handle perceived demands, whether real or not. McGrath (75) adds that the stress or threat only occurs when the consequences of failure to meet the demands are important; or rather, when they are perceived by the person to be important. He further adds that an individual may deal with threat or psychological stress (i.e., the anticipation of adverse consequences arising from failure to meet demands) purposely or otherwise by avoiding the consequences, by fulfilling the demands at a tolerable cost, or by altering his perception of demands, of capabilities, and/or consequences.

It is now commonly known that for some people, stress-provoking situations, especially if continued over an extended period of time, may even lead to physical illness and psychiatric disorder (76).

Child welfare workers have long considered the social environment as having both potentially supportive and stressful implications for the psycho-social survival of the child and his family system. In specifically addressing the psycho-social characteristics and environments of Hispanics, Padilla et al. state that ". . . the Spanish-speaking, surnamed as a group, are only partially acculturated and marginally integrated economically and, as a consequence, are subject to a number of high-stress indicators" (77). They add that:

> . . . these indicators, known to be correlated with personality disintegration and subsequent need for treatment intervention, include: (a) poor communication skills in English; (b) the poverty cycle, limited education, lower income, depressed social status, deteriorated housing and nominal political influence; (c) the survival traits from a rural agrarian culture which

are relatively ineffectual in an urban-technological society; and . . . (e) the very stressful problems of acculturation to a society which appears prejudicial, hostile and rejecting.

Given the demographic profile of many Hispanic families in the United States which shows that a majority are characterized by low income, low educational achievement, a high rate of unemployment, inadequate housing, and lower age at time of marriage, it would appear that many Hispanic children and their families are constantly besieged by a wide range of psycho-social stresses that have negative effects on the quality of life, psycho-social development, and efforts to cope. It is for these reasons, among others, that adequate supportive and supplemental child welfare services are so relevant for Hispanic children and their families. When such services are not readily available, Hispanic families become more vulnerable to the problems of marital separation and divorce, lower educational achievement, increased parent–child conflict, child abuse and neglect, psychological, social, and acculturative stress, negative self-concept, low self-esteem, and dysfunctional coping efforts such as alcohol and substance abuse.

When socioeconomically oppressed families are not afforded quality child welfare services, they are in essence further victimized by society. The resulting consequences all too often involve a great deal of unnecessary human suffering and remedial services that simply strive to "pick up the pieces" in a stopgap fashion.

Ethnic-Sensitive Child Welfare Practice

Although more has been written about the Hispanic family, especially during the last twenty years than ever before, the specific child welfare needs and problems of Hispanic children have not received adequate attention. A review of most texts on child welfare underscores the cursory attention devoted to Hispanic children and their families. However, when compared to other human service professions, social work has historically been more sensitive to the needs and problems of Hispanics, although even in social work it was not until the late 1970s that more focused attention was devoted to the needs of culturally diverse client populations in general.

One of the major unresolved issues pertinent to child welfare practice with Hispanics is how the worker might go about operationalizing social work values, principles, knowledge, and skills in a manner congruent with the clients' ethnicity. Along this same vein, one of the frequent concerns of recent research in service delivery to Hispanics has been their underutilization of supportive child welfare services and involuntary overutilization of substitute services. Reasons cited for underutilization have included a range of social, economic, and cultural attributes of Hispanics, as well as ineffective service delivery efforts by traditional social service agencies and organizations.

According to Leigh (78), "It has become increasingly evident that to be effective in service delivery, the social worker of today, and of the future, must be sensitive to ethnic considerations and competent in dealing with ethnic concerns." He further adds that "ethnic competence" is defined as the knowledge and skills which enable the worker to understand and utilize ethnic information in daily practice. Ethnic information is considered to include the ethnic client's world view, customs, language, common history, family patterns, relationship and parenting styles, values, and other characteristics associated with ethnicity.

Obviously, if supportive, supplemental, and substitute child welfare services are to more adequately address the child welfare needs of Hispanic children and their families, such services must take into account the psycho-social and economic needs and cultural attributes and diversity of the growing Hispanic population in the United States.

Counseling Services

The principle of "least restrictive environment" posits that child welfare service providers have an ethical responsibility to do everything possible to help children and families remain intact. Supportive services, considered to be the least restrictive in comparison to supplemental and substitute services, are intended to "support, reinforce, and strengthen the ability of parents and children to meet the responsibilities of their respective statuses" (79). Supportive services, then, exemplify the belief that the best place for a child is at home with his or her nuclear or extended family. When we consider the inadequacy of supplemental and substitute services for Hispanic children, the need for quality, culturally relevant supportive services becomes quite apparent. While supportive services include a wide range of informal (that is, self-help) and formal home-based (that is, provided to children while living in their own homes) interventions, the present review will focus on the relevance of formal counseling services and also the use of informal natural support systems among Hispanic families. According to Olenick (80):

> The role of psychotherapy in promoting mental health among low-income Hispanic families and children should be primarily to support efforts in the area of prevention. Traditional one-to-one treatment over an extended period of time does little to improve the community's mental health because opportunities for change are required now . . . .

While the need for and merits of prevention in Hispanic communities is indisputable, there continues to be an ongoing need for remedial child welfare counseling services.

Inclan and Herron (81), in addressing the counseling needs of Puerto Rican adolescents, posit that:

> A valid psychological assessment of Puerto Rican adolescents requires an understanding of relevant sociocultural issues. The experience of these adolescents often differs significantly from that of mainstream White American adolescents, and needless to say, there is wide individual variation among Puerto Rican adolescents.

They add that "Cultural factors, values, and clashes between parental and adolescent generations cannot be overemphasized as necessary considerations in the assessment and treatment of minority group adolescents and Puerto Rican adolescents in particular." They recommend that "Therapists working with poor minority adolescents need to understand that more than one worldview competes for these clients' attention as a viable life course."

In essence, proponents of child welfare services that take Hispanic culture into account have proposed several strategies for accomplishing such a goal. One strategy involves increasing the accessibility of services by utilizing bilingual and bicultural staff. Another strategy proposes that the counseling services received by Hispanics be congruent with their culture. And a third approach has been to focus on modifying culturally prescribed attitudes and behaviors that do not enhance the Hispanic person's ability to function, i.e., sub-assertiveness. In summary, the child welfare needs of Hispanic children and their families can be viably addressed through the use of formal counseling services as long as such services are individualized to incorporate the cultural attributes and needs of Hispanic clients whether they be individuals, couples, families, groups, or communities.

However, formal supportive services are often turned to only after the Hispanic person has made an effort to resolve his or her child welfare needs and problems through the use of informal social support resources when available within the family or in the indigenous community.

Delgado et al. (82) in discussing natural support systems as sources of strength in Hispanic communities, list four specific systems: (1) the extended family, consisting of blood relatives and a wide-ranging constellation of "adopted" relatives who fulfill both formal and informal functions within the extended family. In their view, the family is perceived as the primary social support for family members, especially in times of crisis; (2) folk healers; (3) religious institutions, both organized (the Catholic church) and alternative religions (e.g., Pentecostal, Seventh Day Adventist, Jehovah's Witness, etc.); and (4) merchants' and social clubs.

Valle and Bensussen, in their view of Hispanic networks, social support, and mental health, identify three different types of social networks (83): 1. aggregate networks that consist of large or small, formal or informal, groups which form naturally in the community; relationships here are between non-kinship group members with implicit rights and obligations accruing to the participants. Examples include peer and self-help (i.e., alcohol and substance abuse self-help groups). Another example is a Hispanic parents' self-help group. The purpose of such a group is to help Hispanic parents cope with conflicts between Hispanic and Anglo cultural systems and values, discrimination, inadequate housing, inflation, and poor schooling (84); 2. kinship networks for which membership is achieved via birth, adoption, or marriage. Examples include the nuclear, extended or modified-extended family systems; 3. linkpersons such as may be found in *compadrazgo*, a system of ritual co-parenthood, friends, neighbors, and individuals with formally designated health and counseling roles in the community, i.e., *curanderos* (healers), *yerberos* (herbalists), *sobadores* (masseuses), and *espritualistas* (spiritual counselors). According to Valle and Bensussen:

All three types of networks have one common helping or "socially supportive characteristic" which stands out—namely, the brokering function of the principal natural helpers within the network (85).

Given today's challenging context for parenting and the psycho-social, cultural, and economic attributes of many Hispanic children and their families, there is an ongoing need for both formal supportive services as well as culturally syntonic informal social support resources. Neither should exist to the exclusion of the other.

Maltreatment and Hispanic Children

In a comprehensive six-state (California, Florida, Illinois, Michigan, New York and Texas) study of Hispanic children conducted by the National Latino Child Welfare Advocacy Group (NLCWAG) to assess the child welfare needs of Latino children and families, a five percent increase in incidents of child abuse and neglect was noted between 1993 and 1994 in five of the six states included in the study. Furthermore, almost half (48.8%) of the nation's cases of Hispanic child maltreatment occurred in California and Texas in 1994 (86).

The NLCWAG study also identified several major weaknesses in the capacity of the child welfare system to meet the needs of Hispanic children. These included: a greater tendency to ignore Hispanic parental rights, an insufficient number of appropriate foster care placements, a lack of commitment to cultural diversity, a lack of culturally specific programs for Hispanics, inadequate funding, lack of uniformity in agency policies, and inadequate monitoring of service delivery (87).

Alcohol and Drug Use Among Hispanic Youth

Recent studies suggest that the downward trends in drug, alcohol, and tobacco use by adolescents nationwide that occurred during the 1980s have begun to reverse, especially since 1992. Drawing from data from the combined years of 1994 and 1995, Hispanic twelfth graders reported the highest use of heroin and most forms of cocaine. And, among the younger students, Hispanic eighth graders reported the highest lifetime, annual, and 30-day usage of most drugs such as marijuana, hallucinogens, cocaine, heroin, tranquilizers, and steroids and the highest daily use of marijuana (88).

Hispanic eighth graders also reported the highest usage of alcohol and were more likely to engage in daily drinking and heavy drinking (i.e., five or more drinks in a row in the past two weeks). Possible reasons cited for such high rates of alcohol and drug use among younger Hispanics were: the high dropout rates among Hispanics which tend to occur after the eighth grade and the use of alcohol and drugs at younger ages. Hispanic eighth graders also had the highest rate of lifetime and 30-day cigarette smoking (89). High rates of alcohol and drug use among young Hispanics suggest the more timely preventive and remedial ethnic-sensitive child welfare services.

Family Preservation and Family Reunification Programs

Family preservation programs that focus on strengthening families to prevent out-of-home placement of children have developed in the fields of child welfare, mental health and juvenile justice (90). Families generally served by such programs include families in serious crisis, families that are no longer able to cope with problems that threaten family stability, families in which a decision may have been made by an authorized public social-service agency to place a child outside the home, and families whose children are in temporary out-of-home care and are being reunited (91).

In preliminary studies, the use of intensive family preservation services (IFPS) for reuniting families has been found to be effective. In one recent experimental study of intensive family preservation services serving children who were in foster care for more than 30 days and who were assigned randomly to receive a three-month IFPS intervention, the children were reunited more quickly, in higher numbers, and remained in the home for a greater number of days, using a 12-month follow-up period compared to the control-group youth (92).

While IFPS programs are not a "cure-all," it makes sense to use such programs, especially when they are ethnic-sensitive, to enable Hispanic families to stay together to avoid unnecessary placements outside the home and to reunite families after a child has been removed.

Foster Care

As a form of substitute care, foster care is ideally thought of as a temporary service provided to children unable to obtain adequate care at home. According to Costin and Rapp (93), "the primary reason why children come into foster care is found in family breakdown or incapacity, exacerbated by severe environmental pressures." Frequently, there is a combination of circumstances necessitating foster care; the latter might include conditions such as inadequate support networks to help families maintain their equilibrium; poverty; inadequate community resources (a lack of supportive and supplemental services); and a disruption of a family's usual level of psycho-social functioning.

Unfortunately, children from at-risk Hispanic families tend to receive foster care that is less than ideal. Kadushin and Martin, addressing this problem, state that, "Providing appropriate services for minority children has proved to be a problem in foster care for a variety of reasons . . . children of minority heritage whose families face extensive poverty—black, Hispanic, Native American children—are overrepresented in substitute care" (94). They further add that " . . . minority children, particularly, are less likely than whites to have a clear foster-care plan . . . . and stay in care longer, an average of a year or more, and . . . wait in foster care for more lengthy periods before being adopted." In a study by Jenkins et al. (95), the median time spent in foster care by Hispanic children was twenty-six months, which was six months longer than for white children.

Another area of concern regarding foster care as it pertains to Hispanic children is the unavailability of bilingual, bicultural homes. The loss of proficiency in Spanish and the insidious erosion of the Hispanic child's ethnic identity are often consequences of non-Hispanic foster home placements.

In summary, foster care, as it is currently provided to Hispanic children, leaves much to be desired. More specifically, there is a need for foster care that is higher in quality, more culturally syntonic, and more effective in helping children to be reunited with their natural families.

In a recent report (96), it is estimated that through the year 1990, about 85 percent of the children in foster care in New York were African-American or Hispanic, and that for this reason minority youngsters have frequently been placed in foster care situations that do not match the dominant social characteristics of the children's biological families. The report notes that minority youngsters tend to remain in foster care for long periods.

As a practical solution, Vidal (97) suggests that social service workers be aware of the institution of godparenting as a natural community support system and use it as a resource for permanency planning. Another option is the licensing of relatives and extended family members as foster parents. Such a practice could help temper the trauma experienced by Hispanic children when removed from their nuclear family environment even for temporary periods.

Adoption

According to Kadushin and Martin (98):

> One of the most serious problems in the field of adoption concerns children who are or who might be legally free for adoption, who could benefit from and contribute to normal family living, but who are difficult to place because they belong to a minority group (black, Chicano, American Indian, and so on).

Costin and Rapp (99) concur that, "Proportions of children of racial minorities who need permanent homes through adoption are high." Kadushin and Martin (100) add that as a result "large numbers of minority group children continue to live in impermanent substitute care settings when they could benefit from placement in permanent homes in the community." Without a higher rate of subsidized adoptions, many potential Hispanic adoptive families are less likely to adopt due to low income, employment instability, inadequate housing, etc.

Recommendations for increasing the rate of intra-racial/intra-ethnic (i.e., within the same ethnic group) adoptions include: more assertive outreach into minority communities by adoption agencies; vigorous educational campaigns designed to emphasize the need for minority adoptive homes; modifications in agency procedures, including agency and attorney fee schedules; the reduction of unnecessary "red tape" (without compromising the safety of children or quality of services); the utilization of minority social workers whose racial and ethnic backgrounds are more congruent with those of minority communities; and a reevaluation and revision of "standard, traditional" criteria used to "qualify" potential minority adoptive families.

Without the implementation of more effective and humane policies, procedures, and strategies for finding acceptable adoptive homes for Hispanic children—many of whom have been considered "unadoptable" due to age and other special needs, such as physical, mental, and emotional handicaps—many of these children will unnecessarily remain in foster care and institutional placements. Such a practice only serves to further subject Hispanic children to the continued inimical effects of institutional racism, discrimination, and neglect due to ethnicity and social class.

Summary

Quality, ethnic-sensitive child welfare services for Hispanic children and their families are a right. Such services are imperative to help Hispanic families remain intact. However, when placement outside the home is temporarily indicated, concerted efforts must be made to reunite the family as quickly as possible. This will only occur when family reunification is one of the primary goals of foster care placement, and ongoing therapeutic contact is maintained with the child's family system.

When a Hispanic child can not be reunited with his parents, and parental rights have been abdicated or terminated, timely efforts should be made to find a quality, culturally appropriate adoptive home. This, however, will require assertive, well-planned efforts to recruit Hispanic adoptive parent families.

With the projected increase of Hispanic populations in the United States, the need for quality supportive, supplemental, and substitute child welfare services for Hispanic families will increase. Such a challenge can only be met through the availability of ethnic-sensitive child welfare services that enhance instead of hinder the psycho-social and cultural functioning of Hispanic families.

Endnotes

1. Dorothy V. Harris, "Renewing Our Commitment to Child Welfare," *Social Work* 33 (1988): 483.
2. Patricia Turner Hogan and Sau-Fong Siu, "Minority Children and the Child Welfare System: An Historical Perspective," *Social Work* 33 (1988): 493.
3. Hogan and Siu, "Minority Children," p. 493.
4. Ibid., p. 495.
5. Children's Defense Fund, *The State of America's Children: Yearbook 1998.* Washington D.C.: Author .

6. U.S. Bureau of the Census, "Persons of Spanish Origin in the United States," March 1985 (Advance Report). *Current Population Reports, Population Characteristics,* Series P-20, No. 403 (Washington, D.C.: Government Printing Office, 1985).

7. U.S. Bureau of the Census, The Hispanic Population of the United States: March 1991. *Current Population Reports, Population Characteristic Series P-20, No. 455.* Washington, D.C.: U.S. Government Printing Office, 1991.

8. G. J. Church, "A Melding of Cultures," *Time,* July 8, 1985, pp. 36–39.

9. National Council of La Raza, *State of Hispanic America 1991: An Overview.* Washington, D.C.: National Council of La Raza.

10. U.S. Bureau of the Census, *1990 U.S. Census Population and Housing Summary Tape File 3 A,* 1996.

11. T. Nuno, C. Dorrington, and I. Alvarez, *Los Angeles County Hispanic Youth Health Assessment Report, 1998,* p. 1–2 (note: this means chapter 1, page 2; this is the way the pages are numbered throughout the document by the authors).

12. Cary Davis, Carl Haub, and Jo Anne L. Willette, "U.S. Hispanics: Changing the Face of America," in *The Hispanic Experience in the U.S.: Contemporary Issues and Perspectives,* eds. Edna Acosta-Belen and Barbara R. Sjostrom, pp. 107–136.

13. Davis, Haub, and Willette, "U.S. Hispanics," p. 27.

14. S. Gordon, *The Sexual Adolescent* (North Scituate, MA: Duxbury Press, 1973.)

15. Davis, Haub, and Willette, "U.S. Hispanics," p. 39.

16. Nuno, et al., p. 1–2.

17. Ibid., p. 40.

18. Ibid., p. 40.

19. Ibid., p. 39.

20. Ibid., p. 42.

21. Ibid., p. 42.

22. Nuno, et al., p. 1–3.

23. Ibid., p. 1–3.

24. Ibid., p. 42.

25. L. Grebler, J. W. Moore, and R. C. Guzman, *The Mexican American People: The Nation's Second Largest Minority,* p. 351.

26. N. Murillo, "The Mexican-American Family," in *Chicanos: Social and Psychological Perspectives,* eds. C. A. Hernandez, M. J. Haug, and N. N. Wagner, pp. 15–25.

27. W. Madsen, *The Mexican-Americans of South Texas* (New York: Holt, Rinehart and Winston, 1964).

28. Murillo, p. 19.

29. Ibid., p. 20.

30. Grebler, Moore, and Guzman, p. 128.

31. M. Montiel, "The Chicano Family: A Review of Research," *Social Work* 18 (1973): 23.

32. Grebler, Moore, and Guzman, pp. 352–53.

33. Ibid., pp. 356–57.

34. S. E. Keefe, A. Padilla, and M. L. Carlos, "The Mexican American Extended Family as an Emotional Support System," in *Family and Mental Health in the Mexican-American Community,* eds. M. J. Casas and S. E. Keefe (Los Angeles: Spanish-speaking Mental Health Research Center, University of California at Los Angeles, Monograph No. 7, 1978), 65.

35. Keefe, Padilla, and Carlos, "The Mexican American Extended Family," p. 63.

36. Grebler, Moore, and Guzman, p. 355.

37. Keefe, Padilla, and Carlos, "The Mexican American Extended Family," pp. 57–8.

38. Grebler, Moore, and Guzman, p. 354.

39. Ibid., p. 355.

40. Ibid., p. 354.

41. Carlos Vidal, "Godparenting Among Hispanic Americans." *Child Welfare* 67 (Sept.–Oct. 1988): 453–59.

42. Grebler, Moore, and Guzman, pp. 472–75.

43. F. X. Acosta, "Ethnic Variables in Psychotherapy: The Mexican-American," in *Chicano Psychology,* ed. J. L. Martinez, p. 217.

44. Keefe, Padilla, and Carlos, "The Mexican American Extended Family," p. 56.

45. J. Jorge Klor de Alva, "Telling Hispanics Apart: Latino Sociocultural Diversity," in *The Hispanic Experience in the U.S.: Contemporary Issues and Perspectives,"* eds. Edna Acosta-Belen and Barbara R. Sjostrom, pp. 107–36.

46. Klor de Alva, "Telling Hispanics Apart: Latino Sociocultural Diversity," p. 127.

47. J. S. Ruiz, *Clarifications of the Concepts of Machismo and Hembrismo: Significance for Social Work Practice with Chicanos,* pp. 34–67.

48. Ibid., p. 55.

48. Ibid., p. 56.

50. Ibid., p. 68–82.

51. A. Delgado, "Machismo," *La Luz* (December 1974): 6.

52. R. Delgado, *An Exploratory Study of Marital Satisfaction, Psychological Stresses and Coping Preferences of Married Mexican American Males,* p. 147.

53. C. Martinez and H. W. Martin, "Folk Diseases Among Urban Mexican-Americans," *Journal of the American Medical Association,* 196 (1966): 161–64.

54. A. Kiev, *Curanderismo: Mexican-American Folk Psychiatry.*

55. P. Ruiz and J. Langrod, "The Role of Folk Healers in Community Health Services," *Community Mental Health Journal* 10 (1976): 392–98.

56. E. Gonzales, "The Role of Chicano Folk Beliefs and Practices in Mental Health," in *Chicanos: Social and Psychological Perspectives,* eds. C. A. Hernandez, M. J. Haug, and N. N. Wagner, pp. 163–81.

57. Kiev, *Curanderismo,* p. 148.

58. Ibid., pp. 149–74.

59. Martinez and Martin, "Folk Diseases Among Urban Mexican-Americans," pp. 161–64.

60. Ruiz and Langrod, "The Role of Folk Healers in Community Mental Health Services," pp. 392–98.

61. Ibid., p. 394.

62. Ibid., p. 394.

63. Ibid., p. 395.

64. Gonzalez, "Chicano Folk Beliefs," p. 264.

65. R. B. Edgerton, M. Karno, and I. Fernandez, "Curanderismo in the Metropolis: The Diminishing Role of Folk-Psychiatry Among Los Angeles Mexican-Americans," *American Journal of Psychotherapy* 24 (1970): 124–34.

66. E. Le Vine and A. M. Padilla, *Crossing Cultures in Therapy: Pluralistic Counseling for the Hispanic,* p. 150.

67. Ibid., p. 150.

68. Guadalupe Gibson, "Child Welfare and the Welfare of Mexican-American Children," in *Human Services for Mexican-American Children,* ed. Andres A. Tijerina, p. 22.

69. A. M. Padilla, R. A. Ruiz, and R. Alvarez, "Delivery of Community Mental Health Services to the Spanish-speaking Surnamed Population," in *Delivery of Services for Latino Community Mental Health,* ed. R. Alvarez, pp. 12–13.

70. J. Szapocznik and W. Kurtines, "Acculturation, Biculturalism and Adjustment among

Cuban-Americans," in *Acculturation: Theory, Models and Some New Findings,* ed. A. M. Padilla, p. 146.

71. Oscar Ramirez, "Mexican American Children and Adolescents," in *Children of Color: psychological Interventions with Minority Youth,* eds. J. T. Gibbs, L. N. Huang, and Associates, p. 234.

72. P. M. Insel and W. T. Roth, *Health in a Changing Society,* p. 555.

73. J. McGrath, ed., *Social and Psychological Factors in Stress,* pp. 15–17.

74. R. S. Lazarus, *Psychological Stress and the Coping Process,* pp. 179–85.

75. McGrath, *Social and Psychological Factors in Stress,* p. 18.

76. B. S. Dohrenwend and P. Bruce, ed., *Stressful Live Events: Their Nature and Effects.*

77. Padilla, Ruiz, and Alvarez, "Delivery of Community Mental Health Services," pp. 11–38.

78. J. W. Leigh, Jr., "The Ethnically Competent Social Worker," in *A Handbook of Child Welfare: Context, Knowledge, and Practice,* eds. J. Laird and A. Hartman, p. 449.

79. A Kadushin and J. A. Martin, *Child Welfare Services,* p. 83.

80. C. Olenick, "Observations on the Effectiveness of Psychotherapy for Low-Income Hispanic Families and Children," in *Proceedings of Puerto Rican Conferences on Human Services,* eds. D. J. Curren, J. J. Rivera, and R. B. Sanchez (Washington, D.C.: National Coalition of Spanish-Speaking Mental Health Organization, 1975), p. 150.

81. J. E. Inclan and D. G. Herron, "Puerto Rican Adolescents," in *Children of Color: Psychological Interventions with Minority Youth,* eds. J. T. Gibbs, L. N. Huang, and Associates. (San Francisco: Jossey-Bass, 1980), p. 259.

82. M. Delgado and D. Humm-Delgado, "Natural Support Systems: A Source of Strength in Hispanic Communities," *Social Work* 27 (1981): 85–89.

83. R. Valle and G. Bensussen, "Hispanic Social Networks, Social Support and Mental Health," in *Hispanic Psychological Perspectives and Social Work Practice,* ed. Rodolfo Arevalo (Needham Heights, MA: Ginn Press, 1988), p. 227.

84. A. M. Leon, R. Mazur, E. Montalvo, and M. Rodrieguez, "Self-help Support Groups for Hispanic Mothers," *Child Welfare* 63 (May–June 1984): 261.

85. Valle and Bensussen, "Hispanic Social Networks," p. 229.

86. R. M. Ortega, C. Guillean, and L. Gutierrez Najera. Latinos and Child Welfare/Latinos y El Bienestar del Nino, Voces de la Comunidad, cited in T. Nuno, C. Dorrington, and I. Alvarez, *Los Angeles County Hispanic Youth Health Assessment 1998,* p. 7–4.

87. Nuno, et al., p. 7–4.

88. Nuno et al., p. 4–1.

89. Nuno et al., p. 4–1.

90. P. J. Pecora, "Are Intensive Family Preservation Services Effective?" in E. Gambrill and T. J. Stein, eds., *Controversial Issues in Child Welfare,* p. 290.

91. Ibid., p. 291.

92. Ibid., p. 296.

93. L. B. Costin and C. A. Rapp, *Child Welfare: Policies and Practice,* p. 335.

94. Kadushin and Martin, *Child Welfare Services,* p. 441.

95. S. Jenkins et al., "Ethnic Differentials in Foster Care Placement," *Social Work Research and Abstracts* 19 (Winter 1983): 43.

96. Foster Care 1984, "A Report on the Implementation of the Recommendations of the Mayor's Task Force on Foster Care," *Race and Ethnicity Special Concerns,* 1984.

97. C. Vidal, "Godparenting Among Hispanic Americans," pp. 443–459.

98. Kadushin and Martin, *Child Welfare Services,* p. 592.

99. Costin and Rapp, *Child Welfare,* p. 426.

100. Kadushin and Martin, *Child Welfare Services,* p. 593.

Bibliography

Acosta, F. X. "Ethnic Variables in Psychotherapy: The Mexican-American." In *Chicano Psychology*, ed. J. L. Martinez, New York: Academic Press, 1977, pp. 215–232.

Children's Defense Fund Reports. July 1989. "Hispanic Children in America," pp. 4–5.

Children's Defense Fund. *The State of America's Children: Yearbook 1998.* Washington D.C.: Author.

Church, G. J. "A Melding of Cultures," *Time,* July 8, 1985.

Costin, L. B., and Rapp, C. A. *Child Welfare: Policies and Practice,* 3/e. New York: McGraw-Hill Book Company, 1984.

Davis, Cary, Haub, Carl, and Willette, Jo Anne L. "U.S. Hispanics: Changing the Face of America." In *The Hispanic Experience in the U.S.: Contemporary Issues and Perspectives,* Edna Acosta-Belen and Barbara R. Sjostrom, eds. New York: Praeger Publications, 1988, pp. 107–136.

Delgado, A. "Machismo." *La Luz* (December 1974): 6.

Delgado, R. *An Exploratory Study of Marital Satisfactions, Psychological Stresses and Coping Preferences of Married Mexican-American Males.* Unpublished doctoral dissertation. University of Southern California, 1984.

Dohrenwend, B. S. and Bruce, P., ed., *Stressful Life Events: Their Nature and Effects,* New York: Wiley, 1974.

Edgerton, R. B., Karno, M., and Fernandez, I. "Curanderismo in the Metropolis: The Diminishing Role of Folk-Psychiatry Among Los Angeles Mexican-Americans." *American Journal of Psychotherapy* 24 (1970): 124–134.

Gibson, Guadalupe. "Child Welfare and the Welfare of Mexican-American Children," in *Human Services for Mexican-American Children,* edited by Andres A. Tijerina, pp. 9–40. Austin, Texas: Center for Social Work Research, School of Social Work, the University of Texas at Austin, 1978.

Gonzales, E. "The Role of Chicano Folk Beliefs and Practices in Mental Health," in *Chicanos: Social and Psychological Perspectives,* C. A. Hernandez, M. J. Haug, and N. N. Wagner, eds., Saint Louis: The C. V. Mosby Company, 1976, pp. 263–81.

Gordon S. *The Sexual Adolescent,* North Scituate, MA: Duxbury Press, 1973.

Grebler, L., Moore, J. W., and Guzman, R. C. *The Mexican-American People: The Nation's Second Largest Minority,* New York: The Free Press, 1970.

Harris, Dorothy V. "Renewing Our Commitment to Child Welfare." *Social Work* 33 (1988): 483.

Hogan, Patricia Turner, and Siu, Sau-Fong. "Minority and the Child Welfare System: An Historical Perspective," *Social Work* 33 (1988): 493.

Insel, P. M. and Roth, W. T. *Health in a Changing Society,* Palo Alto, California: Mayfield, 1976.

Kadushin, A. and Martin, J. A. *Child Welfare Services,* 4/e, New York: MacMillan Publishing Company, 1988.

Keefe, S. E., Padilla, A., and Carlos, M. L. "The Mexican-American Extended Family as an Emotional Support System," in *Family and Mental Health in the Mexican-American Community,* M. J. Casas and S. E. Keefe, eds. Los Angeles: Spanish Speaking Mental Health Research Center, University of California at Los Angeles, Monograph No. 7, 1978, pp. 49–68.

Keefe, S. E., Padilla, A., and Carlos, M. L. "Emotional Support Systems in Two Cultures: A Comparison of Mexican-Americans and Anglo-Americans." In *The Chicano Community: Psychological Theory and Practice,* J. M. Herrera, ed., New Haven: Yale University Press, 1976.

Kiev, A. Curanderismo: *Mexican American Folk Psychiatry.* New York: The Free Press, 1968

Klor de Alva, J. Jorge, "Telling Hispanics Apart: Latino Socio-cultural Diversity." In *The Hispanic Experience in the U.S.: Contemporary Issues and Perspectives,* edited by Edna Acosta-Belen and Barbara R. Sjostrom, New York: Praeger Publications, 1988, pp. 107–136.

Lazarus, R. S. *Psychological Stress and the Coping Process.* New York: McGraw Hill, 1966.

Le Vine, E., and Padilla, A. M. *Crossing Cultures in Therapy: Pluralistic Counseling for the Hispanic.* Monterey, California: Brooks/Cole Publishing Company, 1980.

Leigh, J. W., Jr. "The Ethnically Competent Social Worker." In *A Handbook of Child Welfare: Context, Knowledge, and Practice,* J. Laird and A. Harman, eds., New York: The Free Press, 1985, pp. 449–59.

Lum, D. *Social Work Practice and People of Color: A Process-Stage Approach.* Monterey, California: Brooks/Cole Publishing Company, 1986.

Madsen, W. *The Mexican-Americans of South Texas.* New York: Holt, 1964.

Martinez, C., and Martin, H. W. "Folk Diseases Among Urban Mexican-Americans," *Journal of the American Medical Association* 196 (1966): 161–164.

McGrath, J., ed., *Social and Psychological Factors in Stress,* New York: Holt, Rinehart and Winston, 1970.

Montiel, M. "The Chicano Family: A Review of Research." *Social Work* 18 (1973): 22–31.

Murillo, N. "The Mexican-American Family." In *Chicanos: Social and Psychological Perspectives,* C. A. Hernandez, M. J. Haug, and N. N. Wagner, eds., Saint Louis: The C. V. Mosby Company.

National Council of La Raza. *State of Hispanic America 1991: An Overview,* Washington, D.C.: National Council of La Raza, 1991.

Nuno, T., Dorrington, C., and Alvarez, I. *Los Angeles County Hispanic Youth Health Assessment Report,* Washington, D.C.: National Coalition of Hispanic Health and Human Services Organizations (COSSMHO), 1998.

Ortega, R. M., C. Guillean, and L. Gutierrez Najera. "Latinos and Child Welfare/Latinos y el Bienestar del Nino, Voces de la Comunidad," cited in Los Angeles *County Hispanic Youth Health Assessment* by T. Nuno, C. Dorrington, and I. Alvarez, Washington, D.C.: National Coalition of Hispanic Health and Human Services (COSSMHO), 1998, Chapter 7, p. 4.

Padilla, A. M., Ruiz, R. A., and Alvarez, R. "Delivery of Community Mental Health Services to the Spanish Speaking Surnamed Population." In *Delivery of Services for Latino Community Mental Health,* R. Alvarez, ed., Los Angeles: Spanish-Speaking Mental Health Research Center, University of California at Los Angeles, Monograph No. 2, 1975, pp. 11–38.

Pecora, P. J., and T. L. Rznepnici, "Are Intensive Family Preservation Services Effective?" in *Controversial Issues in Child Welfare,* E. Gambrill and T. J. Stein, eds., Boston: Allyn and Bacon, 1994, pp. 290–309.

Ramirez, Oscar. "Mexican-American Children and Adolescents.: In *Children of Color: Psychological Interventions with Minority Youth,* edited by Gibbs, J. T., Huang, L. N., and Associates, San Francisco: Jossey-Bass Publishers, 1989, pp. 224–229.

Ruiz, J. S. *Clarification of the Concepts of Machismo and Hembrismo: Significance for Social Work Practice with Chicanos.* Unpublished doctoral dissertation. University of Denver, 1975.

Ruiz, P., and Langrod, J. "The Role of Folk Healers in Community Mental Health Services." *Community Mental Health Journal* 10 (1976): 392–398.

Szapocznick, J., and Kurtines, W. "Acculturation, Biculturalism and Adjustment Among Cuban-Americans." In *Acculturation: Theory, Models and Some New Findings,* edited by A.

M. Padilla, Boulder, Colorado: Published by Westview Press for the American Association for the Advancement of Science, AAAS Selected Symposium 39, 1980, pp. 139–160.

U.S. Bureau of the Census. The Hispanic Population of the United States: March 1991. *Current Population Reports, Population Characteristics,* Series P-20, No. 455, Washington, D.C.: U.S. Government Printing Office, 1991.

U.S. Bureau of the Census. Persons of Spanish Origin in the United States: March 1985 (Advance Report). *Current Population Reports, Population Characteristics,* Series P-20, No. 403. Washington, D.C.: U.S. Government Printing Office 1985.

Vidal, Carlos. "Godparenting Among Hispanic Americans." *Child Welfare* 67 (September–October 1988): 453–59.

CHAPTER

8 Child Abuse and Neglect

CYNTHIA CROSSON TOWER

Fitchburg State College

One of the most difficult issues facing the child welfare worker is that of child abuse and neglect. The first time one observes a badly beaten child, walks into a home reeking of human waste and garbage, or hears a child recount the details of sexual molestation by a parent, the neophyte worker may wonder at his or her choice of profession. Although the trend is toward having a special unit of workers trained in protective services to handle the investigation of such cases, the generalist may nevertheless come in contact with abuse or neglect situations either at intake or for case management on an ongoing basis. In some smaller offices, protective services cases may be integrated into a general caseload. The worker seeing a family for other reasons must also be sensitized to recognizing where abuse

193

or neglect becomes an issue. Maltreatment is not always the presenting complaint. Rather it may be at the root of other, more obvious problems. In addition, as our society becomes more diverse, the protective worker increasingly is called upon to understand cultural differences in child rearing. Some of these may constitute abuse or neglect according to U.S. laws.

For these reasons, it is vital that the child welfare generalist be familiar with the signals pointing to abuse, the needs and motivations of the parent, and procedures used in intervention.

Historical Background

To truly understand maltreatment, we must see it within a historical context. Child abuse and neglect are an age-old phenomenon. Children have been killed, maimed, beaten, and seduced throughout history—sometimes in the interest of cultural mores, or sometimes purely due to the pathology of the abuser.

In our earliest history, children were regarded as chattels—the property of their parents, who governed them to the point of control over their life or death. Early religions saw children offered as sacrifices; Abraham, for example, intended to sacrifice his son Isaac to his God. Infanticide, the killing of babies and young children, served as a form of population control when children were unwanted, deformed, or not of the preferred sex. Native American tribes practiced a ritual of plunging babies into frigid water to test their ability to survive (1).

Children were expected to be obedient, and disobedience could be dealt with severely. Educators as well as parents were allowed—even expected—to punish children harshly. Inglis states that:

> Schoolmasters in colonial Boston were conscious of the need to maintain the great English tra-
> dition of "education through pain" and, if anything, added refinements to the flagellant tools
> they had inherited from the old country. One Bostonian invented an instrument called a
> "flapper"—a heavy piece of leather six inches in diameter with a hole in the middle which
> was fixed to a wooden handle. Every stroke on a bare bit of flesh raised an instant blister (2).

Our forefathers, influenced certainly by Calvinist tradition, felt that such "discipline" was needed to transform children into God-fearing individuals who would later become productive adults.

Early cultures also found the sexual misuse of children acceptable. In early Greece pederasty (men using boys sexually) was practiced extensively. Boys of afflu-ent or noble families were initiated into their sexuality by adult lovers, reportedly in preparation for the youth's destiny as future soldiers. The benefactor in turn offered protection to his youthful charge. Young girls (often as young as nine or ten) promised to convents in the middle ages became the sexual playthings of monks. To disclose this practice was tantamount to excommunication for these postulates (3).

Not only were children beaten and sexually abused, they were exploited in other ways. Authors such as Charles Dickens and Jonathan Swift have made us aware of the injustices perpetrated upon children. Dickens, a reformer and child advocate in his own right, describes in *Oliver Twist* the failing of the apprentice system—a practice that involved placing children at early ages with masters who would teach them a trade. Unfortunately, these masters were not always interested in more than the child's production power. Some masters extracted from their charges, by whatever means they saw fit, work that often surpassed the child's developmental abilities.

The Industrial Revolution increased the need for children as inexpensive labor. Children were brought to the New World to work not only in factories, but at unhealthy jobs (e.g., mining, chimney sweeping) which necessitated their smallness and dexterity. Children did find advocates, however. In the late 1800s the settlement houses—especially Jane Addams' Hull House in Chicago—took on the task of curbing the exploitation of children through child labor.

It was in 1874, just prior to this time, that the first efforts were made to protect children from being physically beaten. In fact, the course of social service history was changed by Mary Ellen Wilson, an eight-year-old girl who was being cared for by foster parents. Mary Ellen's screams as she was beaten had been heard by neighbors. She had been seen scantily clad and shivering outside the locked door of her apartment. But no one knew how to intervene. A "friendly visitor," Etta Wheeler, finally brought the situation to Henry Bergh of the Society for the Prevention of Cruelty to Animals. The outcome of the case was the birth of a new agency, The Society for the Prevention of Cruelty to Children (SPCC), in early 1875. Today the SPCC continues to advocate for maltreated children with prevention as well as treatment efforts (4).

Following the example set by the SPCC, the American Humane Association, another agency dedicated to the protection of animals, created a children's division in 1887 to aid in the coordination of many of the voluntary service organizations that had begun to spring up throughout the United States. The emphasis of these new agencies was on rescuing children from the horror of abuse. Toward this end, these advocates for children fostered legal statutes that would seek to protect children from abusive caretakers. Little concern was expressed over the needs of those caretakers.

Despite the rapid increase in the founding of protective agencies during the late 1800s and early 1900s, the public's interest turned in other directions from the 1920s on. It was not until the 1950s that child abuse again became a concern, and this was due largely to the efforts of several physicians. In 1946, John Caffey, a radiologist questioning the unexplained fractures detected by the x-rays of several young children, concluded that they must have been intentionally inflicted. Physicians became interested in Caffey's work, until in 1962, Dr. C. Henry Kempe of the Department of Pediatrics at the Colorado School of Medicine published an article outlining what he termed the "battered-child syndrome" (5). Kempe contended that children with these unexplained breaks had been subject to abuse at the hands of caretakers. His writings stimulated active interest by other physicians as well as social workers until well into the 1970s. By 1974, the federal government took its stand through the Child Abuse Prevention and Treatment Act, which authorized funding for projects devoted to the identification, treatment, and prevention of child abuse and neglect. By 1978 protective agencies were in place in all fifty states (6).

Today child abuse and neglect is addressed extensively in federal grants and publications. The state of the art in child protection has progressed considerably since the time of Mary Ellen. Until recently, however, we have tended to look at child abuse and neglect from a majority perspective. Only in the last few years have the researcher and the practitioner considered the detection and treatment of child abuse and neglect within a cultural context. Understanding the cultural implications inherent in the treatment of minorities is vitally important to the protection of children.

Defining Child Maltreatment

Child maltreatment is frequently divided into several categories: physical abuse, physical neglect, sexual abuse, and emotional abuse.

As summarized in Table 8.1, each of these categories has specific characteristics and should be considered individually.

Physical Abuse

Definition.   Most sources would agree that physical abuse refers to "non-accidental injury inflicted by a caretaker." Two dilemmas arise, however, with this definition.

1. *What is the difference between discipline and abuse?* Is physical punishment as a form of discipline considered abusive? This is a point which has created much controversy worldwide. Some years ago Sweden passed a law prohibiting the hitting of children for any reason. In the United States, however, many families use physical punishment as part of their child-rearing practices. Only five states outlaw corporal punishment in schools.

   One argument suggests that abuse is a matter of degree. If a child is hit to the point where bruises are left on the skin for a prolonged period of time, this is abusive. Some state statutes do not recognize that the child has been abused if the bruises are not present after 24 hours.

   Other definitions recognize intent as an important factor. If a caretaker intends harm to the child, the act would be considered abusive. The problem with this interpretation becomes more obvious in the following example.

Case Example: Diedre

Two-year-old Diedre was brought to the hospital by her mother. The palm of the child's hand had been severely burned on the family's wood stove. When asked how it had happened, the mother explained:

"I told her not to touch that stove. She kept going nearer until I just grabbed her hand and showed her how it'd hurt. She won't go near that stove again, I'm sure."

Diedre's mother did not set out to intentionally harm her child. Her intent was to teach her a valuable lesson. It was the means that were abusive.

2. *When are cultural practices abusive?*

Case Example: Alphonso

Juan Hernandez was indisputably the head of his family. In his native land, children never questioned their father's authority. But peer pressure here in the United states had caused 9-year-old Alphonso to disobey with increasing frequency. Feeling that his son's behavior could be tolerated no longer, Mr. Hernandez gave him a beating which brought the family to the attention of the school and initiated a report to protective services.

Culturally, Mr. Hernandez was within his patriarchal rights to deal with his son as he saw fit. Yet in his adopted culture, his practices were questioned.

Gray and Cosgrove cited ". . . physical discipline, most often for disobedience which followed after several verbal warnings" (7) as one of the most frequently reported types of abuse for Mexican Americans. The use of corporal punishment is just one cultural practice that is subject to reports of abuse. Similarly, the Vietnamese practice a ritual called *cao gio,* coin rubbing: A hot coin is dipped in oil and rubbed on the skin. The purpose is to cure illness, ward off spirits, or in general promote well-being (8). The results are ugly marks which are often reported to social service agencies.

While the results of such practices may be considered by law as abusive, it is important to understand the meaning of these cultural customs to the abuser.

Symptoms

Physical abuse is detected from a variety of symptoms. Bruises make up a large category of symptoms. Although it is possible for a child to sustain bruises from play, these are often centered on exposed areas of the body, such as the knees, shins, elbows, hands, etc. When bruises appear on the less likely areas of the body such as upper arms, back, face, head, upper legs, genitalia, abuse should be at least considered. This is not to say that a fall might not cause an injury to the face or head, for example. But if a child frequently sustains bruises in this area, abuse, or even poor supervision, is possible. Some abusers use objects, such as coat hangers, cords, sticks, or belts, to inflict pain. Bruises in the shape of objects or that radiate around the body (from cords, ropes, etc.) attest to the use of instruments. Bruises change color according to their ages. A new bruise is red, but turns blue about six to twelve hours later. In 12 to 24 hours, the injury will become blackish-purple. A dark greenish tint develops around four to six days, and finally a pale green or yellow between five to ten days means that the bruise will soon be healed (9).

It is important to note that the above colorings may be more difficult to discern on darker skin pigmentation. Other types of bruises may result from human bite marks (adult size), pinch marks, fingernail scratches and choke marks.

Fractures, first discovered by radiologists, are also indicative of abuse. Sometimes a child's bones are broken imperceptibly and left untreated. The result is calcium deposits around the fracture, which can be detected by x-ray. Spiral fractures

TABLE 8.1   **Physical and Behavioral Indicators of Child Abuse and Neglect***

Type of Child Abuse/Neglect	Physical Indicators	Behavioral Indicators
PHYSICAL ABUSE	Unexplained bruises and welts: • on face, lips, mouth • on torso, back, buttocks, thighs • in various stages of healing • clustered, forming regular patterns • reflecting shape of article used to inflict (electric cord, belt buckle) • on several different surface areas • regularly appear after absence, weekend, or vacation • human bite marks • bald spots Unexplained burns: • cigar, cigarette burns, especially on soles, palms, back, or buttocks • immersion burns (sock-like, glove-like, doughnut-shaped on buttocks or genitalia) • patterned like electric burner, iron, etc. • rope burns on arms, legs, neck, or torso Unexplained fractures: • to skull, nose, facial structure • in various stages of healing • multiple or spiral fractures Unexplained lacerations or abrasions: • to mouth, lips, gums, eyes • to external genitalia	Wary of adult contacts Apprehensive when other children cry Behavioral extremes: • aggressiveness, or • withdrawal • overly compliant Afraid to go home Reports injury by parents Exhibits anxiety about normal activities, e.g., napping Complains of soreness and moves awkwardly Destructive to self and others Early to school or stays late as if afraid to go home Accident prone Wears clothing that covers body when not appropriate Chronic runaway (especially adolescents) Cannot tolerate physical contact or touch
PHYSICAL NEGLECT	Consistent hunger, poor hygiene, inappropriate dress Consistent lack of supervision, especially in dangerous activities or long periods Unattended physical problems or medical needs Abandonment Lice Distended stomach, emaciated	Begging, stealing food Constant fatigue, listlessness or falling asleep States there is no caretaker at home Frequent school absence or tardiness Destructive, pugnacious School dropout (adolescents) Early emancipation from family (adolescents)

TABLE 8.1 (*Continued*)

Type of Child Abuse/Neglect	Physical Indicators	Behavioral Indicators
SEXUAL ABUSE	Difficulty in walking or sitting	Unwilling to participate in certain physical activities
	Torn, stained or bloody underclothing	Sudden drop in school performance
	Pain or itching in genital area	Withdrawal, fantasy or unusually infantile behavior
	Bruises or bleeding in external genitalia, vaginal, or anal areas	Crying with no provocation
	Venereal disease	Bizarre, sophisticated, or unusual sexual behavior or knowledge
	Frequent urinary or yeast infections	Anorexia (especially adolescents)
	Frequent unexplained sore throats	Sexually provocative
		Poor peer relationships
		Reports sexual assault by caretaker
		Fear of or seductiveness toward males
		Suicide attempts (especially adolescents)
		Chronic runaway
		Early pregnancies
EMOTIONAL MALTREATMENT	Speech disorders	Habit disorders (sucking, biting, rocking, etc.)
	Lags in physical development	Conduct disorders (antisocial, destructive, etc.)
	Failure to thrive (especially in infants)	Neurotic traits (sleep disorders, inhibition of play)
	Asthma, severe allergies, or ulcers	Behavioral extremes: • complaint, passive • aggressive, demanding
	Substance abuse	Overly adaptive behavior: • inappropriately adult • inappropriately infantile
		Developmental lags (mental, emotional)
		Delinquent behavior (especially adolescents)

are especially suspect, as these indicate that the limb has been twisted forcefully. For the most part, babies do not sustain fractures under normal conditions. When infants and children receive fractures, there is usually swelling and discomfort. Healthy children will complain to a parent. It is not likely that such an injury sustained in normal activity would go undetected. Thus, when previously untreated fractures are later discovered, the situation should be investigated.

Some abused children sustain head injuries or skull fractures. These can be extremely serious, since blood can collect around the surface of the brain as a result; this is referred to as a subdural hematoma. Often children experiencing these types of fractures vomit, have seizures, or lose consciousness (10). Of particular concern is the shaking of babies and young children to the point that it causes head injuries. Brought to public attention by the well-publicized trial of an English nanny, the "shaken baby syndrome" has gained national attention. Shaking a baby can cause not only fractures, but detached retinas, subdural hematomas, and even death (11).

Burns are also characteristic of child abuse. It is often the infant or young child who is the victim here. Social workers report that the most frequent tool to burn with is the cigarette. While one cigarette burn may attest to a careless moment, multiple burns, especially on the abdomen, bottom of the feet, genitals, and other inaccessible areas, are usually deliberate. Children may also be burned by scalding water or other liquids, hot pokers, irons, heating grates, or radiators.

Children demonstrate a variety of behaviors which suggest that they may be abused. Infants who are abused may exhibit a shrill cry which does not change according to their needs. As the abused children grow older, motor and social development become delayed. They may become withdrawn, displaying an apparent incapacity to enjoy life. Some parents are able to care for young dependent infants, but abusive behavior begins when their child becomes more autonomous as a toddler or at school age. Abused children will learn to be compliant in order not to stimulate parental abuse. Their conflict may manifest itself in other ways, however. Some children wet the bed (called *enuresis*) while others soil (*encopresis*). They may begin to have difficulty in learning and have problems in school. Some demonstrate compulsive behavior. Almost all abused children demonstrate low self-esteem.

Table 8.1 describes other physical and behavioral indicators of physical abuse.

It is important when identifying symptoms of abuse that the social worker consider the family's cultural heritage. A knowledge of cultural practices may give some helpful clues to the origin of the symptom.

Abusive Parents

Abusive parents have a variety of motivations for harming their children. Some see their abuse of their children as synonymous with discipline; this is how the parents themselves were raised. For example, disobedient behavior for Joe Helfsted was met with a beating by his father.

> I'll never forget the look he'd get on his face. He'd just stare at me. And then he'd take off his belt and really wallop me. But it worked. It works on my kid too.

Mr. Helfsted had difficulty initially understanding how his behavior toward his son could be termed abusive. Nor did he know other methods of coping with the boy's "rebellious behavior."

Some parents are overwhelmed by the stresses of their lives. One young mother described her husband's drinking, his job losses, and her own poor health as precipitating factors that led to the deterioration of her ability to cope with her four children, all under six. Certainly the closeness of their ages and the stresses of having four children so young and dependent may have added to her feelings of being overwhelmed. Her anger and frustration were manifested at first by screaming at and finally by hitting her children. Her guilt over her behavior only intensified her problems.

Many abusive parents have never been nurtured properly themselves and have difficulty nurturing their children. Ray Helfer, noted pediatrician and expert in child abuse detection and treatment, contends that if parents have not learned five basic tasks themselves, they will find parenting overwhelming (12).

He describes these tasks as:

1. *Learning how to get their needs met appropriately.* If no one has taught the parent how to recognize his or her own needs and how to ask to have them met, the parent may just assume others know what he or she wants. For example, a child asks for a drink. If the parent does not respond, the child may have to ask again and again. Eventually the child may have a tantrum, to which the parent responds. The child learns that extreme behavior—the tantrum, is the way to get one's needs met. As an adult, such a person may know only how to respond with extremes. Therefore, when this parent's own child does not behave, the parent's reaction is to strike out rather than talk.

2. *Learning the difference between feelings and behavior.* All parents have moments when they are angry with their children, but there are other ways to deal with this anger than by hitting. But some parents have never learned any way to express anger, other than through violence.

3. *Learning how to make decisions.* When people are not taught decision making in their childhood (through something as simple as "Would you prefer peanut butter or bologna for lunch?"), they grow up to be adults who feel paralyzed when faced with the need to decide something. They also feel vulnerable and out of control, and may strike out at more vulnerable individuals—often their children.

4. *Learning that they are responsible for their own actions and not the actions of others.* Some people are given messages throughout their childhood like "If it hadn't been for you, your father wouldn't have left me," or "Because of you I had to marry your father, and now we're miserable." Such messages make children feel guilty and to blame. Eventually this becomes overwhelming. As adults they may be confused over what they actually can control and what they cannot. Some even repeat these messages to their own children.

5. *Learning to delay gratification.* When a childhood is not a happy, consistent one, where patience is rewarded by pleasure, one learns to take that pleasure whenever it's available. The abusive parent wants to feel good *now*, and may want immediate obedience from children *now* as well.

Parents who have not learned these tasks may feel extremely needy themselves. Their resulting poor self-concept may cause them to look to others for validation. They want to "look good" in other's eyes and their children, as extensions of them, must appear so also. This may translate into high expectations of children. If their children "look good," parents may feel they are seen as good parents. When their children misbehave, they feel they are seen as failures.

Most abusive parents feel out of control, dependent, and have low self-esteem. Often they isolate themselves from those around them. Many parents turn to their children to nurture them as their own parents did not. This creates a role reversal between parent and child.

When one parent in a family is abusing a child, it would seem that the other parent would step in. Yet the non-abusive parent often feels the same helplessness, low self-esteem, and dependency as the abuser. He or she may feel powerless to intervene.

Very few parents abuse their children sadistically. For those who do, the child has often become someone on whom the parent expresses the rage he or she has harbored for a lifetime—the rage of unmet needs and perceived injustices.

Abused Children

Why are some children abused and some not? It is not always easy to say. Sometimes a specific child reminds the parent of another person who has caused conflicts for the abuser. Or the child's behavior or personality is difficult for the perhaps already overwhelmed parent to handle. For example, children with attention deficit disorder with hyperactivity are at risk for abuse when parents are unable to cope with their inability to concentrate and their extreme activity level. Not only are children with a variety of disabilities at higher risk for abuse but Bonner et al. found that children with disabilities may not be identified by child protection agencies and may therefore not receive the appropriate services once they do come to the attention of social services (13). Most experts contend that what causes one child to be abused while his siblings are not may have to do with an intricate balance of personal and situational factors.

Physical Neglect

Definition.   The role of the parent is to meet the child's basic human needs. These are: adequate food, clothing, shelter, medical care, educational needs, supervision and protection, and moral guidance. The failure to meet these needs is considered to be physical neglect. Polansky, Holly, and Polansky offer a more inclusive definition.

Child neglect may be defined as a condition in which a caretaker responsible for the child either deliberately or by extraordinary inattentiveness permits the child to experience available present suffering and/or fails to provide one or more of the ingredients generally deemed essential for developing a person's physical, intellectual and emotional capacities (14).

Operationalizing such a definition—especially in view of the cultural diversity of the United States—becomes more of a problem. Many cultures define the meeting of basic needs differently. For example, the freedom a Native-American child has on the reservation comes from the parents' knowledge that the community will assume responsibility when they are not available. In the dominant American culture, letting one's child run freely and perhaps leaving him or her for long periods of time would be considered neglectful.

Gray and Cosgrove found in their study of ethnocentric practices of child rearing that Mexican Americans were cited more for neglect than for any other type of maltreatment. Neglect in these instances took the guise of "lack of adequate supervision." The authors theorized that, culturally, Mexican-American parents expect the extended family to assume responsibility for the children in the parents' absence. With the family's immigration to the United States and their isolation from extended family members, very young children were being left with siblings far too young (e.g., seven to eight years old) to be responsible for their care. This, by law, was neglect (15).

Symptoms.   Lack of supervision, according to child abuse laws, would fall into the category of neglect despite cultural variations. What other symptoms point to neglect?

Children who are neglected often exhibit poor hygiene, are inappropriately dressed for the weather, or are constantly hungry. They may satisfy their hunger by stealing food. Some children exhibit physical signs of malnourishment; e.g., they look emaciated, with a distended stomach.

Case Example: Sally Wells

Martha Wells and her 18-month-old daughter Sally were seen by the juvenile court. The case had originally been brought to the attention of social services when her 6-month-old son was rushed to the hospital and died soon after. The cause was given as malnutrition due to severe neglect. Now Sally was brought in by her mother. The child was barely able to sit, let alone walk or crawl. She gazed around the room with casual disinterest. Her limbs were extremely thin while her stomach was distended. She reminded the onlookers of posters they had seen of starving children in struggling Third World countries.

Developmentally, neglected children are also often significantly delayed. Since healthy development necessitates stimulation by a caretaker as well as adequate nutrition, neglected children fall short on both counts.

Many neglectful parents place little emphasis on school. Their children, therefore, are often absent and may drop out of school at an early age. Neglected children are also not protected from inadequate housing standards, poor sanitation, and unsafe conditions, as described in the following:

Case Example: Mrs. Smith

During our first home visit Mrs. Smith had a frying pan full of grease on the electric burner. Before long we smelled smoke. The grease had caught fire and ignited towels and diapers that were thrown over a rope stretched over the stove. Mrs. Smith stood clutching the baby, screaming, but otherwise immobilized. The Head Start teacher took the baby out the front door, while the caseworker threw the blazing skillet out the back door and pulled the clothes from the line before the ceiling could catch fire. Throughout all this, Mrs. Smith remained helpless, crying and wringing her hands. Two weeks later, another fire in the living room burned out one whole end of the room.

Of course the house itself was always cluttered and incredibly dirty. Rubbish was piled in one end of the living room. During one visit, a large rat was observed slipping through the unfinished baseboard and into the pile of trash. The mother remained quite unconcerned, continuing to sit and rock the baby (16).

Not attending to a child's medical needs is also neglectful. Certainly poverty and the inability to access adequate medical care prevent some families from seeking medical attention. In addition, some religious groups, such as Jehovah's Witnesses and Christian Scientists, demand the right to handle medical situations in their own manner. In some cases courts have intervened and actually overturned the rights of parents when it was felt that the child's life was at risk.

Another issue that has caused increased concern over the last few years is that of babies who are drug addicted at birth. Controversy rages over whether to charge mothers who intentionally take drugs during pregnancy, and if so, whether this practice should be considered abusive or neglectful. The plight of drug-addicted babies will undoubtedly be a problem of foremost importance in the 1990s.

Certainly the practices of many cultures are interpreted as neglect. For example, inherent in Native-American child-rearing practice is the belief that children must learn from experience, and that adults should offer little overt guidance. Gray and Cosgrove described an incident at a pow-wow when a small child, observed by his mother and several other adults, stuck his finger in the fire. His subsequent burned finger did prevent future behavior of this type, but might also have come into question by adults not familiar with the Indian philosophy (17).

Neglectful Parents.   Neglect remains the least defined type of maltreatment, despite the efforts of Polansky et al. at definition through the Childhood Level Living Scale (CLL). The CLL was developed to assess the maternal care in families with children aged between four and seven. Questions were directed to an assessment of such issues as the physical care of the child, supervision, medical care safety issues, living conditions, cleanliness, and so on. From the use of this scale among both rural and urban families, Polansky and his colleagues were able to determine what type of parents are neglectful and suggest implications for treatment (18).

These researchers felt that there were five types of neglectful mothers (fathers were not specifically addressed as they tended not to be present):

1. *The apathetic futile mother* is one who demonstrates an emotional numbness. Her own unmet needs in childhood make it difficult for her to feel competent. She believes that there is not much that is worth doing in life; for example, children who are fed now will just be hungry later. She is hard to reach because of her concrete understanding and inability to conceptualize on any but the most basic level. Social workers often feel frustrated working with this client as her depression is infectious.

2. *The impulse-ridden mother* is manipulative, defiant, restless, and cannot tolerate stress or frustration. She acts impulsively and finds the consistency necessary by parenting almost impossible. She has never learned to achieve inner controls and remains childlike and impulsive.

3. *Some mentally retarded mothers* are also neglectful. It is important to realize that many retarded parents with adequate supports can parent well, but some low-functioning parents do not have these supports. The mothers studied by Polansky et al. demonstrated a marked inability to function in their parenting role of meeting even the most basic of their children's needs.

4. *Some mothers exhibit reactive depression*—that is, some event (especially loss) has rendered them temporarily incapable of parenting. They may have had intense depression and have been preoccupied with their own grief or stress.

5. *A few neglectful mothers are psychotic*, exhibiting thought disturbances, bizarre behavior, severe anxiety and often withdrawal (19).

Case Example: Edna Todd

Edna Todd was brought to the attention of social services after police responded to a call reporting that her 3-year-old son was running through the house naked and screaming. Neighbors feared he was being abused. Investigation uncovered the fact that the child was mimicking his mother, who was having paranoid hallucinations. The house was unkept, littered with rotting food and human excrement. The mother sat rocking and mumbling to herself, seemingly unaware that anyone was in the room other than herself.

Whatever the category, neglectful parents exhibit immaturity and inability to meet their children's needs. They find it difficult to form more than superficial relationships. They lack judgment to parent and often have not had parenting models in their own childhoods. Neglectful parents can be difficult to treat therapeutically, as they lack insight into their own actions.

One of the problems with the current literature on neglect, and even with the research to date, is that neglect has been framed from a white middle-class perspective with little room for cultural variations. For this reason much more attention should be paid by future researchers to this area.

Sexual Abuse

Definition.   Sexual abuse has been defined by Kempe and Kempe as ". . . the involvement of dependent, developmentally immature children and adolescents in sexual activities they do not comprehend, to which they are unable to give informed consent or that violate the social taboos of the family roles" (20). Mrazek suggests that the term sexual abuse refers to ". . . activities which are detrimental to the normal development of the sexuality of the child or which control or inhibit his/her sexual self determination" (21). These definitions may cover touching a child sexually, exposing a child to sexual acts, or using a child in the production of or exposing a child to pornography (22).

Child sexual abuse has been defined and redefined since the mid-1970s. Much has been written, making a brief treatment of the problem exceedingly difficult.

Symptoms

Children who have been sexually abused will often demonstrate specific symptoms no matter who has abused them. Physically, sexual abuse can be detected from pain or tears in the genital area or can be associated with frequent urinary tract or yeast infections. Sexually transmitted diseases of various types are also indicative of sexual abuse in young children, as they can only be transmitted through the contact of mucus membranes or their secretions. Gellert et al. call for guidelines to test for HIV antibodies in the victims of pediatric sexual abuse (23).

Behaviorally, children who are sexually abused may withdraw or be secretive. Some children begin to do poorly in school, while others use school as a place to excel. They may cry without provocation or exhibit self-damaging behavior, such as anorexia, bulimia, or suicide attempts. It is not unusual for children to act out their sexual victimization by molesting younger children or exhibiting age-inappropriate sexual knowledge.

When children are abused by parents, they often feel betrayed—unable to trust adults. Generational boundaries in incestuous families become blurred, and often the child is placed in the role of the caretaker and demonstrates pseudo-maturity. Although the symptoms may be similar, sexual abuse can actually be divided into several categories.

- familial abuse or incest
- extra-familial molestation or rape
- exploitation through pornography production, prostitutions, sex rings, or cults
- institutional abuse

Incest.   has been much publicized, dispelling the myth that children are abused only by strangers. In fact, a high percentage (some sources maintain it is as high as 60–70 percent) of sexual abuse is perpetrated by parents or older siblings. Finkelhor, a leading researcher in the field of child sexual abuse, contends that children (especially girls) with stepfathers are most vulnerable to abuse, even if the stepfather is not the perpetrator (24).

Incest (like other forms of sexual abuse where the perpetrator is known by the child) often progresses from seemingly benign behavior (e.g., tickling, observing the child in the bath, etc.) through more obviously sexual and damaging behavior (such as mutual masturbation, oral sexual stimulation, and anal or vaginal intercourse). It should be noted that most incestuous cases have gone on for between one to three years prior to disclosure, and that many never reach the point of anal or vaginal intercourse (25).

The most common incestuous pattern is thought to be father–daughter incest—a phenomenon that has been considered extensively in the literature since Sandra Butler's *Conspiracy of Silence* in 1978 (26).

Experts continue to debate about the personalities of the participants. The father is described as controlling and tyrannical by some authors, and as ineffectual and overly dependent by others (27). He is usually someone who lacks the communication skills and maturity to deal with adults on other than the most superficial level. Most such fathers have been socialized throughout their own childhoods to feel inadequate. They equate affection with sexuality. They expect that their wife will meet all their needs. When she is unable to do so, due to her own craving to satisfy unmet needs, the problems between them intensify.

In the midst of marital conflicts, the father seeks out a nonconflictual partner in his daughter. Certainly society's emphasis on sexual prowess and performance does little to help this already insecure individual feel more adequate in his sexual relationships with adults. To him, a child provides a loving, accepting, sexual partner. It is unlikely that the incestuous father would seek sexual satisfaction from an adult (e.g., a prostitute) outside the home. This type of father is surprisingly "moral" and conservative. On the other hand, new research suggests that some incestuous fathers have approached children other than their own.

Incestuous fathers are masters at rationalization and manipulation. For this reason the abuse can often be difficult to detect. Alcohol and drug abuse can be a problem for such a father, but rather than actually precipitating the abuse, the altered affect appears to supplement his rationalization.

The mother in an incestuous family has been the subject of much controversy. Does she know her daughter is being abused? Current thinking emphasizes her prior knowledge less than her inability to support and protect the child after disclosure. This mother often feels inadequate and dependent upon her husband. She may have few skills and seeks to be cared for herself. If she is financially dependent upon her husband—which she often is—it is even more difficult for her to support her child. Her own magical expectations that she will be loved and pampered add to her own denial. Many of these mothers were abused themselves as children.

The daughter in this triangle often sees her mother as cold and unavailable. The attention, all but compounded with sex, she receives from her father fills her need for affection and nurturing. As she grows older, she may even discover she can barter with her sexual favors. She often feels that her compliance with her father is holding the family together and she, like others in the family, fears loss and loneliness.

Most of the information compiled about mother–daughter incest is from adult survivors who describe their experiences in childhood. From the limited material available, theorists postulate that the abusing mother is usually a very disturbed woman who sees her daughter as an extension of herself. For this reason the sexual abuse takes on an almost masturbatory quality (28). The father in such cases is usually absent, if not physically, at least emotionally.

The father in father–son incest is usually homosexual, bisexual, a pedophile (one who is predominantly interested sexually in children), or someone who uses the sexual relationship as a power tool over his son. This type of incest is also rarely reported. Incest of this type creates special problems for the young boy, as it sets up for him confusion about his own sexual identity. Adult survivors describe childhoods full of confusion and chaos.

Case Example: Carl

Carl's father began fondling him when he was five. At first Carl resisted, but fearful of his father's response, eventually complied. He describes sexual advances from his brothers, too, and feels that they had learned their behavior earlier. Sex permeated the family's life; only his mother and sister seemed exempt.

Mothers in such families are often unavailable to the family emotionally.

Cases of mother–son incest have also been reported in limited numbers. However, the close relationships of mothers and sons following the mounting number of divorces increases the likelihood (29). Mothers in the absence of a spouse turn to their sons for comfort—a relationship that in incestuous families takes on sexual overtones. This creates guilt and confusion for the son. Nasjleti suggests that victims of such incest may demonstrate aggressive problems—rape, wife battering, or child rape in later life (30).

Sibling incest is long felt to be benign in what Russell calls the "myth of mutuality" (31). In fact, some younger siblings do feel exploited by the attentions of their older brothers or sisters. Finkelhor found that 30 percent of his sample of women involved in sex with older brothers were left with negative feelings (32). Sibling abuse was either due to curiosity or was a power play in order to control or humiliate (33).

The recent research in incest—and indeed all forms of child sexual abuse—tends to be focused on the white majority. Little has been done to date to consider the implications of cultural mores on the incidence of abuse (34).

Extrafamilial Abuse.   is the term given to the molestation or rape of children by those outside their homes. The degree of trauma to a child depends largely upon the child's relationship with the perpetrator and the degree of violence involved. Children can be abused by a variety of people. In a study by Russell in 1984 of 930 adult California women who had been abused before the age of 18, 15 percent were molested by strangers, 40 percent by acquaintances, 14 percent by friends of the family, and 18 percent by a friend or date of the victim. Of these women, most reported being abused by males (35). New research tells us that boys are almost as vulnerable as girls for abuse, but more vulnerable to abuse from people outside their homes. In addition, boys are usually abused at younger ages—a median age of 8.5—than girls—a median age of 12.4 (36).

Who abuses children outside their homes? Groth classifies abusers into two categories, fixated and regressed (37). The fixated abuser is one who is attracted sexually primarily to children (often termed a pedophile). Such perpetrators are threatened by interactions with age mates and feel inadequate to cope with life. Children become almost an obsession to these individuals. They have often been abused themselves as children. Fixated abusers tend to prefer boys, becoming almost like "children themselves" with their victims.

The regressed abuser is one who has made at least a tentative adjustment to life and his peers. In many cases, he has married, but finds this relationship in constant conflict. Overwhelmed by his feelings of powerlessness, this abuser turns to children, usually female, whom he elevates to the role of "miniature woman." The regressed abuser, unlike his fixated counterpart, does feel guilt over his deviant behavior.

While both types of abusers prey on children both in and out of the home, the fixated or pedophile is usually felt to have more unrelated victims.

In incestuous relationships, the child is usually cajoled or bribed into compliance. Extrafamilial abusers also cajole and bribe, but may in addition use threats or even force.

Children are also *exploited through the production of pornography, prostitution, sex rings, and cults.* Often pornography is a by-product of the other types of exploitation. A child is lured into posing for suggestive or sexual photos and often blackmailed into more serious crimes (e.g., prostitution) by the threat of exposure to parents or police. Sex rings (when one or more adults is involved sexually with several under-age victims) exist to produce pornography, prostitution, or sexual gratification of the adults (38).

Children become lured into pornography, sex rings, and prostitution often because their own lives are filled with chaos and abuse:

Case Example: Noreen

Noreen was ten when she began to spend all her after school hours at the local arcade. She found this preferable to going home and being beaten by an alcoholic father or being expected to perform sexual favors by her two older brothers. Sex was nothing new to Noreen. She had been an observer of her parents' drunken sexual encounters since she was quite young. There was little chance to avoid seeing what went on in their small apartment.

Noreen was attracted to 30-year-old Sam immediately. He gave her candy and cigarettes and eventually took her to his apartment to "meet his friends." His friends proved to be a group of children, not much older than Noreen, who

*made "movies" with him. Before long Noreen was "making her own money,"
helping Sam and his friends and their movies and selling sexual favors to older
boys.*

The exploitation of children appears to cross all cultural lines.

Over the last years newspapers have been filled with reports of the institutional abuse of children. Day-care settings such as the much-publicized Manhattan Beach, Calif. case in 1984, became the scene of the multiple abuses of children. Despite the fact that in this case the defendants were acquitted due to insufficient evidence, the toll on the victims and families of the victims was significant. Jan Hollingsworth's 1986 book, *Unspeakable Acts,* chronicles the Miami case of day-care proprietors Iliana and Frank Fuster who were convicted. The Fusters murdered animals and employed other scare tactics and drugs to sexually abuse numbers of young children (39).

The perpetrators in such cases are usually found to have abused scores of children prior to disclosure. Certainly, sexual abusers would be attracted to settings in which children are most vulnerable. Left by their parents in the care of day-care operators, the children often assume that whatever is asked of them is condoned by their family. The seriousness of the cases of the mid-80s stimulated additional research into the causes of such abuse and pointed to the need for more effective interviewing techniques with young children.

Cults are sometimes settings in which children fall prey to sexual abuse. In *Michelle Remembers,* Smith and Pazder chronicle the experience of a young woman who lives through a myriad of abuses at the hands of a satanic cult (40). As more of these cases become documented, practitioners face the challenge of how to treat them.

Emotional Abuse

Definition.   Emotional abuse can refer to belittling, humiliating, rejecting, undermining a child's self-esteem, and generally to not creating a positive atmosphere for a child. Garbarino, Gettman, and Seeley define emotional abuse as "a pattern of psychically destructive behavior" which takes the form of 1) rejecting, 2) isolating, 3) terrorizing, 4) ignoring, and 5) corrupting—stimulating, and reinforcing deviant behavior (41). The parent who constantly refers to his or her child as "stupid" or "a real jerk," compounding the effect of these terms by telling the child that he or she "can do nothing right," is emotionally abusive. Studies show that this belittling behavior causes emotional scars that can be observed in later life.

Symptoms.   Children who are emotionally abused may demonstrate a variety of behaviors. They may exhibit low self-esteem by constantly demeaning themselves. Or they may become self-destructive, either passively (by using drugs, alcohol, etc.) or actively (anorexia nervosa, suicide attempts, etc.). Some children withdraw, while others strike out destructively. Children may also become overachievers, seeking compulsively to prove their worth.

Tower gives the following example:

Case Example: Sally

Sally demonstrated her abuse by a perpetually sad expression. She looked as if she had just been beaten, but her father never touched her. Instead he berated her: "how did I ever deserve a girl? Girls are lesser beings." He had cut her hair in an unbecoming style, saying there was no point in trying to make an ugly girl look any better. He demanded complete obedience and subservience, including having her stand beside him as he ate to cut and salt his food. He rationalized this activity by saying that her only hope in life was to be useful to a husband, if in fact anyone would want her. Even when Sally scored 160 on an IQ test, her father assured her the teachers were wrong—she was only a girl. Unfortunately she believed him (42).

Children who are emotionally maltreated may also exhibit somatic complaints such as asthma, hyperactivity, and ulcers.

Abusive Parents.   Parents who emotionally abuse children are often insecure individuals who use their abuse to control. They may be threatened by the child or his or her abilities, or may see the child as a miniature of themselves or of their spouses.

Unfortunately, because emotional abuse is difficult to prove, it often goes unaddressed by social service agencies. More recently, however, many states are proposing statutes which would operationalize the definition of emotional abuse and thus make it measurable.

Exposure to Domestic Violence.   Children who are not themselves beaten may be the innocent observers of violence in their homes. In the last decade, we have become aware of the magnitude of the impact that domestic violence has on children. Graham-Bermann and Levendosky found that children who observed their mother being beaten develop many of the symptoms of post-traumatic stress disorder such as irritability, difficulty concentrating, hypervigilance, heightened startle response, or intrusive memories. Many of these children either develop a violent pattern of behavior or go to great lengths to avoid violence in later life (43). The witnessing of violence inflicted on a parent can have effects that mirror those of their abused peers.

Scope of Child Abuse and Neglect

It is difficult to determine exactly how prevalent abuse and neglect have become in the United States today. Even if we are able to compile seemingly accurate statistics, we know that abuse, especially sexual abuse, is grossly under-reported.

The most comprehensive study to determine the degree of maltreatment was undertaken in 1979–80 by the National Center on Child Abuse and Neglect.

Physical abuse, sexual abuse, emotional abuse, physical neglect, educational neglect, and emotional neglect were all considered. From the responses to this survey given by children's protective agencies, the rate of children abused or neglected appears to be at least 652,000 children per year (44).

The American Humane Association reports that cases of reported maltreatment have increased from 416,000 in 1976 to 1,928,000 in 1985 (45). The Child Welfare League of America reports an increase of reports of physical abuse and neglect of 16 percent between 1983 and 1984 and an increase of 59 percent in the reporting of sexual abuse nationwide between those same years (46).

It is questionable, however, if the increased number of reports reflects an upswing in the incidences of abuse or neglect. Rather the public and the child welfare professional, due to increased awareness, may be less hesitant to report.

Certainly we know that one out of three girls and one out of five boys is vulnerable to sexual abuse prior to the age of 18. Researchers and practitioners both postulate that the incidence of abuse of boys probably equals that of girls, but boys are less likely to report (47).

The scope of reports of sexual abuse in day care has recently been outlined by Finkelhor, Williams, Burns, and Kalenowski through a grant funded by the National Center on Child Abuse and Neglect. From January 1983 to December 1985, the team located and analyzed hundreds of cases. They found that within this two-year period, 270 child-care facilities documented cases of sexual abuse with 1,639 children as victims. Given the fact that there are 229,000 child-care facilities nationwide, the researchers estimated that only a rate of 5.5 children in 10,000 were abused in centers. Of the victims, 62 percent were girls while 38 percent were boys. Of the abusers, 40 percent were women; 60 percent were men (48). Given the fact that approximately 120,000 cases of sex abuse were reported in 1985 alone, the incidence of reported cases in day care is not as significant as the media has represented.

Cross-culturally, Lindholm found that black children were more likely to be physically abused and less likely to be sexually abused than white or Hispanic children. Such abuse took the form of whippings, beatings, and lacerations with flexible objects, using discipline as the rationale. White children were more likely to present bruises, usually made by feet or hands rather than objects. Hispanic parents tended to bruise and whip with either flexible objects or hands and feet (49).

Leung and Carter, in their study of child abuse among Chinese, Native Americans, and Anglo-Canadians, concurred that the white parents were more likely to leave bruises as well as inflict fractures. For the Native Americans, bruising was followed closely by children presenting as failure to thrive. Almost all Chinese parents who abused children bruised or scratched them (50).

Hampton, on the other hand, found that Hispanics had a higher level of sexual abuse than white and African-American parents he studied. All ethnic groups demonstrated physical neglect as the highest form of maltreatment, African-American parents having a slightly higher rate than the other two groups (51). Mothers tended to abuse more frequently than fathers in Hampton's study, as well as in the Leung and Carter sample.

Pierce and Pierce studied African-American and white children who had been sexually abused. Black children in this study were abused at a slightly higher rate than white children and at a younger age, 8.7 years compared to 11.1 years for whites (52).

Obviously, researchers differ in their conclusions about the cross-cultural implications of abuse and neglect, but it is encouraging that the number of studies of ethnic differences have increased in the last few years.

Social Service Intervention

The goal of social service intervention is obviously to stop the abuse and ensure the future safety of the children. It is important, however, that the total case be understood—not only from the perspective of the harm to the child, but also the motivations of the parents, as well as the total cultural context of the family system. Only then can we hope to treat the family effectively.

Reporting

Reports are made by those professionals mandated (called *mandated reporters*) by state and federal law to bring the protective agency's attention to abusive or neglectful families. State laws designate who those particular professionals are. For example, every state in the United States mandates that school personnel report child maltreatment. Social service personnel are usually also included in the mandated. Penalties for not reporting (from no penalty in only one state, to fines and jail terms in others) are also outlined in the state statutes. The requirements for reporting also differ, from "suspicion" to "reasonable cause to believe."

Lindholm found that African-American (26.8 percent) and white (25.1 percent) children were reported at about the same frequency, while Hispanic children were more often reported (32.5 percent). Hospitals were most likely to report African-American children, followed by Hispanic and white children (53). Leung and Carter found that medical personnel were most likely to report whites (65 percent) and Native Americans (65 percent), while schools were most likely to be the reporters of Chinese families (60 percent) (54). Social service reports attest to the usual over-reporting of minority groups compared to whites.

In many states, reports can also be made by nonprofessionals; how earnestly these reports are received and investigated differs from state to state. Reports, whether by mandated reporter or private citizen, are made by phone and/or in writing to the designated social service agency—the department of social service, child protective services, etc. The intake worker who receives the report must then determine if the case should be screened in or substantiated or if it should be referred elsewhere or closed. Child protective agencies for the most part deal with in-family abuse and neglect. Many states and countries do not service cases of extrafamilial sexual abuse or exploitation. The social worker must also determine if the child is safe in the home and if the family will respond to treatment. These decisions are usually made through a series of interviews, visits, and phone calls to family members, the abuser, the victim, and "collaterals," that is, neighbors, school personnel, and others who might have information.

Case Example: Jenny Johnson

A report came in from a local school that 10-year-old Jenny Johnson told the school nurse that she was being sexually abused. Susan Davis, caseworker, took the call, and from the information given by the school decided to investigate. Susan went first to the school, where she spoke with Jenny's teacher, the school nurse, and finally Jenny. She saw Jenny in the nurse's offices where she apparently felt comfortable. Jenny's teachers had related that her grades had dropped significantly and she seemed secretive and preoccupied. Jenny had befriended the school nurse (who often monitored recesses) and often talked with her when she had a problem. Yesterday Jenny had walked stiffly and complained that "she hurt" and asked to see the nurse. Mrs. Rawlings, the school nurse, questioned her about her "hurt" and was amazed when Jenny blurted out that her father had been "messing with her" and had "hurt her bad." Now Jenny talked to Susan Davis, tearfully glancing periodically at the nurse for support. She related that her older sister had recently (six months earlier) become pregnant and left home, leaving Jenny to assume much of the housework and the care of her 6-year-old brother. Her father had been unemployed for several months and her mother worked as a waitress and bartender evenings.

Shortly before her father left, Jenny stated that he had started coming to her room and fondling her. He told her that her mother thought he was a failure and he needed Jenny to feel better. He urged her to keep their relationship secret. When the fondling progressed to attempts at intercourse Jenny found it painful and begged for her father to stop. The previous night, when she cried and tried to resist, he had raped her. Jenny's father was described by school personnel as a somewhat violent man who raised Doberman pinschers to train as attack dogs. He had terrorized the neighborhood.

After talking with Jenny, the social worker had to decide if it was safe for Jenny to return home. Since the school day had not yet ended, Susan Davis hurried to decide what her next plan would be. Immediately, she called the Johnson home. Mrs. Johnson was home alone and agreed to see her. If Mr. Johnson, described as a violent man, had been home, the caseworker would have had to decide if she should ask him to come to her office or bring the police to ensure her own safety.

Jenny's mother, although at first shocked, acknowledged that her daughter might be telling the truth. She stated that she had always wondered about her husband's relationship with her older daughter, too. She did express some fear of her husband, however.

In some states, a report of sexual abuse necessitates police intervention and/or a report to the district attorney. While at one time children were automatically removed when abuse was found, the current trend is toward removal of the perpetrator if the non-abusing parent is able to believe, support, and protect the children. Fathers may then be served with a restraining order to legally ensure their removal.

Assessment and Case Management

After the initial assessment of risk to the child, the caseworker begins to look at family strengths and weaknesses to determine what treatment plan will be most effective. Neglect has probably gone on for years, if not generations, and may not be immediately volatile. In addition to making a thorough assessment, the caseworker benefits by taking time to gain the client's trust. Physical abuse may present more of a danger to the child. Careful consideration should be given to how safe the environment is. Disclosures of the situation can augment the abusive behavior.

In cases of sexual abuse disclosure, the family often goes into acute crisis. The perpetrator and the victim may both be at risk for suicide attempts, or the family may mobilize its resources and decide to fight the allegation by hiring an attorney. Families tend to deny and rationalize the abusive behavior, and will often protect the perpetrator and scapegoat the child.

As the caseworker begins to assess the family, it will be important to consider their cultural background. Does the family place particular emphasis on the extended family? Would other family members be resources? For example, African-American families call upon extended family members—aunts, uncles, cousins, grandparents, etc., in times of stress. The Asian respect for the father and value on family harmony make the treatment of sexual abuse (which fortunately is rare in this population) particularly difficult. Asians also believe that the role of the child is to obey without question. Punishment, however severe, for disobedience is condoned by the family. The family is a resource for both Hispanic and Native-American cultures (55).

Another consideration in assessment, case management, and treatment is the client's view of authority figures. While Asians respect authority and Hispanics revere it, Native Americans value the group rather than prominent individuals. To appear the expert to a Native American is to lose rather than gain his or her respect (56).

The possible placement of children is a factor that must also be weighed. If the children cannot be protected at home, they may need to be placed in foster homes. What will this separation mean to the children, as well as the parents? For Asians, placement may mean that they perceive themselves as failures. To fail as a parent is the ultimate shame—a "loss of face." Suicide is an acceptable solution among many Asian cultures (e.g., Chinese, Japanese) to this humiliation. The caseworker must be aware of this fact.

If children are placed, the social worker must prepare both the family and the parents for separation. Indeed, the reality of the benefits of separation is carefully weighed against the pain, fear, confusion, and anxiety caused by the move vs. the safety of the child in his or her biological home. Pellegrin and Wagner comment that in sexual abuse cases, it is the mother's inability to believe the child's allegations and her unwillingness to comply with treatment that create a need for removal (57). Certainly, in such instances, it is not only the child's removal from a familiar setting, but also the dynamics at home that must be considered in the placement process. Unfortunately, thorough preparation is not always realistic or possible, but the competent worker will accomplish as smooth a transition as possible, given whatever circumstances warrant it.

Court Intervention

Some states require that every case of abuse or neglect be heard before the juvenile or family court. Other states initiate an abuse report involving the court only when the child is in imminent danger or when the parents will not cooperate.

Case Example: Jenny Johnson (Continued)

In the case of Jenny Johnson, Jenny's father had complied with the order for him to leave his home. However, he made nightly calls to his wife expounding upon the injustices he felt had been done to him. He used a combination of pleadings and threats, until the mother broke her appointment with caseworker Susan Davis to discuss a treatment plan. Mrs. Johnson refused to answer the phone, and the school felt that Mr. Johnson was spending time at the house. Fearing for Jenny's safety, the caseworker filed a petition in juvenile court for Jenny's protection. The family was notified that they must appear in court the next day.

In the state in which Jenny's family resided, it was also necessary to file a criminal complaint against Mr. Johnson. This is usually only done in cases of sexual abuse.

Juvenile court is used as leverage to ensure that the family complies with treatment recommendations. One problem with the caseworker filing court petitions is that he or she is transformed in the family's eyes from helper to adversary. The authority and power represented by the court, however, often jolt the family into recognition that they must make changes.

The court involvement follows a process that may differ slightly from state to state and court to court. There may be a "show cause" hearing to determine if the case should be dealt with further. An adjudication or identification hearing follows, at which time the evidence indicating that abuse or neglect exists is presented. Some courts then appoint an investigator to further study the case and generate a report outlining recommendations. These recommendations are presented at a dispositional hearing, at which time the court decides where the child will reside, who will have legal custody, and what type of treatment the family will receive. Subsequent hearings are then scheduled to allow the social worker overseeing the case to attest to the family's progress. Cases may be dismissed by the court at any time in the process, provided it is determined that there is no further evidence of continued maltreatment. Abuse and neglect cases are heard before a judge in a closed courtroom (i.e., only the participants, their attorneys, and court officials are allowed to be present). Children, in accordance with the 1974 Child Abuse Prevention and Treatment Act, must be provided with representation by an attorney. The judge hears the facts and receives progress reports on the parents' treatment progress. Some parents are able to respond to and benefit from treatment under the watchful eyes of the court. Others still cannot demonstrate that they will be able to parent effectively. If the court is given "clear and convincing" evidence of their lack of consistency in motivation or ability to care for their children, parental rights can be terminated. Under these circumstances, children will be placed or remain in foster care, or they may be subsequently released for adoption (58).

Case Example: Jenny Johnson (Continued)

Mrs. Johnson was able to respond to treatment. The court ruled that Jenny could remain in her home if Mrs. Johnson and she attended a mother–daughter therapy group. In addition, the mother was not to allow her husband access to Jenny. In the meantime, the criminal court ordered that Mr. Johnson attend treatment regularly or be sent to the house of correction.

He continued to harass both his wife and daughter. His violent outbursts became more frequent, until one day he greeted his wife at the door with a gun. The eventual outcome was his sentencing.

Although court intervention does have advantages in supplying some degree of leverage and providing service that sometimes might not be otherwise available, there are drawbacks. Kadushin and Martin state that there are seven areas of concern.

1. Court intervention makes the client-social work contacts seem more adversarial than therapeutic.
2. The orientation of the social worker (human service) and the court (legal) are different.
3. Social workers must explain and justify their interventions to others who see the case from a distinctly different vantage point.
4. Sharing control of the case can lead to frustration for the worker.
5. Client confidentiality may be compromised.
6. Social workers are vulnerable to cross-examination from opposing counsel.
7. Many workers find it difficult to adopt a legal orientation that deals in facts. Social workers have often been trained in subjective rather than objective truths (59).

It should be noted that Native Americans use tribal codes to deal with abusive and neglectful situations. The federal government has empowered them to establish legislative bodies, such as courts, that hear abuse cases. Different tribes determine how they will respond to this right. Some handle cases totally independently, while others cooperate with state and private agencies (60).

Treatment

What types of treatment are used with abusive and neglectful families? In the initial assessment, the social worker has determined what the client needs to be able to parent more effectively. The services may be concrete. The use of homemakers may eliminate stresses on otherwise overwhelmed parents. Day-care services may provide much needed space to accomplish daily tasks. Transportation may enable parents to keep medical appointments. Some parents can parent if a case manager or case aide is there to support them. One neglectful mother was able to respond to her children if she knew that once a week she would have someone who was there to talk exclusively to her. The case aide also showed this mother games she could play with her children, recognizing that her client too needed to learn to play.

Counseling can be effective to help the client gain insight into his or her problem. Although some do benefit from individual therapy, the treatment of choice for physically and sexually abusive parents is group therapy. Physically abusive families respond well to exposure to other parents or couples who are experiencing the same stresses. Sexual abuse perpetrators are effective in confronting the denial and rationalization of other perpetrators. Mothers and daughters in sexual abuse situations benefit by coming together with other mothers and daughters in the hope of strengthening their relationships. Groups are usually led by professionals, skilled in groupwork and with experience of the population being treated. These groups may be open-ended (continuing on) with open membership (anyone can join at any time), or closed (a set number of people begin and end together) and time limited (meeting for a predesigned number of weeks).

Also exceptionally effective is the self-help approach, represented by organizations like Parents Anonymous and Parents United. Parents Anonymous was begun by an abusive mother with social service support and now has groups all over the United States. Modeled on Alcoholic Anonymous, these groups are sponsored by social service agencies or social workers and give support to abusive parents. Parents United sprang from the work of Henry Garrett in Santa Clara, Calif. He found self-help groups helpful in the treatment of sexually abusive families. Although not quite as strong in some parts of the United States, Parents United too has branches from coast to coast.

The social worker treating families must also be sensitive to cultural mores. We expect parents to be motivated and interested in keeping their children or having them returned from foster care. Different cultures may respond differently, however. For example, Native Americans culturally protest that which they dislike with silence. Thus, the Native Americans who do not respond, do not come for appointments, or visit their children in foster care, are seen by the culturally uneducated as disinterested or uninvolved. Even if they do keep appointments, Native Americans have their own conception of time. A morning appointment may translate as anytime in the morning rather than 9:00 A.M. sharp. It may be necessary for the worker to stress the need for punctuality (61).

Deeply religious African-American or Hispanic clients may feel that events will transpire at "God's will." To the social worker, this attitude may appear to be resistant or to demonstrate a lack of motivation, just as the Native American's patience can be interpreted as inactivity.

Confrontation is often used in the treatment of abuse and neglect cases. The high value many Hispanics place on relationships causes them to avoid confrontation as a perceived threat to these relationships. Native Americans consider directness rude. Before discussing sensitive topics they bring up peripheral issues, often to the frustration of a hurried social worker. Some Asians are offended by direct eye contact. Sensitive topics such as sexuality are also difficult for Asians to discuss (62).

There is much controversy over what constitutes success in treatment. Is halting the abuse enough? Treatment should be considered successful when these conditions are met:

1. The abuse/neglect has stopped.
2. The parent has insight into what caused it.
3. The parent has developed alternative coping mechanisms to help avoid future abusive or neglect behavior.
4. The parent has learned when and how to reach out for help in the future.
5. The parent gets some pleasure and satisfaction out of parenting.

Jenny Johnson's family was able to terminate after several years of therapy. Mrs. Johnson continued as a member of a self-help group where she found the support to eventually divorce her husband. She knew that if she needed help in the future, it was there for her. Although her relationship with Jenny was not ideal, it had improved considerably. Jenny, in addition to the mother–daughter group, had attended a group of children who were also victims of abuse. In time she gained confidence and accepted the reality that she was not to blame for her father's abuse of her.

It would be nice to think that we could produce model parents by our interventions. The fact is that some parents can only be helped to parent in a very minimal way. As long as children can be assured of safety and of having their needs met adequately, there may be little else we can offer. Survivors tell us that if we do *not* intervene, the results of abuse fester and may significantly inhibit their adult lives.

Problems

As we consider the mandate to intervene when we perceive that children are being maltreated, several issues surface.

1. *How to agree upon a definition of abuse, in a culture that is called the "great melting pot."* The United States continues to gather immigrants and to shelter a variety of ethnic groups, each with their own values, mores, and child-rearing practices. Gray and Cosgrove point out a variety of cultural variations that make a clear and inclusive definition of maltreatment difficult. For example, Mexican Americans and Vietnamese both use nicknames describing some

physical characteristic of the child as a form of affection. Often these names seem derogatory and suggest emotional abuse. Japanese-American children are expected to use all their free time studying, yet they are intentionally not praised in any way so as to encourage humility (63). In mainstream American culture, the practices of these groups might appear abusive or neglectful. Can we judge other cultures by our laws? Until now, the answer was that the majority rules. It was assumed that someone living in this country had to conform to the expectations. But as we anticipate what has been termed *the browning of America,* the increase of non-white populations, can we expect the same conformity?

2. *Abuse and neglect as under-addressed causes.* One primary arena where the symptoms of maltreatment have become obvious is in the schools. Granted, with the increased training of teachers, there is more recognition that some discipline problems dealt with at face value in fact stem from the underlying cause of abuse or neglect. But we have much work ahead of us before these symptoms are dealt with effectively. Teachers must be helped to become even more sensitive to children's problems (64). Often overwhelmed by excessive paperwork, the concerned teacher feels helpless to intervene in children's lives. Many teachers have never had training in the detection of abuse and neglect. Certainly such training could be an important prerequisite for their certification.

3. *The threat of sexual abuse prevention "backlash."* Sexual abuse prevention is primarily in our schools and supported by our communities. Yet some complain that children will be overstimulated or frightened by strangers. Despite the findings of Finkelhor and Strapo (65) that prevention information did no harm to children, the debate rages. Some critics comment that we should be teaching normal, healthy sexuality before we teach children what can go wrong, i.e., about sexual abuse.

4. *Role definition and duplication of effort among professionals.* Despite our progress in intervention and treatment methods, there are still overlaps in service, as well as huge gaps into which many clients fall. If clients are not of the right socio-economic status or from the exact area, or do not have the appropriate diagnosis, they may not be able to receive service. On the other hand, we discover that multi-problem families—often masters at enlisting the help of professionals—are being served by several agencies and a variety of workers, each espousing a different view of what should be done. Better communication and more emphasis on case management might alleviate this problem somewhat. How can we teach clients effective communication skills if we do not demonstrate them ourselves?

5. *Continuity of service from the system.* Bureaucracy governs much of the practice of social work. Although vital to the functioning of agencies, the bureaucratic structure brings with it red tape, eligibility criteria, and shuffled cases. People become numbers—their problems, case records, and clinical diagnosis. It becomes the role of the social worker to advocate for the client with the system. Yet at best protective services are a difficult field. Adding this type of

advocacy to the stresses of a daily caseload can become overwhelming. Burnout and high worker turnover are the result. No sooner has the client learned to trust, when the worker leaves and he or she is faced with one more adjustment.

6. *Delays and confusion in the court system.* Even if the social agency processes a case immediately, it may take as long as two years for a case referred to the court system to be heard. This backlog (more common in criminal court than in juvenile court) can intensify the impact of the abuse on the victim. Such delays can create stresses for families and render them unable to support the child.

Trends

Increasingly, we recognize that the best way to combat abuse and neglect is through primary prevention. Sexual abuse prevention in schools has been one of the most recent interventions. Finkelhor and Strapo (66) review evaluations of a variety of such programs to determine how our efforts could be improved. The trend is also toward the recognition that we must teach children how to be future parents. High schools and junior highs answer this need by courses in child development and segments on parenting skills. Instead of fragmented prevention efforts, the next step will be combining our efforts.

The trend in responding to maltreatment, especially sexual abuse, is away from punishment in favor of treatment. There is increased recognition that incarcerated perpetrators gain little in prison without treatment. Slowly, therapy groups are being formed in prison settings to respond to this need. The trend is also toward more creativity in treatment. New approaches borrow techniques from other fields. There is increased research that recognizes cultural and racial differences and examines ways of treating cultural and racial minorities. Also, there is an increased emphasis on improving the intervention system, especially in the courtroom. These efforts are not enough. Unless our intervention strategies are constantly evolving, we cannot hope to provide answers for the future.

The intervention and treatment of child abuse and neglect has come a long way in the last several decades, but there are many challenges ahead. Anne Cohn Donnelly, of the National Committee to Prevent Child Abuse, suggests that the emphasis has shifted from people expecting the government to devise programs to solve the problem of child abuse and neglect to people looking for their own individual and collective solutions. There has been a decline both in the use of corporal punishment by parents (by 15 percent) and in the number of parents verbally abusing their children (17 percent). An increasing number of professionals have dedicated themselves to work in protective services. The American Professional Society on the Abuse of Children (APSAC) increased its membership to around 5,000. Prevention efforts have increased significantly as well (67). Despite these laudable efforts, Donnelly contends that the challenges are myriad. People have become more critical of the work and the worker, and this fact may have impacted the types of funds that are available. Quality control is mandatory as the critics demand to know how their money has been spent.

There are societal changes that also influence the future of service provision in child protection. As a society, we have become more socially isolated. Social isolation is one factor that is positively correlated with abuse and neglect. And as our families undergo change with an increase in divorce, parenting teens and single parents, children have fewer adult figures on whom to depend (68).

We continue to recognize that the best way to combat abuse is through primary prevention. But now this prevention demands that communities strive together to meet the challenge of isolation, duplication, and the struggle for diminishing funds. It is only by working together that we will make a difference for abused and neglected children from all cultural backgrounds.

Endnotes

1. C. H. Kempe and R. Helfer, *The Battered Child;* L. de Mause, *The History of Childhood: The Untold History of Child Abuse.*

2. R. Inglis, *Sins of the Fathers,* p. 29.

3. F. Rush, *The Best-Kept Secret: Sexual Abuse of Children;* L. de Mause, *The History of Childhood: The Untold History of Child Abuse.*

4. B. Nelson, *Making an Issue of Child Abuse;* I. Sagatun and L. Edwards, *Child Abuse and the Legal System.*

5. G. Williams, "Child Protection: A Journey Into History," *Journal of Clinical Child Psychology,* vol. 12 (Winter 1983): 236–243.

6. Nelson, *Making an Issue of Child Abuse.*

7. E. Gray and J. Cosgrove, "Ethnocentric Perception of Child Rearing Practices in Protective Services," *Child Abuse and Neglect,* vol. 9 (1985): 389–396.

8. Ibid.

9. J. David, *Help Me, I'm Hurt,* C. Crosson-Tower, *Understanding Child Abuse and Neglect,* p. 8.

10. K. Faller, M. L. Bowden, C. O. Jones, and M. Hildebrandt, "Types of Child Abuse and Neglect," in K. Faller *Social Work with Abused and Neglected Children,* pp. 13–31.

11. C. Crosson-Tower, *Understanding Child Abuse and Neglect.*

12. R. E. Helfer, *Childhood Comes First: A Crash Course in Childhood for Adults,* pp. 59–60.

13. B. Bonner et al., "State Efforts to Identify Maltreated Children with Disabilities: A Follow-up Study," *Child Maltreatment* Vol 2(1) (1997): 52–60.

14. N. F. Polansky, C. Holly, and N. A. Polansky, *Profile of Neglect: A Survey of the State of Knowledge of Child Neglect,* p. 5.

15. Gray and Cosgrove, "Ethnocentric Perception."

16. N. E. Polansky, C. DeSaix, and S. Sharlin, *Child Neglect: Understanding and Reaching the Parent.*

17. Gray and Cosgrove, "Ethnocentric Perception."

18. N. Polansky, M. A. Chalmers, E. Buttenweiser, and D. Williams, *Damaged Parents: An Anatomy of Child Neglect.*

19. Polansky, DeSaix, and Sharlin, *Child Neglect.*

20. R. S. Kempe and C. H. Kempe, *The Common Secret - The Sexual Abuse of Children and Adolescents,* p. 9.

21. P. B. Mrazek, "Definition and Recognition of Child Sexual Abuse: Historical and Cultural Perspectives," in *Sexually Abused Children and Their Families*, eds. P. B. Mrazek and C. H. Kempe, pp. 5–15.

22. C. Crosson-Tower, *Understanding Child Abuse and Neglect*.

23. G. A. Gellert, M. J. Durfie, and M. Berkowitz, "Developing Guidelines for HIV Antibody Testing Among Victims of Periodical Sexual Abuse," *Child Abuse and Neglect*, vol. 14-1 (1990): 9–17.

24. D. Finkelhor, *Child Sexual Abuse*.

25. S. M. Sgroi, *Handbook of Clinical Intervention in Child Sexual Abuse*.

26. S. Butler, *Conspiracy of Silence*.

27. J. Herman, *Father-Daughter Incest*; B. Justice and R. Justice, *The Broken Taboo: Sex in the Family*; A. Mayer, *Incest: A Treatment Manual for Therapy with Victims, Spouses and Offenders*.

28. S. Forward and C. Buck, *Betrayal of Innocence: Incest and Its Devastation*; C. Crosson-Tower, *Understanding Child Abuse and Neglect*.

29. R. S. Kempe and C. H. Kempe, *The Common Secret*.

30. M. Nasjleti, "Suffering in Silence: The Male Incest Victim," *Child Welfare* vol. 49-5 (1980): 269–275.

31. D. Russell, *Sexual Exploitation*.

32. Finkelhor, *Child Sexual Abuse*, p. 178.

33. For a more extensive discussion of this type of incest see C. Crosson-Tower, *Understanding Child Abuse and Neglect*.

34. Gray and Cosgrove, "Ethnocentric Perspectives."

35. D. Russell, *Secret Trauma: Incest in the Lives of Girls and Women*, p. 188.

36. Finkelhor, *Child Sexual Abuse*, p. 161.

37. A. N. Groth, "Patterns of Assault Against Children and Adolescents" in A. Burgess, A. N. Groth, L. L. Holmstrom, and S. M. Sgroi, *Sexual Assault of Children and Adolescents*, pp. 3–24.

38. A. Burgess, A. N. Groth, and M. P. McCausland, "Child Sex Initiation Rings," American Journal of Orthopsychiatry, vol. 51-1 (Jan. 1981): 110–119.

39. J. Hollingsworth, *Unspeakable Acts*.

40. M. Smith and L. Pazder, *Michelle Remembers*.

41. J. Garbarino, E. Gittman, and J. W. Seely, *The Psychologically Battered Child*, p. 8.

42. C. C. Tower, *How Schools Can Combat Child Abuse and Neglect*, p. 32.

43. S. Graham-Bermann and A. Levendosky, "Traumatic Stress Symptoms in Children of Battered Women," *Journal of Interpersonal Violence*. Vol 13(1) (1998): 111–128.

44. U.S. Department of Health and Human Services, Children's Bureau, National Center on Child Abuse and Neglect, *National Study of the Incidence and Severity of Child Abuse and Neglect*, p. 171.

45. American Humane Association, *Highlights of Official Child Neglect and Abuse Reporting 1985*.

46. Child Welfare League of America, *Too Young to Run: The Status of Child Abuse in America*.

47. Finkelhor, *Child Sexual Abuse*; E. Porter, *Treating the Young Male Victim of Sexual Assault: Issues and Intervention Strategies*; M. Lew, *Victims No Longer*; M. Hunter, *Sexually Abused Boys*.

48. K. Stephens, "The First National Study of Sexual Abuse in Child Care: Findings and Recommendations," *Child Care Information Exchange* 60 (March 1988): 9–12.

49. K. J. Lindholm, *Child Abuse and Ethnicity: Patterns of Similarities and Differences*, p. 41.

50. S. M. Leung and J. E. Carter, "Cross Cultural Study of Child Abuse Among Chinese, Native Americans and Anglo-Canadian Children," *Journal of Psychiatric Treatment and Evaluation*, vol. 5 (1983): 37–44.

51. R. L. Hampton, "Race, Class and Child Maltreatment," *Journal of Comparative Family Studies,* vol. 18-1 (Spring 1987): 113–126.

52. L. H. Pierce and R. L. Pierce, "Race as a Factor in the Sexual Abuse of Children," *Social Work Research and Abstracts,* vol. 20 (Summer 1984): 9–14.

53. Lindholm, *Child Abuse and Ethnicity,* p. 28.

54. Leung and Carter, "Cross Cultural Study of Child Abuse," p. 40.

55. Doman Lum, *Social Work Practice and People of Color: A Process-Stage Approach.*

56. W. Thorne, "Child Abuse and the Native American/Cultural Dimensions to Multidisciplinary Interventions," workshop at The National Symposium on Child Victimization, Anaheim, CA, April 30, 1988.

57. A. Pellegrin and W. Wagner, "Child Sexual Abuse: Factors Affecting Victim's Removal from Home," *Child Abuse and Neglect,* vol. 14-1 (1990): 53–60.

58. For more information on the court process, see D. N. Duquette, *Advocating for the Child in Protection Proceedings.*

59. A. Kadushin and J. Martin, *Child Welfare Services,* pp. 281–282.

60. C. R. Wichlacz and J. G. Wechsler, "American Indian Law on Child Abuse and Neglect," *Child Abuse and Neglect,* vol. 7 (1983): 347–350.

61. A. Morales and B. Shaefer, *Social Work: A Professional of Many Faces;* Thorne, "Child Abuse and the Native American."

62. Ibid.; Lum, "Social Work Practice."

63. Gray and Cosgrove, "Ethnocentric Perception."

64. For a teacher-centered approach, see C. C. Tower, *How Schools Can Combat Child Abuse and Neglect.*

65. D. Finkelhor and N. Strapo, "Sexual Abuse Prevention Education: A Review of Evaluation Studies," in D. S. Willis, E. W. Holder, and M. Rosenburg, eds., *Child Abuse Prevention.*

66. Ibid.

67. A. Donnelly, "We've Come a Long Way, But the Challenges Ahead Are Mighty," *Child Maltreatment.* Vol 2(1) (1997): 6–11.

68. Ibid.

Bibliography

American Humane Association. *Highlights of Official Child Neglect and Abuse Reporting 1985.* Denver, CO: American Humane Association, 1987.

Bonner, B., Crow, S. M., and Hensley, D. L., "State Efforts to Identify Maltreated Children with Disabilities: A Follow-up Study," *Child Maltreatment.* Vol 9(1) (1997): 52–60.

Burgess, J. A., Grath, A. N., and McCausland, M. P. "Child Sex Initiation Rings." *American Journal of Orthopsychiatry* 51-1 (Jan. 1981): 110–119.

Butler, S. *Conspiracy of Silence.* San Francisco: Valcano Press, 1978.

Carter, I., and Parker, L. "Intra-familial Sexual Abuse in American Indian Families," in Patton, M. P., *Family Sexual Abuse,* Newbury Park, CA: Sage, 1991.

Child Welfare League of America. *Too Young to Run: The Status of Child Abuse in America.* New York: Child Welfare League of America, 1986.

Crosson-Tower, C. *Understanding Child Abuse and Neglect,* Boston: Allyn & Bacon, 1999.

Davis, J. *Help Me, I'm Hurt.* Dubuque, Iowa: Kendell Hunt Publishing Co., 1982.

de Mause, L. *The History of Childhood: The Untold History of Child Abuse,* New York: Peter Bedrick, 1988.

Donnelly, A. C. "We've Come a Long Way, But the Challenges Ahead Are Mighty." *Child Maltreatment* Vol 2(1) (1997): 6–11.

Duquette, D. N. *Advocating for the Child in Protection Proceedings.* Lexington, MA: Lexington Books, 1990.

Faller, K., Bowden, M. L., Jones, C. O., and Hildebrandt M. "Types of Child Abuse and Neglect" in Faller, K., *Social Work with Abused and Neglected Children.* New York: Free Press, 1981, pp. 13–31.

Finkelhor, D. "Sex Among Siblings: A Survey of the Prevalence, Variety and Effects," *Archives of Sexual Behavior* 9-3 (1980): 171–194.

——— *Child Sexual Abuse.* New York: Free Press, 1984.

——— and Strapo, N. "Sexual Abuse Prevention Education: A Review of Evaluation Studies." In D. S. Willis, E. W. Holder, and M. Rosenburg, eds., *Child Abuse Prevention.* New York: Wiley Duke, 1988.

Forward, S., and Buck, C. *Betrayal of Innocence: Incest and Its Devastation.* New York: Penguin Books, 1978.

Garbarino, J., Guttman, E., and Seely, J. W. *The Psychologically Battered Child.* San Francisco: Jossey-Bass, 1986.

Gellert, G. A., Durfee, M. J., and Berkowitz. "Developing Guidelines for HIV Antibody Testing among Victims of Pediatric Sexual Abuse." *Child Abuse and Neglect.* 14-1 (1990): 9–17.

Graham-Bermann, S. A., and Levendosky, A. A., "Traumatic Stress Symptoms in Children of Battered Women," *Journal of Interpersonal Violence* Vol 13(1) (1998): 111–128.

Gray, E., and Cosgrove, J. "Ethnocentric perception of Childrearing Practices in Protective Services." *Child Abuse and Neglect* 9 (1985): 389–396.

Groth, A. N. "Patterns of Assault Against Children and Adolescents." In A. Burgess, A. N. Grath, L. L. Holmstrom, and S. M. Sgroi, *Sexual Assault of Children and Adolescents.* Lexington, MA: Lexington Books, 1978, pp. 3–24.

Hampton, R. L. "Race, Class and Child Maltreatment." *Journal of Comparative Family Studies* 18-1 (Spring 1987): 113–126.

Helfer, R. E. *Childhood Comes First: A Crash Course in Childhood for Adults.* East Lansing, MI: Ray E. Helfer, 1976.

Herman, J. *Father-Daughter Incest.* Cambridge: Harvard University Press, 1981.

Hollingsworth, J. *Unspeakable Acts.* New York: Congdon and Weed, 1986.

Hunter, M. *Sexually Abused Boys.* Lexington, MA: Lexington Books, 1990.

Inglis, R. *Sins of the Fathers.* New York: St. Martin Press, 1978.

Justice, B., and Justice, R. *The Broken Taboo: Sex in the Family.* New York: Human Services Press, 1979.

Kadushin, A., and Martin, J. *Child Welfare Services.* New York: Macmillan, 1988.

Kempe, C. H., and Helfer, R. *The Battered Child.* Chicago: University of Chicago Press, 1968 (3rd ed. 1980).

Kempe, Ruth S., and Kempe, C. H. *The Common Secret - The Sexual Abuse of Children and Adolescents.* New York: Witt-Frjeeman, 1984.

Leberg, E., *Understanding Child Molesters,* Thousand Oaks, CA: Sage, 1997.

Leung, S. M. R., and Carter, J. E. "Cross Cultural Study of Child Abuse Among Chinese, Native Indians and Anglo-Canadian Children." *Journal of Psychiatric Treatment and Evaluation* 5 (1983): 37–44.

Lew, M. *Victims No Longer.* New York: Nevraumont Publishing Company, 1988.

Lindholm, K. J. *Child Abuse and Ethnicity: Patterns of Similarities and Differences.* Los Angeles: Spanish Speaking Mental Health Research Center, 1983.

Lum, Doman. *Social Work Practice and People of Color: A Process - Stage Approach.* Monterey, CA: Brooks/Cole Duke Company, 1986.

Mayer, A. *Incest: A Treatment Manual for Therapy with Victims, Spouses and Offenders.* Holmes Beach, FL: Learning Publishing, 1983.

Morales, A., and Sheafer, B. *Social Work: A Profession of Many Faces.* Boston: Allyn & Bacon, 1983.

Mrazek, P. B. "Definition and Recognition of Child Sexual Abuse: Historical and Cultural Perspectives." In *Sexually Abused Children and Their Families,* edited by P. B. Mrazek and C. H. Kempe. New York: Pergamon Press, 1981, pp. 5–15.

Nasjleti, M. "Suffering in Silence: The Male Incest Victim." *Child Welfare* 49-5 (1980): 269–275.

Nelson, B. *Making an Issue of Child Abuse.* Chicago: University of Chicago Press, 1985.

Pellegrin, A., and Wagner, W. "Child Sexual Abuse: Factors Affecting Victim's Removal from Home." *Child Abuse and Neglect,* 14-1 (1990): 53–60.

Pierce, L. H. and Pierce, R. L. "Race as a Factor in the Sexual Abuse of Children." *Social Work Research and Abstracts* 20 (Summer 1984): 9–14.

Polansky, N. A., Chalmers, M. A., Buttenweiser, E., and Williams. D. *Damaged Parents: An Anatomy of Child Neglect.* Chicago: University of Chicago Press, 1981.

———. DeSaix, C., and Sharlin, S. *Child Neglect: Understanding and Reaching the Parent.* New York: Child Welfare League of America, 1972.

Polansky, N. F., Holly, C., and Polansky, N. A. *Profile of Neglect: A Survey of the State of the Knowledge of Child Neglect.* Washington, DC: Department of Health, Education, and Welfare, 1975.

Porter, E. *Treating the Young Male Victim of Sexual Assault: Issues and Intervention Strategies.* Syracuse, NY: Safer Society Press, 1986.

Rush, F. *The Best-Kept Secret: Sexual Abuse of Children.* New York: McGraw-Hill, 1980.

Russell, D. *Sexual Exploitation.* Beverly Hills: Sage, 1984.

——— *Secret Trauma: Incest in the Lives of Girls and Women.* New York: Basic Books, 1986.

Sagatun, I. J., and Edwards, L. P. *Child Abuse and the Legal System.* Chicago: Nelson Hall, 1995.

Sgroi, S. *Handbook of Clinical Intervention in Child Sexual Abuse.* Lexington, MA: Lexington Books, 1982.

Smith, M., and Pazder, L. *Michelle Remembers.* New York: Pocket Books, 1987.

Stephens, K. "The First National Study of Sexual Abuse in Child Care: Findings and Recommendations" *Child Care Information Exchange* 60 (March 1988): 9–12.

Thorne, W. "Child Abuse and the Native American/Cultural Dimensions to Multidisciplinary Interventions." Workshop at The National Symposium on Child Victimization. Anaheim, CA: April 30, 1988.

Tower, C. C. *How Schools Can Help Combat Child Abuse and Neglect.* Washington, DC: National Education Association, 1987.

U.S. Department of Health and Human Services, Children's Bureau, National Center on Child Abuse and Neglect. *National Study of the Incidence and Severity of Child Abuse and Neglect.* Washington, DC: U.S. Government Printing Office, 1981.

Wichlacz, C. R., and Wechsler, J. G. "American Indian Law on Child Abuse and Neglect." *Child Abuse and Neglect* 7 (1983): 347–350.

Williams, G. "Child Protection: A Journey into History." *Journal of Clinical Child Psychology* 12 (Winter 1983): 236–243.

9 The Practice of Child Welfare in the Rural Setting

BY CHARLES L. BAKER

President and C.E.O.
Presbyterian Child Welfare Agency, Buckhorn Children's
Foundation, Buckhorn, KY

The story is told of an elderly woman who lived alone in an isolated cabin. During a severe snow storm that had lasted for days on end, the Red Cross sent two National Guardsmen in a jeep to see if she needed help. The journey was long and hazardous, but their fear that she could be cold and hungry kept them going. Finally they stopped in front of the cabin, pounded on the door and shouted over the noise of the wind, "Ma'am, we're from the Red Cross!" She opened the door just a crack and shouted

back, "I'm sorry boys, I'm not going to be able to help you this year. It's been a real hard winter."

Rural people are independent, and they are often both more ingenious and more caring than city folks. They can also be nosy and conservative, but if you have a flat on a small rural road, the first car along will probably stop to help. When you visit in rural homes, the poorest of them will probably offer you a cup of coffee and something to eat, but the child welfare worker requires special skills for working with rural people, for they will not easily admit to needing our help or volunteer much personal information. They are part of America's heritage of independence and self-sufficiency.

Rural America often seems to be both the best and the worst of child welfare work. The crushing weight of poverty on clients, the lack of basic services and the worker's feeling of professional isolation can be overwhelming, but a strong and self-reliant Child Welfare Worker can look forward to the satisfaction of becoming a respected member of the community and making a powerful difference in peoples' lives. In this chapter we will look at both sides of the coin. Here we enumerate many of the major issues of child welfare service in rural America, including the issue of child neglect. We also discuss some of the skills the child welfare professional can utilize to make rural child welfare work the most rewarding of any in our field. This work is neither for those dependent upon a professional support group nor for the child welfare specialist, but it will challenge and reward the generalist who wants to be deeply involved in the community and in the lives of people he/she serves.

America: A Rural or Urban Nation?

Until the census of 1970, population trends in this century had shown a growing exodus of Americans from their rural roots to the cities. In 1970, census data seemed to indicate what many called a *rural renaissance*, as large numbers of people seemed to be rediscovering the joys of small town living. Small towns and rural areas grew at a faster rate than metropolitan areas. The 1980s showed a slowing if not a reversal of that trend. Now in the 1990s rural areas are again showing widespread population gains. Three of four nonmetropolitan counties in the US gained population between 1990 and 1994 (1). This population shift to rural areas may be long-term since many retirees are moving to rural America.

With "the purple mountain majesties" and "the amber waves of grain," from the hymn by Katherine Bates, *O Beautiful for Spacious Skies*, we are reminded of one strong element of our natural self-perception—we have a rural heritage. Join this perception with the popular belief that a rural lifestyle is friendlier and slower-paced, and many of us are attracted to rural living. After all, few are enchanted with urban crowding, crime, and traffic. Most of us, however, are motivated by economics—we live where the jobs are, and the pace of job growth has been faster in rural and suburban areas than in urban areas. Therefore, for those of slightly more independent vision, there are child welfare problems to be solved and child welfare jobs waiting in rural America. According to the 1995 Population Survey of the U.S. Bureau of Census, there were 36 million persons living in poverty. Of these, 16 million are white, 10 million are black, and 9 million are of Hispanic origin. Of the total, 14 million, 39 percent are children under 18 years of age, with 17 percent under the age of 6.

Eight million of the nation's poor live in suburban or rural areas, and assuming the same ratio of children, there were 3.1 million poor children under 18, 1.4 million under 6, living in rural America in March of 1995 (2). Certainly, with poverty often linked to child abuse and neglect, there are an abundance of child welfare issues in rural America.

As a cautionary note in the following discussion of the child welfare problems of rural areas, we should not lose sight of the very real positive aspects of life in the country. Many of the romantic ideas of rural living can be true; however, our purpose here is to attempt an understanding of the nature of the major issues and concerns facing children and their families in this setting. Wanda Urbanska and Frank Levering's book, *Moving to a Small Town, A Guidebook for Moving from Urban to Rural America* (3), is an excellent tool for those who are considering the exciting option of becoming a rural Child Welfare Worker. In chapter one of the book, the authors will "help you determine if you're good small-town material." Are there things you feel are missing in your current life? Such things as:

- Spending more time with family
- Knowing neighbors better
- Getting to know people in multiple contexts, over time
- Being a part of a community
- Feeling that you—one person—can make a difference
- Yearning for more time in which to tap into and develop your creativity
- Doing work that has an immediate, tangible impact
- Feeling safe in your home and in public places
- Spending more time out-of-doors or being in better touch with nature
- Having time to explore the spiritual dimension of life
- Leading a more harmonious and organic—less fragmented—life
- Slowing the pace of your life

If you are seriously considering such a move, ask your yourself and your family these questions:

- Do you have an open mind?
- Would you like to settle in one place for the rest of your life?
- Do you enjoy telling stories and hearing them told?
- Are you a joiner? Are you prepared to roll up your sleeves and go to work for the community?
- Are you willing to accept the fact that your life is not entirely your own?

While an answer in the affirmative to the above questions might predict success, a "yes" answer to the following questions may be cause for concern:

- Are you an elitist?
- Do you treasure your anonymity?
- Are you able to keep your thoughts to yourself, or do you find yourself saying the first thing that comes to your mind?

In Chapter Six, *Making a Place for Yourself,* you can tackle the most difficult and delicate challenge that awaits you if you decide to move to a small town—making a place for yourself in this foreign land—learning the art of crossing cultures. This insightful chapter is good reading, not only for those brand new to small town or rural life, but also for those of us who have already moved and too often forget our manners and revert back to our "city ways." Here we learn valuable lessons in how to behave in a community. There are actions we should definitely take and ones we should avoid. These include:

- Don't prejudge. Learn to wait until you understand the history and the context.
- Don't say you know how things should be. Give advice very carefully, and only when asked.
- Don't expect everything from the city to be in the small town. Bagels and expresso are not available in most small towns.
- Cultivate a giving attitude. Everyone is prepared to help.
- Seek input from the old guard. There definitely is reverence for the wisdom of age and experience in rural America.
- Don't be the first voice to speak. Wait, then wait again.
- Avoid directness of speech. Because rural people see each other in so many different contexts, they have learned not to offend each other.
- No more "throw away" people. In a small town, everyone has a job and a role in the community. They all "belong."

Two members of the same Appalachian family were complaining about the "black sheep" of the family. He had embarrassed everyone by having his name in the newspaper, arrested again for "being drunk in a public place." Following a discussion of a number of his most infamous escapades, the eldest of the two ended the discussion with this remark, "Yeah, but he's airn (ours)." In the context of family and the rural community, you always belong, no matter what you do.

The positive behaviors which must be cultivated include:

- Slow your pace. Drive slower and learn to wave.
- Cultivate drop-in's, and make it a point to socialize. You don't just buy something at the drug store, you visit with the pharmacist.

- Be part of a conspiracy of kindness. Teach yourself to smile and speak to strangers.
- Forgive.
- Donate.
- Join.

Rural living is not right for everyone, but a small town can be the safest place to be a child, the most supportive place to be parents, the most creative place to be a working adult, and the most comforting place to grow old. A small town is "family" at its very best.

Child Welfare Issues in the Rural Environment

Child welfare workers in rural America usually work for a governmental agency, a state, or a county child welfare or social services department. Even though there are many unique elements and issues in rural child welfare work, workers who wish to specialize in this endeavor will have to primarily be self-educated since there are few training or educational opportunities available. A 1987 study of rural practice content in the curriculum of both undergraduate and graduate social work education revealed "significant abandonment of preparation for rural practice has taken place," especially in undergraduate programs (4). The major child welfare issues in the rural environment include those of minority culture, poverty and associated child abuse and neglect, and the widespread neglect of rural concerns by state and federal government. *Rural children and families in need are largely ignored, but when they are noticed, they are viewed as poor and part of minority culture.*

Poverty

Poverty is increasing, and children are suffering more than any other age group. The Children's Defense Fund reports that one of each five children now live in poverty, and for preschoolers the ratio is one in four (5). For rural children the figures are even more frightening. Children are suffering the most as a result of the rise in poverty rates, but statistics from four very different states illustrate the crisis for children in rural America. In the farm state of Kansas, 11.5 percent of the school-aged children in rural areas were living in poverty compared to 9.7 percent in urban areas. The urban children of New Mexico have a tragic poverty rate of 19 percent, but the rate for rural children exceeds 25 percent. While the census data shows 12.3 percent of Kentucky's urban children are living in poverty, the rate for rural children is at 21.8 percent. In Georgia, poverty among urban children is a shocking 17.3 percent, but that of rural children is still higher at 25 percent (6).

The impact of poverty on children is devastating. In the largely rural state of Maine, a study of children's deaths (7) over a four-year period revealed the death rates for low-income children as substantially higher than those for other children.

The ratio of poor children who died by fire was 4.9 to 1, in motor vehicle accidents; it was 2.2 to 1, and for all accidents it was 2.6 to 1. Poor children died of homicide at a ratio of 5 to 1, and of disease related causes at 3.5 to 1. Only in the category of suicide did the ratio of poor children not exceed other children's deaths, at 1 to 1.6. For all causes, 3.1 poor children died for each other child who died in Maine during the years of 1976–1980. These statistics illustrate our nation's lack of commitment to serving the poor. Poor children are all too often paying the ultimate price of inadequate resources.

Minorities

Many of America's pockets of rural poverty are also communities of cultural minorities. In Georgia, for example, many of the rural poor are black; while only 11.7 percent of the population of the United States is black, in Georgia, 26.5 percent of the rural poor are black. Of the rural poor in New Mexico, 8 percent of the population is American Indian, 37 percent is Hispanic and only 53 percent is white (8). Statistics are not kept on the percentage of rural West Virginia, Kentucky, Virginia, North Carolina, Georgia, and Tennessee people who might be classified as poor Mountaineers, but stereotypical television programs and reruns, like *The Beverly Hillbillies* and *Hee Haw*, are potent testimony to the cultural prejudice still imposed upon these proud people and their children.

Ignored

A serious look at the homes of many of the rural poor will uncover little evidence of the involvement of the state or federal government. The basic elements of infrastructure needed to raise healthy children are not available. Pure drinking water, sewers, fire and police protection, and garbage pick-up are the basic services a government provides for citizens in a civilized society, but the homes of poor rural Hispanics, Mountaineers, American Indians, and blacks go without even these most basic services.

> *Quality problems persist, particularly in the chronically poverty-stricken areas of southern states, Appalachia, the Ozarks, Indian trust land, and along the Mexican border. And residents of metropolitan America still occupy a disproportionate share of the nation's housing units with physical problems, with people of color affected most of all. Metropolitan areas, with 22 percent of the nation's population, have 29 percent of its occupied substandard units.*

"Physically deficient housing" is defined by the U.S. Dept. of Housing and Urban Development as *units with severe physical problems related to plumbing, heating, electricity, maintenance, or hallways, or moderate physical problems related to plumbing, heating, maintenance, hallways, or kitchen.* Well over 2 million rural families live in these conditions. In rural areas under 2,500 population, fully 17 percent of families who rent live in severely or moderately physically deficient homes.

Racial and ethnic concerns persist; while African-American households comprise about 8 percent of all rural households, they occupy 23 percent of all substandard rural housing units. Rural Hispanic households, too, suffer a high degree of housing problems; over 18 percent live in substandard units. Almost two of every five American Indians residing in rural areas lived below the poverty line. Nearly twelve percent of Native American households in rural areas lived without complete plumbing in 1990.

Water supply and sewage disposal problems are much more common in rural than urban areas. A 1990 report of the Environmental Protection Agency states that $110 billion is needed to construct new and improve existing wastewater treatment facilities in communities with less than 10,000 people (9). This lack of the basic elements of civilized living is often shocking to urban visitors. They may ask the question, *In the wealthiest nation on earth, how can so many people lack the basic governmental services of public water supply, public sewers, garbage service, fire and police protection?* There is only one possible answer and that is the failure of government from the federal through the state and local levels to provide for the needs of all citizens. By illustration, nearly every home in the United States now has access to electric power. The National Rural Electric Cooperative was founded in 1942 by President Roosevelt and funded by Congress to deal with war time shortages of electric power. Since that first step to address the need for utilities in rural areas, Congress has failed to create similar organizations for safe drinking water, sewers, etc. The RWA (Rural Water Authority) and the RSA (Rural Sewer Authority) were never formed. It is not surprising that rural Americans often feel ignored and exploited when rural areas provide valuable minerals for industry, farm produce for the nation, and timber for construction with little from government in return.

Speaking of the colonial nature of coal mining in his classic book, *Night Comes to the Cumberlands,* Harry Caudill speaks of how industry removes rural natural resources to the industrial sections of the country, while returning little of lasting value to the people of the region. There are no water or sewer systems, no schools or libraries left behind, but *"They have brought economic depression, to be sure, and it lies like a grey pall over the whole land. But a deeper tragedy lies in the depression of the spirit which has fallen upon so many of the people, making them, for the moment at least, listless, hopeless and without ambition"* (10). Given this incredible neglect of people's most basic needs by all levels of government, it's not surprising that the child welfare worker, who often represents a government agency, may be viewed by the rural poor with great suspicion.

Poverty or Neglect?

Given the high degree of poverty and the inadequate living conditions in many rural areas we are quite appropriately concerned that many children may be in danger of abuse and neglect. Neglect is of especially great concern to the rural child welfare worker, however; the definition of "neglect" is often vague. One definition is: *Neglect is a lack of attention to the physical and/or emotional needs of a child and a fail-*

ure to use available resources to meet those needs (11). But it is crucial to our understanding of these issues that we clearly distinguish between the family that is
merely poor and the family that is neglectful! This issue is one of the most complex
facing child welfare practitioners today. Many believe that children are permanently damaged to at least some degree by the mere fact of growing up in a home
of abject poverty. The effects of inadequate diet, poor hygiene, lack of stimulation,
and parents with low self-esteem are seen as permanently damaging to the child.

Others argue that most poor parents do an excellent job of parenting under
terrible conditions. Poor parents are seen as very similar to other parents. They are
strongly motivated to provide for their children even when economic issues force
great sacrifice. Where does the truth lie? Here are a few of the relevant facts.

> *There is little debate that the poor are malnourished. The Public Voice for Food and Health*
> *Policy conducted a major survey of the rural poor assessing dietary intake, actual circulat-*
> *ing levels of nutrients, low birthweight and infant mortality rates. Their findings were com-*
> *pared with equivalent measures for the population as a whole. Their analysis found the*
> *rural poor in much worse condition than the population as a whole with the gap between*
> *the two growing (12).*

There has been a good deal of attention paid to the effect of child rearing
practice on child development. Children who experience severe maternal deprivation, including lack of attention and physical contact, become unable to communicate. Those who suffer from milder forms of parental neglect, including a
deficit of cognitive or effective stimulation, are thought by many to be handicapped, at least in public school performance if not in later vocational and social
interactions as well (13). Research in early brain development has strongly suggested that parenting practices, especially from the ages of 0 to 3, can play a critical role in a child's growth and development—even in the creation of a child's
potential as an adult to be healthy and productive. In their ground breaking book,
Ghosts From the Nursery, The Roots of Violence, Robin Karr-Morse and Meredith S.
Wiley noted:

> *Depressive, or otherwise neglectful, or abusive patterns each teach an infant a maladaptive*
> *series of behaviors that can exacerbate the neurologically based predispositions toward atten-*
> *tional and impulse-regulation deficits. These pathological interactions form the basis of the*
> *child's "cortical map" or basic learned programming in the frontal lobes of the brain during*
> *the first year after birth.*

They report on one study of twenty-five homicidal youth which found that
96 percent of these most violent youth were reared in chaotic families (14).

The issue is complex, and the child welfare practitioner must keep attention
focused both on the general needs of the community and its families—diet, sanitation, etc., and also work closest with those families who are not providing their
children with the attention, stimulation, and protection they need to grow to
become healthy, productive adults. Where there is a lack of adequate housing,

health, education and social services, the basic issue may be one of "community neglect" (15), and the worker and her/his agency have an obligation to remember the systemic issues and to push government agencies for improvement. Meanwhile, the child welfare worker's daily focus is with the individual families who must assume the responsibility of improving their parenting practices. Distinguishing which parents are neglectful is difficult. Norman Polansky, in his work with rural families in Appalachia, has devised a Childhood Level of Living Scale (16), which is of great assistance in this process. This comprehensive approach has five or more items under the following categories:

Childhood Level of Living Scale

Part A—Physical Care

- I. Comfort
- II. Safety
- III. State of Repair
- IV. Hygiene
- V. Feeding Patterns
- VI. Safety Precautions
- VII. Disease Prevention
- VIII. Use of Medical Facilities
- IX. Clothing
- X. Sleeping Arrangements
- XI. Regularity of Provision for Rest
- XII. Grooming
- XIII. Home Comforts

Part B—Emotional/Cognitive Care

- XIV. Cultural Artifacts
- XV. Parental Play with Child
- XVI. Promoting Curiosity
- XVII. Consistency in Encouraging Superego Development
- XVIII. Level of Disciplinary Techniques
- XIX. Providing Reliable Role Image
- XX. Providing Reliable Evidences of Affection

This complex view of the family and its functioning reveals the major areas of physical and emotional neglect and provides the child welfare worker with a clear perspective of which problems need attention. The damage inflicted on children by chronic neglect is appalling. Here is the story of one victim of the author's acquaintance who came to the attention of our residential treatment program several years too late to rectify many of his problems or to assist his family in providing the care and attention he needed.

Johnny's Story

Johnny was referred to us with a long history of violence. His record indicated that he had had dozens of fights at school, not only with other students, but with teachers and the principal as well. When Johnny came to the Children's Center we soon discovered that he fought because he was scared. In fact, I have never seen anyone as terrified of school and anything associated with it as Johnny was.

You see, Johnny came from a very poor family and had to wear hand-me-down clothes. A lot of rural kids wear hand-me-downs, but Johnny's were from his older sister. Inevitably, when Johnny wore his sister's shirts or pants, he would be teased and ridiculed by the other children. Not surprisingly, Johnny, who also had a severe speech impediment and couldn't successfully compete in a verbal battle, would ball up his fists and go after anyone who teased him about his clothes.

Johnny's school had one hard and fast rule—any student caught fighting in school would be paddled. So nearly every day that Johnny went to school he was first humiliated, then got into a fight and subsequently was paddled. It was no wonder he was terrified of school.

When Johnny arrived at the Children's Center, he had all his belongings in a small paper sack. He was wearing the only pair of blue jeans he owned, and a completely worn-out pair of sneakers. When our nurse gave him his physical examination, she found his painfully thin body covered with scratches and scars, the evidence of a life of pain and suffering. She also discovered the reason for his severe speech impediment. Johnny was nearly deaf from long-neglected infections in both ears. Ear surgery was scheduled, and in time, Johnny's hearing was restored and, with speech therapy, his speech improved. He never overcame his fear of school, but in our on-campus school he did learn to read.

Of course, many staff members demonstrated their care for Johnny's well-being, but caring is best illustrated by Alice, a child care worker, who within a few days of Johnny's arrival, took him on his first shopping trip. The budget for that initial shopping trip was $50. The first place they visited was the shoe department to get Johnny a good practical pair of shoes, in the right size, to replace his worn out sneakers. The problem was that Johnny immediately fell in love with a beautiful pair of cowboy boots. They were the right size, but hardly practical, and the price was $50!

When Alice returned she apologized. She said, "I was so torn. He really needed some good shoes and a pair of jeans, but I knew he probably never had anything he really wanted. So I got the shoes and the jeans, but we got the boots too! I'm sorry I didn't stay within the budget." What chance does a budget have against a pair of cowboy boots?

Johnny has been *permanently* damaged by neglect. He completed the residential treatment program, and, a year later, still had an improved self-image and had kept some of his new skills. He always had a winning smile and a delightful sense of humor, but it's not possible to estimate what he might have been without the toll of neglect. Today he is barely literate and has little real hope of ever earning much above minimum wage.

It's entirely possible that Johnny will neglect and abuse his own children because that's what he learned at home. There's a strong likelihood he will need to receive some level of public support for the rest of his life. Perhaps the saddest note is that his "dreams" are handicapped—he has very limited ambitions. To achieve his full potential, Johnny needed the intervention of a skilled rural child welfare worker many years earlier.

Rural Child Welfare Practice Implications

The rural Child Welfare Worker must be a generalist in orientation, a professional with a wide range of skills and a commitment to social work values in a variety of services (17). Child protection, adoptions, foster care, juvenile probation, and general court work may be all in a day's work for a rural child welfare worker as an employee of a public agency. Arrangements differ, but the public worker may be the only person in a county office, or in some cases, one of a small team located in a small town which serves the outlying county or district. Seldom will there be an interdisciplinary team with whom to consult or a group of colleagues with whom to share case load problems and solutions. Often he/she will be serving as the team and supervisor, too (18). Somewhere in the hearts of many social workers lurks the desire to work with sophisticated urban clients who have interesting but not critical problems, who keep appointments in the worker's office and who pay handsomely for 30 minutes of counseling. Perhaps some such jobs exist. This is not the daily life of the rural child welfare worker. He or she must be much more flexible and mobile, and is more likely to deal with both critical and chronic problems of families and children. Much of the worker's time will be spent out of the office, visiting in clients' homes. Many times, the interventions he/she makes will be crucial to provide a healthy future for the children and the family, and the worker knows there is no one else to make these interventions, for these are clients for whom the worker may be the only hope. The worker may be the only representative of a better, healthier society, the one caring individual who can make a positive difference.

There are several attitudes and skills which the rural Child Welfare worker needs to develop in order to be successful. The worker must have:

1. basic trust in the resources and support of the local community
2. understanding and appreciation of the cultural heritage of the people to be served
3. skill in individual counseling
4. skill in small group work
5. skill with juveniles
6. skill in the art of building a network of consultants and resources outside of the community.

Community Resources

Rural Child Welfare Workers often envy the multitude of resources available to child welfare workers in the city. Urban workers know, however, that the very best of those resources have long waiting lists and complicated admissions criteria. Good urban workers specialize in developing relationships with the staff of the best resources for the future benefit of their clients. Good rural workers do the same, only their resources are different.

The personal attitude of the rural child welfare worker is the key to successful resource-building. You will have to initiate most of the relationships; you will be observed carefully by the community; and your actions and words will be considered and discussed by your clients and other members of the local community after you leave.

The rural Child Welfare Worker must be open to finding resources anywhere. After spending the hours needed to build a relationship, the owner of the local general store may be a tremendous repository of information about the parenting practices of many a local family. *You* become the only real representative of your public agency, and if he trusts you, he may extend credit to a particular family with whom you're working. If she thinks *you* are trustworthy, she may make a confidential child protection report. If he respects *you*, he may begin to accept your notions of better parenting practice, and support your stance when clients ask his opinion. Any of these gestures of friendship from a community leader can be the one crucial item you need to make a real difference in the life of a family. Neighbors know each other in rural areas, and many may be willing to become involved if they like or respect the worker. In the self-imposed isolation typical of them, neglectful parents may need the worker to go with them to meet the neighbors and solicit their assistance. Good neighbors will help with babysitting and rides to the doctor. The rural worker should always wave and speak with the neighbors on subsequent visits. In a close-knit rural community, many people will know when you're visiting, therefore it's a better idea for the neighbors to view the worker as a pleasant, competent professional who helps families rather than a person who "takes children from their parents."

Religious life is extremely important in most rural communities. You will probably find the pastor or priest of each little church friendly and cautiously open to being of assistance. They can be your best resource. Here are only some of the resources rural churches can provide for the Child Welfare Worker:

1. Ministers may not wish to serve in a screening capacity for requests for food or rent money. They are aware that in a small community feelings may be hurt and families with needs may be embarrassed to ask for assistance. The child welfare worker may arrange to act in the screening role, serving as a confidential liaison between the church's small charitable funds and the clients' needs. With the right relationship, the pastor will trust you, first not to ask them for assistance unless you feel there is a true emergency, and second, to keep the source of funds confidential so they don't have more requests than can be filled.

2. At your request, churches may run notices in Sunday bulletins and make other announcements when you have a family that needs items such as used furniture, clothing, etc. Again, you serve as the collector of the needed items and keep the source of the gift confidential.

3. Small-town churches often have day care centers in their basements or Sunday school rooms during the week. These are usually designed to benefit working parents only, but day care is a marvelous resource for the preschooler who is in need of more stimulation than he is receiving in his marginal home situation. When adequate funds are not available, perhaps several churches, on your recommendation, will join forces to provide a scholarship for a child to attend day care.

4. Summer camps provided by scouting organizations or 4-H can be an excellent educational and socializing experience for school-age children from a neglectful home situation. Churches or individual church members may be motivated to fund a camp scholarship.

Given the importance of personal relationships, resources in the rural community are not transferable. Each worker must develop his/her own relationships within the community. The skillful child care professional can continue to develop community resources while carefully guarding the dignity and confidentiality of the clients. It will take years to build the influence and relationship networks with elected officials and others of community influence that are needed for changes on the macro level. These contacts can develop into successful applications for water projects, sewer lines, and other major assistance for the community you serve. This kind of lasting impact on a community is often possible only for the child welfare worker who practices in a rural area. Every community has resources, waiting for development by the child welfare worker.

In his essay, *The Work of Local Culture,* the novelist, poet and farmer Wendell Berry describes how we are rapidly losing our sense of community, easily apparent in cities and suburbs, and now even in rural America. He believes that our basic national values are threatened when families no longer plan for sons and daughters to return "home" to live and work in the home town. In his view, local culture is built multi-generationally, just as rich soil is built from generations of leaves and other organic matter.

A human community, too, must collect leaves and stories and turn them to account. It must build soil, and build that memory of itself—in lore and story and song—that will be its culture. These two kinds of accumulation of local soil and local culture, are intimately related.

A very real part of the work of the rural child welfare worker then must be this building of local culture and community. The dismantling of the federal welfare state, by granting fewer dollars but more programmatic freedom to state governments, is quickly being copied by states passing along fewer dollars but more freedom to local governments and communities. A rural child welfare worker who is willing to join in the life of the community, over the long haul, has an opportunity to contribute to the lasting difference Berry describes.

In this difficult time of failed public expectations, when thoughtful people wonder where to look for hope, I keep returning in my own mind to the thought of the renewal of the rural communities. I know that one revived rural community would be more convincing and more encouraging than all the government and university programs of the last fifty years, and I think that it could be the beginning of the renewal of our country, for the renewal of rural communities ultimately implies the renewal of urban ones . . . . It would have to be done not from the outside by the instruction of visiting experts, but from the inside by the ancient rule of neighborliness, by the love of precious things, and by the wish to be at home (19).

This author has had an opportunity to participate in the rebuilding of community in the Appalachian town of Buckhorn, Kentucky. The Buckhorn Children's Center, where the author is employed, has been a part of the community since 1902, but as a part of the Presbyterian Child Welfare Agency, the organization had long restricted its own definition of service to the traditional child welfare programs of residential care, foster care, and day care. The area had long suffered from a lack of safe drinking water, since the ground water in the area contains an unhealthy concentration of the mineral barium. The Children's Center and the local public school found ways to remove Barium from well water, but the process was expensive and inefficient. As the Children's Center began redefining its role to include the building of local community, a collaboration emerged. The Children's Center joined with the public school, the Buckhorn Lake State Park, and the U.S. Corps of Engineers (who manage the dam of Buckhorn Lake) to cooperatively fund the construction of water lines to each of the four partners. Then a federal grant was secured to pay for the additional construction of water lines to citizens' homes in the area, most of whom had never been able to afford the process of removing barium from their own wells. Safe, inexpensive drinking water and fire hydrants are now provided to the entire area. As an essential part of this process, the local community was incorporated into the Village of Buckhorn, and the Village Council believes that many more improvements will result through collaboration and citizen involvement. Local 24-hour ambulance service is already a reality and the dreams of a new fire station and family/community recreation center are forming.

Rural Child Welfare Workers and traditional child welfare agencies can be change agents for improved quality of life if we are willing to commit ourselves to becoming collaborators and partners, rather than specialists and bureaucrats, and if we are willing to engage ourselves and our own families in the process of community building. Such a process is not over at five o'clock each day, it is a life's work, for it includes the building of a healthy physical and social environment for all of our children.

Cultural Heritage

In light of the earlier discussion concerning minority groups, it's obvious that the Child Welfare Worker who is of the same cultural heritage as the clients served will have the easiest task in building initial relationships. Of course, this is not always possible, and a worker of a different race or culture, who is sensitive to the heritage of the clients, can also build successful relationships. In the author's opinion the successful child welfare worker only need acquire three specific talents to communicate successfully with another culture.

1. *Quiet Observational Skills.* The skill of listening quietly while observing individual, family, or group interaction is a necessity. The worker may need to spend several hours in the general store, not interacting, but quietly observing the mores and interactions of community members. Since community members themselves often spend hours here as well, regular visits to the general store can be an important use of time as the worker makes initial contact with potential clients and potential resources.

2. *An Ear for Dialect.* Obviously the worker who is working with Hispanic or American Indian clients who cannot speak English must learn to speak their language. Not so obviously perhaps, there are many spoken versions of English that also need to be learned. The worker from Massachusetts who spends three years in Mississippi and still sounds like he is very recently arrived from Massachusetts will not communicate with clients nearly as well as the worker who can speak both "languages." Rural communities often speak a local version of English that is highly idiomatic. Some words and phrases will be unknown to visitors, and outsiders, in their defensiveness, often label the natives as ignorant and backward. The rural child welfare professional will do well to remember that he/she is the stranger who must learn to communicate, rather than acting as the "ugly American" in Paris who complained about "all these ignorant foreigners who can't speak English!" Certainly many rural people will understand standard English, but in the emotional situations faced by the child welfare worker, the sounds of familiar speech rhythms and accents will be all the more comforting and supportive. Rural communities are traditional and conservative. They are suspicious of strangers, often with good cause. Sounding like an outsider can be detrimental in working with new clients and potential resources.

Looking like an outsider can also be a problem. The new bank employee will try to dress like other employees, to not offend customers or the supervisor. The rural child welfare worker should also give some thought to how he/she dresses. A pin-striped suit will be out of place, but a mistaken attempt to dress like the client will be degrading to the client. Comfortable, clean, neat, and conservative clothes are appropriate. Dress to demonstrate your respect for the client and the local culture.

3. *Finding a Local Consultant.* If you are new to a particular culture, it's important that one of the first resources you develop is a relationship with someone with whom you can informally discuss cultural elements you don't understand. The best person for this role is someone that you like and respect immediately, who is a native of the area, and who has, preferably, lived or traveled outside of the particular rural community at sometime in his/her life. This may often be an older person, who has developed the ability to be able to speak both the local dialect and standard English and can interpret for you. However, you will want to reevaluate your choice of consultant regularly to be sure you are not becoming involved with someone who is not respected by the community.

The excellent manual, *Cross-Cultural Skills in Indian Child Welfare*, developed by the Northwest Indian Child Welfare Institute, clearly articulates how the values of American Indians must also be understood by the non-Indian in order for her/him to be successful in this largely rural practice (20).

Each culture has specific characteristics of language and behavior that can be learned in specialized training sessions, by reading and through observation. There are two crucial mistakes to avoid. First, don't think the major responsibility lies with the client—you have the primary obligation of communication. Second, and related to the first, don't ever assume you've learned all you need to know about a culture—there are subtleties that an outsider can never learn.

Interviewing

The rural child welfare worker must be an expert in the skills of interviewing. Child welfare workers often undervalue this group of skills. *There are no other skills as valuable.* For without them, the worker is left guessing as to which services to force on an unwilling client. In the last analysis, only the client's perception of the worker's concern will motivate the client to participate in the process, and these interviewing techniques are designed to promote the worker as someone who is at least interested enough to listen.

Assessment and Observation

In a rural setting, the child welfare worker may initially find the image of "welfare worker" even worse among his/her clients than that found by the urban worker. In many locations the state or county agency has universally given the title of "social worker" to most of its frontline employees, whether or not these employees have the values, knowledge, or skills of the profession. Now many of the rural poor expect harsh and insensitive treatment at the hands of any worker associated with these agencies. This makes the assessment task especially difficult.

On the first visit with a family the worker may have to rely extensively on objective observations, such as those identified earlier in Polansky's *Childhood Level of Living Scale*. In a rural setting the extended family is also of great importance. The grandparents may be a part of the solution or the genesis of the problem, and their involvement must be assessed carefully. It is a rare rural family who does not have extensive contact with the extensive family.

Joining with the Client

To successfully engage the rural client in the helping process, the Child Welfare Worker must find a way to join with the client. "Joining" is a level of involvement that demonstrates to the client that the worker is genuinely concerned. This demonstration of concern can be expressed verbally by the skills of "identifying feelings" and "goal recognition" (21) or through *action* via client advocacy or physical service provision by the worker. In essence, the worker is always modeling the attitudes and actions of a caring individual. This modeling both aids the process of joining and uses the worker as an example of the kind of person the client may wish to emulate.

All rural child welfare workers, as a part of their education and training, should have numerous opportunities to practice interviewing techniques and be videotaped while doing so. Videotaping will allow the worker to view his/her own actions and interactions.

Video Home Training

A new method of both developing child welfare worker skills and for working with families has just become available in the United States. **Video Home Training** (22) was developed in the Netherlands and has spread across Europe because of its effectiveness in early intervention. The method involves the use of a camcorder by a video home trainer to tape a brief period of interaction between parent(s) and child(ren). Returning to the office, this tape segment is microanalyzed by the trainer and his/her supervisor to identify the parents' level of communication with the child. The key principle in the work of the video home trainer is *how well does the parent respond to the child's initiatives.*

After analysis, the trainer uses the videotape to provide the parent with feedback exclusively on the positive elements of communication the parent is already using. The impact of this joining with the parent as a collaborator and partner is spectacular.

Video Home Training is available in the United States in the states of Massachusetts, New York and Kentucky. Expansion across the nation is expected to follow within the next five years. Eighteen months of initial training and ongoing consultation are necessary to keep the model authentic.

The rural child welfare worker must have excellent communication skills. These skills include:

Joining Through Verbal Skills

Identifying feelings is perhaps the most important skill of interviewing. The worker helps the client to label and own the feelings expressed while beginning to identify some of the reasons for the feelings. The worker paraphrases or restates the feelings heard and names a possible reason the client may have for feeling this way. These statements by the worker are always in the form of a question so the client can confirm or correct the worker. This skill procedure is never complete unless all three steps are present:

1. The client makes a statement.
2. The worker interjects a question which
   a. identifies a feeling and
   b. states a reason or reasons for such a feeling.
3. The client confirms or corrects the worker's statement.

In a rural situation where clients are distrustful of outsiders and often prove to be passive when angry or depressed, this skill is a powerful tool for the child welfare worker. As a general rule, the worker should gather the important facts of the situation only after the client's feelings have been identified.

To illustrate this skill, here are two client statements followed by possible responses from three workers. Worker A's response is unskilled and not likely to help in forming a helping relationship. Worker B demonstrates only some minimal skill, and Worker C responds skillfully and is more likely to join with the client quickly in the helping process.

I. *Client:* "I probably shouldn't have hit him that hard, but he knew I was having a bad morning with his little sister, and he kept on pestering me anyway."

Worker A: "Did you hit him with your hand or your belt?"

Worker B: "He made you mad?"

Worker C: "You regret hitting him so hard, but you were frustrated because he kept pestering you. Is that right?"

II. *Client:* "Seems like the welfare check just won't last all month, and Billy, my husband, hasn't been able to find work. It just keeps me torn up."

Worker A: "When did Billy last work?"

Worker B: "It's really been difficult for you."

Worker C: "You keep feeling worried and down because Billy hasn't worked and there isn't enough money. Is that how it is?"

Many inexperienced workers complain about this skill. Some say the interchanges are phony and awkward, and others say the skill may be fine for some settings, but they have so many cases there isn't enough time for this process. New workers must realize that at first the skill is awkward, just as riding a bike is awkward when one is first learning. With practice this soon passes, but *the process of identifying feelings in this way is crucial.* There is no other way to assure that the worker hears what the client wants understood, nor for the client to face his/her own feelings, which may have been denied until now.

Workers who find themselves pressured to sacrifice the quality of their work for quantity must identify the source of the pressure. Is the pressure coming from the agency or the worker him/herself? The worker who is pressuring herself to do more is sacrificing today's client for a client who may be more needy tomorrow. This action will only result in today's client requiring even more attention later. When the agency is the source of the pressure, the worker is advised to question the wisdom of such policy. Will more active cases lead to additional workers? Is the agency committed to quality care for clients? The worker has a right to know the reasons behind such a policy.

Goal recognition is the next step in the verbal process of joining with the client. The worker assists the client in identifying his or her overall goal and the intermediate objectives for achieving this goal. Rural clients are likely to be much more interested in practical outcomes than an insight-oriented, subjective outcome. The goal recognition process includes the exploration of a variety of possible outcomes until the client identifies a goal that is desirable and achievable. If the client feels overwhelmed and sees little that is achievable, he/she will need the worker's assistance in identifying goals that can be accomplished.

Goal recognition follows naturally after the worker has identified the client's feelings and gathered the facts. For example, a possible goal recognition statement in the first situation above might be:

> *Worker:* "Now let me see, your son has been frustrating you quite a bit lately, and you would like to find some other way to teach him to do better without hitting him. Is that right?"

Such a statement not only gives a direction for the process to follow, it also serves as a summary of what has been covered in the interview so far. The worker may then offer some help for solving a problem that the client has identified. This will have a much greater chance of success than a "required" solution that the worker orders the client to follow because the worker has the authority to attempt to exercise such power. The solution might include parenting classes offered by the worker to a small group of parents, or a pamphlet to read and discuss on a later visit. In a rural area, the worker may be the only source of help.

Joining Through Action

Physical service provision can be a very clear way of demonstrating the Worker's concern for the client. Such service includes finding food for clients, finding clothes, locating rent money, finding employment, and providing transportation. The worker's own community resources, as discussed earlier, often will be the only emergency resources available for clients in need, but the use of major resources such as AFDC and Food Stamps should be explored with the client. Research has demonstrated that these resources are severely underutilized in rural areas (23).

Transportation is a major need in many rural areas. Public transportation is seldom available and, until neighbors or other volunteers can be identified, the worker may be the client's only source of transportation. The worker can often utilize the provision of transportation as an excellent method of joining with the client. While traveling to the grocery store, the doctor's office, or the food stamp office, the worker can also learn a great deal about the client's organizational, budgeting, and parenting skills.

Homemaker or parent aide service is an excellent example of joining through action. Homemaker services can be the primary treatment service in a good many neglectful rural families. The homemaker excels in modeling and in the provision of physical services. When one homemaker was asked by the author to describe her service, she replied, "Well I arrive with a bucket, a bottle of Lysol, and two pairs of rubber gloves, and say, 'We've got to get started on this kitchen.

It's just not healthy for your kids when things are this dirty.' You see, I work right with the Mother, and she learns that I care enough to pitch right in and help her."

A skillful homemaker, working in tandem with the worker, can protect the children by engaging the client in a very practical experience of learning to parent. Potential homemakers are easily located in rural areas. They are the strong and ingenious women who have managed to do an excellent job of raising their own children under the very difficult conditions of rural poverty. Many of these women are more than willing to pass along their knowledge and skill to younger mothers. They are happy to share their knowledge of gardening, canning, child rearing, and home management to someone in need. The devotion and dedication of these women serves as an inspiration to all of us in the child welfare profession. They demonstrate the best of our society, often in the worst of situations (24).

Mary's Story

Two child welfare workers, the team's homemaker, Mary, and I were sharing lunch in the small office of a rural county one day. The phone rang, and a shy voice asked for Mary.

When she returned from her call, Mary had a tear in her eye. She told us that the woman on the phone was a client of about two years ago. At the time of initial referral, this woman was extremely shy and withdrawn, almost a recluse. A neglectful parent, she lived in an isolated house. She was very embarrassed about her appearance, had no friends, and only distant relatives. Mary worked with her and her three children for over a year, one or two visits per week. Eventually her self-confidence improved and she had become involved in her children's school and had been able to make friends with other mothers.

She had telephoned Mary to share another accomplishment. As she put it, "Mary, I finally ordered something out of the catalogue today, and I knew you were the only person who would know how big a step that is for me. You remember when I was afraid to try new things on my own. I couldn't have done it without your help."

This would be a small, insignificant task for most of us, but Mary and her client knew that, in this instance, this was a great accomplishment, and an example of growing self-confidence. Mary is a true child welfare professional. She has had a wonderful influence on the lives of hundreds of rural clients.

Small Group Work

The child welfare worker may be the only resource in many rural settings. Small groups can be an effective way of stretching this resource! There are many clients with similar problems who can benefit from a small group of six to twelve individuals, including: adolescents with school problems or with juvenile court difficulty, parents who have been abusive, school-aged children in foster care, mothers who are overwhelmed and neglectful, farm families with financial difficulties, women who have been abused, and families who need to improve their parenting practices.

The school or the church is a logical place to meet and the group members can come from the worker's own caseload. The worker can invite each one individually, and ensure that everyone has transportation. It's important for the worker to remember about the extended families of the rural community and not invite relatives unless each agrees that the situation would be comfortable.

Because of the close-knit nature of the rural community, confidentiality will be an important issue. The worker must stress the importance of keeping all information within the group at the first meeting and often thereafter. A group member who spreads confidential information out of the group will probably destroy all trust among the members (25).

There are several stages through which groups pass as a natural growth process, and the Worker's role changes accordingly. In the beginning or *formative stage,* the worker is quite active in helping define the general purpose for the group and modeling good group behavior, including going around the circle soliciting input from each member. In the middle or *rule setting stage,* the worker's involvement decreases as members define topics to discuss, leadership, and attendance rules. These can be stormy times, but the process is necessary. Some members may drop out at this stage, and the worker may fear nothing will come of this group. As the group reaches the later or *working stage,* members can confidently share and support each other. The worker's role is minimal at this time, and he/she must be content to allow the group members to have the fun of mutual problem solving and support. Eventually, individual members must be encouraged to leave the group's support. Each group seems to have a personality and life of its own and although it's difficult, it is sometimes possible to add members after the group has been through the middle stage.

If another worker is available, a co-leader of the opposite sex can add to the effectiveness of the group. So many things are going on in the group that two heads and two observers are very helpful. The leaders should always meet prior to and following each session to plan their roles and discuss progress. Co-leadership is especially helpful to the worker inexperienced in group work.

Services to Juveniles

The rural Child Welfare Worker in a one or two person office may be called upon by the Court to provide services to juveniles in the community who have come to the Court's attention through any of a variety of ways including: Status offenders who have run away from home or experienced behavior problems in school, dependent children who have been neglected or abused and need the worker's supervision to prevent acting out, and delinquents who have committed crimes and need treatment in the community to prevent institutionalization.

The rural worker is likely to have only the resources he/she has developed, but the creative worker will find this can fit very well with the two philosophies of individualized treatment and the least restrictive placement alternative. Such a worker will also naturally place emphasis upon involving the community wherever possible in the solution of problems.

In the development of treatment plans, the rural worker will be advised to rely not on the type of offense prompting the referral, but rather on his/her own assessment of the adolescent's needs. The following categories of developmental maturity in juveniles may be helpful:

I. *Impulsive:* Juveniles who are known by their extremely immature and impulsive behavior. Often victims of severe neglect, their parents are immature and impulsive as well.

II. *Conforming:* Young people who have a weak self image and are anxious to conform to the expectations and negative suggestions of their peer group.

III. *Controlling:* The highly peer oriented juvenile who has a strong identification with negative values.

IV. *Emotional:* Juveniles who are more mature than many others and whose problems are strongly tied to emotional issues in their families.

The following goals for each category of juvenile are the broad based approaches under which services can be provided:

Impulsive—To develop in the client some minimal measure of conformity by strengthening self-control. To increase the client's ability to understand the relationships between his needs and his behavior. To carry this out, the rural worker must establish him/herself, in the view of the client, as a supportive person, to protect the client from being scapegoated and to reduce the client's sense of isolation and rejection.

Conforming—For the client to recognize and differentiate his or her feelings, and to accept the legitimacy of feelings. To become aware of his impact on others and their impact on him. To become more confident in decision making, to become more aggressive. To establish a positive self-image. For the worker to be seen as a giving, caring, non-threatening adult. To demonstrate that he is empathic and has affection for the client. To demonstrate nurturing and non-threatening involvement in the relationship.

Controlling—The client should demonstrate more direct expression of dependency needs and reduction of his or her fear of close relationships with others. He should be able to describe a more accurate cause and effect connection between his own behavior and the response of others to him. He should demonstrate acceptance and conformity of the adult authority system. Over time, he should demonstrate a change in self-definition in the direction of non-delinquency and personal worth. The worker *must* demonstrate the ability to exert friendly but firm parental control and the ability to act promptly and appropriately in order to provide controls. He or she must demonstrate the ability to make definitive decisions and act upon them. In addition, the worker must be able to demonstrate empathy in nonverbal ways and describe an understanding of the dependency needs underlying the juvenile's facade of "distance."

Emotional—Short-term immediate goals include: establishment of a treatment contract between the juvenile and the worker or between the family and the worker. This includes a moratorium on acting-out behavior and a specified and agreed-upon plan regarding initial placement, job, school, etc. Long-range goals include: the elimination of delinquency by reduction or resolution of internal conflicts, the ability to demonstrate a changed self-image in the direction of a sense of personal worth, to see a mature person as other than a "bad" person, to demonstrate an ability to relax, and not need to always "run" from problems, to verbalize increased self-knowledge and increased awareness of complex patterns in others. For these children, the rural worker should be internally oriented and comfortable with his or her identity as a counselor. The worker should demonstrate patience and an ability to persevere, to not be easily distracted from the treatment focus by the juvenile's defenses. The worker should demonstrate a willingness to make her/himself open and emotionally available to the young person.

Consultants and Resources Outside the Community

No generalist can be an expert in all services he or she will be called upon to provide, and no rural child welfare worker can hope to function well without a list of specialists to call upon. Attendance at conferences is crucial for the rural worker in building a network of consultants, mostly urban, who can advise the rural worker by telephone. The rural worker will probably need advice in such areas as sexual abuse, juvenile work, adoptions, the law, and the use and abuse of medications. Specialists are often flattered and pleased to be of assistance to a rural generalist whom they respect for knowing so many things and having the courage to be independent.

New Technologies in Rural Practice

The technology of social work is the relationship.

Perhaps it is true that there is nothing new under the sun, but at least, there are some currently popular technologies that lend themselves to the rural practice of child welfare. It is apparent and generally accepted that many services designed for urban practice are not effective or efficient in a rural setting. For example, the isolation and transportation problems of rural settings make the food stamp program difficult for clients to access. The Public Voice found that the rural poor participate in the program "often at 40 percent the per capita level received by the urban poor" (26).

In addition, the use of large institutions, now frowned upon by most of the profession, remains popular for rural workers, perhaps because of the perceived lack of other resources. The highly specialized treatment programs, popular in many urban areas, are not options for rural areas because of insufficient numbers of clients and staff to keep such programs fully operational. Several of the most recent innovations, however, which strongly individualize service are also highly adaptable for rural populations. These include programs variously described as therapeutic foster care, intensive family support services, video home training, and special preschools.

Therapeutic Foster Care

Foster care has continued to come under strong criticism from those who believe children have been separated from their parents too soon and have stayed too long in foster care. There are some other voices who now say the system itself is at fault when children, for whom home return is not an option, are moved from foster home to foster home by agencies who seem to have no understanding of commitment or of the connection between multiple disruptions and emotional distress. Somehow separation and loss are concepts that are reserved for death and dying. Separation has become a way of life for many children in the child welfare system. A few agencies are committed to investing in better selection, more training and higher pay for foster parents, and they are creating what are called therapeutic foster homes, which have the extra intensity and agency back-up and support needed to care for very troubled children. One of the leaders in this field has been the Casey Family Program. Started and based in Seattle, this program has spread to a number of states.

Rural families, who are close-knit, have large extended families, and are involved in the community, have the potential to become good therapeutic foster families. With proper support services and consultation available, perhaps a rural family may be better prepared to handle the stress associated with accepting a difficult child into their home. That has certainly been the case with "David."

David's Story

David was at risk from the moment he was born. As the child of alcoholic parents, he was born with fetal alcohol syndrome and his early years were filled with suffering and neglect. His two younger brothers died soon after they were born; his father and then his mother died also. He spent some time in several foster homes before placement with an adoptive family.

His adoptive family proved to be as bad as his natural family. This time David was physically and sexually abused, the adoption was terminated and he was placed in a psychiatric hospital for treatment. After seventeen unhappy months in the hospital, child advocates brought suit to have him placed in a less restrictive setting. So, at the age of fourteen, he came to the Children's Center

Very slowly he began to trust his therapist and the child care staff. He was very guarded and not able to show any spontaneity. At first he was so frightened of the other boys he had to eat all meals in his own room, but slowly he began to make friends. Finally he didn't need the light on in his room all night, and six months after admission he was able to attend one period of public school a day, for the first time in five years.

Four months later he could attend public school all day and began to have very short visits to a potential therapeutic foster family in our rural community. He was afraid but excited too. It took a long time for him to stay overnight and eventually a weekend. Gradually he began staying most weekends with the family, and a month later he could spend the week with the family and return to the Children's Center on weekends.

Now David has just celebrated his fifteenth birthday. He is living full-time with his therapeutic foster family, but often makes visits back to the campus. To some, the therapeutic foster home and the support services he still needs may seem expensive, but they are only one sixth of the hospital costs, and he now has a good chance to grow up to become a healthy productive adult.

A Healthy Beginning

The most important time in the child's life is the period from birth to age five. If a child doesn't get the nourishment and stimulation he or she needs during this time, much of the child's potential will be lost. Hawaii's intensive home visiting program, Healthy Start, offers states an excellent model for establishing a voluntary, universal home-visiting program for all new parents. It should be noted that Hawaii is largely a rural state and this model works particularly well in rural environments where the home visitors are from the same area and culture. To a certain extent, the success of this model lies in the manner in which the program complements and builds upon some unique features of the state's social services and health care systems and cultural context. It is equally true, however, that Hawaii's program works because it has successfully adopted several of the best practice standards suggested by repeated evaluations of home-visitor services or interventions with new parents.

The National Committee on Prevention of Child Abuse has adapted Hawaii's model and incorporated additional research in the development of a structured approach to serving at risk infants and mothers. This program, called Healthy Families America, begins with an assessment of risk factors in the maternity ward.

Summary

There are the familiar problems in rural child welfare of poverty, neglect, and abuse. These are exacerbated by the lack of traditional resources and the neglect of rural problems by national and state policy makers. We have seen that in this environment the effective worker must be creative, able to function independently, and possess skills in developing community resources, individual counseling and group work. Since many clients are members of minority groups, the worker must also often learn to understand and appreciate values, culture and language patterns different from his/her own.

We have looked at the issue of child neglect in rural areas and at some of the newer ideas and programs designed to address this problem. In any setting, changes are made in families and children through *relationships,* and we have noticed that the close-knit, family-oriented, rural community is especially inclined towards the development of relationships with a worker who demonstrates skill and caring.

Kathy Miles, M.A., is a talented professional in a small town in a rural area. She spent her childhood on a farm, and after her graduate training she had an urban practice. Now living on her own farm, she has done extensive work with substance abuse, spouse abuse cases, and abused and neglected children. In an interview with the author, Ms. Miles commented on the differences in rural and urban work with families:

> *Rural families generally have a broader concept of "family" than urban families. They not only see the importance of the extended family of grandparents, uncles, aunts, and others—they have a greater appreciation of how family history impacts the present and the future. Consequently, rural families have less resistance to involving their extended family in the therapeutic process. Urban families are much more tied to the immediate family and the present, therefore they sometimes artificially limit their own understanding and their resources for change. Rural families also seem more open to story telling in therapy.*
>
> *As might be expected, the personal values and lifestyle of the therapist have a strong impact on her practice in the community. Rural families select a therapist based not so much on professional reputation as on personal values and reputation. The marriage counselor who is personally experiencing the latest in a series of divorces may also experience a loss of referrals.*

It would be a mistake to end this chapter without a reminder that the rural child welfare worker should expect to learn a great deal from the wisdom of his rural clients. A formal education is not the only source of knowledge, nor a sure indicator of intelligence. The humorist, Loyal Jones, is fond of telling this story:

> *When the warriors in President Johnson's skirmish against poverty came, they had their own ideas about us. They did a lot of good, but they too were not content to help us with education, social services, and jobs. They also wanted to change us. They had discovered values, thanks to sociology, and they plotted endlessly for ways to intervene in the cycle of poverty that was the current targetal thrust. We toyed with them too. One well-dressed poverty fighter, driving a fancy car, was asked by a mountain man what he did.*
>
> *"I'm with the War on Poverty," he said.*
>
> *"Looks like you won," the mountaineer observed.*

The VISTA workers living with mountaineers wrote back home about all of the things mountain people didn't know about, like museums, subways, and art galleries. Their hosts talked with each other in wonder about people who didn't know how to milk a cow, plant a garden, slaughter a hog, or piece a quilt (27).

Child welfare work is enormously challenging and vital to our survival as a nation. Our children are our future, but in rural America, we are failing to care for them in a way that gives them the opportunity to grow to become the competent, caring adults our world so desperately needs.

For those with the courage and the commitment, rural child welfare work can be the rewarding work of a lifetime.

Endnotes

1. K. M. Johnson and C. L. Beale "The Rural Rebound Revisited," *American Demographics*, July 1995.

2. U.S. Bureau of the Census, Housing and Household Economic Statistics Division, March 1995 *Current Population Survey.*

3. Urbanska W., and Levering F. *Moving to a Small Town, A Guidebook for Moving from Urban to Rural America.* New York: Simon & Schuster, 1996.

4. K. L. DeWeaver, M. L. Smith, and M. A. Hosang, "Has Social Work Education Abandoned Preparation for Rural Practice?," *Human Services in the Rural Environment,* Spring 1988, p. 28.

5. Children's Defense Fund, *A Call for Action to Make Our Nation Safe for Children: A Briefing Book on the Status of American Children in 1988,* Washington, D.C., p. iii.

6. Public Voice for Food and Health Policy, *Profiles of Rural Poverty: Facing Barriers to the Food Stamp Program,* Washington, D.C., 1987, pp. 21, 49, 101.

7. Maine Department of Human Services, *Children's Deaths in Maine,* Augusta, Maine, 1983, p. 10.

8. Public Voice for Food and Health Policy, *Profiles of Rural Poverty: Facing Barriers to the Food Stamp Program,* Washington, D.C., 1987, pp. 51. 103.

9. Housing Assistance Council, *Information Sheet from the 1991 American Housing Survey* (AHS), under a Cooperative Agreement with the U.S. Department of Housing and Urban Development.

10. H. M. Caudill, *Night Comes to the Cumberlands,* Boston: Atlantic-Little, Brown, 1963, p. 325.

11. N. Falconer and K. Swift, *Preparing for Practice, The Fundamentals of Child Protection,* The Children's Aid Society of Metropolitan Toronto, 1983, p. 49.

12. Public Voice for Food and Health Policy, *Rising Poverty, Declining Health: The Nutritional Status of the Rural Poor,* Washington, D.C., 1986, p. 1–5.

13. George Thomas, *Poverty in the Nonmetropolitan South: A Causal Analysis,* Lexington, MA: D.C. Heath and Co., 1972, p. 59–60.

14. Karr-Morse, R. and Wiley, M. S. *Ghosts from the Nursery, Tracing the Roots of Violence,* New York: Atlantic Monthly Press, 1997.

15. Child Welfare League of America, *Standards for Child Protective Service,* Washington, D.C., 1973, pp. 7–8.

16. N. A. Polansky, C. DeSaix and S. A. Sharlin, *Child Neglect: Understanding and Reaching the Parent, A Guide for Child Welfare Workers*, Washington, D.C., Child Welfare League of America, 1972, pp. 74–75.

17. M. J. O'Neil, *The General Method of Social Work Practice*, Englewood Cliffs, NJ, Prentice-Hall, Inc., 1984, p. 30.

18. *Encyclopedia of Social Work*, 1974, s.v. "Rural Social Work."

19. Berry, Wendell. *What Are People For?* San Francisco: North Point Press, 1990.

20. Northwest Indian Child Welfare Institute, *Cross-Cultural Skills in Indian Child Welfare, A Guide for the Non-Indian*, Portland, OR, 1987.

21. J. M. O'Neil, *The General Method of Social Work Practice*, Englewood Cliffs, NJ, Prentice-Hall, Inc., 1984, pp. 82–87, 89–91.

22. Biemans, H. *Video Home Training. Theory, Method and Organization of SPIN*. In F. Kool, S. van Rees & J. van Lieshout eds., The power to change lies within the families. Rijswijk: Ministry of Welfare, Health and Culture (International Seminar for Innovative Institutions).

23. Public Voice for Food and Health Policy, *Profiles of Rural Poverty: Facing Barriers to the Food Stamp Program*, Washington, D.C., 1987, p. ix–xi.

24. Farley, O. W., et al. *Rural Social Work Practice*, Free Press Fields of Practice Series, New York, 1982, pp. 120–141.

25. Ibid., pp. 120–141

26. Public Voice for Food and Health Policy, *Profiles of Rural Poverty: Facing Barriers to the Food Stamp Program*, Washington, D.C., 1987, p. ix.

27. Loyal Jones and Billy Edd Wheeler, *Curing the Cross-Eyed Mule*, Little Rock, AR, August House, 1989, pp. 18–19.

Bibliography

Berry, Wendell. *What Are People For?* San Francisco: North Point Press, 1990. Essays that focus on the generally unrecognized principle that the quality of urban life is directly proportional to the quality of rural life. Mr. Berry is also a poet, a novelist and a farmer.

Caudill, Harry M. *Night Comes to the Cumberlands*. Boston: Atlantic-Little, Brown, 1963. An analysis of the problems of Appalachia, written by an insider who can see the issues and love the people.

Children's Defense Fund. *Falling by the Wayside: Children in Rural America*. Washington, D.C., 1992. The facts and figures of children's poverty in rural America.

Falconer, Nancy and Swift, Karen. *Preparing for Practice, The Fundamentals of Child Protection*. The Children's Aid Society of Metropolitan Toronto, 1983. Written for Canadian practice, but applicable in the United States with an excellent chapter on counseling in different cultures.

Farley, O. William, et al. *Rural Social Work Practice*. Free Press Fields of Practice Series. New York, 1982. A discussion of social work with individuals, families and groups in the rural setting.

Karr-Morse, R., and Wiley, M. S. *Ghosts from the Nursery, Tracing the Roots of Violence*, New York: Atlantic Monthly Press, 1997. A compilation of the research that makes clear the connection between abuse and neglect in the first two years of life and violent behavior in youth.

Northwest Indian Child Welfare Institute. *Cross-Cultural Skills in Indian Child Welfare, A Guide for the Non-Indian.* Portland, OR, 1987. A handbook for practice with Indian clients with a sensitivity to cultural differences that has much wider applications.

O'Neil, Joan Maria. *The General Method of Social Work Practice.* Englewood Cliffs, NJ: Prentice-Hall, Inc., 1984. A holistic view of social work practice.

Polansky, Norman A., Desaix, C. and Sharlin, S. A. *Child Neglect: Understanding and Reaching the Parent, A Guide for Child Welfare Workers.* Washington, D.C., Child Welfare League of America, 1972. The classic work on child welfare practice in the rural setting.

Thomas, George. *Poverty in the Nonmetropolitan South: A Causal Analysis.* Lexington, MA: D.C. Heath and Co., 1972. Out of print but available in reference, this is a breathtaking analysis of the root causes of rural poverty.

Urbanska W., and Levering F. *Moving to a Small Town, A Guidebook for Moving from Urban to Rural America,* New York: Simon & Schuster, 1996. Essential reading for every person who is considering the move to a better life in nonmetropolitan America.

Zinn, Howard *A People's History of the United States, 1492—Present.* New York: HarperCollins Publishers, 1995. Extensive coverage of the contributions of farmers, miners and poor people to the American definition of democracy, in spite of the considerable efforts of politicians and capitalists.

10 The Year 2000 and Beyond: Summary and Future Directions

NEIL A. COHEN

Cal State Univ, Los Angeles

WITH CARLOS SOSA

Cal State Univ, Los Angeles, and former Deputy Director, Los Angeles County, Department of Children and Family Services

The overall objective of this book has been several-fold: first, to provide in-depth information about the evolution of child welfare policies, programs, and services in the United States; second, to examine child welfare policies and practices from a generalist perspective; and third, to present culturally appropriate and sensitive forms of child welfare assessment and intervention, particularly for the undergraduate student who may be considering entry into the field of child welfare.

Tracing the roots of child welfare from the "child-saving" and "child-rescuing" movements of colonial times to the present-day emphasis on "the best interests of the child," we have acknowledged the change of concern, which has moved from fear of children's idleness and dependency to today's focus on children's rights and that the best opportunity for optimum growth and development most often is in their own home.

Throughout, we have examined the provision of child welfare from a perspective of an array of programs and services, ranging from supportive to supplemental to substitute interventions. Emphasis today is on providing children and youth with the least restrictive environment with focus on family preservation and family reunification and family maintenance. Child welfare practice is guided by the principles of prevention, deinstitutionalization, permanency planning, normalization, family preservation and managed care.

Emerging Trends

As we move into the first decade of the twenty-first century, we can point with satisfaction to the progress made in providing a more decent standard of living for many of the children and youth in the United States. Immunization, medical advances, increased knowledge concerning child development, and increased legal rights of children have all added to the quality of life enjoyed by the future generation of this country. Yet, as this book has described and examined throughout, serious public issues and private problems continue to tear at the fabric of society and its child-rearing institutions.

The family institution with traditional extended and nuclear components has undergone substantial change. Divorce and blended, reconstituted, alternative family patterns are now part of the language of family systems. The single-parent, female-headed household—an exception in the past—is becoming a way of life for increasing numbers of children.

Demographers project that half of all first marriages made today will end in divorce. Sixty percent of second marriages will probably collapse. One-third of all children born in the past decade will probably live in a stepfamily before they are 18. Twenty-five percent of the children today are being raised by a single parent.

We have examined in this book how child welfare policies, programs, and services are called upon to intervene and bring about positive change in those children and youth whose families are often subjected to the broader social problems of inequality, poverty, hunger, unemployment, underemployment, lack of affordable, decent child day care, teenage pregnancy, family violence, alcoholism, drug abuse, and lack of adequate education, health, housing, and mental health.

Since the beginning of the 1980s, our nation has been immersed in a significant reduction of its social program spending, reflected in cutbacks in such programs as AFDC, Food Stamps, SSI, and Mental Health Care, etc. AFDC no longer exists as it has since 1935; it has been profoundly transformed into TANF, a work-driven, benefits-limited program. These were the very programs that have provided a system of mutual support for families beset by a host of social problems coupled with the increase of family violence and drugs. It should come as no surprise, then, that children coming into the child welfare system are described as more troubled and more troublesome.

We are in a time of residual responses to social problems where the social welfare system, of which child welfare is an integral part, is called upon to intervene in a secondary, reactive manner. Too often the victim is blamed and the locus of change is predicated on changing the individual, rather than on imparting change on those societal conditions that may have had a large part in bringing about the social problems in the first place.

How social welfare would be considered a primary, first-line institution, predicated on a goal of social problem prevention, can be illustrated by the example of a proposal of a National Family Policy that could include:

1. Child and family allowances with payments scaled to the number of children in each family
2. Guarantees of mothers of full job protection, seniority, and benefits upon their return to work after maternity leave
3. Pay equity for working women
4. Cash payments to mothers for wages lost during maternity leave
5. Full health programs for all children
6. National standards and provision of decent, affordable child day care

Generalist Practice

We have discussed and examined child welfare from a generalist perspective in the belief that this framework is the most relevant and functional for baccalaureate students. It stresses that students focus their perceptions and conceptions for practice on people and environments as a unitary system. As Germain states, "People are regarded as biological and psychological beings engaged in continuous exchanges with the social environments, physical settings, and cultural contexts" (1).

It is intended that the baccalaureate child welfare worker learn and apply a general method of working with people and their environments, with limited but significant goals and circumscribed skills of moderate complexity. The B.A. child welfare worker should be skilled in general service provision, in assessing and managing readily amenable and accessible person–environment needs and problems, and in making informed judgments about when to refer more complex or intractable problems to the M.S.W. practitioner or other human service specialists.

Baccalaureate child welfare workers should be prepared to relieve life problems and environmental needs not requiring complex interventions. According to Germain (2), they should be capable of:

providing reassurance, support, and tangible resources; link[ing] people to for-
mal and informal helping systems; furnish[ing] needed information; and
work[ing] collaboratively with others in assuring continuity, coordination, and
comprehensiveness in basic social welfare services.

In every stage of the generalist model—i.e., assessment, data collection, engagement, intervention, evaluation, and termination—the three focal points of problem, person, and environment need to be explored as well as their dynamic interaction. Generalist child welfare workers also need to have a sensitivity to gender as well as to other diversity variables of ages and stages, endowment and personality, value systems, class, race and ethnicity, and geographic location.

In addition to sensitivity, effective child welfare generalists should possess vision of what could be, as well as what is and has been; warmth; hope; as well as purpose and skills. They need to be self-aware, capable of respecting the worth and dignity of all individuals, provide positive role models and endeavor to empower their clients to become independent, self-sufficient, and better functioning individuals.

Cultural Awareness

Minority children and adolescents are the most rapidly growing segment of the youth population in America; yet very little literature has been available to enlighten child welfare workers about their problems and needs. This book, and particularly the chapters focusing on African-American, American Indian, Asian-Pacific, and Hispanic children and families, has endeavored to provide knowledge and insight concerning the values, traditions, customs, and family patterns of people of color—particularly as they relate to implications for child welfare policy and practice.

A major theme that has been established is the fallacy of perceiving minority children and families as homogeneous, stereotypic entities. There is no model Asian/Pacific family, nor African-American, nor Hispanic family, nor American Indian family. There are as many differences within each of these minorities as there are similarities between them and white society. Thus, we have not made reference to "the" African-American family, "the" Hispanic family, "the" American Indian family, nor to "the" Asian/Pacific family. There are rich, poor, fully acculturated, non-acculturated, first-, second-, third-generation minority families, rural/urban, educated, uneducated, monolingual, bilingual families, etc.

What does become quite clear, however, is that these families often have been victims of discrimination, prejudice, and other forms of oppression. The need for child welfare services often comes as a result of minorities experiencing differential access to goods, services, and resources in society—including housing, health, mental health, education, and legal and social services.

One theme that manifests itself in examining people of color is the high value placed on the family. It is recommended that child welfare practice emphasize the positive social functioning both of the family as a unit and of its individual members, and concern itself also with the provision of a supportive social environment. Services need to be culturally appropriate, with sensitivity about emphasizing the family system and also emphasizing advocacy and case management. Recognition needs to be given to the unique cultural characteristics and the interdependence of people and their resource systems.

African-American Families

One of the most important characteristics of African-American children and families is their heterogeneity. There is *not* one African-American family but rather many African-American families which run the gamut from the traditional two-parent structure to various combinations of reconstituted families as well as single-parent families. Yet a disproportionate number of African-American children and families are poor, and they are more likely to be consumers of child welfare services.

Child welfare workers need to identify and work with the strengths of the client. Common features of African-American families that have been described as strengths include strong kinshop bonds, strong work orientation, adaptability of family roles, and high achievement orientation and religious orientation.

The strong extended family bonds have traditionally provided African-American families with mutual aid beyond the nuclear family structure. The concept of strong kinship bonds extends to the "family of friends and neighbors." This "Harambee Spirit" of togetherness, love, brotherhood, and sisterhood promoted with self-help initiatives in African-American communities is a significant characteristic of African-American families that can be used to empower them.

Child welfare workers can utilize the natural support networks in the African-American community combined with basic social work knowledge and skills to assist African-American families to develop a sense of control and power over their lives through increased effectiveness in the performance of valued social roles, thereby empowering the client system.

American Indian Families

There are 554 federally recognized tribal groups, 304 federal reservations, and over 100 non-federally recognized groups in approximately 1,959,234 American Indians and Alaska Natives. Cultural values associated with the American Indian community emphasize a familial and collective orientation. The cultural system is transferred through culturally based religious, healing, linguistic, artistic, educational, and organizational activities. The reader is reminded that great diversity characterizes "Indian country" with regard to tribal affiliation, language, land base, social and political history, and access to resources.

Social workers are encouraged to use a cultural perspective in examining and analyzing issues affecting American Indian and Alaska native children and families as it promotes understanding of the role of culture as a resource and strength.

In describing and analyzing the Indian Child Welfare Act of 1978, the authors conclude, that despite criticism of the ICSW, the act is and has been successful in fulfilling Congress's intent, which as to halt the destruction of American Indian families and preserve and bring strength and stability to American Indian families.

Indian children demonstrate great vulnerability on almost every demographic marker, many of which are directly related to the losses experienced as a result of contact with nonnatives, federal policy, relocation, and the boarding school legacy. As a result, child welfare and other social policies must strive to protect the legal and political rights of American Indians on and off the reservation; and must acknowledge the role of culture and support the sovereign rights of Indian nations and the right to self-determination.

Asian/Pacific Families

In working with Asian/Pacific families, of which there are some 60 separate ethnic groups and sub-groups, the child welfare worker needs to be aware that economic hardships, problems of adaptation, and lack of familiarity with social resources contribute to difficulties for immigrant Asian/Pacific children and their families.

There is a reluctance among Asian/Pacific families to seek professional help for emotional or mental problems outside the family network. Going "outside" for help with family problems is seen as bringing shame or "loss of face" to the family. Family honor is a most important value and it must be understood and respected by child welfare workers. In the Asian/Pacific family, the preferred way to meet the needs of the child is to focus from the outset on the needs of the family. It is also very important to recognize the status of fathers in Asian/Pacific families and to actively include them in any plans for the family.

Hispanic Families

Hispanics are a socio-culturally diverse group, constantly in a state of flux, and include Mexican Americans (or Chicanos), Puerto Ricans, Cubans, and people from other Spanish-speaking countries of Latin America and Spain.

In main, Hispanic families fall below the general U.S. population in economic well being, associated with higher divorce rates, lower educational achievement levels, and higher unemployment rates. These circumstances dictate the need for more adequate supportive, supplemental and substitute child welfare services.

The family, particularly among Mexican Americans, is of central importance, is seen as providing emotional support and material security, and is turned to first for help by family members. Child welfare workers should capitalize on the family's strengths and acknowledge and understand the Hispanic father's usual position of authority and respect afforded him by the children.

Child welfare workers should also be familiar with the role of *compadrazgo* (godparents), the church, *machismo,* and folk medicine (*curanderismo*) in Hispanic culture and utilize this knowledge in working with the Hispanic family.

Child welfare services can more effectively meet the needs of Hispanic children and their families by (1) recognizing Hispanic parental rights; (2) assuring the appropriateness of foster care placements; (3) ensuring such services are individualized to incorporate the cultural attributes and life experiences of Hispanic clients; (4) increasing funding; (5) assuring uniformity in agency policies; and (6) improving monitoring of service delivery.

The Practice of Child Welfare in the Rural Setting

Child welfare workers in rural environments must also be sensitive and knowledgeable about minority cultures, as a significant number of rural inhabitants are African Americans, American Indians, and Hispanics. In addition, workers will be providing services to a population that is poorer than the national average and with far fewer resources, and a population which appears to be growing. In the 1990s, 75 percent of the non-metropolitan counties in the United States gained population.

The rural child welfare worker must be a generalist in nature. It is not uncommon to be called upon to provide child protection, adoptions, foster care, juvenile probation, and general court work services as part of one's everyday caseload as a public-sector child welfare worker. Often, the worker is the only child welfare professional working in a small town or even in a rural county.

The rural child welfare worker needs to develop the following attitudes and skills in order to be successful: (1) a basic trust in the resources and support of the local community; (2) understanding and appreciation of the cultural heritage of the people to be served; (3) skill in individual counseling; (4) skill in small group work; (5) skills with juveniles; and (6) skill in the art of building a network of consultants and resources outside of the community.

It is suggested that the successful rural child welfare worker acquire three specific talents to communicate successfully with another culture: (1) quiet observational skills—the ability to spend time observing, listening, without interacting; (2) an ear for dialect—the need to be able to communicate and understand the local idioms and language; and (3) the ability to find and develop a trusting relationship with a local consultant.

Rural child welfare workers must be able to work independently, be creative and resourceful, and have the capacity to engender trust by becoming highly familiar with the local culture, language patterns, and day-to-day concerns and issues of the local people. This takes time and patience, requires sensitive interviewing skills, and the ability to provide the necessary help without detracting from the dignity and worth of the individual.

Child Maltreatment

One of the most difficult issues facing the child welfare worker in urban or rural settings is child maltreatment or child abuse and neglect. These are a widespread problem in our society. The American Humane Association reports that cases of reported maltreatment have increased from 416,000 in 1976 to 1,928,000 in 1985. The figures of reported maltreatment dramatically increased to 3.1 million children in 1996. The reports were substantiated for at least 969,000 cases of child abuse and neglect in the United States in 1996 up from 775,677 cases in 1990 (3).

We have endeavored to provide a detailed examination of the etiology of child maltreatment, as well as definitions of physical abuse, emotional abuse, sexual abuse, neglect, and their concomitant symptoms, manifestations, and consequences. The importance of understanding child maltreatment in a cultural context has been stressed, with the need for child protective services workers to be sensitive to cultural differences in child-rearing practices while, at the same time, assuring the safety of the children involved.

Child welfare workers use a variety of assessment tools to determine whether there is no risk, low risk, intermediate risk or high risk. Child factors and family factors have to be assessed. For the child, these include the child's age, severity and frequency of abuse or neglect, and the type and location of any injury.

Family factors include the caregiver's emotional and physical health, including possible substance abuse, degree of cooperation, parenting skills and knowledge, past history, home environment, availability of support systems, and strengths and weaknesses of the family (4).

Increasingly we are recognizing that the best way to combat abuse and neglect is through primary prevention. This prevention demands that communities strive together to meet the challenge of isolation, duplication, and the struggle for diminishing funds. Sexual abuse prevention in schools has been one of the most recent interventions. The trend is also toward the recognition that we must teach children how to be effective future parents. Coursework in junior and senior high schools can help to answer this need by courses in child development and segments on parenting skills. There is also need for parent training courses for teenage couples beyond that which is provided in schools.

The trend in responding to maltreatment, especially sexual abuse, is away from punishment in favor of treatment. While emphasis must always be on protecting the child, helping the abusive/neglecting individual(s) is crucial in curtailing the cycle of abuse. Self-help groups such as Parents Anonymous and Parents United are seen as effective intervention techniques.

Conclusions

Child welfare personnel, programs, and services are involved in working with our society's most precious resource—children and youth, who will become the future of our nation. This challenge becomes even more important as our society continues to age, with fewer children and more elderly becoming a demographic reality with each passing generation.

We have seen the 1980s and 1990s reflected by a marked shift from child-centered to family-focused services; increased networking among child and family services providers; widespread training for foster parents, child care workers, and social work staff; and more attention to respecting the cultural diversity of clients.

We have seen, at the same time, an increase in poverty among women and their children, a rise in homelessness, malnutrition, drug use, HIV/AIDs, school dropouts, family and youth violence, teenage pregnancies, and family dislocation. Children coming into the child welfare system are considered more troubled and more troublesome and increasing numbers come from families with domestic violence, including child abuse and neglect and substance abuse problems. Nearly 480,000 children are estimated to be currently in out-of-home placement, a figure which has grown by approximately 19 percent between 1990 and 1995 and continues to grow into the onset of the twenty-first century.

A particularly troubling finding in an HHS 1997 study was that while about the same number of children were in foster care in 1977 and 1994, there was a 60 percent decline in the number of children receiving in-home services (5). Agencies have been able to serve fewer children at home, even while we champion the virtues of a "least restrictive environment" and family preservation. Child Welfare is increasingly becoming protective services for battered and abused children, with the practice realities revolving around out-of-home care for greater numbers of children and youth. The call for more timely, relevant, and effective child welfare services has never been greater.

The first edition of this book cited CWLA's Out-of-Home Care Task Force Report to the CWLA Board of Directors in September 1989 recommending a need for greater and more flexible funding. While there have been some programmatic funding increases, welfare "reform" and cuts to food stamps, SSI, and Medicaid reflect a turning away from the needy and those at-risk. The challenge is how to provide relevant, timely, and effective services to children, families, and communities in the face of diminishing social welfare resources and an increasingly politically conservative climate.

We need to acknowledge that the child welfare system is not equipped to handle these problems alone. In order to build families, there is need to build and strengthen communities through interagency and community participation. As Schorr so cogently proposes in her book, *Common Purpose* (6), the well-being of children, families, and communities are inseparable. To strengthen families, one needs to combine action in the economic, service, education, physical development, and community building domains. What is needed, therefore, is the "adoption of a broad, noncategorical, nonideological, comprehensive approach" (7).

There is need also to add to our existing knowledge through further research which examines the sequence of events that promote stress and impede the inability to cope with life, resulting in social isolation. Why do families fail to use available services? What services provided to what children and families under what circumstances provide the desired results?

Too little attention is spent on studying and discussing the successes we have achieved in working with children and families. Perhaps we need to study successful children reared under adverse circumstances rather than focusing on corrective intervention to enhance the quality of life. These efforts, according to Rutter and Schorr (8), have a greater potential for developing preventive intervention and a comprehensive social policy.

We need further studies of methods of practice used with families in protective and preventive services. The use of multiservice family centers, short-term and long-term intensive casework services, multidisciplinary teams, comprehensive services combined with outreach and advocacy, group services, lay services, parent education, and various types of contracting bear further examination.

We need to use the computerized tracking systems that have been developed to provide data that can be analyzed to add to the knowledge in the field. In addition, child welfare practitioners can greatly assist the total research effort by testing findings in the field and by keeping an organized record of results.

As we begin our twenty-first century journey, we have seen significant strides take place in the field of child welfare. Children's rights, re-emphasis on the sanctity of the family, family preservation, managed care, permanency planning, normalization, deinstitutionalization, and prevention have all helped to shape the nature of child welfare policy and practice. To the extent that the problems of institutional racism and sexism, inadequate health care and child day care, and non-quality education receive higher national priority, the tasks confronting child welfare programs and staff will become easier.

Child advocacy groups such as the Child Welfare League of America, the Children's Defense Fund, and, more recently, Children Now in California have lobbied steadfastly and valiantly in this regard. Yet, these problems are a fact of life in America and will continue to place heavy demands on the child welfare system. There are no easy solutions to these complex problems, but sensitive, committed, and well-trained generalist child welfare workers can make a positive difference in enhancing the quality of life for our children—the future of our country.

Endnotes

1. Carel B. Germainn, "Foreword," in Maria Joan O'Neil, *The General Method of Social Work Practice*, p. xi.
2. Ibid., p. xii.
3. U.S. Department of Health and Human Services, National Center on Child Abuse and Neglect.
4. Christian M. Hansen, et al., "Can We Protect Children from Abuse? A Review of Three Cases." *Child Welfare* LXVIII, no. 6, Nov./Dec. 1989: 615–621.
5. U.S. Department of Health and Human Services, *National Study of Protective, Preventive and Reunification Services Delivered to Children and Their Families: Final Report, 1997.*
6. Lisbeth Schorr, *Common Purpose: Strengthening Families and Neighborhoods to Rebuild America,* 1997, p. 361.
7. Ibid., p. 362.

8. S. Rutter, "Protective Factors in Children's Responses to Stress and Disadvantage." In M. W. Kent and J. E. Rolf, eds., *Primary Prevention of Pathology*, vol. 3: *Social Competence in Children*, 1979, and Lisbeth Schorr, *Within Our Reach: Breaking the Cycle of Disadvantage*, 1988.

Bibliography

Balcerzak, Edwin A., ed. *Group Care of Children: Transitions Toward the Year 2000.* Washington, D.C.: Child Welfare League of America, 1989.

Edelman, Marian Wright. *Families in Peril. An Agenda for Social Change.* Cambridge, Mass.: Harvard University Press, 1987.

Germain, Carel B. "Foreword." In Maria Joan O'Neil, *The General Method of Social Work Practice.* Englewood Cliffs, N.J.: Prentice-Hall, 1984.

Hansen, Christian M., et al. "Can We Protect Children from Abuse? A Review of Three Cases." *Child Welfare* LXVIII, no. 6, Nov./Dec. 1989: 615–621.

Rutter, S. "Protective Factors in Children's Responses to Stress and Disadvantage." In *Primary Prevention of Pathology*, edited by M. W. Kent and J. E. Rolf., vol 3. *Social Competence in Children.* Hanover, N.H.: University Press of New England, 1979.

Schorr, Lisbeth, *Common Purpose: Strengthening Families and Neighborhoods to Rebuild America*, New York: Anchor Books, 1997.

———. *Within Our Reach: Breaking the Cycle of Disadvantage*, New York: Anchor Books, 1988.

U.S. Department of Health and Human Services, National Center on Child Abuse and Neglect, N.D.

———, *National Study of Protective, Preventive, and Reunification Services Delivered to Children and Their Families:* Final Report, 1997.

INDEX